Women Seers of the Ṛgveda

Women Seers of the Ṛgveda

Mau Das Gupta

DK PRINTWORLD
Publishers of Indian Traditions

Cataloging in Publication Data — DK

[Courtesy: D.K. Agencies (P) Ltd. <docinfo@dkagencies.com>]

Das Gupta, Mau, 1968- **author.**

Women seers of the Ṛgveda / Mau Das Gupta.
pages cm
Includes bibliographical references (pages).
ISBN: 9788124608685

1. Rishis in the Vedas. 2. Hindu women in literature. 3. Hindu civilization. 4. Vedas. Ṛgveda – Criticism, interpretation, etc. I. Title.

DDC 294.59212046 23

ISBN: 978-81-246-0868-5
First published in India, 2017

Printed and published by:
D.K. Printworld (P) Ltd.
Regd. Office: *Vedaśrī*, F-395, Sudarshan Park
(Metro Station: Ramesh Nagar), New Delhi – 110 015
Phones: (011) 2545 3975, 2546 6019
e-mail: indology@dkprintworld.com
Website: www.dkprintworld.com

Preface

THOUGH scholars have devoted their time and energy to the study of a literary appreciation of *Ṛgveda* and have authored many books and articles, the colourful mind of the women seers of the age, vibrant with all its will and woe, sorrows and happiness, hopes, despair and aspirations, reverberating in the hymns ascribed to them, has largely remained unexplored in the male-dominated society. In my limited capacity I have made a humble attempt to fill a very small part of this vital gap, by concentrating on the sociocultural conditions reflected in the writings of the Ṛgvedic *ṛṣikā*s, a study of which must be deemed a desideratum.

My work on this book was started in 1993 when I joined the Jadavpur University for a PhD degree as a University Grants Commission (UGC) awardee of the Junior Research Fellowship of the Government of West Bengal. I worked there till I joined my service in February 1997. After a gap of about five years, when my time was mostly consumed by my service in West Bengal Education Services at the Lady Brabourne College, Calcutta and when I was passing through one of the critical periods in my personal life, the second phase of my research in this direction began in mid-2002 when I came in touch with Abhijit Ghosh, MA, PhD, a teacher of Sanskrit in Jadavpur University. Eventually I was registered in the same year as a PhD research scholar there in the Faculty of Arts, to work with him. In 2005 the UGC sanctioned for this research a grant meant for the Minor Research Projects (MRP), for which I am very grateful. This also acted as an obligatory force for me to finish the marathon started in 1993. The findings of the project were submitted to the UGC as the final report of the MRP in 2007.

In course of my research, besides consulting original Sanskrit texts, I tried to go through a vast amount of secondary literature as well, in English, Bengali, Hindi, German, French and Marathi, sometimes with the assistance of my supervisor. I now humbly present before the scholarly world this book which embodies the fruits of my labour for the past several years, done in conditions not always favourable for academic studies.

My learned guide Dr Abhijit Ghosh supervised the work patiently and astutely over a long period of time, always generously giving me valuable information and invaluable suggestions. I have met a few persons who are characterized by such impressive meticulousness, industriousness and trustworthiness in their dealings with their students. Anyone who knows about the research conditions in India, where one would be happy to have even a fraction of the resources and assistance which are regarded as a matter of course in Western Europe and America, cannot but be amazed at the thoroughness with which my supervisor lovingly guided the young generation working with him, sparing no pains to procure for them even the most obscure sources from various corners of the world by means of often incredible labour and resourcefulness: he has been simply in an altogether different league. It is a great loss for the Sanskrit scholarly world that a sudden and untimely death took him away from us in 2013.

My father Dipankar Das Gupta, who was a linguist of the Anthropological Survey of India, has been the inspiration behind all my academic efforts. So far as this dissertation is concerned, he suggested the lay-out of the study of the higher constituents in sentences of the select texts in my dissertation. I have been fortunate that he could see me earning my PhD in 2008 just a year before he passed away.

Mr Debasis Majumdar, an electrical engineer and my relative, lent me a helping hand in preparing the charts and graphs in Chapter 7 of the thesis. Dr Shilpa Sumant of the Tilak Maharashtra University of Pune took the trouble of copying materials from her university library and sending them to me. Grateful thanks are due to all of them for their kind assistance, as also to the staff of the Kolkata libraries I used, including those of the Gol Park Ramkrishna Mission Institute of Culture, the Asiatic Society, the Lady Brabourne College, and the Central and the Sanskrit Department's libraries of the Jadavpur University.

I am grateful to my present employers at University of Calcutta in supporting me in every way to publish my thesis. Prof. Suranjan Das, the former Vice-Chancellor of Calcutta University, took no time to sanction a financial grant from the UGC XIIth plan for the publication of this book. My heartfelt gratitudes are due to D.K. Printworld for their wonderful endeavour to publish the book with a perfectionist's attitude. I feel personally indebted to Mr Susheel Kumar Mittal to have encouraged me to update the work with latest research information and to have borne with patience the long time I took for going through the proofs. My affectionate thanks are due to Nandit Desai, for designing the cover of this book, which projects the strength and trust of an archetypal Indian woman.

Kolkata, March 2016 **Mau Das Gupta**

Contents

Preface v

Abbreviations xiii

1. **Introduction** 1
   - Romaśā 2
   - Lopāmudrā 3
   - The Rivers 4
   - Aditi 4
   - Viśvavārā 5
   - Śaśvatī 7
   - Apālā 8
   - Sikatā and Nīvāvarī 11
   - Yamī 11
   - Ghoṣā 13
   - Agastya-svasṛ 16
   - Sūryā 17
   - Indrāṇī 19
   - Urvaśī 20
   - Dakṣiṇā 21
   - Saramā 22
   - Juhū 23
   - Vāc 23
   - Rātri 25
   - Godhā 26
   - Indrāṇī Again 27

Śraddhā 28
Indra-mātṛs 29
Yamī Again 29
Śacī 30
Sārparājñī 31
Vasukra-patnī 32
Niṣat and Upaniṣat 33
Śrī 33
Lākṣā 34
Medhā 35

2. Traditional Expositions vis-à-vis Modern Interpretations of the Concerned Ṛgvedic Hymns: Some Major Differences **37**

3. Socio-Cultural Aspects of the Select Hymns and the World-view of the Women Seers **106**

The World of Women in the Ṛgvedic Age 124
Were Girls Condemned in the Ṛgvedic Family? 124
Chastity was not a Necessity for Ṛgvedic Women 126
Proof of Incest in Ṛgvedic Age 128
The Institution of Marriage 130
Woman in Her Role as Mother 135
Plight of Women if and When they Lost their 135
Husbands 135
The Subjects that Women Learnt 139
Women at War 140
Weltanschauung of the Female Seers 141
Summing Up 145

4. Mythological Aspects of the Select Texts **146**

Myth and Mythology and the Ṛgvedic Context 146
Trends in Indian Mythological Researches 147
Gods vis-à-vis Mortals 148
Mythification and Ritual 149

Vedic Mythology 150
Mythological Tracks in the Literature of the Ṛgvedic Female Seers 153
Romaśā 153
Lopāmudrā 154
Vipāś and Śutudrī 156
Aditi 156
Viśvavārā 160
Śaśvatī 161
Apālā 162
Yamī 164
Wife of Vasukra 167
Ghoṣā 168
Agastya's Sister 171
Sūryā 172
Indrāṇī 178
Urvaśī 181
Dakṣiṇā 184
Saramā 184
Juhū 188
Vāc 189
Rātri 192
Godhā 192

5. Liturgical Peculiarities of the Select Texts 194
The Hymn Ascribed to Niṣat and Upaniṣat 205

6. Literary Appreciation of the Select Texts and the Poetic Imageries Therein 206
Chief Elements of Oral Poetry Found in Select Texts 206
A Survey of the Figures of Speech Used in the Select Texts 213
Imageries Found in the Select Texts 225
What is Imagery? 225
Imagery Turning into "Symbol" or "Leitmotif" 228
The How of Ṛgvedic Imagery 229

An estimate of Individual Imageries in the Literature of the Ṛgvedic Women Seers 231
Citrakalpa 235
Imageries of Female Seers vis-à-vis those of Some Male Seers 236

7. A Study of the Language and Stylistics of the Text 239
Analysis IA: A Study of the HC Orders in Select Verses of the Female Seers 240
Analysis IB: A Brief Study of the HC Orders in Select Verses of Male and Female Seers 256
Select verses of some male seers 256
Select Verses of Female Seers 260
Analysis II: A Study of the Negative Sentences in Verses Ascribed to Male and Female Seers 266
Select Verses of Male Seers 266
Select Verses of Female Seers 269
Analysis III: A Study of the Interrogative Sentences inVerses of Male and Female Seers 276
Select Verses of Male Seers 276
Select Verses of Female Seers 278
Findings from the Above Analyses 285

Epilogue **286**

Bibliography **289**

Index of English Terms **298**

Index of Sanskrit Terms **306**

Abbreviations

AiBr	*Aitareya Brāhmaṇa*
AiUp	*Aitareyopaniṣad*
AnukrBh	*Anukramaṇikā-Bhāṣya*
ĀpDhS	*Āpastamba-Dharmasūtra*
ĀpGS	*Āpastamba-Gṛhyasūtra*
ĀpŚrS	*Āpastamba-Śrautasūtra*
ĀrṣA	*Ārṣānukramaṇī*
ĀśvŚrS	*Āśvalāyana-Śrautasūtra*
AV	*Atharvaveda*
BṛUp	*Bṛhadāraṇyakopaniṣad*
BhGS	*Bhāradvāja-Gṛhyasūtra*
BhP	*Bhāgavata Purāṇa*
BṛhD	*Bṛhaddevatā*
DhtP	*Dhātupāṭha*
GDhS	*Gautama-Dharmasūtra*
GGS	*Gobhila-Gṛhyasūtra*
GPBr	*Gopatha Brāhmaṇa*
JBr	*Jaiminīya Brāhmaṇa*
KātŚrS	*Kātyāyana-Śrautasūtra*
KauṣBr	*Kauṣītaki Brāhmaṇa*
KauśS	*Kauśika-Sūtra*
KhGS	*Khādira-Gṛhyasūtra*
MS	*Maitrāyaṇī Saṁhitā*
Nigh	*Nighaṇṭu*

Nir	*Nirukta*
Pāṇ.	Pāṇini
PMS	Pūrvamīmāṁsā-Sūtra
ṚV	*Ṛgveda*
SD	*Sāhitya-Darpaṇa*
ŚGS	*Śāṅkhāyana-Gṛhyasūtra*
Śiś	*Śiśupālavadha*
ŚPBr	*Śatapatha Brāhmaṇa*
SV	*Sāmaveda*
TĀr	*Taittirīya Āraṇyaka*
TBr	*Taittirīya Brāhmaṇa*
TS	*Taittirīya Saṁhitā*
VS	*Vājasaneyi Saṁhitā*
VasS	*Vasiṣṭha-Sūtra*

1

Introduction
An Account of the Hymns of the Women Seers in R̥gveda

In both the lists, as given by *Br̥haddevatā* (2.82-84) and *Ārṣānukramaṇī* (10.100-02), one comes across names of no less than 27 women seers from *R̥gveda*, who are authors of hymns: Ghoṣā, Godhā, Viśvavārā, Apālā, Upaniṣad and Niṣad, Brahmajāyā Juhū, Agastya's sister, Aditi, Indrāṇī, Indra-mātr̥s, Saramā, Romaśā, Urvaśī, Lopāmudrā, the rivers, Yamī, a wife named Śaśvatī, Śrī, Lākṣā, Sārparājñī, Vāc, Śraddhā, Medhā, Dakṣiṇā, Rātri and Sūryā Sāvitrī. Of these female seers some are doubtlessly mythical characters, some are non-human objects while again some are celestial beings. For instance, Sūryā Sāvitrī, Saramā and Yamī are, according to scholars, of mythological provenance, whereas Nadī, Dakṣiṇā, Medhā, Rātri, Śraddhā and Vāc are considered either to be non-human objects or personified abstract ideas. Similarly, Urvaśī, Aditi, Indramātr̥ and Indrāṇī of *R̥gveda* X.86 are celestial beings. Apart from them, one finds only a few poetesses who can be considered to be women in flesh and blood; they are Romaśā, Lopāmudrā, Viśvavārā, Apālā, the sister of Agastya, the wife named Śaśvatī, Ghoṣā, Godhā and to some extent Yamī of X.10 and Indrāṇī of X.145, 159. In addition to the lists given in *Br̥haddevatā* 2.82-84 and *Ārṣānukramaṇī* 10.100-02, some more female seers are found in *R̥gveda*: one is the wife of Vasukra and the seer of X.28.1. Sikatā and Nīvāvarī, too, are two women seers to whom *R̥V* IX.86.11-20 have been ascribed. An account of the female seers and the hymns or verses composed by them, in the order of the latter's occurrence in the Saṁhitā text, is the subject of the present study.

Romaśā

Romaśā and Lopāmudrā are only to be met in the first book of *Ṛgveda*. According to tradition, Romaśā is the seer of I.126.7. The *Bṛhaddevatā* alludes her to be the wife of King Svanaya Bhāvayavya (III.155), who has been praised more than once in *Ṛgveda* for his bounteous nature. The entire hymn I.126 itself is a praise for gifts, addressing King Svanaya, the last two stanzas of which are a dialogue of the royal couple, but these two stanzas seem to have no apparent connection with what precedes. They rather actually comprise a bedroom conversation between a man and a woman, than a dialogue of the royal couple as mentioned in *Bṛhaddevatā*. The internal evidence of these two stanzas does not agree with what *Bṛhaddevatā* says. Griffith (1896-97: 652) suggests that here the seventh stanza of the hymn should have preceded the sixth, because the seventh stanza reveals the speakers' unfamiliarity with each other, which is why the woman has to highlight her youth to the man in order to lure him, and what the man says undoubtedly presupposes their first meeting. He eventually comes to the conclusion that "these two look like a fragment of a liberal shepherd's love song".

Jamison and Brereton (2014: I.291) hold that this hymn is a single composition of Kakṣīvant who, praising the gifts of Svanaya who gave him ten maidens along with other gifts, gives a brief literary description of the sexual encounter he had with one of the girls he received from the king. The final verse of this hymn contains "the ostensible and crudely seductive speech of the woman herself".

Disputes prevail over the actual name of the poetess of I.126.7, since nowhere in the verse has the term "Romaśā" been used as a proper noun. The speaker (a woman) in the verse says, "I am hairy all over the body" (*sárvāhám asmi romaśā́*). Traditional commentators take the adjective *romaśā* to be the name of the seer. But some modern Indian interpreters are reluctant to accept this hymn in its face value, and think that the word does not at all refer to a woman but has been used to mean "[a land] covered with grass" (Sarasvati and Vidyalankar 1977: 3.5651).

Lopāmudrā

The next female seer of the first book of *R̥gveda* is Lopāmudrā. *R̥gveda* I.179 is a dialogue hymn, the first four stanzas of which are ascribed to the ascetic couple Lopāmudrā and Agastya. The first two stanzas are attributed to Lopāmudrā where she seeks her husband's communion in order to make their marriage a success. This hymn carries the fragment of an ancient story which is fortunately not completely lost but can be restored from citations in later literature. After she has practised penance for a long time, Lopāmudrā approaches her husband with the plea that since her youth is on the wane, if not almost worn off, it is high time that the husband should now approach the wife. To persuade her ascetic husband toward the mundane conjugal life, Lopāmudrā cites examples from the past and appreciates those ascetics who could make a proper balance between their asceticism and married life. She is answered by her husband, but a disciple of the sage overhears their secret conversation and consequently observes an expiatory ritual for his sin, as can be gathered from the final couple of stanzas.

The authorship of *R̥gveda* I.179.1-2 is not much questioned. Indian tradition and modern scholarship of the East and the West almost unanimously agree on this point. Both Sāyaṇa and his predecessor Veṅkaṭamādhava follow the footsteps of *Br̥haddevatā* and *Sarvānukramaṇī*, and hold Lopāmudrā to be the seer of the first two stanzas of *R̥gveda* I.179. But Durga on *Nirukta* 5.1.3 ascribes in addition the fourth stanza beginning with *nadasya mā rudhatam* to Lopāmudrā. Incidentally, Griffith thinks the fifth stanza of this hymn is rather superfluous in character, but this does not affect the text in question.

Bergaigne (1878-83: 2.394) observes that the present hymn has a mystic meaning. Agastya is identifiable with the celestial Soma while Lopāmudrā represents fervent prayer, who after long efforts succeeds in drawing Soma down from his secret dwelling place.

The Rivers

In the third book of *Ṛgveda* the thirty-third hymn is ascribed to the rivers, who according to *Bṛhaddevatā* and *Ārṣānukramaṇī* come under the list of the female seers. A detailed discussion of this hymn is not necessary as it has been stated earlier that being non-human objects the rivers named Vipāś and Śutudrī are hardly relevant to any socio-cultural study. Still, in this hymn which is a conversation between the Sage Viśvāmitra and the aforesaid rivers, is found a very typical feminine mannerism in the speech of the rivers, e.g.

> *ní te naṁsai pīpyānéva yóṣā máryāyeva kanyā̀ śaśvacái te*
>
> We bend down before you like a nursing mother and like a maiden bending to embrace a man. — v. 10

Griffith suggests that this hymn is of some historical value as it contains a relic of the traditions of the Aryans regarding their eastward progress in the land of Five Rivers.

Aditi

Aditi is the sole female seer to be met in the fourth book of *Ṛgveda*. *Ṛgveda* IV.18 is a dialogue hymn, the speakers being Indra, Aditi and Vāmadeva. Here again Aditi cannot be regarded as a mundane woman but a celestial being — the mother of the gods. Aditi holds a very exalted position in the Vedic religion, and is considered to be the primary source of all divine beings. *Nirukta* 4.22 says: *aditir adīnā deva-mātā*, where *adīnā* has been paraphrased by Sāyaṇa as *akhaṇḍanīyā*, i.e. "unimpaired". While introducing this hymn, Sāyaṇa narrates a legend from Ṣaḍguruśiṣya's *Sarvānukramaṇī-Bhāṣya* which may be summarized as follows:

> Having attained knowledge already during his gestation period, the great Sage Vāmadeva decided not to be born in the usual way,

> but to come into the world through his mother's side. Coming to know of his intention, his mother prayed for the help of Goddess Aditi, the mother of Indra, whereat Aditi with her son came to her and had a talk with Vāmadeva to dissuade him from his fatal intention.

Sarvānukramaṇī, however, does not make specific attribution of the stanzas of this hymn to individual speakers. *Sarvānukramaṇī-Bhāṣya* has tried to do this though apparently without much success.

Griffith considers this hymn to be made up of somewhat incoherent fragments. Following *Sarvānukramaṇī-Bhāṣya*, Sāyaṇa and Veṅkaṭamādhava have ascribed only seven hemistichs of this hymn to Aditi, wherein she admits that after she had given birth to Indra, she left her child at a secret place as if to hush up a sin, even as Indra by his own valour rose up from there to become a hero unparalleled in heaven and earth. Aditi goes on to glorify her son's exploits, and narrates further how in spite of every hindrance he succeeded in slaying his enemies and achieved the highest position in both the worlds. The desertion of the child Indra by Aditi has been mentioned no less than thrice in this hymn — viz. in the fifth, eighth and tenth stanzas. A glimpse of the social position of women at the age of *Ṛgveda* is contained in the utterance of Aditi: *avadyám iva mányamānā gúhākar índraṁ mātā́* (*ṚV* IV.18.5). It suggests that the birth of a child in some cases was considered to be *avadyá* (of reproach) even by its mother.

Viśvavārā

The next woman seer of *Ṛgveda* is Viśvavārā of the family of Atri, who authored V.28. She is indeed a woman of this earth and has no definite legendary background, and hence her hymn occupies a very important place among the works of such female seers. *Bṛhaddevatā* tells not much about this hymn and its seers, and only mentions that the Atris, having dispelled the eclipse of the sun decreed by Svarbhānu, praised Agni with twenty-seven hymns, viz. *Ṛgveda* V.1-28 (V.12). Macdonell (1904: 2.169 fn.) rightly points out that this number "twenty-seven" includes the twenty-eighth hymn of the fifth book of *Ṛgveda* as well, because the Āprī hymn, no. V.5, has to be left out of account, and thus the series of twenty-seven hymns covers the hymn of Viśvavārā as well.

Jamison and Brereton (op. cit. II.689) do not consider Viśvavārā a female poet since her name is extracted from *viśvavārā* "bringing all desirable things" in vs. 1. which describes the sacrificial ladle. The hymn, they contend, is a compilation of *sāmidhenī* verses from the Atri tradition brought together to accompany the kindling of fire.

Veṅkaṭamādhava in his commentary on *Ṛgveda* has related another myth to the above poetess. "The sun having disappeared", says he, "Atri gave birth to the Dawn (Uṣas), whence Ātreyī Uṣā (the Dawn born of Atri) was called Viśvavārā." The nomenclature Viśvavārā in the first stanza of this hymn is explained by Sāyaṇa as "she who repels all the enemies of the nature of sin" (*viśvavārā sarvam api pāpa-rūpaṁ śatrum* [sic] *vārayitrī*). Griffith, too, hesitates to accept Viśvavārā as the author of the hymn, and comments: "[T]his hymn is *ascribed* to a *supposed* Viśvavārā, a lady of the family of Atri" (emphasis added). In passing, it may be mentioned that Dayananda (Sarasvati and Vidyalankar 1977: 1.219-20) interprets Viśvavārā of V.28.1 as "the lady who chooses or selects the whole universe" (*yā viśvaṁ vr̥ṇoti sā*), and too boldly asserts that "she refers to cosmic light, or one who brings the entire creation into appearance".

The hymn of Viśvavārā consists of six stanzas, in which the poetess exalts the glory of Fire and prays to him for marital happiness and security in life. In comparison with the other hymns of female seers, the present hymn has some liturgical value as well.

The exact meaning of the controversial expression *jāspatyám* at V.28.3 has been hotly debated by scholars. Of the indigenous scholars, Sāyaṇa takes it to denote "the duties of husband and wife", while his predecessor Veṅkaṭamādhava considers the term to mean "the married couple". Griffith, almost after Veṅkaṭamādhava, prefers to translate it by "the household lordship", while Geldner 1951: 2.24, rather following Sāyaṇa, renders it by "*Haushaltung*". Whatever its exact meaning might be, the word evidently connotes "a married couple" and in this stanza the authoress yarns from her household deity Agni after a well-balanced marital partnership. A more significant, nay wonderful, aspect as regards a woman's rights in that age can be detected in the hymn that refers to the poetess *herself* offering oblation to the fire with a sacrificial ladle. This hymn perhaps offers evidence that in ancient Ṛgvedic society a woman, just as a man, could herself pay homage to God uttering the (same) *mantra*s.

Śaśvatī

In the sixth and seventh books of *Ṛgveda* one does not meet any female seer. In the eighth book, which is called the "Pragātha Maṇḍala", two poetesses are found. The first poetess is the wife of King Āsaṅga named Śaśvatī. *Ṛgveda* VIII.1 is a considerably long hymn, of thirty-four stanzas, where the final stanza alone is attributed to Śaśvatī. She has been spoken of as Nārī Śaśvatī at *Bṛhaddevatā* 2.83. The epithet in *Nītimañjarī* has been explained as "the one among women, who is distressed when her husband is distressed and who rejoices when he rejoices" (vide Macdonell 1904: 2.55). Sieg in Sagenstoffe cites this *Nītimañjarī* passage where Śaśvatī of *Ṛgveda* VIII.1.34 has been quoted as an example of a *nārī* (vide o.c., l.c. with ref.). Macdonell, however, in his translation of *Bṛhaddevatā* 2.83, interprets the word simply as "wife".

Jamison and Brereton (op. cit. II.1021-22) are of the opinion that 'Śaśvatī' is not the name of the woman but an attributive adjective of the female who expresses happy surprise at the sight of the penis of an unidentified man. Since there is no context for this brief description of sexual adventure with such provocative direct speech; they are inclined to accept it as a part of the *dānastuti*, contained in the preceding three verses, and it praises the gift of a woman to the poet because women are often mentioned as part of the poet's spoils in *Ṛgveda*.

The *Sarvānukramaṇī* relates the following legend on this hymn. A prince named Āsaṅga, the son of King Playoga, had been turned into a woman owing to a curse of the gods, but later with the favour of Sage Medhātithi of Kaṇva family restored to manhood by the power of penance. On that account he offered abundant riches to the seer (*ṚV* VIII.1.30-33), and was praised and congratulated on restoration of his manhood by his wife Śaśvatī, the daughter of Aṅgiras (*ṚV* VIII.1.34). *Bṛhaddevatā* does not give any details about Āṅgirasī Śaśvatī. Sarasvati and Vidyalankar (1977: 1.220) suggest that Śaśvatī might not be the historical seer of this *mantra*, but since words have been put into her mouth, she has been called a *ṛṣikā* thereof.

The stanza attributed to Śaśvatī bears a typical Ṛgvedic naïvety found in the hymns of Romaśā, Lopāmudrā or Yamī of *Ṛgveda* X.10. Here she praises her husband's signs of manhood in an unhesitant language, which hardly shows any cover of sophistication.

Apālā

The next poetess to be found in the eighth book of *Ṛgveda* is Apālā of the family of Atri. She is the seer of the entire hymn VIII.80 (91). A fascinating legend about her has been narrated by Sāyaṇa in the preface of his commentary on this hymn. Apālā, it is said, being afflicted with a skin disease was repudiated by her husband, whereupon she returned to her father's hermitage and practised severe austerities for long, seeking Indra's favour. Once while she had gone for a bath in the river, intending to make a *soma*-offering to her tutelary god, she found, on the way back home, some *soma* plants which she plucked up and chewed as she walked. Indra, having heard the gnashing sound of her jaws, took it for the sound of *soma*-grinding stones and came at once to the girl. He asked her if there were any stones pounding *soma* in the vicinity, to which she informed him of the fact, and he turned away. She called him back, and offered him a drink from her mouth itself. At her insistence, Indra, now fallen in love with her, drank the *soma* as she had wished. Being triumphant at this incident, Apālā jubilantly exclaimed, "I have been repudiated by my husband and yet Indra comes to me!" Thereupon Indra granted her three boons of her choice, and she prayed Indra make her father's bald head and barren field, as also her own person that was devoid of hair due to skin disease, sprout. Indra, at this request of her, dragged her first through the wide hole of his chariot, then through the narrower hole of the cart and finally through the still smaller hole of the yoke, and she cast off three skins one after another, of which the first became a hedgehog, the second an alligator and the third a chameleon, while Apālā herself was given a sun-like skin. Going by his own acknowledgement, Sāyaṇa owes this story to the now lost *Śāṭyāyana Brāhmaṇa*.

A detailed discussion of this hymn is preserved at *Bṛhaddevatā* 6.99-107. The narrative manner in which *Bṛhaddevatā* relates the legend to *Ṛgveda* VIII.91 is indeed a delightful reading. The story in the present text is somewhat different from the one narrated by Sāyaṇa. There was once a girl Apālā, says *Bṛhaddevatā* 6.99, the daughter of Atri, suffering from an acute cutaneous disease, whom Indra saw in the lonely hermitage of her father, and as usual fell in love with her. Having known the intention of Indra through penance, *Bṛhaddevatā* 6.100-07 go on to say, Apālā came out, with a vessel to fetch water. On the way she found a *soma* plant and lauded it. This part of the event has its nucleus in the commencing stanza of *Ṛgveda* VIII.91 (*kanyà vā́r avāyatī́,* etc.). She pressed *soma* in her jaws and then with the next stanza (v. 2) invoked Indra, who sucked it from her mouth, and relished cakes and other delicacies at her house. He was thereafter praised by Apālā with the following three *mantras* (vv. 3-5). In the remaining portion of the hymn (vv. 6-8), she requested him to grace her with abundant hair and faultless limbs and fair skin. Pleased with her praise Indra passing her through the apertures of the carriage and of its yokes drew her forth thrice, whereupon she became fair skinned. The rest of this legend tallies with that in Sāyaṇa's version. This hymn has been called "Itihāsa" (a traditional account) by Yāska and Bhāguri, says *Bṛhaddevatā*. Śaunaka regards this hymn as addressed to Indra.

Sarasvati and Vidyalankar (1977: 1.220-21; 1982: 10.3553) derive *apālā́-* from root *pā́l-*, meaning "protection", and attribute to the word the meaning of "an unmarried girl". This is a pointer to the assumption that Apālā was yet to get protected, or, in other words, was yet to be married. However, far-fetched this meaning may apparently look, the epithet *kanyā̀-* at the commencing stanza would seem to suggest that Apālā was a maiden. In contradistinction to this, the expressions *patidvíṣaḥ* and *yatī́ḥ*, however, are congruous to the legend given in *Śāṭyāyana Brāhmaṇa* and *Bṛhaddevatā*, since, as is but expected, both Sāyaṇa and his predecessor Veṅkaṭamādhava take these words to connote "being repudiated by her husband". Even if the above etymology be accepted, one may wonder that even a woman repudiated by her husband, too, needed proper protection, and was living like a maiden at her parental house. Griffith, using different terminologies, explains *patidvíṣaḥ* as "hostile to our lord", which eventually means "disliked by my husband".

This hymn of Apālā is very popular, perhaps because of the dramatic touch it possesses and the simplicity yet earnestness with which she invokes her God. It instantly gives the reader a feeling that the girl and the God whom she lauds are very intimate to each other, and their relation is not one of the worshipper and the worshipped. The same note strikes in the hymns of Ghoṣā (*ṚV* X.39-40), where addressing the Aśvins she blames them for not coming to her, and further asks for their favour to grant her a heroic husband. But, the Apālā hymn has attracted much more attention than the hymn of Ghoṣā, probably because of its dramatic treatment and lyric poetry, as well as the mystic myth underlying its contents.

Hanns Peter Schmidt (1987: 1-29) in his intriguing discussion on the Apālā hymn has convincingly established that Apālā was an adolescent suffering from acne performed a female-puberty rite to appease Indra and ultimately conjugated with him. The gist of the findings of Schmidt can be quoted here: "The hymn is not only a legendary account of a girl's growth into nubility put in analogy with the reawakening of nature, but also a rather human and touching document inasmuch as it offers a glimpse into the girl's private worries and fantasies while she is preparing herself for the event she is half dreading, half yearning for to be a woman and wife." (p. 29)

Sikatā and Nīvāvarī

In *R̥gveda* IX.86.11-20, two women seers, Sikatā and Nīvāvarī, are witnessed to have composed ten *mantra*s. Unfortunately, however, neither the internal evidence of the hymn nor the tradition comes to our help as regards their identities. *Br̥haddevatā* is completely silent about them. Apart from the dialogue hymns (save the single *mantra* of Śaśvatī and Agastya-svasr̥, and the one-and-a-half *mantra*s of Godhā), only in this hymn of a heterogeneous character is found so many number of *mantra*s composed by the *r̥ṣikā*s among the ones composed by their male counterparts. Only, if eros is considered to be one of the salient features of the literature ascribed to female seers, these ten verses are not devoid of it (cf. v. 16).

Yamī

Most of the hymns attributed to the female seers are accumulated in the tenth book of *R̥gveda Saṁhitā*: among total twenty-eight of them, eighteen are to be met in this book alone. The poem of Yamī Vaivasvatī (X.10) is the first among such hymns, a colloquy of Yama and Yamī, the offspring of Vivasvant. Here Yamī in very passionate words provokes her brother Yama to share physical pleasure with her as she is anxious to gift him a child, whereat Yama refuses her calmly, saying that such a relation between brother and sister is unethical and forbidden. This hymn is remarkable for many reasons. In spite of possessing every feature of a lyric poem, it has never neither been cited in any of the later Vedic texts, nor been utilized as the source of any classical Indian literary piece, since perhaps during the classical age of Sanskrit literature, the topic was not considered palatable. Though the epics and Purāṇas contain many an instance of the conjugal relation between blood relations — e.g. Arjuna's and even Lord Kṛṣṇa's marriage with their maternal cousins, respectively Subhadrā and Rukmiṇī, in *Mahābhārata*, besides umpteen such references in Buddhist literature as well (collected by Sen: 1950 in his book, passim) — gradually this system must have become unpopular and the moral values turned against such cases. This apathy of the society for sexual relation between brother and sister is first attested in *Ṛgveda* X.10. Though Yamī is not ashamed of approaching her own brother, and boldly asserts that in the past such a relation was quite in vogue, Yama turns her request down. But as he never blames Yamī for her desire, it appears likely that Yama is as if standing on the threshold of a new epoch (cf. *ṚV* X.10.4, 6 & 10), trying to introduce his newly-acquired moral values to the society, connecting them to the rules of the ancient gods of Ethos, viz. Mitra and Varuṇa. In the tenth stanza of this hymn says Yama: "Subsequent ages will come, when a sister will choose one who is not a brother" (as Wilson 1850: VI renders *ā́ ghā tā́ gacchān úttarā yugā́ni* । *yátra jāmáyaḥ kṛṇávann ájāmi*). Yāska at *Nirukta* 4.20 explains this *mantra* thus: "Surely there will come those future ages, when kinsmen will behave like strangers" (following Sarup: 1920-27). Wilson's translation (1850: VI.29) of this stanza, though chiefly following Sāyaṇa, will corroborate the proposed placement of Yama on the threshold of an era of new moral values. Curiously and erroneously in the present writer's opinion, Griffith understands this stanza diametrically differently: "Sure there will come succeeding times when brothers and sisters will do acts unmeet for kinsfolk". Jamison and Brereton (op. cit. III.1383) translate line ab as "later generations will come, in which Kin will perform the unkindred (act)."

In keeping with the indigenous tradition, Roth (1850: 423ff.), among the Westerners, for the first time took Yama and Yamī to be twin brother and sister, as their names suggest. He considered them as the first human pair, the originator of the human race, just as the Hebrew conception closely related the parents of mankind by making the woman formed from a portion of the body of the man. *Bṛhadāraṇyakopaniṣad* presents the same myth about the origin of woman. Being lonely in the beginning of the universe, says *Bṛhadāraṇyakopaniṣad* 1.4.3, man did not find any joy in life, and longed for a companion and divided himself into two parts, one of which became the husband and the other, the wife. Roth ingeniously relates this old Upaniṣadic story of the origin of mankind with the hymn of Yama and Yamī, where Yamī says: "Even in the womb the creator made us husband and wife" (X.10.5). On the other hand, Müller (1864: 510) takes Yama as "the day" and Yamī as "the night", and according to his interpretation, the night in this hymn implores her brother the day to make her his wife, and he refutes. He does not seem to regard Yama and Yamī to be the first couple of mortals, the Indian Adam and Eve, as nowhere in the Vedas Yama and Yamī have been mentioned as such, though Yama referred to himself as the first mortal who had departed to the celestial world after death.[1] Following Müller, Muir (at Griffith 1896-97: 2.392 fn.), too, refuses to accept Yama as the first mortal, but both of them believed that this idea developed only in a later phase of Indian religious thought.

Sarvānukramaṇī and *Bṛhaddevatā* both say that Yama and Yamī were the offspring of Vivasvant, and Yama rejected Yamī who solicited him with a view to sexual intercourse in the hymn beginning with *o cit sakhāyam,* etc.

On the evidence of *Ṛgveda* X.13.4 it can be assumed that Yama yielded to Yamī's proposal (cf. Jamison and Brereton s.v.).

Ghoṣā

Ghoṣā, Kakṣīvant's daughter, is the seer of two Ṛgvedic hymns, X.39-40, both consisting of fourteen stanzas each. The very next hymn (X.41) is attributed to her son Suhastya Ghauṣeya. These are addressed to the Aśvins, the twin celestial physicians. Ghoṣā, the

[1] Cf. Yima, the first mortal king mentioned in *Avesta: Haomo Yašt,* Yasna 9.4.

legends say, was afflicted with leprosy and could not get married. She became sixty years of age in her father's house, when to make life worth-living with husband and sons she prayed for the favour of Aśvins in these two hymns (*BṛhD* 7.41-47). Ghoṣā's songs are significant as they contain important pieces of information regarding the status of aged unmarried women in the Vedic society. (In addition, in the couple of hymns composed by Ghoṣā, a number of myths have been mentioned, most of which are to be found in *ṚV* I.112, 116-18; IV.16; V.78; VI.62 and VIII.5.)

In her hymns, Ghoṣā alludes to the glorious deeds of the Aśvins like their helping and rescuing men in distress, and further begs for her own welfare. This story finds further mention in *Ṛgveda* I.117.7, where its seer Kakṣīvant, described as Ghoṣā's father, exalts:

> *ghóṣāyai cit pitṛṣáde duroṇé pátiṁ jū́ryantyā aśvināv adattam*
>
> The twin divines gave a husband to Ghoṣā, who had grown old in her father's house.

The term *amājúra-* in X.39.3 has been explained by Sāyaṇa as "the girl who gets old in her father's house", while another ancient commentator Udgītha derives this word from *amā* (house) and root *jṝ́-* (to get old), the compound thereby meaning "a girl who rots in her [father's] house" (cf. also *Nighaṇṭu* 3.4). Some stanzas of the two consecutive Ghoṣā hymns from the 10th book are very specific so far as her intense urge for getting a good husband is concerned, like 39.6 (*iyáṁ vāṁ ahve śṛṇutáṁ me aśvinā́,* etc.); 39.14 (*etáṁ vāṁ stómam aśvināv,* etc.); 40.4 (*yuvā́ṁ mṛgéva vāraṇā́,* etc.); 40.5 (*yuvā́ṁ ha ghóṣā páry aśvinā,* etc.); 40.9 (*jániṣṭa yóṣā patáyat kanīnakó,* etc.); 40.10 (*jīváṁ rudanti ví mayante,* etc.); 40.11 (*ná tásya vidma tád u ṣú prá vocata,* etc.); 40.12 (*ā́ vām āgant sumatír vājinīvasū,* etc.); 40.13 (*tā́ mandasānā́ mánuṣo duroṇá,* etc.); and 40.14 (*kvà svid adyá katamā́sv aśvínā,* etc.).

The impulse with which Ghoṣā invokes her gods is unique in character in so far as she requests somewhere like a child to its parents (cf. *R̥V* X.39.1 & 6) and tries elsewhere to propitiate them as a woman would her lover.[2] Ghoṣā's songs are noteworthy also on account of the intimate tone in which she accuses the Aśvins for not coming to her (cf. *R̥V* X.39.1 & 6, and what has been said on *R̥gveda* VIII.91 above). The two stanzas, viz. X.40.10-11, in which she expresses her longing for a married life are indeed touching:

> There are men, who empathize for the life (of their wives lying terminally ill), and get them admitted to holy places for treatment. Earnestly they wish them a long life, and hold them in their embraces and ask their elders to pray for (her) recovery. Upon such husbands, the consorts shower their love and yarn for their embraces.
>
> O twin divinities, we have never experienced this relationship; would you kindly guide? Could you tell us how it is when the youth sleeps in the bride's chamber? We would love to reach the home of our darling, young husbands, this is our longing.
>
> — tr. Sarasvati and Vidyalankar 1984: 12.4197

An intense lyricism flashes forth at X.40.9, where Ghoṣā prays:

> The bride, [O Aśvins,] has been born, let the husband approach (her), and may the plants of wondrous beauty spring up straightway after the rain: for him may the streams flow as down a deep descent and may he, the invulnerable, have the manliness of a husband over her.

Following his predecessor Veṅkaṭamādhava, Sāyaṇa explains *kanīnaká-* in the above verse as "a husband desiring a wife" (*kanyā-kāmaḥ patiḥ*), while Griffith renders the word as "an infant", explaining the verse thus:

> The woman hath brought forth, the Infant hath appeared, the plants of wondrous beauty have straightway sprung up. To him the rivers run as down a deep descent, and he this day becomes their master and their lord.

---

[2] Cf. *R̥V* X.39.14: *nyàmr̥kṣāma yóṣaṇāṁ ná márye*, *R̥V* X.40.2: *śayutrā́ vidháveva devárarn máryaṁ ná yóṣā*, and X.40.6: *niṣkr̥táṁ ná yóṣaṇā*.

Once again Griffith suggests an allegorical meaning for the word *yóṣā-*, viz. "the water of the cloud" and interprets *kanīnaká-* as the lightning or the infant of the water of the cloud.

Thus Ghoṣā is found longing for a family with a husband and of course a male child, and she might have composed hymns which afterwards even acquired application in sacrificial rituals, viz. in *prātar-anuvāka* and *āśvina-śāstra* (also see below Chapter 5), but it is evident from her songs that she herself felt incomplete and helpless without husband and son.[3]

Agastya-svasṛ

The next female seer is Agastya-svasṛ of X.60. This is a heterogeneous hymn: its first five verses are ascribed to the seers called Bandhus of the family of Gaupāyana, the sixth verse is attributed to their mother Agastya-svasṛ or the sister of Agastya, while the remaining six verses are again ascribed to the previous seers according to *Sarvānukramaṇī*.

Bṛhaddevatā 7.82.95 relates a story to *Ṛgveda* X.57-59. It speaks of the four brothers named Bandhu, Subandhu, Śrutabandhu and Viprabandhu, who were priests of King Asamāti of the Ikṣvāku clan. Once the king dismissed them to appoint two other priests called Kirāta and Ākuli, at which the Bandhu brothers felt offended and took recourse to black magic for the king's destruction. On hearing this, the king's newly-appointed priests put Subandhu to death, at which the other three Bandhu brothers composed these hymns to safeguard their lives and to bring Subandhu back to life.

In *Ṛgveda* X.60, with the first four verses the Bandhus praise Asamāti to appease him, the deity of these verses hence being Asamāti himself. In the fifth verse Indra is invoked for the welfare of the king. The sixth verse is again addressed to the king: the mother of the Bandhus praises Asamāti in this stanza beginning with *agástyasya nádbhyaḥ,* etc. Thus praised, the king, ashamed,

---

[3] Cf. *ṚV* X.39.6: *ánāpir ájñā asajātyā́matiḥ* | *purā́ tásyā abhíśaster áva spṛtam* ||

went to the Gaupāyanas. The following five verses are meant for Subandhu's resuscitation, which the last one, i.e. v. 12, endorses.

Unable to discover any apparent connection in between, Griffith refuses to accept that the final six verses of this hymn are really sequel to the preceding ones, an assumption which the miscellaneous metres of the various stanzas would also seem to point to: Gāyatrī has been used for the first five verses, while the rest — except the eighth and ninth which are in Paṅkti — are in Anuṣṭubh.

It is evident from the indices of *Ṛgveda* that the index-makers completely ignored preserving the name of the poetess of *Ṛgveda* X.60.6, since she bore no personal name, and was known merely after her brother and according to *Bṛhaddevatā* also after her sons. In her verse, too, she appeases the king and sings the glory of his bestowing wealth on her sons. Even in this verse of a mere twelve words, the speaker does not forget to mention the name of Agastya in order to inspire awe in the king, so that he may forget his rudeness toward her offspring.

Sūryā

Ṛgveda X.85 is the famous marriage hymn ascribed to Sūryā Sāvitrī, the daughter of Savitṛ. In this hymn, in general Sūryā describes her marriage with Soma. Most of the verses of this hymn are down to the present days recited in the marriage rituals of the Hindus. This hymn provides a picture of the ancient Indian wedding which persists till date and has hardly undergone any significant changes. The bride is blessed in this hymn to reign over her in-laws and to beget ten mighty sons, and she is urged to look after her husband as her eleventh child. Apart from this, some details of the early Hindu marriage customs are also to be found in this hymn. For example, the bride was taken to her groom's house by a flower-decorated chariot, and she was dressed in special clothes meant for the ceremony, which were termed as "the garment of the bride" (*vadhvò vā́sasā*: v. 30).

Some important documents about the marriage system in early India are attested by this hymn. It is apparent that early marriage was not the norm in those days. The coveted position occupied by the bride in her in-laws' house can also be assumed. The hymn also informs that the father used to give presents for the daughter at the time of wedding (v. 13). The system of slaughtering cows was practised on the occasion of wedding, and so on and so forth. The fortieth verse has given rise to a dispute if polyandry was actually in vogue in ancient India. The stanza explicitly tells that the bride was married to three husbands before her present marriage, and her previous husbands were Soma, Gandharva and Agni respectively. But most of the scholars are reluctant to consider this verse as indicative of polyandry in ancient India. In their opinion, since those three husbands of the bride are divine beings, they can hardly be accepted as the real husbands of a mortal bride. *Gobhilīya-Gṛhyasūtra-Pariśiṣṭa* 2.17-20, *Vasiṣṭha-Smṛti* 28.5-6, *Baudhāyana-Smṛti* 2.2.58, *Atri Saṁhitā* 90 and finally *Yājñavalkya-Smṛti* 1.71 have shed considerable light on this controversy. They assert that the maiden is given chastity by Soma, while Gandharva gives her learned and pleasant speech and Agni makes her all clean. The maiden achieves all these things during various stages of her adolescence (vide Sen 1950: 44-46).

This hymn, of forty-seven stanzas, and the two parallel Atharvavedic hymns, viz. XIV.1-2 respectively of sixty-four and seventy-five verses, are all about the marriage of Sūryā. These hymns, all important for sociological studies, are altogether very valuable documents of the Vedic marriage system, discussed in detail again in the later Gṛhyasūtras.

Ṛgveda X.85, though ascribed to Sūryā, sounds very much to be spoken to her, and moreover appears to be a description of Sūryā's marriage by a spectator, not her. In *Nirukta*, this hymn is explained as having a link with the following Indra-Indrāṇī-Vṛṣākapi hymn (*ṚV* X.86). Yāska at *Nirukta* 12.9 suggests that the origin and nature of Sūryā (in his opinion, the wife of Sūrya) has been explained in the next hymn, Vr̥ṣākapi being none other than Sūrya himself.

Indrāṇī

Now, X.86 is a complicated hymn, with seemingly incoherent and rather unintelligible stanzas, remarkable for the poetic refrain *víśvasmād índra úttaraḥ*. Tilak (1903) has even used the hymn to ascertain the Arctic home of the Aryans, interpreting it astronomically. Sāyaṇa ascribes eleven stanzas of this hymn to Indrāṇī, the wife of Indra. (Abhijit Ghosh, in a personal communication suggested that in association with Sarasvatī, as also with the Vedic trio of lunar goddesses, viz. Rākā, Kuhū and Sinīvālī, she was perhaps connected with progeny, fertility and the like.) *Sarvānukramaṇī* does not specifically ascribe the stanzas to any particular seers, and *Br̥haddevatā* 7.141, too, does not speak much of this hymn. It only mentions that this hymn is addressed to Vr̥ṣākapi, and this "brown bull" is at the same time both Indra and Prajāpati. Though in *Br̥haddevatā* 2.67 Vr̥ṣākapi is stated to be one of the seven names of Sūrya and the celestial form of Agni. Yāska, too, in *Nirukta* 12.27 explains Vr̥ṣākapi as the Sun. Griffith, sub *R̥gveda* X.86, remarks:

> Vr̥ṣākapi — literally 'the strong ape', or 'the male ape' — appears to be a sort of intermediate between a demi-god and a demon; but it is not easy to determine his nature.

In the footsteps of Yāska and *Br̥haddevatā* 2.67, he further adds that he also appears to be the setting sun, which draws up vapour and irrigates with mist. Bergaigne 1878-83: 2.270 holds Vr̥ṣākapi as a mystic sacrificer. However, Sāyaṇa following his predecessor Veṅkaṭamādhava considers Vr̥ṣākapi as the son of Indra.

A loosely connected meaning and sequence is strenuously apprehended from this hymn. Indrāṇī is furious with Vr̥ṣākapi who has monopolized the offerings that should have been presented to Indra, but Indra is very much kind to his devotee Vr̥ṣākapi and tries to cool down Indrāṇī, but she is again cross with Vr̥ṣākapi because of his amorous assault to her. She wishes him to be hunted by hounds and wants herself to rend his head in pieces. Indra tries to convince her that Vṛṣākapi is his friend and he does not enjoy without him, but from the twenty-first stanza it is comprehended that finally Indra had to bid him farewell.

Indrāṇī in this hymn can hardly be identified with a human being. So, though she deserves no detailed discussion in connection with the socio-cultural aspects of the select hymns, some interesting stanzas of this hymn still needs to be mentioned, e.g. the ninth verse — where Indrāṇī is angry with Vṛṣākapi because he considers her unprotected like a woman without husband. The next verse informs that since the days of yore women used to go to feasts and general sacrifices.

Urvaśī

Ṛgveda X.95 is the colloquy of Purūravas and Urvaśī. Urvaśī was, Sāyaṇa informs, a celestial nymph who, cursed by Mitra and Varuṇa according to legends, had to come down to earth. Purūravas, the son of Ila, fell in love with her. Urvaśī consented to live with him on condition that he would take care of her two pet rams and that she should never see him unclothed. They lived together for four years. Once the *gandharva*s decided to bring her back and so they stole one of her rams by night. At this, Purūravas jumped out of his bed without getting dressed, even as the *gandharva*s sent on him a flash of lightning to show Urvaśī him naked. The conditions being broken, Urvaśī instantly vanished. Purūravas was very depressed at her separation and wandered in search of her. He found her with a few *apsaras*es in the form of geese in the Mānasa Lake, and he implored her to come back to him. She, however, refused to return to earth and consoled him saying that he would unite with her again in heaven after his death. Briefly hinted in *Kāṭhaka Saṁhitā*, the story was retold in *Śatapatha Brāhmaṇa* 11.5.1. It also finds place in *Baudhāyana-Śrautasūtra* and in a modified version in Ṣaḍguruśiṣya's commentary on *Sarvānukramaṇī* and at *Bṛhaddevatā* 7.148-52.

In classical Sanskrit literature like *Harivaṁśa*, *Viṣṇu Purāṇa*, *Kathāsaritsāgara* and above all the immortal drama *Vikramorvaśīya* of Kālidāsa this story is again dealt with.

This hymn carries a very ancient Indo-European myth. The archetype is found in Urvaśī's assuming the form of a goose which is more clearly revealed in the same story of *Śatapatha Brāhmaṇa*. The *Śatapatha Brāhmaṇa* story is in all likelihood the older version of this legend (vide Bhattacharya 1987: 125). This hymn became extremely popular in later literature for the dramaticality and romanticism contained in it.

Urvaśī being a celestial nymph would not seem ordinarily to be a subject of socio-cultural study, but by all means she evidently articulates a few noteworthy references in her dialogues which may help the reader ascertain the position of women in that age. Urvaśī being a woman herself says or is made to say:

> With women there can be no lasting friendship. Hearts of hyenas are the hearts of women. —*R̥V* X.95.5

Purani (1963: 157-78) is not willing to accept Urvaśī as a celestial nymph of the later Purāṇas, but in his work, on the lines of Aurobindo according to his own statement, he is inclined to accept the psychological meaning suggested not only by the context but by the etymology of the word as well. Thus, for him Urvaśī implies "wide enjoyment" or "infinite delight", while the name Purūravas denotes "the many voiced [human being crying aloud for satisfying his desires]". Urvaśī the divine delight came to Purūravas, a man seeking for mundane pleasure, who chanced to experience the heavenly joy once but failed to recognize it, and consequently it forsook him.

Dakṣiṇā

R̥gveda X.107 eulogizes *dakṣiṇā* or the honorarium offered by the institutors of sacrifices to the priests who perform the ceremonies. This *dákṣiṇā* is the subject matter, i.e. the deity of this hymn, but the personified Dakṣiṇā, regarded as Prajāpati's daughter, is in the same breath enjoined as its seer, the alternative seer being Divya of the race of the Sage Aṅgiras. *Bṛhaddevatā* 8.22 says that with this hymn Dakṣiṇā Prājāpatyā praised herself. Here, Dakṣiṇā is doubtlessly a personified concept, and should not be considered in a socio-cultural study, the more so, since the hymn, not even indirectly, supplies any clue of its author.

Saramā

Ṛgveda X.108 is the famous colloquy between Saramā and the Paṇis. Saramā is the messenger of Indra, whom Sāyaṇa characterizes as the "divine bitch" (*devaśunī-*). She is by no means a woman of this soil. According to the legend narrated in *Bṛhaddevatā* 8.24-36a, the demons called Paṇis dwelt on the other bank of the Rasā, who carried off Indra's cows and hid them away. Bṛhaspati noticed it and informed Indra of the matter, when Indra sent Saramā to the Paṇis as his messenger. *Bṛhaddevatā* 8.30-35 give a somewhat different story than that found at Sāyaṇa. The hymn as interpreted by the latter means to say that Saramā made efforts to frighten the Paṇis by telling them about the might of Indra — whose cows they had stolen. The shrewd Paṇis tried to make friends with her, cajoling her saying: *svásāraṁ tvā kṛṇavai* (we will make you our sister) (v. 9c), but Saramā, not to be persuaded, sternly refused the offer of their brotherliness and advised them to get away to a far-off place, as her masters Indra and Bṛhaspati were advancing in order to vanquish them and regain the cattle.

Bṛhaddevatā 8.30-35 go on to say that the Paṇis offered Saramā the milk of the stolen cows which she drank, and then returned to Indra. Indra asked her about the cows but Saramā, who was under the influence of the milk given by the demons, replied "negatively" (i.e. probably, she denied any knowledge of the stolen cows at the Paṇis' place) to her master. Enraged, Indra kicked her with his foot — presumably at her belly — whereat she, throwing the milk out, went back trembling to the Paṇis. Indra, following her footsteps, reached where the Paṇis were, and, having smitten them, brought back his cows. This story of *Bṛhaddevatā*, however, does not tally with the hymn of *Ṛgveda*.

Noteworthy is the reference to the fraternity offered by the Paṇis to Saramā in this hymn. This suggests that even in the days of yore, brotherhood and sisterhood could be diplomatically exploited to keep up self-interests. The firmness with which Saramā refused to fall in the sentimental trap laid by the Paṇis is also remarkable.[4]

Das (1927: 188-207), however, thinks that the words of the Paṇis: "we shall make thee our sister" is characteristic of the courteous attitude of men towards women and has become a part of Indian social etiquette.

Juhū

Ṛgveda X.109 is composed by Juhū, the wife of *Brahman* (i.e. Brahmā), the alternative seer of this hymn being Ūrdhvanābha, the son of *Brahman*. Wilson (1850: 6.385) comments on this hymn: "a curious and not very intelligible legend is said to form the subject of the *sūkta*". Brahmajāyā Juhū is completely a mythical character. Sāyaṇa relates that Juhū or Vāc, the wife of Bṛhaspati who is identified with *Brahman*, had been deserted by her husband. The gods then consulted together as to find out how to expiate his sin. And, ultimately they restored her to him. The very first stanza of this hymn tells about the sin of *Brahman* (*brahmakilviṣá*) which was exclaimed by the Sea, the Wind (Mātariśvan), Fire and the heavenly Floods. The interpreters hold that this sin of *Brahman* resulted in Juhū's losing her husband's affection and he abandoned her. The desertion of wife was considered as the husband's sin.

Vāc

Ṛgveda X.125 is the famous hymn addressed to the goddess of speech (Vāc) and ascribed to Vāc herself, proclaimed as Āmbhṛṇī, i.e. the daughter of Sage Ambhṛṇa. This hymn is popularly known

---

[4] Cf. *ṚV* X.108.10a: *nấháṁ veda bhrātṛtvám nó svasṛtvám.*

as Devī-Sūkta, *Bāṣkala-Mantropaniṣad* and *Saptaśatī* or *Caṇḍī* of *Mārkaṇḍeya Purāṇa* being based thereon. *Bṛhaddevatā* 2.87 says that the group of female seers (*ṛṣikās*) which incorporates the appellation Vāc sang forth the evolutionary form of the Self, which is why whosoever of this group the seer of a hymn be, also becomes its deity. Thus in this hymn Vāc herself praised her as the deity.

The mystic exaltation expressed in this hymn of Vāc, which declares the identification of Self with the entire universe, is somewhat strange in the predominantly practical and polytheistic age of *Ṛgveda*. Nevertheless, it is altogether not unattested, and has also been expressed in various ways especially in Puruṣa (*ṚV* X.90) and Hiraṇyagarbha (*ṚV* X.121) hymns. In the present hymn a systematic philosophical thinking is lacking, but a very emotional realization of what is transcendental is found. Darmesteter in Darmesteter and Mills (1887: 1.lxxviii) suggests that the word from above, i.e. Vāc, is either a weapon that kills, or a revelation that teaches, a suggestion, however, unacceptable to Chatterji (1945). Curiously, Sarasvati and Vidyalankar (1977: 1.223-24) suggest that either the name Vāk [*sic*] as the female seer is conjectural, or the female seer derived her name only after the hymn on which she had worked as an interpreter or *saṁhitākāra*. In this connection it needs to be noted that according to the editors of this edition, the seers are no composers of the Vedas but only interpreters thereof. The traditionalist commentators like Ṣaḍguruśiṣya and Sāyaṇa, however, take Vāc as the daughter of Sage Ambhṛṇa.[5]

Though some present scholars are unwilling to accept Vāc as a human being instead of speech personified, it is rather difficult to agree with them. The spontaneous use of the feminine gender in first person raises serious doubts if this hymn should indeed be attributed to a personified idea, or must be ascribed to a woman who finds within herself the Supreme Cause of the universe.

[5] *ambhṛṇasya maharṣer duhitā vāṅ nāmni brahmaviduṣī* Sāyaṇa on *ṚV* X.125.1, and *vāṅ nāmāmbhṛṇī ambhṛṇasya maharṣeḥ putrī* Śaḍguruśiṣya on the same.

Nirukta, the earliest Vedic exegesis, lends support to the latter supposition by classifying all the Vedic hymns under three groups, viz. (i) indirectly addressed, (ii) directly addressed, and (iii) self-invocations, and further declaring only three hymns in the entire *R̥gveda* to belong to the third category (*Nir* 7.2.3),[6] the present hymn being one of them.

Under a divine spell Āmbhr̥ṇī uttered this hymn, where she exceeds every mundane limit and finds herself in the highest heaven, and feels as if touching the sky with her summit, *utā́mū́ṁ dyā́ṁ varṣmáṇópa spr̥śāmi* (v. 7). This spiritual experience is not common to ordinary people, and it suggests that Āmbhr̥ṇī was an ascetic, and her words like "Whomsoever I desire, him I make mighty, him the priest, him the seer, him the sage", appears to give credence to this assumption.[7]

Wallis (1887: 85) observes that in this hymn Āmbhr̥ṇī identifies herself with the Speech incarnate (i.e. Vāc) as exalted in the fourth verse of famous Jñāna-Sūkta of Br̥haspati (*R̥V* X.71.4), where Vāc is the Word, the first creation and representation between man and God.

Rātri

Rātri is said to be the seer of *R̥gveda* X.127. As her epithet Bhāradvājī suggests, she is from the family of Bharadvāja. It must be mentioned that the alternative seer of this hymn is Kuśika, the son of Sobhari. The deity is Rātri herself. The ritualistic application (*viniyoga*) of this hymn is its recital at a sacrifice offered in the early morning by one who has had unpleasant dreams during the night (*ApGS* 9.5.8, vide below in Chapter 6). Rātri, however, can hardly be accepted as the author of the hymn, because she is evidently a personified idea (i.e. night), who has been glorified in this hymn.

---

[6] *tās trividhā r̥caḥ pratyakṣakr̥tāḥ parokṣakr̥tāḥ ādhyātmikyaś ca.*

[7] *yáṁ kāmáye táṁtam ugráṁ kr̥ṇomi* | *táṁ brahmā́ṇaṁ tám ŕ̥ṣiṁ táṁ sumedhā́m* || — *R̥V* X.125.5cd

This hymn is noteworthy for the lyricism and the poetic imageries it contains, such as, *rā́trī vyàkhyad āyatī́ purutrā́ devy àkṣábhiḥ,* etc. (v. 1), or, *rā́tri stómaṁ ná jigyúṣe* (v. 8). These lines, however, show clearly that the lauder and the deity are not identical, since in the entire hymn first person is used only to denote the seer who is seeking the favour of Goddess Rātri.[8]

Godhā

The next woman seer is Godhā, to whom have been attributed the last half of the sixth stanza and the entire seventh stanza of *Ṛgveda* X.134. The other seer of this hymn consisting of seven stanzas is Māndhātṛ, the son of Yuvanāśva. The deity of this hymn is Indra, but according to *Bṛhaddevatā* 8.48 the deity of verse 7 thereof is All Gods or Viśvedevāḥ, while *Sarvānukramaṇī* is totally silent about this stanza.

Unfortunately, nothing is known of Godhā, as *Bṛhaddevatā* and other sources of legends do not shed any light on her. The metre of *Ṛgveda* X.134 is generally Mahāpaṅkti of forty-four syllables, only verse 7 being composed in Paṅkti of forty syllables. A refrain starting with *devī́ jánayitry ajījanat* is repeated in all the stanzas except the last one. All this would seem to suggest that the author of the seventh stanza is different from that of the rest of the hymn. The first hemistich of the final stanza, with insignificant variants, reappears at *Sāmaveda* I.176, but strangely, the deity of the Sāmavedic version is different (Indra). These are almost conclusive indications that the last stanza was at least a somewhat later addition. Tradition recognizes Godhā as the author also of the second half of the sixth stanza. This, however, seems unacceptable, as it contains the refrain of the previous stanzas. In view of all this, it will be more prudent to accept the final stanza to be composed by a seer other than Māndhātṛ, and the name of this seer, following the tradition, is but Godhā.

---

[8] Cf. *ṚV* X.127.4, 6-8.

Ṛgveda X.134.7 strikes a familiar note of intimacy with the god invoked, as heard also in the hymns of Apālā and Ghoṣā. Here in this stanza Godhā says:

> O gods, we never injure you, nor do we ever disturb you, we are obedient to the commandments of the holy texts, closely we clasp and cling to you, cling to your sides, beneath your arms.

A typical mannerism of speech found in the hymns of the women seers of *Ṛgveda* in general is attested especially in the third line of this stanza.[9]

Indrāṇī Again

Ṛgveda X.145 is attributed to Indrāṇī, a hymn aimed at getting rid of a rival wife. The proper realm of such hymns is in fact *Atharvaveda*, and not *Ṛgveda*, as it is used as a spell. *Āpastamba-Gṛhyasūtra* 9.5.8 prescribes that a woman who wishes to get rid of a co-wife must recite this hymn silently three times in bed before she embraces her husband. This hymn is termed as *sapatnī-bādhana* by *Sarvānukramaṇī*, where it has also been declared to be esoteric (*upaniṣad*). *Bṛhaddevatā*, which has in 8.55 elaborately dealt with this hymn, adds to it another epithet, viz., evolutional (*bhāva-vṛtta*), whereon Macdonell (1904: 2.308 fn.) comments: "The term seems to be applied to this hymn as it contains spells connected with wives", the expression otherwise being reserved for hymns dealing with birth or cosmogony.

In this hymn of six stanzas, a potential herb *pāṭhā* (on whose identification vide Das 1987 with references) is eulogized by the seer, praying to the herb the destruction or rather expulsion of her rival co-wife so that her husband remains loyal and faithful to her alone.

---

[9] Cf. *ā́ caná tvā cikitsāmáḥ*, etc. (*ṚV* VIII.91.3); *kuvíc chákat kuvít karát*, etc. (*ṚV* VIII.91.4); *iyáṁ vām ahva*, etc. (*ṚV* X.39.6); *ā́ téna yātam*, etc. (*ṚV* X.39.12); *ráthaṁ yā́ntam*, etc. (*ṚV* X.40.1); *kúha svid doṣā́*, etc. (*ṚV* X.40.2); *yuvā́ṁ mṛgéva*, etc. (*ṚV* X.40.4); *ná tásya vidma*, etc. (*ṚV* X.40.11).

This hymn, as internal evidences show, is in all probability composed by a woman. The first personal usage in the first stanza clearly suggests that the very woman uttering this hymn practises the spell on her rival. The desperate desire to do away with the co-wife, graphically expressed in this hymn, poignantly hints at the acute mental agony which wives at the polygamic age of *Ṛgveda* suffered from the unstable, rather fickle, affection of their husbands towards them. In addition, they remained in constant fear of the possibility of their rival wives snatching from them the position in the family held so far by themselves alone. The jealousy and apathy of the first wife for her rival new comer(s) are well reflected in the fourth stanza, where Indrāṇī even refuses to utter her rival's name. In all the remaining verses, save the final one, she expresses, again and again, her desire to be superior to her rival, and begs of the herb to drive her co-wife away into a far distance. How she craves for her husband's affection is evident from the last stanza where she stops with these utterances:

> As a cow hastens to her calf, so may your spirit speed to me:
> hasten like water on its way.

This hymn is remarkable in the Ṛgvedic literature, in so far as it gives vent to the despair of a neglected wife in her own words. The best wishes for a bride heard of in the famous hymn of Sūryā Sāvitrī (*ṚV* X.85) — where she was blessed to become the queen of her in-laws (v. 46) — seemingly prove to be turned to dust in this incantation of Indrāṇī meant for banishing her rival wife, in order to get back the position she had previously had in her husband's household.

Śraddhā

Ṛgveda X.151 is attributed to Śraddhā of the family of Kāma, who is also the deity of the hymn. Wilson (1850: 6.475) takes the seer Śraddhā Kāmāyanī to be an obvious allegory. For him, she is nothing but the Faith of the family of Love, a view accepted also by Griffith. This short hymn beautifully describes the glory of Śraddhā, and can be classed with the hymns of Dakṣiṇā, Rātri and Medhā, where personified concepts have been invoked and lauded, and the seers are also named after the goddesses praised in the hymns.

Indra-mātr̥s

R̥gveda X.153, of five stanzas, has been ascribed to Indra-mātr̥s, obviously mythological beings. Sāyaṇa, following *Sarvānukramaṇī*, comments that these mothers of Indra are the sisters of gods. Both Wilson (1850: 6.478) and Griffith (1897), however, think that the controversial word *devajāmayaḥ* of *Sarvānukramaṇī* denotes not the sisters but the consorts of the gods. *Br̥haddevatā* 8.59 merely says in passing that Indra is the deity of this hymn, and prefers to remain silent about its seer(s).

This hymn starts with an allusion to Apasyuvaḥ, who, swaying about, came near to Indra at his birth and shared his great heroic might. Jamison and Brereton (op. cit. III.1637) state that "the first verse of this hymn presents a tender image of unidentified females rocking the baby Indra, and verse 2 continues with a more conventional treatment of his birth." The word *apas-yú-* (?) was rendered by Sāyaṇa as "desirous of (fulfilling their) work". But Griffith (1897) suspects that this expression might even mean the water-goddesses. The following stanzas engage themselves with a description of Indra's might and glory. This hymn might have an allusion to a fragment of the story told in *R̥gveda* 4.18, where Aditi, the mother of Indra, admits that after his birth she left him in a secret place as if to conceal a sin. It may not be too bold to assume that the abandoned child was brought up by some women, eventually to be known as "the mothers of Indra".

Yamī Again

R̥gveda X.154 is attributed to Yamī, the daughter of Vivasvant. The deity or the topic of the hymn is the state of the dead. This Yamī is probably to be identified with the female seer of *R̥gveda* X.10, viz. Yamī, the sister of Yama. Sarasvati and Vidyalankar (1977: 1.221) are reluctant to accept Yamī as a historical seer, but claims Yamī to be a mere conjectural nomenclature. *Bṛhaddevatā* 8.59 declares this hymn to be evolutional (*bhāvavṛtta*).

In the five stanzas of this hymn the seer prays that the dead man may depart to the noble souls of the other world. Addressing Yama, the regent of the world of the dead, the seer prays that the departing man may go to the great souls for whom all the good things mundane flow forth, to them who have achieved heaven through great fervour, and to the heroes who lost their lives in battle, or to them who were great sacrificial donors, to the first followers of cosmos (*ṛta*) who continue to uphold it, or to that heaven which is inhabited by the penance-rich Fathers and the sages who protect the Sun.

Though traditionally Yamī Vaivasvatī of *Ṛgveda* X.10 and the seer of *Ṛgveda* X.154 are equated with each other, the humane passion found in *Ṛgveda* X.10 in the words of Yamī imploring Yama to make her his consort, is conspicuous by its absence in the present hymn. The fourth stanza of this hymn is in a sense akin in style to *Ṛgveda* I.179.2, the verse of Lopāmudrā, in spite of the fact that the theme happens there to be entirely different. The present hymn contains no information by which one can get any idea whatsoever as to the social position of the seer.

Śacī

Ṛgveda X.159 goes in the name of Paulomī Śacī who is also acclaimed as none other than Indrāṇī herself, the one whom *Ṛgveda* X.145 is ascribed to. Literally speaking, this is a song of exultation by Śacī over her rival wives, says Wilson (1850: 6.467), but the word *śácī-* in fact means "heroic act; exploit", and this hymn metaphorically is a praise of Indra's glorious activities. *Bṛhaddevatā* 8.63 states that in this hymn Paulomī lauds her own virtues and those of her co-wives, though, strangely, in the entire corpus of the hymn, not a single virtue of the fellow-wives is spoken of.

If both *Ṛgveda* X.145 and X.159 are attributed to Indrāṇī or Paulomī Śacī, the possibility of an intimate connection between these two can be considered. In the first hymn the seer expresses her desire to get rid of a rival wife, while in the present hymn her desire appears to have already been achieved, as she repeatedly calls herself triumphant and free from her co-wives. In fact, this hymn is a song of victory by a wife who seems to have won her husband's affection after a tough battle fought with her co-wives. She is not only successful in winning her husband's love, she now even declares that she rules over him. She is successful in every aspect of life, such as, she has mighty sons who defeat enemies, and a daughter who is also ruling like a queen (probably over her in-laws).

This hymn is obviously of a different tune in contradistinction to the other hymns composed by the women seers. In other hymns, women have expressed their desire of overcoming the barriers, and have prayed for a heroic yet affectionate husband and mighty sons, but in this hymn Paulomī announces her achievements in a boastful language. In the hymn of Āmbhr̥ṇī Vāc alone can the glory of the seer herself be said, though not in the same breath, to be so proudly stated.[10]

Sārparājñī

R̥gveda X.189 is ascribed to Sārparājñī, and she herself or the Sun is the deity thereof. In this short hymn of three stanzas Sārparājñī, identified by the commentators with Kadrū who is Kaśyapa's wife and the fabulous mother of the snakes, praises herself as the Sun personified, or even the Sun-god at that. This hymn reappears, among other places, also in *Vājasaneyī Saṁhitā* (3.6-8), where Uvaṭa and Mahīdhara hold Agni to be the deity of the first line of the commencing stanza, and Agni in the form of the Sun, of the rest of the *mantra*.

All the commentators unanimously take the word *gauḥ* in the first stanza to stand for the Sun. This stanza contains a picture

---

[10] Cf. *ahám rā́ṣṭrī saṁgámanī vásūnām* (*R̥V* X.125.3a).

which is rather agreeable to a motherly woman. It says that this moving Sun, or literally "the spotted bull", has arrived and sat before (his) mother in the east, to advance next to (his) father, the heaven. Wilson would love to identify the Mother in the east with the Earth, while Griffith would prefer to take it as the Dawn. In the rest of the hymn, the glorious deeds of the Sun are depicted in a metaphorical language.

This Sārparājñī appears very likely to be a mythical being, though only the first stanza of this hymn may have a remote possibility of being composed by a real woman, and ergo, any socio-cultural study of this hymn would seem pointless.

Vasukra-patnī

Vasukra-patnī is the seer of *Ṛgveda* X.28.1, though, curiously enough, she has not been enlisted as such in *Bṛhaddevatā* 2.82-84. *Bṛhaddevatā* 7.30-31, however, recognize and confirm her authorship. *Sarvānukramaṇī*, at one with *Bṛhaddevatā*, says that Vasukra is the son of Indra, his wife hence being Indra's daughter-in-law. In this dialogue hymn, the latter is the speaker of one but the very first verse. According to legends, her father-in-law Indra was actually present, in disguise though for reasons unknown, at her sacrifice, but she, without any knowledge thereof, complained that all the other gods had come to attend her sacrifice, but Indra, her very father-in-law, was conspicuous by his absence. The concerned dialogue between Indra and Vasukra took place in the background of an attempt on Indra's part to assure her that he in fact had not ignored her.

Sarasvati and Vidyalankar (1977: 1.221) hold Vasukra and his wife both to be conjectural seers. This hymn of twelve stanzas apart from the first verse is somewhat obscure, being mystic in character. The words of Vasukra's wife, however, would rather urge one believe this hostess of the sacrifice to be a woman of this soil, who gets anxious at the absence of her honoured guest, her father-in-law, at the function arranged by her.

Niṣat and Upaniṣat

In addition, mention must be made of the other five female seers, who are in all the composers of four *khila*-hymns of *Ṛgveda*. The first two of them are Niṣat and Upaniṣat, the composers of the *khila* beginning with *prá dhā́rā yantu mádhuno ghṛtásya*. This hymn of seven stanzas is one of the ancient Sauparṇa hymns, addressed to the Aśvins. These eleven Sauparṇa hymns occurring after *Ṛgveda* I.73 are, according to the *Khilānukramaṇī*, composed by the authors of the Sauparṇa race. Kashikar (in Sontakke and Kashikar 1933-51 (1946): 4.902 (& l.c. fn.)) thinks that these *khila*s must be very old since they originally stand unconnected whatsoever with the rituals in which they have been prescribed by the Brāhmaṇas, Śrautasūtras and Gṛhyasūtras, so far as their contents are concerned, are used in the rituals only secondarily (cf. also the voluminous study of Charpentier (1920) thereon). This hymn of Niṣat and Upaniṣat has also been cited in *Āśvalāyana-Gṛhyasūtra* 3.12.14 and in *Aitareya Brāhmaṇa* 8.10.4.

In this hymn Niṣat and Upaniṣat sing the glory of Aśvins, citing their illustrious exploits, as have also been found in the hymns of Ghoṣā (*ṚV* X.39-40), and prayed for an adorable son. In this hymn there is a mention of Aśvins fulfilling Ghoṣā's desire. There should hardly be any scope of doubt as regards the authorship of the hymn, since the seers have themselves announced their names in the colophon, i.e. the concluding stanza.

Śrī

The next *khila*-hymn by Śrī is to be found after *Ṛgveda* V.87. This *khila* is the well-known Śrī-Sūkta. This hymn addressed to Goddess Śrī is often read and recited in India since time immemorial. This hymn, it should be recorded that, is not as old as the forementioned *khila* of Niṣat and Upaniṣat. This hymn must have been composed in the background of a newly-commenced worship of Śrī and Lakṣmī introduced in the Yajurvedic age. Kashikar (op. cit. 4.897-99 & 930 fn.) suspects that this hymn must have been affected by later supplements. There is a commentary of Vidyāraṇya on the first fifteen verses of the hymn. There is also a dispute regarding the exact number of stanzas thereof. In Aufrecht's edition there are twenty-three stanzas while in Müller's edition there are twenty-nine, with a considerable number of variant legomena. The Vaidika Saṁśodhana Maṇḍala edition (vol. 4, p. 907), however, reduces the number to nineteen.

Bṛhaddevatā 5.91 calls this hymn a benediction, but also remarks that it may alternatively be employed to banish ill luck. Whatever that may be, the hymn actually praises Śrī or the goddess of fortune and describes her beauty and grace. She is invoked for the welfare of the seer, who cannot hence be the goddess herself, as there is a clear distinction between the worshipper and the worshipped. Internal evidence suggests that the speaker of the prayer is not a woman.[11] The seer prays for worldly pleasures, such as fame, wealth, sons, obedient servants and power, all the common male desires especially of that age.

Lākṣā

The *khila*-hymn of Lākṣā, the deity whereof is also Lākṣā, comes after *Ṛgveda* X.137. *Bṛhaddevatā* has thrice spoken of this deity, in 1.129, 2.84 and 8.51. The name Lākṣā has been mentioned in *Bṛhaddevatā* 1.129 along with the names of Bhūmi, Anumati, Dhenu, Sītā, etc. She is a deity belonging to Indra's sphere.

Lākṣā or Lac is a deity of the herbs, whose glory has been eulogized in this hymn where the welfare of the seer is also prayed for (for the nature of the herb/worm, vide Griffiths (2009: 53-56), introducing *Paippläda Saṁhitā* VI.4 used to heal wounds with lac, with ample bibliographical references). This hymn is popular on account of the beautiful lyric it possesses. Anyway, the seer does not seem to be the deity herself, but there is no other clue with the help of which anything about the seer can be inferred.

---

[11] Cf. vv. 2, 7, 10, 17, 19 of the Śrī hymn.

Medhā

The *khila*-hymn of Medhā comes after *Ṛgveda* X.151 (i.e. the hymn of Śraddhā). The deity is Medhā or Merit, of whom the seer prays for her (?) own wisdom. This hymn is mentioned at *Bṛhaddevatā* 2.84 and 8.58, and also at *Ṛgvidhāna* 4.14.1 as Medhā-Sūkta. This hymn, too, falls under the category of hymns addressed to Śraddhā, Dakṣiṇā and Śrī, since in all these hymns, personified concepts have been praised as deities and the seers are also known after the deities whom they have worshipped in their songs.

Summing up, in view of the account given above, it can be presumed that there were at least some female seers who were the women of this earth and soil, and consequently the hymns composed by them are vibrant with their will and woe, joys and sorrows, hopes and despair, aspirations and frustrations, triumphs and failures. Altekar (1962: 10) suggests that some of the female seers of *Ṛgveda* may have been mythical personages, but internal evidence shows that Lopāmudrā, Viśvavārā, Apālā, Sikatā, Nīvāvarī and Ghoṣā were surely women in flesh and blood, who once lived in Hindu society. He says further, that the authors of *Ṛgveda* X.145 and 159 were doubtlessly ladies, though it may be questioned if their real names were indeed Indrāṇī and Śacī as recorded by tradition. A close scrutiny of the hymns may, however, tempt one to conclude that, in addition to the seers who in Altekar's view were real women, also Romaśā, Śaśvatī, Vasukra-patnī, Agastya-svasṛ, Vāc, Godhā, Niṣat, Upaniṣat and to some extent even the Yamī of *Ṛgveda* X.10 were women of this soil. Their hymns contain wonderful materials for estimating the position of poetesses in ancient Indian civilization.

Interestingly, mere statistics will prove that most hymns ascribed to women seers find place in the two late books of *Ṛg-veda*, viz. the first and especially the tenth (one such hymn being pre-penultimate in the latter book). The majority of the seers of the few *ṛṣikā*-hymns to be found in the *vaṁśa-maṇḍala*s are not human beings but mythical figures. Of only the two such hymns appearing in the heterogeneous eighth book, one occurs even much after the Vālakhilya hymns. This assumes some significance when it is remembered that many scholars, including Macdonell (1900: chap. III), perhaps rightly, think that at one stage *Ṛgveda* ended just before the beginning of the Vālakhilya hymns — widely considered, not being commented upon by Sāyaṇa, to originally be outside the corpus of *Ṛgveda* — i.e. with the forty-eighth hymn of book 8. This is a pointer to the fact that in a certain rather late stage the society of the age became so permissive that hymns even composed by female seers were allowed to be incorporated in the sacred texts.

2

Traditional Expositions vis-à-vis Modern Interpretations of the Concerned Ṛgvedic Hymns

Some Major Differences

THIS chapter attempts at pointing out some major differences between the interpretations of indigenous commentators and those offered by the modern scholars on the expositions of the concerned Ṛgvedic hymns and verses composed by women seers.

In the book 1 of *Ṛgveda*, only two female seers' compositions are found: I.126.7 and 179.1-2, ascribed to Romaśā and Lopāmudrā respectively. Since both the hymns are of the dialogue type, and in case of such hymns, it is necessary to ascertain the authorship of the individual stanzas, in this chapter an attempt has been made to ascertain the authorship of the select hymns, sometimes even stanza-wise.

I.126.7

The seer of 126.7 is, as said above, Romaśā. In this hymn of seven stanzas, the first five verses are ascribed to Kakṣīvant, while the seer of verse 6 is King Bhāvayavya and the seventh one goes by the name of his queen, viz. Romaśā. According to a traditional legend (*BṛhD* 3.140-54), Kakṣīvant, the son of seer Dīrghatamas Aucathya, while returning from his teacher's hermitage on completion of his study, met King Svanaya Bhāvayavya on the way. The king liked the youth very much and honoured him with his daughters and wealth. On the next morning Kakṣīvant rushed to his father to inform of his good fortune and asked him to pray for the sake of King

Bhāvayavya, who had bestowed affection and prosperity on him. Thus in the preceding hymn, I.125, a praise of gifts (i.e. *dānastuti*, or *nārāśaṁsī* as termed by *Bṛhaddevatā* 3.154) by Kakṣīvant and his father Dīrghatamas is found.

Kakṣīvant is seen again at the next hymn, praising King Svanaya Bhāvayavya with the first five stanzas, whereat the next and last two stanzas contain an intimate erotic conversation between two lovers, who have been identified as King Svanaya and his wife Romaśā. Śākapūṇi, an ancient Niruktakāra who precedes Yāska, thinks that these two stanzas constitute a dialogue of Indra and the king with Romaśā. But Śākaṭāyana, another of Yāska's predecessors, thinks that in this couple of verses a story of a husband and wife, who were in contact with Indra, has been told (cf. *BṛhD* 3.155-56). According to *Bṛhaddevatā* 4.1-4 Indra was present at the time of this conversation. *Bṛhaddevatā* states that it was Indra who questioned the queen jokingly, whether she had (pubic) hair or not, at which the queen out of her childish nature replied, "Clasp me closely, O Mighty one" (*úpopa me párāmṛśa,* etc.) at verse 7. Then the king soothed her with the previous stanza, i.e. the sixth verse of the present hymn.[1]

These last two stanzas visibly have no connection with the preceding five, as thereat the gifts of Svanaya to his son-in-law have been described in detail. In the initial *mantra* the seer says:

> I compose with delight a number of praises for King Bhāvya alias Svanaya, who lives on the bank of the River Sindhu, who, unhurt by anyone and desirous of fame, grants me thousands of Soma sacrifices.

---

[1] *tatas tam arthaṁ harivān viditvā* | *priyaṁ sakhāyaṁ svanayaṁ didṛkṣuḥ* |
abhy ājagāmāśu śacīsahāyaḥ | *prītyārcayat taṁ vidhinaiva rājā* ||

abhy ājagāmāṅgirasī ca tatra | *hṛṣṭā tayoḥ sā caraṇau vavande* |
indraḥ sakhitvād atha tām uvāca | *romāṇi te santi na santi rājñi* ||

sā bālabhāvād atha taṁ jagāda | *upopa me śakra parāmṛśeti* |
tāṁ pūrvayā sāntvya nṛpaḥ prahṛṣṭo |
anvavrajat sātha patiṁ pativratā || — *BṛhD* 4.1-3

In the following four stanzas, Kakṣīvant gives a list of the gifts he received from the king and describes them explicitly, among which there was a good number of well-trained horses, hundreds of gold coins, 60,000 cows, ten chariots and ten brides as well.

The two concluding stanzas of this hymn, however, strike a different note. At verse 6 a man is heard speaking about his lady-love:

> This girl, fit to enjoy, has been fully accepted by me (or, this girl has embraced me deeply); she gets stuck to one like a she-mongoose who has given birth to children; being moistened with desire she gives me hundreds of erotic embraces.[2]

Or, a bolder translation of the modern scholars may be considered:

> She who, when squeezed and squished, keeps stinking like a mongoose – fusing (with me), the woman to be enjoyed . . . gives me hundreds of "spurts".
>
> — Jamison and Brereton 2014: I.292

The woman shots back to her lover in the following stanza:

> Come close to me, give me a close hug, and do not consider me to be a minor. I am hairy all over the body (i.e. quite enjoyable), just like a ewe of the Gandhāras.[3]

Again, going the with modern translators where "the last verse (7) contains the ostensible and crudely seductive speech of the woman herself" – (saying)

> Feel me up – keep going further. Don't belittle my "little things [= private parts]. I am entirely hairy, like a little ewe of the Gandhāris." — Jamison and Brereton 2014: I.292

According to Griffith the above two stanzas appear to be a fragmentary piece of a popular song, as these have no apparent

---

[2] *ā́gadhitā párigadhitā* | *yā́ kaśīkéva jáṅgahe* |
dádāti máhyaṁ yā́durī | *yā́śūnāṁ bhojyā̀ śatā́* || — ṚV I.126.6

[3] *úpopa me párā mṛśa mā́* | *me dabhrā́ṇi manyathāḥ* |
sárvāhám asmi romaśā́ | *gandhā́rīṇām ivāvikā́* || — ṚV I.126.7

connection with what precedes and are composed in a different metre. The first five verses are in Triṣṭubh of eleven syllables, while the rest two are in octosyllabic Anuṣṭubh. Griffith considers these couple of verses to be "a fragment of a liberal Shepherd's love song", where the seventh stanza should have preceded the sixth (vide p. 2 in Chapter 1). This hypothesis of Griffith, however, is rejected by Jamison and Brereton who consider the entire hymn a composition of Kakṣīvant himself.

The importance that has been traditionally attached to this hymn, however, should not be altogether ignored. The myths and legends about the seers of the hymns, their families and the gods they invoked can hardly be totally conjectural in character, since they have come down to the present age from a very ancient period.

The followers of the spiritualistic method of interpreting the Vedas have attempted to present a comprehensive meaning of this hymn so that it can be looked upon as a single coherent song. Sarasvati and Vidyalankar (1977: 1.203-05) claim that their English translation of the text is based on the interpretations of Dayananda and Aurobindo, the two renowned exponents of this method. The translators see in the seer Kakṣīvant of I.126.1-5 a representative of the people of his country, who on behalf of his countrymen accepts a bounty from a king, desirous of fame, who performed 1,000 noble deeds for the benefit of his subjects. Kakṣīvant prays here for the welfare of his people and sings the glory of the donor. Sarasvati and Vidyalankar (1977: 3.565) explain I.126.6-7 in the following manner:

> The benevolent measures, applied with determination and firmness, would sustain a state, and keep enemies away as under the fear of corporeal punishment and give to me, the dedicated worker, hundreds of benefits.

[The state speaks to the people in ecstasy:]

> Approach me, listen to me, deem me not immature; I am hairy everywhere, like a ewe of an enchanted hilly tract.

The word *bhojyā́* in I.126.6d has been interpreted by Sāyaṇa as "a girl fit to enjoy" (*bhogayogyā*), but in the above rendering it is explained as "the benevolent measures". In this interpretation, thus, the stanza cannot be taken as referring to an individual woman. The words *yā́śūnām śatā́* occurring at the same verse have been understood by Sāyaṇa to mean "hundreds of sexual unions",[4] while his predecessor Veṅkaṭamādhava explained *yā́śu* as "sons, by whom fame is acquired",[5] and accordingly the phrase *yā́śūnām bhojyā́ śatā́* ought to mean "hundreds of enjoyments for the sons". And, the whole verse speaks of a wife who brings good fortune and prosperity to her husband. According to Veṅkaṭamādhava, if this couplet is to be taken as a conversation between Bhāvayavya and Romaśā, the phrase in question will eventually point to "a woman capable of giving birth to sons". It may be noticed that in the aforesaid translation the word *yā́śu* has been interpreted as "benefit", and the final stanza has been assigned to "the state". The spiritualists take delight to discover in this hymn a note of patriotism which reaches its climax in the concluding stanza.

Since these two stanzas contain an intimate conversation of two lovers on love sport, they might better be accepted as a fragment of another song that has been inserted in this poem, as indicated by Western scholars. As held by the traditional commentators, they might also be an integral part of the same poem, of which the former portion glorifies a king's benevolence and the later part comprises a colloquy of the king himself with his queen in private.

The question regarding the authorship of the final stanza, i.e. whether Romaśā is really the name of the queen, a female seer of the list furnished by *Bṛhaddevatā* 2.82-84, or a mere adjective to the speaker herself, remains, however, unsolved. Ludwig (1876) on the verses concerned thinks that the name mentioned in the final

---

[4] *yāśūnāṁ sambhogānāṁ yaśa iti prajananānāma tatsambandhīni karmāṇi yāśūni bhogāḥ* — Sāyaṇa on *ṚV* I.126.6

[5] *yaśa āhartṛṇāṁ putrāṇām* — Veṅkaṭamādhava on *ṚV* I.126.6

couplet is Yādurī and not Romaśā, and ventures to suggest that the word (*semen genitale*; *effundens*) may be the name of a slave girl. Though there is no external evidence to support this hypothesis, it is true that in this stanza *romaśā́* has been used as an adjective. It also cannot be confirmed from the verse itself that Romaśā is the speaker's nomenclature. Anyway, from the internal evidence and the content and spirit of the verse, it seems to be a woman's utterance. Geldner (1951: 1.175 n.) on vv. 6f. remarks that the Indian tradition wrongly took these two verses to constitute a dialogue between the king and his queen called Romaśā, and takes *romaśā́-* literally as an adjective, following Sāyaṇa. He further says that her hairiness is the sign of puberty, and points out that flirting with an *ajātalomnī* was forbidden at *Gobhila-Gṛhyasūtra* 3.5.3.

I.179.1-2

Lopāmudrā is the other poetess to be met in the book 1 of *Ṛgveda*. The commencing two stanzas of *Ṛgveda* I.179 are ascribed to her. Like the last one, this is also a dialogue hymn, of six stanzas. The first two stanzas are said to have been uttered by Lopāmudrā, addressing husband Agastya. The next two stanzas are his reply. The remaining two verses are ascribed to a disciple of Agastya, who overheard the preceding secret erotic conversation between his teacher and his wife, and confesses his sin in the fifth stanza. In the final stanza the disciple speaks of the consequence and significance of the couple's union.

Śaunaka at *Bṛhaddevatā* 4.57-59 narrates this incidence in the following way. Desirous of a secret union, with her, the seer (i.e. Agastya) started to talk to his wife, the illustrious Lopāmudrā, when she had bathed after her courses (*ṛtau*). At this, she, with the two stanzas beginning with *pūrvī́ḥ,* etc. (*ṚV* I.179.1-2), expressed her desire. Then Agastya, also wishing for enjoyment, cajoled her with the next two stanzas (i.e. vv. 3-4). The disciple (of the seer), by the power of austerity, became aware of the whole affair of the craving couple. But afraid that he had committed a sin (*enas*) by listening (*śrutvā*) to their erotic dialogues, the disciple sang the last two stanzas (i.e. vv. 5-6), as a sort of confession and expiation.[6]

Bṛhaddevatā 4.60, however, relates to the sequel of the aforesaid conversation not to be found in the text of *Ṛgveda* I.179, since it says:

> The preceptor and his wife, lauding and embracing him, kissed on his head, and smiling, both of them told him, "You are sinless, son".[7]

Sarvānukramaṇī of Kātyāyana says that the first four stanzas of the concerned hymn are a conversation of Lopāmudrā and Agastya, while the final couplet was spoken by a disciple who had listened to this erotic conversation.[8] The metre of the first four stanzas and the last one is eleven-syllabic Triṣṭubh, and the fifth stanza is in nine-syllabic Bṛhatī. The deity of the hymn is Rati (Eros).

Sāyaṇa, like his predecessor Veṅkaṭamādhava, follows *Bṛhaddevatā* 4.57-59 and comments on *Ṛgveda* I.179 that the first two verses belong to Lopāmudrā and the following two are uttered by her husband Agastya. But Durga, while commenting on *Nirukta* 5.1.3, asserts that the fourth stanza comes from Lopāmudrā (on *nadásya*, etc. He says: *lopāmudrāyā iyam ārṣam* [*sic*] *sābravīd agastyaṁ bhartāram abhipretya nadasya*, etc.). The fifth stanza has been suspected by Griffith to be rather superfluous in character, as

---

[6] *ṛtau snātām ṛṣir bhāryāṁ | lopamudrāṁ yaśasvinīm |*
upajalpitum ārebhe | rahaḥsaṁyogakāmyayā ||

dvābhyāṁ sā tv abravīd | ṛgbhyāṁ pūrvīr iti cikīrṣitam |
riraṁsus tām athāgastya | uttarābhyām atoṣayat ||

viditvā tapasā sarvaṁ | tayor bhāvaṁ riraṁsatoḥ |
śrutvainaḥ kṛtavān asmi | brahmachāry uttame jagau ||
— *BṛhD* 4.57-59, tr. Macdonell (1904)

[7] *praśasya taṁ pariṣvajya | gurū mūrdhny avajaghratuḥ |*
smitvainam āhatuś chobhāv | anāgā asi putraka || — *BṛhD* 4.60

[8] *pūrvīḥ ṣaḍ jāyāpatyor lopāmudrāyā agastasya ca dvṛcābhyāṁ ratyarthaṁ saṁvādaṁ śrutvāntevāsī brahmacāry antye bṛhatyādi apaśyat.* — *Sarvānukramaṇī* 2.12

its connection with the rest of the hymn is not very apparent.

According to Bergaigne (1878-83: 2.394), this hymn has a mystical meaning, where Agastya is identifiable with the celestial Soma, and Lopāmudrā represents fervent prayer, who after long labour succeeds in drawing the Soma down from his secret-dwelling place.

In stark difference from the general traditional assumption of who the speakers of the various *mantra*s are, Geldner (1951: 1.257f.), ingeniously following only the textual indications and ignoring all other external myths, assigns the verses 1-2 and 4 to Lopāmudrā and verses 3, 5 and 6 to Agastya.

In Sāyaṇa's explanation, the first stanza means:

> Since many years I have been toiling day and night, through age-inducing dawns. The old age impairs the beauty of the limbs. Let husbands approach their wives.[9] (For line d, see Jamison and Brereton 2014: I.380: "Bullish (men) should now come to their wives".)

This is why, to seduce her ascetic husband, Lopāmudrā says further in the second stanza:

> Even the law-fulfiller ancient sages, who with the gods declared eternal statutes, begot (progeny), without thereby violating (their vow of continence). Therefore let the wives be approached by their husbands.[10] (For line c, cf. Jamison and Brereton, op. cit. "even they got out of harness, for they did not reach the end.")

In response, in the third stanza Agastya consoles his wife by saying:

> We have not toiled in vain, since the gods protect all. Both of us will surpass all of our challengers. Exerting together we may triumph in many conflicts.

---

9 *pūrvī́r ahám̐ śarádaḥ śaśramāṇā́* | *doṣā́ vástor uṣáso jaráyantīḥ* |
minā́ti śríyam̐ jarimā́ tanū́nām | *ápy ū nú pátnīr vṛ́ṣaṇo jagamyuḥ* ||
— *ṚV* I.179.1

10 *yé cid dhí pū́rva ṛtasā́pa ā́sant* | *sākám̐ devébhir ávadan-n-ṛtā́ni* |
té cid ávāsur nahy ántam āpúḥ | *sám ū nú pátnīr vṛ́ṣabhir jagmyuḥ* ||
— *ṚV* I.179.2

In the fourth stanza the sage expresses his desire that had been restrained so far by austerity, and welcomes his wife to share conjugal pleasure with him:

> Desire arising either from this cause (i.e. the company of the wife) or from that one (i.e. the advent of the spring with the accessory stimulants) has come upon me who so far restrained himself by penance. Let Lopāmudrā approach her husband closely, and let the impatient girl enjoy her ascetic husband of great strength.

Also consider the bolder and probably closer translation of the modern scholars:

> [Agastya:] The lust of a mounting bull [/waxing reed = penis] has come to me, lust arisen from here, from there, from everywhere. Lopāmudrā makes the bullish one flow out; the steadfast man does the flighty woman suck while he is snorting.
>
> —Jamison and Brereton, op. cit.

Durga on *Nirukta* 5.1.3 interpreted the stanza just discussed as spoken by Lopāmudrā and not by Agastya and explained it thus:

> Desire for the sage who has been practising penance, springing from my body or from his (Agastya's), has overpowered me, and this princess Lopāmudrā should approach her man. This woman impatient in desire may enjoy her ascetic husband, who is deeply absorbed in meditation.

In the fifth stanza, to expiate his sin, the disciple of Agastya prays to Soma, the deity of joy, that his sins might be forgiven as man is subject to manifold desires. In the last stanza, which also belongs to the disciple, the result of the union of Agastya and Lopāmudrā is described in following way:

> Agastya, being desirous of progeny, offspring and strength, toiled hard with his spade; he fulfilled both kinds of obligations, viz. one of the household life and the other of austerity. And he received genuine blessings of the gods.

The expression *ubhau varṇau* in I.179.6c has been interpreted by

Griffith as "both classes" meaning probably the classes of the priests and of the princes or the institutors of sacrifices, while Bergaigne (1878-83: 2.394) understands it to mean "two forms or essences of Soma, viz. the celestial and the terrestrial". Geldner (1951: 1.258 fn. on 6c), while appreciating Sāyaṇa's interpretation of the phrase as referring to the two stages of life (celibacy and marital status: *kāmaṁ ca tapaś ca*), also pleads for the possibility of the alternative explanation as "*beide Kasten, seine eigene und die seiner Frau, die eine Königstochter war*" (both castes, his own and that of his wife, who was a king's daughter). Jamison and Brereton (2014: I.379) put the dilemma as "ascetic practice and the production of sons".

The entire hymn deals with a problem faced universally by all humans who lead an ascetic life and yet cannot get rid of the natural urges. The ascetic couple Agastya and Lopāmudrā had been living an austere ascetic life for a considerable period, but time ultimately came when it appeared necessary for them to fulfil the demands of a married life. Agastya, though an ascetic, succeeded in making a proper balance between these two radically opposite obligations. This hymn bears the message, that suppressed desires should not be ignored as by nature man is subject to many desires (*pulukā́mo hí mártyaḥ* I.179.5d), and an ideal man is he, who succeeds in nurturing the demands of married life as well as of the life of austerity.

The traditional interpreters are nearly unanimous with Sāyaṇa regarding the meaning of *Ṛgveda* I.179.1-2. Veṅkaṭamādhava, however, had explained *ávāsuḥ* at 2c as *avasitāḥ*, i.e. "ended", the whole sentence thereby meaning "not having seen the end of it (i.e. continence), they also ended their lives",[11] while Sāyaṇa interpreted *ávāsuḥ* as *avakṣipanti retaḥ*, i.e. "ejaculate", etymologizing the word thus: *syatir upasṛṣṭo vimocane vartate* (when preceded by a prefix, the root -*syá* means "to discharge").

[11] *te ca avasitāḥ na hi antaṁ gatas tapasā*
— Veṅkaṭamādhava on *ṚV* I.179.2

III.33

The female seers to be found in the book 3 of *Ṛgveda* are not human beings, but two rivers named Vipāś and Śutudrī (the modern Beas and Sutlej of north-western India). *Ṛgveda* III.33 is a dialogue hymn, whereat the speakers are Sage Viśvāmitra and the above-mentioned rivers. The hymn has thirteen stanzas, of which stanzas 1-3, 5, 7, 9 and 11-13 are ascribed to Viśvāmitra, while the rest four, i.e. stanzas 4, 6, 8 and 10 are allotted to the above rivers incarnate, viz. Vipāś and Śutudrī.

Despite being rivers, these two have been incorporated in the present study, as their names appear in the list of female seers furnished by *Bṛhaddevatā*. These rivers have been held as female beings because the word *nadī-*, and the nomenclatures Vipāś and Śutudrī are all in feminine gender. Though of uncertain authorship the stanzas ascribed to the two rivers exhibit a mannerism which is very feminine in nature. For this reason, too, it will not be totally uncalled for to consider these four stanzas to have been uttered by women.

Ṛgveda III.30 and the following twenty-three hymns are addressed to Indra, but *Ṛgveda* III.33 stands out of the lot as Viśvāmitra and the two rivers are engaged in a dialogue thereat, though a prayer to Indra is also to be found in the sixth and seventh stanzas.[12] *Bṛhaddevatā* 4.105-09 narrate a story as the background of the hymn. At *Bṛhaddevatā* 4.106 it is told that Viśvāmitra, while going with King Sudās who had appointed him as his sacrificial priest, came to the confluence of Vipāś and Śutudrī. The sage addressed the two rivers with the words "Be propitious etc." (*śam* ...).[13] *Bṛhaddevatā* 4.107 points out that in this hymn there appear statements in dual, plural and singular, in the hemistich beginning with "unto, etc." (*ácchā* ..., *ṚV* III.33.3ab) and/or in the successive

---

[12] Vide *Sarvānukramaṇī* 2.18: *ṣaṣṭhīsaptamyos tv indrastutiḥ*.

[13] *purohitaḥ san-n ijyārthaṁ* | *sudāsa saha yan-n ṛṣiḥ* |
vipātchutudryoḥ sambhedaṁ | *śam ity ete uvāca ha* || — *BṛhD* 4.106

*pāda*s beginning with "Down to thee, etc." (*ní te* . . . , 10cd, 11a), and in the singular in reference to the river.[14] And, according to *Bṛhaddevatā* 4.108-09, in the first distich of the hymn as also in the second hemistich of the following *mantra* (i.e. 3cd), with expressions in dual, it is Viśvāmitra who speaks, according to the sacred text (*śruteḥ*). The rivers address him with stanzas 4, 6, 8 and 10. Indra and Savitṛ are the two gods extolled in the sixth and seventh stanzas, the two stanzas to be recognized as incidental in the entire hymn.[15]

Sarvānukramaṇī, too, supports *Bṛhaddevatā* regarding the distribution of the stanzas among their respective speakers:

> *pra parvatānām saptonā saṁvādo nadībhir viśvāmitrasyottītirṣos tatra nadīvākyaṁ caturthīṣaṣṭhyaṣṭamīdaśamyaḥ ṣaṣṭhīsaptamyas tv indrastutiḥ.* — 2.18

Tradition[16] says that Viśvāmitra, originally the family priest of Sudās, the son of Pijavana, amassed a huge wealth through his services to the king. On his way back home, he arrived at the confluence of the Vipāś and Śutudrī, and to appease them so they be fordable, he addressed the rivers with the initial three stanzas of the hymn in question. To this they replied, and a dialogue ensued, after which they allowed him and his followers to cross.

Griffith thinks that this hymn is interesting as it is considered to bear a relic of the memories of the Aryans of their eastward progress in the Land of the Five Rivers. Sāyaṇa interprets that in

---

[14] *pravādās tatra dṛśyante* | *dvivad bahuvad ekavad* |
acchety ardharce paccho vā | *nadīṣv apy ekavan ni te* ||
— *BṛhD* 4.107

[15] *ādye dvṛce dvivatsārdhe* | *viśvāmitravacaḥ śruteḥ* |
etābhir ṛgbhir vā nadya | *ṛṣim bahuvad ūcire* ||
ṣaṣṭhyāṣṭamyā caturthyā ca | *daśamyā cetarā ṛṣeḥ* |
saptamyām ṛci ṣaṣṭhyām ca | *yau devau parikīrtitau* ||
nipātinau tu tau jñeyau, etc. — *BṛhD* 4.108-10

[16] Cf. Yāska at *Nirukta* 2.24 and Sāyaṇa in his introduction to *ṚV* III.33.

the opening stanza Viśvāmitra describes the two rivers, Vipāś and Śutudrī, as "rushing from the flanks of the mountains, eager to reach the sea like two mares with loosened reins, contending each other in speed, and speeding down their waters like two fair mother-cows hastening to lick their calves". According to Geldner (1951: 1.372f.), however, the commencing two stanzas are from "*der Dichter*", i.e. "the poet" who is other than Viśvāmitra.

Yāska at *Nirukta* 2.24 interprets the pr. n. *viśvāmitra-* as *sarvamitra* (friend of all), explains at 9.39 o.c. the word *víṣite* of *Ṛgveda* III.33.1b as *aśve iva vimukte iti vā*, *viṣanne iti vā* (like two mares who are released, or who are out of temper), and derives at 9.26 o.c. the name *Vipāś* – variously as *vipāḍ vipāṭanād vā*, *vipāśanād vā*, *viprāpaṇād vā*, *pāśā asyāṁ vyapāśyanta vasiṣṭhasya mumūrṣataḥ*, *tasmādvipāḍ ucyate* (the Vipāś is so called because it originates "from bursting forth, or from loosening fetters, or from being extended": it is called "fetterless" "because the fetters of the dying Vasiṣṭha were loosened in it"[17]). Dayananda etymologizes the term thus: *yā vividhaṁ patati*, *gacchati vipāśayati vā sā* (a river flowing with a variety of movements and covering a lot of space). The word *śutudrī-* has been derived by Yāska as *śutudrī śudrāviṇī*, *kṣipradrāviṇī, āśu tunneva dravatīti vā* (Śutudrī is a good runner, a quick runner, or it runs swiftly like one who is goaded[18]), and by Dayananda (at Sarasvati and Vidyalankar 1977: 4.1175-77) as *śu śīghraṁ tudati vyathayati sā* (she who troubles rapidly). In passing, it may be noted that Veṅkaṭamādhava suggests an alternative meaning of *hā́samāne* at *Ṛgveda* III.33.1b, viz. "making merry" (*hāsatiḥ . . . harṣakarmā vā*, *harṣamāṇe*).

Praise to the two rivers with a description of their beauty through a suitable simile is met with in the second stanza. It says:

---

[17] Cf. *Mahābhārata*, Ādi-Parvan, vv. 6745-50, where the legend of the rivalry between Viśvāmitra and Vasiṣṭha is narrated.

[18] Cf. *śatadhā vidrutā yasmāc chatadruriti viśrutā* — *Mahābhārata*, Ādi-Parvan 6752

Impelled by Indra soliciting his commands, you two go to the ocean like charioteers (to their goal); flowing together, swelling with your billows, O bright rivers! each of you seeks the other.

In the third stanza Viśvāmitra says that he has attained the most motherly river and he has come to the broad, blessed Vipāś, flowing to a common home together (with Śutudrī) like parent cows hastening to caress their youngling.

In the fourth stanza the rivers speak out:

Fertilizing [the land] with these billows,
We move forward to the home that gods have made for us;
Our flood, when urged to motion, allows no delay;
Of what is the sage desirous, that he addresses the rivers?[19]

The fifth stanza is the sage's reply, translated metrically and beautifully by Griffith:

Linger a little at my friendly bidding; rest, Holy ones, a moment in your journey.
With hymn sublime soliciting your favour Kuśika's son hath called unto the river.

According to Sāyaṇa the phrase *me vácase somyā́ya* in *Ṛgveda* III.33.5a means "to my speech importing the *soma*" (*somasampādine vacase*). In his opinion, Viśvāmitra intended to say that having crossed the rivers he might go to gather the *soma*-plant (*uttiryāhaṁ somaṁ sampādayāmīti*). Sāyaṇa's interpretation is based on *Nirukta* 2.25.

In the sixth stanza the rivers answer him back:

Indra, the wielder of the thunderbolt, dug our channels when he slew Ahi, the blocker-up of rivers. Savitṛ, the lovely-handed god, has led us on our path, and we, obedient to his commands,

---

[19] *enā́ vayáṁ páyasā pínvamānā* | *ánu yóniṁ devákṛtaṁ cárantīḥ* |
ná vártave prasaváḥ sárgataktaḥ | *kiṁyúr vípro nadyò johavīti* ||
— *ṚV* III.33.4

> flow forth expanded.[20]

Durga, while commenting on *Nirukta* 2.26, brings out the import of *Ṛgveda* III.33.6 in this manner:

> He (Indra) is our lord. And, he alone has the right to issue us orders, not you.[21]

But, according to Sāyaṇa the word *savitṛ* in 3c is an epithet to Indra, meaning "the impeller of the whole world" (*savitā sarvasya jagataḥ prerakaḥ*). Yāska, however, takes Savitṛ to be the well-known individual god, viz. the Sun (*devo 'nayat savitā*). Wilson (1850: 3.69-74) and Griffith, too, accept the word to stand for the Sun. Sarasvati and Vidyalankar (1977: 4.1175-77) follow suit and explain the stanza in reference to "the Sun":

> The resplendent Sun, wielder of the sharp rays, defines our course when he slashes obstructive forces blocking the path of waters. The sun leads us on our path, and obedient to his commands we flow as ample streams.

The seventh stanza is again ascribed to Viśvāmitra, wherein he sings the glory of Indra in order to appease the rivers:

> The heroic endeavour of Indra is ever to be celebrated when he rent Ahi in pieces, and with his thunderbolt destroyed the surrounding (obstructors of the rain), when the waters eager for their course flowed forth.

Now pleased with the seer's praise for Indra, the rivers say in the eighth stanza:

> O praiser, never forget this word of yours, the future generations shall re-echo the words with which you have addressed us. O

---

[20] *índro asmā̆ aradad vájrabāhur* | *ápāhan vṛtráṁ paridhíṁ nadī́nām* |
devó 'nayat savitā́ supāṇís | *tásya vayáṁ prasavé yāma urvī́ḥ* ||
— *ṚV* III.33.6

[21] *so 'smākam īśvaraḥ sa evāsmān ājñāpayitum arhati na tvām iti na tava vacanād uparamāmahe* — Durga on *Nirukta* 2.26

> celebrator of holy rites, be favourable to us with solemn prayers, humble us not amongst men (or: don't make us argue in the arrogant fashion of men); salutation be to you![22]

The phrase, *mā́ no ní kaḥ* in line d of the text, has, however, been interpreted variously by scholiasts. Since Veṅkaṭamādhava explained it as *mā naḥ ni kārsīḥ stutyāḥ puruṣeṣu* (do not deprive us of being adorable among men), while Sāyaṇa specifically mentioned that the rivers do not want to argue in the arrogant fashion of men, i.e. they dislike to act as men do (*uktipratyuktir upasaṁvādavākyākhyāpanena nitarāṁ puṁvat mā kārṣīḥ*), Wilson (1850: 3.69-74) chose to interpret it as "treat us not after the arrogant fashion of men", whereas Griffith translated this phrase as "[h] umble us not mid men", and he was followed by Geldner (1951: 1.373) (*setz uns nicht bei den Menschen herab*!).

In the ninth stanza Viśvāmitra addresses the rivers as sisters (*svasāraḥ*) and speaks:

> O sisters, listen kindly to him, who praises you and who have come to you from far away with a wagon and a chariot. May you bow down lowly and become easily fordable, with your floods staying below the axle of the wheels.

The rivers refused his request earlier but now being pleased with his praise they grant his prayer in the tenth stanza, saying:

> O singer of the hymn, we hear your words, that you have come from afar with a wagon and a chariot; we bend down before you, like a nursing mother and like a maiden bending (to embrace) a man.[23]

---

[22] *etád váco jaritar mā́pi mṛṣthā* | *ā́ yát te ghóṣān úttarā yugā́ni* |
ukthéṣu kāro práti no juṣasva | *mā́ no ní kaḥ puruṣatrā́ námaste* ||
— *ṚV* III.33.8

[23] *ā́ te kāro śṛṇavāmā vácāṁsi* | *yayā́tha dūrā́d ánasā ráthena* |
ní te naṁsai pīpyānéva yóṣā | *máryāyeva kanyà śaśvacái te* ||
— *ṚV* III.33.10

The fourth line, *máryāyeva kanyā̀ śaśvacái te*, finds different treatments from scholars. Veṅkaṭamādhava renders it as "like a maiden who bends down to give her lover an erotic embrace" (*kanyā yuvatiḥ maithunāya ninamati*), an interpretation accepted by such Western scholars as Wilson, Griffith, Geldner and others. Contrarily, Sāyaṇa suggests that the embrace of the maiden in this context is not at all erotic but affectionate, which is why he prefers *maryāyeva* to refer to "any man such as her father or brother" (*maryāyeva manuṣyāya pitre bhrātre vā*). Sāyaṇa inducts this idea probably from Viśvāmitra's address to the rivers as *svasāraḥ* in the preceding stanza. Yāska thinks *yayātha* at c to be an equivalent of an imperative *yāhi*, and thus according to him the line would come to mean: "go afar with this chariot". The explanation offered by Yāska (*Nir* 2.27) may apparently sound agreeable, which cannot, however, be justified grammatically. In contradistinction with this, even if the form of the verb is understood as perfect, the meaning would be equally relevant, viz. "we shall listen to your words as you have come from a long distance" (vide Sarup 1967: 37fn).

The final three stanzas (viz. vv. 11-13) are again ascribed to Viśvāmitra. In the eleventh stanza he states:

> Since, rivers (you have allowed me to cross,) so may the Bharatas pass over your united stream, may the people desiring to cross the streams, permitted (by you) and impelled by Indra, pass; then let the course appointed for your going (be resumed): I have recourse to the favour of you who are worthy of adoration.
>
> — as rendered by Wilson 1850: 3.72-73

Here *bharatá* at a has been explained as "the people of same race of Viśvāmitra" both by Veṅkaṭamādhava (*bharatakulajā viśvāmitras tatsahāyāś ca*) and Sāyaṇa (*bharatakulajā madīyāḥ sarve*), but according to Wilson (1850: 3.69-74), who would rather like to take the word literally, Bharatas are possibly nothing more than those who were the bearers of Viśvāmitra's goods and chattels, the more so since his connection with the Bharatas, whose family priest was indeed Vasiṣṭha, is somewhat remote (cf. *Mahābhārata,* Ādiparvan, v. 3734). In the next stanza the sage says:

> The Bharatas seeking cattle fared over: the singer enjoyed the favour of the rivers. May the streams dispensing food produce wealth and abundance, may they fill the fields in full (with water). For cd, the translation of Jamison and Brereton (2014: I.515) may be quoted: "Swell forth, nurturing, very generous; fill your bellies; drive quickly."

In the following final stanza the sage again seeks the benevolence of the rivers and prays with:

> Let your waves so flow that the pins of the yokes be above the waters, may the waters exempt the yokes, and may the two streams — sinless, harmless and undisturbed by anyone — never increase (beyond limits).

IV.18

Much confusion arises in the apportionment of the stanzas to the several speakers of *Ṛgveda* IV.18. According to tradition the speakers are Indra, Indrāṇī and Sage Vāmadeva. *Sarvānukramaṇī* suggests evasively that the seers and the gods of the respective verses are to be understood according to their plausibility.[24] The mythology attached to this hymn will be discussed in the concerned chapter (i.e. Chapter 4 below). *Sarvānukramaṇī* ascribes the second hemistich of the fourth verse and the seventh verse to Aditi, the celestial mother of the gods.

The *Sarvānukramaṇī-Bhāṣya* says that when Vāmadeva refused to be born in the usual manner but insisted on being delivered through the side of his mother, the distressed mother invoked Indra, who with his mother Aditi appeared and dissuaded Vāmadeva from his fatal intention. But *Bṛhaddevatā* 4.130f. say that it was Indra himself, the unborn child (*garbham*) who refused to be born in

---

[24] *yasya vākyaṁ sa ṛṣiḥ* | *yā tenocyate sā devatā* |
— *Sarvānukramaṇī* 1.2

the straightforward way (*añjasā*), and Aditi, anxious for her own welfare, admonished (*anvaśāt*) her son Indra. Sāyaṇa, however, quotes the *Sarvānukramaṇī-Bhāṣya* version of this legend in the preface of the exposition of *Ṛgveda* IV.18, while Griffith accepts the *Bṛhaddevatā* version. This is why according to the latter the main subject of this hymn is the birth and infancy of Indra. He thinks that the commentators erroneously took the stanza as referring to the birth of Vāmadeva, while the real speakers were Vyaṁsa (Indra's father), Aditi (Indra's mother) and Indra himself. As regards the distribution of the stanzas among their various speakers and determining the gods of the verses, Veṅkaṭamādhava follows but the *Sarvānukramaṇī-Bhāṣya*.

Regarding the interpretation of the second hernistich of *Ṛgveda* IV.18.4, Veṅkaṭamādhava and Sāyaṇa are unanimous, rendering it almost with identical wordings. The preceding hemistich thereof, which should be taken as coming from Vāmadeva, says that Indra's mother carried him in her womb for many months and years. Sāyaṇa appears to elucidate Vāmadeva's speech thereat: viz., Indra tormented her mother by making the gestation period stretch over many years. Aditi, being unable to stand the abuse of Indra, speaks to him (Vāmadeva), and says in the following hemistich, viz. IV.18.4cd, that neither there is any god equal to Indra, nor there will be. In this respect Wilson (1850: 3.217-25) defends Sāyaṇa with an explanation that

> Aditi defends her son upon the plea that, as his period of gestation was marvellous, his actions are not to be compared with those of any others.

Griffith (1896-97: 1.416 fn.) to verse 4, however, comments that "it is not clear who the speaker is", Though, Jamison and Brereton (2014: I.586) ascribe the verse to the narrator of the hymn.

The following two stanzas, according to tradition, expound Indra's glory and are ascribed to seer Vāmadeva. The seventh verse, however, is again attributed to Aditi. In the sixth verse the gurgling rivers are asked about "what they are saying, [and] if the waters burst asunder any girdling cloud". In the seventh verse, as if to present a sort of justification for the statement in the preceding verse, a corresponding query has been put:

> Why is it so that the *nivid*s (the prose prayers) eulogize Indra, since whatever sin he committed (in slaying Vṛtra, a brāhmaṇa, explains Sāyaṇa) has [already] been absorbed by the waters; my son with his great thunder (*vadha iti vajranāmaitat*, Sāyaṇa; cf. *Nighaṇṭu* 2.20) slayed Vṛtra and set these rivers free (to flow).

Veṅkaṭamādhava and Sāyaṇa are almost unanimous in explaining the verse, differing only regarding the meaning of *nivid-*. Veṅkaṭamādhava, following *Nighaṇṭu* 1.11: *nivid iti vāṅnāma*, holds the word as mere "speech", and explains line a thus:

> What sin of Indra is spoken by the commoners' speech (*laukikānāṁ vacaḥ kim avadyam indrāya vadanti*), inasmuch as whatever sin (like the killing of Vṛtra and so on) he has performed is sustained by the waters.

He also quotes a verse saying that "the sin Indra had done by slaying Vṛtra, a brāhmaṇa, was shared by the earth, the waters, trees and women in general" (*pāpmānam indrasya mahī jalaṁ ca vṛkṣaś ca kāmaṁ jagṛhuḥ striyaś ceti*), though *Taittirīya Saṁhitā* 2.5.1.1-7 corroborates that "Indra's sin was distributed in three equal shares among the earth, the plants and the womenfolk", and does not enlist the waters among its recipients. Contrarily, Sāyaṇa takes the *nivid*s to be the prose formulae beginning with *marutstotro marudgaṇaḥ,* etc. applied in the Marutvatīya Śāstra, all of these being eulogies to Indra.

V.28

Ṛgveda V.28, according to the Indian tradition, is ascribed to Viśvavārā, Atri's daughter. *Bṛhaddevatā* remains silent about the details of this hymn and at 2.82 only mentions that she is a female seer. *Sarvānukramaṇī* ascribes the hymn to Viśvavārā and informs that she is Ātreyī, a member of Atri's family. Veṅkaṭamādhava, on the other hand, does not consider Viśvavārā as a real woman, and says that the word is only an epithet of Uṣas, the Dawn. He allegorizes the nomenclature in a novel way: the sun having been vanished (eclipsed??), Atri generated the dawn, which is why the dawn born of Atri is styled Viśvavārā Ātreyī, since it was/is greeted by all (*sarvair varaṇiyā*). But, regarding the identity of Viśvavārā, Sāyaṇa follows *Bṛhaddevatā* and *Sarvānukramaṇī.* He thinks that *viśvávārā-* is a proper noun and its derivative meaning is "the woman who dominates all sinful enemies".[25] Geldner (1951: 2.24) explains Viśvavārā as *Allbegehert*.

Griffith is also sceptical about the authorship of this hymn and says that it is ascribed to a *supposed* Viśvavārā, a lady of Atri's family. He suggests that, the sacrificial ladle with which the oil or clarified butter is taken up and poured out (*juhū*) is meant to go eastward (*éti prắcī*), and that, being properly understood, this very ladle brings all blessings (*viśvávārā*).

Going by the metrical variation of the six-versed hymn Jamison and Brereton (2014: I.689) are of opinion that this hymn is not a unified composition but rather a collection of verses from the Atri tradition, brought together as Sāmidhenī verses to accompany the kindling of fire.

Sāyaṇa explains the commencing verse of this hymn thus: the fire, well kindled, sends its flames to the heaven and shines forth, turning downwards. Praising the gods with prayers, Viśvavārā approaches the east with an oblation of clarified butter contained in a ladle. The word *námobhiḥ* in line c has been explained by Veṅkaṭamādhava as "with homage to gods" (*devaviṣayair namaskāraiḥ saha*), while Sāyaṇa takes it as "with laudatory songs" (*namobhiḥ stotraiḥ*). Both the traditional commentators appear to convey the idea that this verse describes a woman (Viśvavārā according to Sāyaṇa and Uṣas according to Veṅkaṭamādhava),

---

[25] *viśvavārā sarvam api pāparūpaṁ śatruṁ vārayitry etan-nāmikā*
— Sāyaṇa

who in fact is offering oblation to gods, chanting *mantra*s herself. But, Griffith thinks that it is the sacrificial ladle (*juhū*), and not any woman, that has been described as going eastward with homage and oblation intended for the gods.

The rest of the hymn sings the glory of Agni. In the second verse Agni is praised with:

> When enkindled, you rule over the immortal world and ensure welfare of the sacrificer; moreover, he, whomsoever you go to, achieves every riches and lays before you the gifts worthy of a guest.

Veṅkaṭamādhava explains *amṛ́tasya* in line a as *annasya* (of food), while Sāyaṇa interprets it as "of waters" (*udakasya*: cf. *Nigh* 1.12), intending the sentence to mean: "you rule over the waters". Griffith, however, prefers to take the word as meaning "of the immortal world". Both the traditional commentators interpret the rest of the verse in an identical manner.

Veṅkaṭamādhava and Sāyaṇa do not differ much regarding the purport of the third verse, too. Only the word *dyumnā́ni* at line b has been explained as *annāni* (food) by Veṅkaṭamādhava, while Sāyaṇa takes it as "riches or flames" (*dhanāni tejāṁsi vā*). Griffith translates this word as "splendours". The word *suyamam* at c has been explained by Veṅkaṭamādhava to be "the perfect unity of a married couple", with an additional comment, viz. "by giving wealth" (*dhanapradānena jāyāpatyor dvandvaṁ suṣṭhu saṁyuktaṁ sam ā kuru*). Sāyaṇa, however, interprets it as "the well-knit bond of husband and wife" (*suṣṭhu niyamanopetam anyonyasaṁśliṣṭam ity arthaḥ*). Griffith preferred Veṅkaṭamādhava's exposition in this regard, and explains it as: "Make easy to maintain our household lordship". This explanation is plausible, since the well-knit bond of husband and wife truly depends on the smooth running of the household with constant finance flowing.

Geldner (1951: 2.24) translates the word *jāspatyam* as *Haushaltung* (housekeeping) and *suyamam* as *Zustande* (accomplished). Jamison and Brereton (2014: II.690) translate line c as : "Let our united household be easy to control."

The word *dyumnávān* in line c of the fourth verse is again differently interpreted by Veṅkaṭamādhava, Sāyaṇa and Griffith. Veṅkaṭamādhava explains it as "food" while Sāyaṇa sticks to "riches" and Griffith prefers the meaning "splendour" for it as he did in the previous verse.

The final verse does not give rise to any dispute among the commentators, so far as its meaning is concerned.

VIII.1.34

Ṛgveda VIII.1.34 is ascribed to Śaśvatī, who traditionally has been held as the daughter of Aṅgiras and the wife of Playoga's son Āsaṅga, the king. *Sarvānukramaṇī* relates a legend to this hymn. King Āsaṅga, turned into a woman owing to a curse of the gods, regained his manhood later through his own penance, as also with the help of Sage Medhātithi of Kaṇva's family. His wife Śaśvatī, witnessing his manhood, praised her husband in joy with the verse *ánv asya sthūrám,* etc. *Bṛhaddevatā* 2.83 calls her as *nārī śaśvatī*. In this connection Macdonell refers to *Nītimañjarī* which defines *nārī* as "one who, among all women, is distressed when her husband is distressed and is joyful when her husband rejoices". However, he translates the word at *Bṛhaddevatā* 2.83 simply as "wife".

According to Jamison and Brereton (2014: II.1021) the last four verses of this hymn stand apart from the rest of it and there too, verses 30-33 form a *dānastuti* and the striking final verse (34) belongs to the same level of colloquial discourse as the preceeding three verses and may well be part of the *dānastuti*. The verse, they hold, "praises the gift" of a woman to the poet. Through her the poet obliquely praises his own equipment.

The deity of this verse ascribed to Śaśvatī is King Āsaṅga himself, as his virility has been eulogized thereat. Veṅkaṭamādhava and Sāyaṇa differ in interpreting line d of the verse. The former explains it as:

he svāmin! pate! mahyaṁ subhadraṁ bhojanaṁ bhogam annapānādikaṁ vā hara iti.

O my lord, do sustain me with good food and drink.

But, Sāyaṇa says the remarks made by Śaśvatī as:

súbhadram arya bhójanaṁ vibharṣi

O my lord, you possess a very pleasant tool for enjoyment.

Sāyaṇa, thereat, explains *súbhadram* as *atiśayena kalyāṇam* (very pleasant), and paraphrases *bhójanam* with *bhogasādhanam* (a tool for enjoyment). The word *sthūrám* in line a has also been differently explained by the two commentators. Veṅkaṭamādhava thinks that it refers to the fat abdomen of the man, and justifies his explanation further by elaborating that "women have thin waists, but men have fat waistlines" (*striyo hi sannatamadhyā bhavanti pumāṁsas tu sthūlamadhyāḥ*). Sāyaṇa, on the other, takes *sthūrám* as an adjective to the genital organ described in this verse. It seems that Griffith hesitated to translate this verse literally and hence brought out only its impression, admitting that Ludwig and Grassmann had translated it more literally. Geldner (1951: 2.281) in his translation follows Sāyaṇa in general.

VIII.91

The next hymn ascribed to a female seer is *Ṛgveda* VIII.91. The seer is Apālā, of Atri's family. The myth attached to this hymn will be discussed in the concerned chapters, viz. Chapters 3 and 4. This, perhaps, is one of the few hymns, which have no significant disputes regarding their authorship. A dispute, however, remains regarding the marital status of the poetess. While some legends say that she was a married woman eventually repudiated by her husband, some other sources consider her to be a maiden.

Veṅkaṭamādhava appears to have taken the word *kanyā̀* in the first stanza as a "maiden". Sāyaṇa, however, interprets it as "a woman" (*kanyā apālā nāma strī*). Griffith, too, renders *kanyā̀* by "maiden". Geldner (1951: 2.414), too, follows the suit as he translates the word as "*Ein Mädchen*" (a maiden). Jamison and Brereton (2014: II.1189), too, consider Apālā an unmarried girl.

The word *vīrakáḥ* in the second verse is explained variously by the commentators. Veṅkaṭamādhava and Sāyaṇa both read it as *vīraḥ* (a hero), Sāyaṇa further explains it as *samarthaḥ* (capable). But, giving some importance to the suffix *-ka-* attached thereto, Griffith translates the word as "the little man". He suggests that perhaps Indra is intended here to stand for the Sun-god. In *Ṛgveda* Indra is invariably merged with the Sun-god (see below, Chapter 4 and see "Vṛtrahā Indra" by Dandekar 1951): an unsure linguistic connection between the name of Indra and the meaning "sun" may be found in the word *ina-*, a synonym of *sūrya-* (cf. *ina-*, originally "energetic, etc.", said of Indra at *Ṛgveda* X.23.6, 44.4, 50.2, but also of the sun, e.g. at *Śiśupālavadha* 2.65: *svargam avatv* ***indra****s tapatv* ***ina****ḥ*, and cf. *ina-kānta-* for *sūrya-kānta* (sun-stone), as privately suggested by Abhijit Ghosh), with the infix *-d-* coming in, as in *su-nara-*: *sun-d-ara-*, *su-narī-*: *sun-d-arī-*, *vānara-*: NIA. *bandar* (Hindi), *bā̃dar* (Bengali), and from European languages as in the pr. n. English *Henry*, German *Heinrich*, sometimes corrupted to *Henrich*, Italian *Enrico*, French *Henri*, but also Dutch *Hen***d***rik*.

The verb *vicā́kaśat* in line b has been derived from the root *-kāś-* (to shine) by Veṅkaṭamādhava and Sāyaṇa, but Griffith takes it as "to see". Hence, the meaning of the word concerned is different in the interpretations of the Eastern and Western scholars.

While explaining the third verse, both the traditional commentators refer to the *Śāṭyāyana Brāhmaṇa*, Sāyaṇa conjectures that Apālā might actually have said that,

> O Indra, I want to know you, but as it is not possible right here on the road, come to my house.

And, according to Sāyaṇa, Apālā, when she, even after having said so, remained unheard by Indra, addressed the *soma* in her mouth to flow for him, slowly in the beginning but quickly later on. But,

Griffith, unlike the Indian commentators, does not forsee the idea of a meeting on the road, and translates 3b as "nor yet can we attain to thee" (*ádhi caná tvā némasi*). Both Veṅkaṭamādhava and Sāyaṇa comment in a like manner on the fourth verse. They interpret it as a prayer of Apālā, whereby she begs Indra's help and wants him to work for her, to make her wealthier. In the second hemistich she says that

> Indra mates with Apālā who had been repudiated by her husband and had to part with him.

Ḅut the word *patidvíṣaḥ* in line c, though explained as a *tatpuruṣa* by Veṅkaṭamādhava and Sāyaṇa (*patibhiḥ dviṣṭā*: Veṅkaṭamādhava, and *patibhiḥ bhartṛbhiḥ bahuvāraṁ dviṣṭā*: Sāyaṇa), has been considered by Griffith to convey the sense of a *bahuvrīhi,* i.e. a secondary descriptive compound, although formally it is doubtless an *upapada-tatpuruṣa*. The final member thereof being a word with a primary suffix (*kṛd-anta*), the accent of the whole compound corresponds to it (*dviṣ-* + *-kvip-*), which is why he translates *patidvíṣaḥ* as "hostile to our lord". Geldner, however, renders the word as "*die wir vom Gatten gehasst leben*" meaning "we live hated by the husband". Jamison and Brereton (op. cit. 1190) translate the word an "husband-haters".

Veṅkaṭamādhava and Sāyaṇa are almost unanimous regarding the purport of the fifth and sixth verses. A *Śāṭyāyana Brāhmaṇa* passage, relevant to these *mantra*s, is quoted by both of them. Griffith, too, does not differ much in this respect.

In their commentaries on verse 7, Veṅkaṭamādhava and Sāyaṇa quote a myth found in *Śāṭyāyana Brāhmaṇá*. In addition, Sāyaṇa says that the word *sū́ryatvacam* in line d means *sūryasamānatvacam* or *sūryasadṛśakāntim*, both meaning "a sun-like appearance". Griffith interprets the word as "bright and clear", and Geldner as "*sonnengleiche*" (sunlike) Cowell (1866), after Aufrecht, suggests that the hole or space of the chariot and cart represents the opening between the four wheels, and the hole of the yoke seems to him to be the opening through which the animal's head passes, corresponding to Homer's exugle 11.19.406.

X.10

Ṛgveda X.10, ascribed to Yama and Yamī, the twin offspring of Vivasvant, is a dialogue hymn. *Sarvānukramaṇī* says that Yamī is the speaker of the six odd-numbered verses while the nine even-numbered verses are ascribed to Yama. However, the Ṛgvedic text itself has a total number of fourteen verses in this hymn, and Yamī and Yama alternatively speak seven verses each. Strewn with a number of obscure words, on the meanings of which commentators often contradict one another, this hymn is difficult to comprehend. The very first verse ascribed to Yamī has a word *jaganvā́n* in line b, which Sāyaṇa interprets as an adjective to Yamī, meaning "I, Yamī, who have come" (*gatavatī*), while Griffith rightly points out that being masculine in form the word is not likely to refer to Yamī. Therefore, Griffith relates the line *tiráḥ purū́ cid arṇaváṁ jaganvā́n* with *vedhā́ḥ* in line c, and translates: "so may the sage come through the air's wide ocean". Sāyaṇa takes *vedhā́ḥ* to be Prajāpati the Creator, and interprets lines c and d thus:

> Let the Creator grant (*ā́ dadhīta*) a very good (*pratarám*) child (*nápātam*) as He might have contemplated for the father (i.e. you Yama) on this earth (i.e. in my womb).

But Griffith thinks that it is Yama who has been referred to by *vedhā́ḥ* which here must mean "the sage", for whom Yamī wants to bear a child. He also insists that the word *kṣámi* should be taken in its face value, viz. "the earth", since Yamī wants to say that unless Yama fulfils her desire, the earth will remain devoid of human inhabitants, and stresses therefore that for the sake of human progeny Yama must conjugate with her.

The second verse, attributed to Yama, does not need a detailed discussion in the present study. Suffice it to mention that the essence of this verse is that Yama does not want that kind of association in which a blood relation is treated otherwise (i.e. like a consort), since the gods who protect the truth keep vigil on them.

A rejected Yamī shoots back in verse 3. She argues that even the immortals desire the mortals to beget progeny and (to make their desire come true) your mind should unite with mine. She keeps insisting that Yama should make love with her as a loving husband does. Sāyaṇa alludes a myth to line d, which runs thus: *jányuḥ pátis tanvàm á viviśyāḥ*, where according to him *jányuḥ* is Prajāpati and the line contains a *luptopamā* (i.e. a variety of simile with a constituent understood). The intended meaning thereupon is:

> As Prajāpati [himself] seduced his own daughter, it will not be improper for Yama to enjoy his own sister in sex.

But Griffith as well as Geldner let go the allusion and translates the line thus: "As a loving husband take thy consort".[26]

In reply Yama turns down her request and says in the fourth verse:

> How can I do such an act which I did never before, how can I talk falsely when I have been telling the truth so long, the Gandharva in the heaven (viz. Sūrya) and the dame of the ether (viz. Saraṇyu) are our origins, hence we are the closest of kin.

Nevertheless Yamī sticks to interpret their relation in her desired way. She says in the fifth verse that the Creator made them consorts even in the mother's womb, and no one can violate His holy ordinances; the heaven and earth also know this (special) relation of theirs. The commentators, however, do not differ much in interpreting this verse.

In the next verse Yama tries to deter Yamī from assuming that their cohabitation is a divine arrangement, and strikes a philosophical note, saying: "Who knows the first day, who has seen it and who has said about it". Perhaps Yama is sceptical about the divine arrangement as spoken of by his sister, but still he cannot

---

[26] "*als Gatte sollst du in deines Weibes Leib eingehen!*" (as a husband you shall enter into the body of your wife!) — Geldner 3.134

disobey the laws of Mitra and Varuṇa, and so warns Yamī by saying: "Why talk in a manner that tempts a man to his doom?"

In verse 7 Yamī comes up with more practical terms, as she naïvely asserts:

> The desire for Yama has taken Yamī, and she wants to reveal her physique to him as a wife does for her man; so like car wheels they should speed up to meet each other.

The commentators do not have much dispute in interpreting this verse.

In a calm determination Yama dejects Yamī again. He declares that the sentinels of gods, who guard over there, never stop, never do they flick their eyelids, and it is not possible to fool them, so Yamī must look for someone else other than Yama, with whom she can speed up like the car wheels.

The real intention of Yamī's reply to these words of Yama contained in the ninth verse has been much disputed by the commentators. Sāyaṇa thinks that Yamī eulogizes Yama and prays for his great achievements; she prays that all the sacrificers may offer oblations for Yama day and night, and the sun may open up his eye once for Yama. Heaven and Earth along with days and nights may remain for Yama, and Yamī, who knows it, may bear the unbrotherly act of Yama (i.e. the sexual union with him). Griffith renders this verse in a different way. His translation runs thus:

> May Sūrya's eye with days and nights endow him, and ever may his light spread out before him. In heaven and earth the kindred pair commingles and on Yamī let it be the unbrotherly act of Yama.

Griffith does not support the idea that Yamī is praising Yama in the first hemistich but suggests that Yamī intends to say that, lest Yama's life be shortened by punishment, the guilt, if any, caused by this act, should belong to her.

In the tenth verse Yama is seen to stick to his principle, he says that:

> Surely days will come when brothers and sisters (*jāmáyaḥ*) will do act unmeet for kinsfolk (*ájāmi*).[27] But O blessed one, do desire another man and not me, make your arm a pillow for someone else and not for me.

Yamī being rejected gives vent to her despair by accusing Yama, she says in the eleventh verse:

> What a brother is he, in spite of whose presence the sister remains uncared for, what a sister is she in spite of whom the brother gets destruction, being impatient with my desire, I repeat these many times, do unite your physique with mine.

Sāyaṇa interprets line b thus: in spite of having a sister when a brother remains unhappy, what kind of sister should be she? A brother and a sister must do anything to make each other happy (*bhrātṛbhaginyoś ca parasparaṁ prītir yena kenacid upāyena avaśyaṁ kāryā*). But Griffith and Geldner too take the word *nírṛti* in line b in the sense of "destruction" (*Verderben*–Geldner). According to him Yamī means to say that unless the brother and sister conjugate the human race will perish. Jamison and Brereton translate *nírṛti* as 'Dissolution'. Wilson (1850: 6.25-30) explains the first hemistich in this way:

> A true brother will not let his sister lack a husband, and a true sister will not let her brother lack a wife.

In the twelfth verse Yama deplores a physical union with his sister, he says it is a sin to have sex with the sister, so she should choose someone other than him to have pleasure, and it is for sure that her brother does not want this (i.e. sexual union between siblings).

In the last verse attributed to her, Yamī reproaches Yama for not fulfilling her wish, she says:

---

27 See Jamison and Brereton (op. cit. III.1383) translating ab as follow: "Later generations will come, in which kin will perform the unkindred (act)."

> Alas, you are indeed a weakling Yama. I do not understand your mind and your heart (since) other (women) do embrace you as a girth (clings to a horse) or a creeper entwines the tree.

Sāyaṇa explains line b in this way, "we do not know your mind or mentality and neither have we understood your heart, i.e. what you are up to". Griffith, however, translates it as "we find in thee no trace of heart or spirit".

Yama consoles Yamī in the final (i.e. the fourteenth) stanza of the hymn with:

> May you embrace someone else O Yamī, may someone else embrace you back, as a creeper clasps a tree, may you wish his mind and he too yours, let your union be a blessed one.

X.28.1

Vasukra-patnī, the wife of Vasukra, is declared to be the author of *Ṛgveda* X.28.1, though *Bṛhaddevatā* and *Ārṣānukramaṇī* do not include her in the list of the female seers but *Bṛhaddevatā* (7.30-31) accepts her as the speaker of X.28.1. *Sarvānukramaṇī* (2.55) too, says that the daughter-in-law of Indra is the seer of the first verse, which speaks of Indra as a third person (*parokṣavad*) and the rest eleven verses are dialogues between Indra and his son Vasukra. In her verse the wife of Vasukra laments that all other gods have come (to the sacrifice arranged by her) but only her father-in-law has not; had he been present he would eat grains and drink *soma* up to his heart's content, and then he could be back home. Sāyaṇa relates a legend to this verse: once Vasukra had arranged for a sacrifice where Indra came in disguise, but Vasukra's wife did not know that Indra was actually present and she prayed with this verse in this way as if Indra was far away from her (*viprakṛṣṭam iva ādyayā astaut*). There is not much difference in its interpretation by various commentators, however the word *arí* in line a has been explained by Sāyaṇa as "lord" (*ariḥ arya īśvaraḥ*) while Griffith takes it as "friend". Geldner (3.171) interprets *arí* as *standesherr* (nobleman). Jamison and Brereton take it as "stranger" (III.1419).

X.39-40

Two consecutive hymns, viz. X.39f. are ascribed to Ghoṣā, the daughter of Kakṣīvant. Both the hymns are addressed to the twin gods, Aśvins. Commentators disagree many times with each other while interpreting these two hymns of fourteen stanzas each. Some disputed places thereat are incoherent and defy comprehension, it is very probable that portions of the original text were lost. Commentators like Veṅkaṭamādhava and Sāyaṇa tried to give a somewhat meaningful commentary thereon, but their interpretations are subjective and conjectural in many places. The myth related to Ghoṣā made them more conscious and pre-conditioned while explaining some of the obscure verses (see below in Chapter 4). A comparative study between the interpretations of Eastern and Western scholars may reveal the abstruseness of these verses.

Jamison and Brereton (III.1439) observe that this hymn has a number of layers, of which at least two are catalogues of good deeds performed by the Aśvins and "these lists are interrupted (in v. 6) by a surprising. 1st person intrusion: a woman (the feminine pronoun *iyám* opens the verse and makes the gender of the speaker unmistakable) calls upon the Aśvins. . . ."

A particular speech style predominates in this couple of hymns, which seems very close to the spoken language, especially in repeating the same words together. In the sentences some words are dropped, as it happens in the colloquial form, and some words are said in such connections that became incomprehensible even to the early commentators. The missing links are yet to be restored to give a full understanding of the hymns. The verses of dubious meaning, where the commentators grossly vary from each other, will be discussed in the present chapter.

The first verse of the first hymn lauds the chariot of the twin gods, the Aśvins. This chariot, interestingly, appears to be the most important element in Ghoṣā's hymns. It has been mentioned and described in many stanzas, and the poetess even prefers to use chariot-centric metaphors. The verse goes thus:

> O Aśvins, your chariot that runs around (*párijmā*) and rolls swiftly (*suvṛ́t*) deserves invocation (*hávyaḥ*) day and night (*doṣā́m uṣā́so*) by the sacrificer (*havíṣmatā*). We, the most constant (followers of you) (*śaśvattamā́saḥ*) invoke (*havāmahe*) that chariot of yours, which, like the name of the father (*pitúr ná nā́ma*), is easy to call on (*suhávam*).

The word *párijmā* in line a is explained by Sāyaṇa as *parito gantā* (which goes everywhere). Griffith translates it as "circumambient", which comes very near to Sāyaṇa's interpretation. Böhtlingk and Roth (s.v.) give a wider sense to the word in calling it "omnipresent" as well as "running or driving around". Jamison and Brereton put it as "earth-encircling". The interpreters, however, are not unanimous in explaining the word *suvṛ́t* in line a. Sāyaṇa interprets it as *suṣṭhu vartamānaḥ* (well placed) taking the root *vṛ́t-* to mean "to exist" (*vartamāne*), but Griffith takes the root in sense of "rolling"[28] and translates *suvṛ́t* as "swiftly rolling".[29] The word *śaśvattamā́saḥ* is interpreted by Sāyaṇa as "we the utmost eternals" (*atiśayena cirantanā vayam*), while Griffith explains it as "we all assembled here".[30]

At 2a, the word *dhíyaḥ* is explained as "acts" (*karmāṇi*) by Sāyaṇa while Griffith prefers to take it as "hymns". There is much dispute among commentators regarding the meaning of line d, i.e. *sómaṁ ná cā́ruṁ maghávatsu nas kṛtam*. Sāyaṇa interprets it as "make us as illustrious (*cā́ruṁ kalyāṇam*) as the *soma*, among the rich people" (*maghávatsu dhanavatsu*), Udgītha, another ancient commentator, interprets it thus: as the Creator has made the Soma/

---

[28] Cf. *suvṛ́tam* in *ṚV* X.85.20, explained as *suṣṭhuvartanam* (rolling swiftly) by Sāyaṇa.

[29] Cf. "Turning or running well", Böhtlingk and Roth, s.v. also cf. Jamison and Brereton: "smooth-rolling".

[30] *śaśvattamá* (most constant or frequent or numerous), Böhtlingk and Roth, s.v.

soma, the god or the plant, beautiful among the gods, likewise you two (the Aśvins) place us among the gods, i.e. get us to the heaven. Sāyaṇa follows his predecessor Veṅkaṭamādhava in interpreting the line in question as "O illustrious Soma, make us respectable among the well-to-do people". But Griffith's translation of this line, considerably different, runs thus: "give our princes treasure fair as *soma* is".

The word *bhága* in the third verse has been variously interpreted by the commentators. Sāyaṇa explains it as "one who gives".[31] Udgītha interprets it as "you two, being pleased, became Bhaga yourself to give her (viz. Ghoṣā) abundantly" (*aśvinau ca tuṣṭau svayam eva bhagatvaṁ gatau paridānāya iti*). It may be recalled that Bhaga is a form of the Sun-god known for his benevolence and bestowing of wealth. But Griffith explains *bhaga* as "bliss".[32] The word *anāśóh* at line b is explained by Sāyaṇa as "of the fasting one" (*anaśanasya*) but Griffith appears more justified in interpreting it as "of the slow".[33] The word *apamásya* in the same line is rendered by Sāyaṇa as "of someone of inferior caste", but Griffith translates it as "he linger[s] last".[34] The word *rutásya* in the final line has been strangely taken by Sāyaṇa as *ṛtasya* meaning "of sacrifice", while the other traditional commentators had taken the word as "of someone who is ailing in disease".[35] Griffith's translation is: "(of) the man with broken bones".[36]

In the fifth verse *arí-* in the final line is the only word regarding the meaning of which commentators differ. Sāyaṇa, like Veṅkaṭamādhava, interprets the word as *gantā* (one who has gone)

---

[31] *bhága* (dispenser), Böhtlingk and Roth, s.v.

[32] Cf. "Good fortune; happiness; welfare; prosperity"—*ṚV*, *AV*, *ŚPBr*, *BhP*: Böhtlingk and Roth, s.v. also cf. Jamison and Brereton.

[33] *an-āśu* (not quick; slow), Böhtlingk and Roth, s.v.

[34] Cf. "The most distant; the last", Böhtlingk and Roth, s.v.

[35] *rogeṇa ārtasyāpi*—Udgītha and *rogād rudataś ca*—Veṅkaṭamādhava.

[36] *rutá* (broken to pieces; shattered; divided), Böhtlingk and Roth, s.v.

(*ṛ́*- "to go") and thinks that it indicates the sacrificer, "the lord of sacrifice" (*patir yajamānaḥ*), while Udgītha assumes that the word means *īśvaraḥ* (the master) and indicates the man who performs the sacrifice. Contrarily, Griffith takes it for "the foe", and thus the explanations of the same line, offered by different commentators, appear diagonally opposite.

In verse 6 the meaning of the word *asajātyā́* in line c is disputed. Sāyaṇa thinks that it denotes "reproachable" (*aśraddheyā*), while Udgītha takes it to mean "not of same class" (*asamānajātīyā*). The word *ámatiḥ*, coming just after *asajātyā́*, has been explained by Veṅkaṭamādhava as "reproachable" (*aśraddheyā*), whereas Udgītha interprets it as "unwise" or "of little intelligence" (*ámatiḥ aprajñā mandabuddhiḥ*). Geldner (3.191) translates *asajātyā* as *ohne Anhang, ratlos* (without attachment, helpless).

Some proper names are mentioned in the seventh verse, which are found in several other hymns of *Ṛgveda* (viz. I.117.20, 24) as well. But, not all of the commentators are inclined to take these as proper nouns, they interpret them rather fancifully. E.g. regarding the meaning of the word *purumitrá* in line b Veṅkaṭamādhava suggests "someone with many friends and relatives" (*mitraśabdotra pradarśanārthaḥ, bahumitrasvajanasya iti…*). But the word has been taken as a proper noun both by Sāyaṇa and Griffith. But, while *vadhrimatī́* in line c has been taken as a proper name by all the traditional commentators. Griffith, in spite of taking it as a proper name, offers its derivative meaning as well, viz. "the weakling's dame".[37] The expression *púrandhaye* at the last line has been explained by Sāyaṇa as "for the woman of wide intelligence" (*púrandhaye bahuprajñāyai*), while Griffith takes it as "to the happy wife". The word *suṣutim* at the same line is explained alternatively by Sāyaṇa and Udgītha as "noble offspring" and "beautiful wealth" (*súṣutiṁ suprasavaṁ śobhanaṁ aiśvaryaṁ vā*) but Griffith sticks to the meaning "noble offspring" only.

---

[37] *vadhrín* (one whose testicles are cut off), and *vadhrimatī́* (a woman who has an impotent husband), Böhtlingk and Roth, s.v.

In the tenth verse *drāvayátsakham* in line c is a governing compound with a participle as its first member. Commentators differ in its explanation. While Veṅkaṭamādhava thinks it to denote "the friends who fight against" (*pratiyoddhāraḥ sakhāyaḥ*), Sāyaṇa reads it as *dravayátsakham* and suggests that, it denotes him who drives away the alliance of the enemy. Udgītha also follows suit, further clarifying it as "who explodes the enemy-army" (*śatrusenānāṁ sphoṭayitāram*). It is, however, Griffith, who offers the most agreeable meaning, viz. "who bore his friend at speed".[38]

In the eleventh verse Griffith takes the word *adite* in line a to mean: "whom none may check or stay" following Sāyaṇa's interpretation *adite adīnau*. According to Sāyaṇa, *áṁhaḥ* in 11b is *pāpam* (sin), while Griffith translates it as "grief". *Rudravartanī* in line c is an epithet to the Aśvins as this word refers to the gods whose ways are full of praise (*rudravartanī stotrayuktamārgau*). Udgītha interprets it as *śabdavadvartmavantau* (the duo whose paths are full of (cheering) sounds). Griffith explains it as "borne on your [Aśvins'] glowing path". The chariot race in which the Aśvins won Sūryā as their bride is hinted at in this verse (cf. *ṚV* X.85). Ergo, *purorathám* at d is explained by Griffith as "foremost in the race". Udgītha's interpretation, however, was in the background of sacrificial settings, which is why he suggests that here *rátha* (chariot) refers to the *havirdhāna śakaṭa*, the cart on which the sacrificial goods are kept, and the entire 11d, according to him, means "the man whom you place with his wife, the dawn, before the cart carrying the sacrificial goods". Both Veṅkaṭamādhava and Sāyaṇa, however, take this line to mean: "whom you place before the chariot with his wife in a *svayaṁvara*" (occasion where the bride chooses the groom).

The second hymn ascribed to Ghoṣā has a questioning style prevailing in many of its verses. In the third verse beginning with

---

[38] Cf. *drú-* (to run, hasten, flee), cf. *DhtP* 22.47. Also see Jamison and Brereton (III.1440) translating it as "one setting its comrades to running".

prātár jarethe, etc. some differences in interpretation are found among the commentators. The phrase *jaraṇéva kā́payā* is explained by Sāyaṇa as "(you two are praised) like two kings who are grown in riches" (*jaraṇau aiśvaryeṇa vṛddhau rājānau*), the word *kā́payā* being interpreted by him as "by the prayer", i.e. "by the song sung in the morning by a herald" (*prātaḥprabodhakasya bandino vāṇī kāpā*). While Udgītha follows Sāyaṇa in explaining it, Veṅkaṭamādhava differs. According to the latter this phrase means "(you two are praised) by the female monkey who has withered as if by leprosy" (*stūyethe kuṣṭhajīrṇayeva kapikulajātayā*). Griffith follows Sāyaṇa in his translation of this phrase. Jamison and Brereton (III.1443) translate it as "like a pitiable [?] old couple." The rest of the verse was also interpreted variously by the commentators. Sāyaṇa interprets: "whose house do you two, worthy to be worshipped, go to? Which sacrificer's sins do you destroy? Whose sacrifice do you attend like two princes?" Veṅkaṭamādhava, unlike Sāyaṇa, does not conjecture any idea of "sacrificer's sin" and interprets *kásya dhvasrā́* as "whose destroyer do you become?" Griffith's translation matches Veṅkaṭamādhava's interpretation, i.e. "whom do ye ever bring to ruin?"

In the fourth verse the word *júhvate* in line c is wrongly interpreted by Sāyaṇa as a verb, i.e. *juhvati* (pays offerings). The word in question is accented on the first syllable; were it a verb, it should have been unaccented.[39] Udgītha rightly takes it as a dative and interprets it as "for the sacrificer who has paid offerings into the sacrificial fire for you two" (*yuvayor arthāya agnau prakṣipate janāya yajamānāya*). Griffith also takes it as an adjective in dative qualifying the noun *jánāya* in line d. He translates it as, "to folk who pay you offerings". Geldner (3.193), too, follows suit. Jamison and Brereton (III.1443) do the same.

Line d of verse 5 is difficult to understand, as a result interpretations vary. Sāyaṇa takes it as:

---

[39] Vide *tiṅṅ atiṅaḥ* — Pāṇ. 8.1.28.

> May you two be able to ward off (*nirasane śaktau*) (the enemies) for my nephew (*árvate*) who is equipped with horse and chariot.

Wilson (1850: 6.134-38) translates this line after Sāyaṇa as "be able (to grant favour) to the son of my brothers who has horses as well as a chariot". Udgītha interprets *árvate* as *svargatiṁ gantre* (for him who has gone to the heaven). Veṅkaṭamādhava takes *árvate* as *bhrātṛvyāya* (for my brother's son). On the other hand, Griffith tries to assign a more cognizable meaning to the phrase that suits the theme of the rest of the hymn, i.e. Ghoṣā's prayer for a heroic husband, marvellously. He translates: "(H)elp me to gain a car-borne chieftain rich in steeds". Jamison and Brereton put it like this: "Will you exert your abilities (for me, as if), for a steed (to win the prize) of horse and chariot?"

A popular phrase often found in *Ṛgveda* is *niṣkṛtáṁ ná yóṣaṇā*, also found at the final line of the sixth verse. Sāyaṇa explains it as "just as a woman carries purified honey". Udgītha's explanation is fanciful: "as a woman who feeds herself keeps prepared food at one place" (*yathā saṁskṛtaṁ āhāraṁ svayaṁhārikā strī kācid ekatra upasaṁharati evam*). Veṅkaṭamādhava explains: "as a young woman carries purified honey in her month" (*yathā niṣkṛtaṁ madhu yuvatī bibharti āsyena*). According to Muir (1870) and Grassmann (1877), the phrase means "as a maid, or a woman, resorts to her rendezvous (with her lover)",[40] while Griffith translates: "as the maid carries it purified in her hand".

The word *saptā́syam* in 8d is explained by Veṅkaṭamādhava and Sāyaṇa as "a movable door" (*sarpaṇaśīladvāram*) qualifying the cloud (*vrajáṁ megham*). Udgītha, however, took it as "cloud with seven openings, i.e. many doors" (*saptamukhaṁ bahudvāram ca*). Griffith translates it as "sevenfold mouth".

The ninth verse is differently explained by the traditional scholars and modern interpreters. Sāyaṇa explains following Udgītha and Veṅkaṭamādhava:

---

[40] Cf. *niṣkṛtaṁ saṅketasthānam*.

> O Aśvins, by your grace this maiden (i.e. Ghoṣā) has become lovely and fit to enjoy, may a husband seeking a bride come near to her, may plants and herbs grow abundantly for him (i.e. the suitor), may rivers run with waters for him, may that invulnerable one be the lord of this (youth of Ghoṣā).

Griffith, however, offers a different meaning to this verse, viz.

> The woman (*yóṣā*) hath brought forth (*jániṣṭā*), the infant (*kanīnakáḥ*) hath appeared, the plants of wondrous beauty straightway have sprung up. To him rivers run as down a deep descent, and he this day becomes their master and their lord.

Here, Griffith suggests that "the woman" in the verse is perhaps the water of the cloud. The infant is the lightning. And, "to him" (*ā́smai*) in the third line may be intended for the sacrificer. According to Brereton (with Jamison 2014 and 2013) the theme of this verse is connected with the third pressing in the classical Soma rites where the fertility of the sacrificing couple is looked for. To make their marriage a success the Aśvins are invoked to grant them a son. Thus the "little lad" who "has taken flight" in the verse in question might be the hoped for child.

Grassmann (1877) places stanzas 10-14 of this hymn in his appendix since they are obscure and, according to him, interpolated as they do not appear to be the sequel to what precedes and be any part of the original hymn. But, the intense longing for a happy married life is so apparent in the tenth and eleventh stanzas that they cannot be altogether rejected as not being a part of Ghoṣā's prayer. In the tenth stanza it says according to Sāyaṇa that

> those husbands who cry aloud for the lives of their dying wives, they take their wives to the sacrifice and take them in long embrace, and they leave their loving offspring for their forefathers. For such husbands the wives give pleasant hugs.

Griffith translates this verse after Lanman (1889: 387), i.e.

> they mourn the living, cry aloud, and at sacrifice the men have

set their thoughts upon a distant cast. A lovely thing for fathers who have gathered here, a joy to husbands, are the wives their arms shall clasp.

X.60.6

Ṛgveda X.60.6 is credited to the sister of Agastya (Agastya-svasṛ), who is the mother of the Bandhus of Gopāyana family. The single verse attributed to her has twelve words altogether; commentators do not differ much in its explanation. In the phrase *agástyasya nádbhyaḥ* Veṅkaṭamādhava explains *nádbhyaḥ* straightway as "for the nephews" (*bhāgineyebhyaḥ*). Sāyaṇa, on the other hand, interprets: "for the Bandhus who make the Sage Agastya happy" (*agástyasya ṛṣeḥ nádbhyaḥ nandayitṛbhyo bandhvādibhyaḥ*). Griffith takes it as "Agastya's sister's sons". Veṅkaṭamādhava explains *arādhásaḥ paṇī́n* as "non-sacrificers" (*ayajamānān*), while Sāyaṇa explained the word *paṇī́n* in line c as "the greedy traders" (*paṇī́n vaṇijaḥ lubdhakān*). Griffith translates *paṇī́n* as "niggards" and so do Jamison and Brereton (III.1472). The verb *akramīḥ* with two prefixes *ní* and *abhí* has been interpreted by the traditional scholars as "defeated" (*abhibhava*: Veṅkaṭamādhava; and *nikṛṣṭam nitarām vā abhibhava*: Sāyaṇa). But Griffith's translation is more literal: "Thou troddest (niggards) under foot".[41] Geldner (3.224) does not translate the word *paṇī́n* and treats it like a proper noun.

X.85

Ṛgveda X.85, a long hymn, is attributed to Sūryā, the daughter of Savitṛ. As stated in the previous chapter, this hymn contains some famous marriage-*mantra*s essential for Hindu nuptial rituals. Of a composite nature, this hymn is composed of a traditional set of forty-seven verses strung loosely together. The scholars consider this hymn to be one of the latest in *Ṛgveda*. Among the traditional commentators Yāska explained only a few verses thereof and only Veṅkaṭamādhava and Sāyaṇa's commentaries

---

[41] Vide *kramu pādavikṣepe — DhtP*

on this hymn are available. However, there is not much dispute among the traditional commentators regarding the meaning of this hymn. The modern interpreters do vary in some places. The following discussion will cover the major differences among the various interpretations.

Veṅkaṭamādhava explains the word *kóśa* in 7c as "the treasure kept in a treasury to be given off" (*dhanādhiṣṭhāne anudeyaṁ dhanam āstām*). The word, however, is not explained by Sāyaṇa. The verse exhibits a metaphor of the bridal chariot. Heaven and Earth are stated there as *kóśa*, the word in Sanskrit having various meanings, only two of which, however, would seem to suit the context, viz. "treasury" and "the interior or inner part of a carriage". Griffith takes *kóśa* to mean "treasury".

In 8b *opaśáḥ* is explained derivatively by Veṅkaṭamādhava and Sāyaṇa: *yena upaśerate sa opaśáḥ* (the thing on which [people] rest), i.e. "pillow". Wilson (1850: 6.276-88) takes it as "the thong of the whip", while Griffith appears to evade the problem by sort of rendering, rather surmising, as "decked the car" or "decked her car", i.e. "formed its canopy". In passing, there is now no doubt about the real meaning of the word, viz. "the circular sliced-bamboo rim", as is clear from the ample discussion on the word at Chowdhury (1931: 62-65, with references).

The phrase *śrótram te cakré āstām* in 11c has been variously interpreted by the commentators. Veṅkaṭamādhava interprets it as meaning "two ears formed two wheels of your chariot" (*śrótraṁ cakrākāram . . . tvadīyasya anasaḥ cakram abhavad dvidhābhūtam*). Sāyaṇa explains: "your (Sūryā's) two ears were the two wheels of the chariot eager to hear the virtues of the bridegroom" (*varasya guṇagrāhiṇī śrotre eva cakre āstām*), further adding that "the chariot being the mind, the ears formed its wheels". Wilson translates it thus: "the two wheels were thy ears". Griffith's interpretation brings out the imagery in this lyrical verse, i.e. "all ears were thy two chariot wheels".

The cluster *aghā́su hanyante gā́vaḥ* in line c of the thirteenth verse generates some disputes. Veṅkaṭamādhava, followed by Sāyaṇa, interprets *hanyante gā́vaḥ* as "the kine given by Savitṛ are beaten by sticks" (*hanyante daṇḍais tāḍyante preraṇārtham*), obviously to get Soma's house. Griffith takes *hanyante* as "are slain" which tallies with the ritual of the Indians slaughtering cows to appease the special guest as well as the bridegroom, the guest hence being called *goghna-* (for whom cows are slain).

Veṅkaṭamādhava and Sāyaṇa identify Sūryā in the seventeenth verse as the wife of the Sun-god, as adoration (*námas*) has been paid to her along with other gods like Agni and others, as also Mitra and Varuṇa. Griffith, however, rightly takes her to be Sūryā, the daughter of Sūrya, the Sun-god, to whom this hymn is attributed and who is described here as the typical bride.

Yāska in *Nirukta* 12.8 explains the twentieth verse of this hymn in the following way: "O Sūryā, ascend this world of nectar, which is very bright, free from impurities, multiform, golden in colour, easy to turn and with beautiful wheels, in order to bring comfort to thy husband" (as rendered by Sarup), Yāska explaining *sukiṁśukám* in this verse as "shining beautifully" (*sukāśanam*), *śalmalím* as "whose impurity has been destroyed" (*śannamalam*) and *viśvárūpam* as "omni-form" (*sarvarūpam*). Yāska suggests alternative meanings, too, of these words, since, according to him, the terms might also have been used for the sake of comparison, viz. "bright like a beautiful *kiṁśuka* flower, soft like the silk-cotton tree". Abhijit Ghosh personally suggested that of the above words, *śalmalí-* should probably be related to the word-group *kalmali-*: *śarmari-* which means "shining; many-coloured; variegated", discussed with ample notes at Chowdhury (1931: 60-62). Yāska explained the second hemistich thus:

> O Sūryā, ascend the world of nectar (*amṛ́tasya*), i.e. of water (*udakasya*). Do so, in order to bring happiness to thy husband.
>
> — tr. Sarup

Veṅkaṭamādhava and Sāyaṇa do not comment on the word *amṛ́tasya*, indicating thereby that they have taken the term in its usual meaning of "nectar" or "immortality". Griffith translates it as "bound for the world of life immortal". Be it noted here that the word *vahatú-* has been explained by Sāyaṇa variously at different places. In the present hymn *vahatúḥ* in verse 13 he interprets as "gifts to the bride from her father", *vahatúm* in verse 14 as "marriage" (*vivāham*), and again *vahatúm* in verse 20 as "carrying", i.e. "journey" (*vahanam ātmanaḥ prāpaṇam*). Sāyaṇa does not discuss in detail the meaning of *vahatúnā* at verse 38, but it seems from the context that he accepted it there in the sense of "the gifts a bride gets from her father" or "the bridal procession". Geldner (3.272), too, does the same.

The word *vyàktām* in the twenty-first verse is an adjective qualifying a pronoun *anyā́m* in line c. Sāyaṇa suggests three meanings for this word, viz. "unmarried" (*anūḍhā*), "fully developed" (*parisphuṭām*) and "devoid of anointments" (*vigatāñjanāṁ*): this indicates that he was not at all sure about any of the alternatives. Quite in contrast with the last alternative, Wilson (1850: 6.276-88) takes the word to mean "decorated with ornaments", while Griffith translates it as "(another) fair one".

The twenty-fourth verse is applied in the *patnī-saṁyāja* part of the Darśapūrṇamāsa sacrifice. At the time of untying the grass-belt from the waist of the sacrificer's wife this verse is uttered (see below Chapter 5, p. 198). The phrase *prá tvā muñcāmi váruṇasya pā́śāt* means I set you free from the noose of Varuṇa. But keeping in mind the marital context of the hymn, Lanman (1889: 89f, 389-90, 398-401) suggests in sharp contrast that the noose may here stand for the tie by which a girl is bound to her father till marriage. It, however, seems that Lanman's explanation has little to do with Varuṇa who at *Atharvaveda* IV.16 is regarded as the Lord of moral upkeep, who punishes the sinners by tying them with his noose.

The sentence *vaśínī tváṁ vidátham ā́ vadāsi* in the twenty-six verse gives illuminating information about the wife's activities and about her place in the society at that time. Veṅkaṭamādhava explains the word *vaśínī* as "independent" (*svatantrā*). According to Sāyaṇa this has a reference to the wife in her capacity to take everyone in the household in her control (*sarveṣāṁ gṛhagatānāṁ vaśaṁ prāpayitrī*) — the commentator was perhaps influenced by the likes of verse 46 of the present hymn — but he was also aware that it could as well mean a wife who is under control of her husband (*patyur vaśe vartamānā*). Griffith's rendering is: "speak as lady to thy gathered people". Geldner (3.271) too follows Griffith as he renders the line: *Du mögest als Gebieterin weise Rede führen*. (May you as a lady lead speech.) Jamison and Brereton (III.1523), however, translate this as: "Exerting your will you will announce the ceremonial distribution."

In the phrase *gā́rhapatyāya jāgṛhi* in verse 27, Veṅkaṭamādhava takes the initial word to mean *gārhapatitvāya*, further clarifying it by *prabhutvāya* (for the lordship). Sāyaṇa follows him in interpreting the phrase as "be alert that you may be mistress of the house" (*gṛhapatitvāya jāgṛhi budhyasva*). Wilson (1850: 6.276-88) renders the same as "be watchful over the domestic fire"; he evidently takes the term *gṛhapati-* to refer to the domestic fire worshipped daily by the householder. Griffith, on the other hand, prefers to take *gā́rhapatyāya* as "for the household", the phrase thus meaning "be vigilant to rule thy household". Jamison and Brereton follow the suit.

In verse 29 *śāmulyàm* has been explained as "a cloth containing the soil of the body" both by Veṅkaṭamādhava and Sāyaṇa (*śarīrācchannasya malasya dhārakaṁ śāmulyaṁ vastram*, and *śamalaṁ śārīraṁ malaṁ, śarīrāvacchannasya malasya dhārakaṁ vastram*, resp.). Wilson (1850: 6.276-88) translates, in parity with the description of Veṅkaṭamādhava and Sāyaṇa, as "the garment soiled by the body". Geldner (3.271) follows suit by translating *śāmulyà* as '*befleckte Gewand*' (stained cloth). But, Griffith takes the word to mean "the woollen robe".[42] Anyway, in his commentary on the second hemistich of the same verse, Sāyaṇa offers an explanation (*ity upacaryate*) that the bridal garment should be discarded lest *kṛtyā́* the female fiend, whose abode is the same garment, may grow her feet and through the person of the wife take on the groom. Griffith follows Sāyaṇa in his translation, whereas Ludwig interpreted the hemistich as "(the magic or evil spell) returns to its originator", thereby ascribing to the sentence a meaning completely opposite to that given by Sāyaṇa.

Disputes prevail regarding the meaning of the thirty-fifth verse beginning with *ā́śásanam,* etc. Veṅkaṭamādhava and Sāyaṇa explain *ā́śásanam* as "placing the husks" (*tuṣādhānam*) and *viśásanam* to mean "being placed on the head" (*śirasi nidhīyamānam*). The term *adhivikártanam* is explained by both of them as "cutting of the (bridal) cloth into three pieces" (*yat tridhā vāso nikṛntanti*). But the actual meanings of these three words are uncertain. Wilson (1850: 6.276-88) renders them respectively by "border-cloth", "head-cloth" and "divided skirt". Griffith's translation also supports Wilson's view, i.e. "the fringe, the cloth that decks her head, and then the triply parted robe". But Weber [1862: 5.195-204 (vide also 178ff.)] and Böhtlingk and Roth (s.v.) think that this passage refers to the carcass of the animal that has been slaughtered for the festivity.[43] In this view, the three words in question mean respectively "the butchering, the cutting up, the severing of limb and joint".[44] Again, to *sūryā́yāḥ paśya rūpā́ṇi* of the same verse, Griffith attributes the meaning "behold the hues which Sūryā wears", while according to Weber, and Böhtlingk and Roth (s.v.) *rūpā́ṇi* may be rendered as "forms".

---

[42] Cf. *śāmulyà* (a woollen shirt), Böhtlingk and Roth, s.v. Though it suggests that the word may be connected with *śamala* (impurity or feces) as in *Lāṭyāyana Brāhmaṇa*.

[43] Also see Jamison and Brereton (III.1521) contending the same; they consider these two verses (vv. 34 and 35) to concern the wedding feast and in particular the cow killed for the feast.

[44] Cf. *śás-* (to cut down; to kill) and *ví-śas-* (to slaughter), see *DhtP*.

The fortieth verse may apparently suppose that polyandry was in vogue in those days, as it says that the bride was obtained first by Soma, then Gandharva was her lord, her third husband was Agni and the man to whom she is being married is her fourth husband (see below Chapter 3, p. 117). But, Grassmann (1877) gives a rational explanation to negate this apparently polyandric reference: as the typical bride Sūryā was first married to Soma, it means that the young maid originally belongs to the custody of Soma. Being her next lord, Gandharva guards her virginity. Then Agni, the sacrificial fire, becomes her lord as she walks round him in the marriage ceremony and gets finally married to her mortal husband.

The term *ápatighnī* in the forty-fourth verse is not explained in detail by Veṅkaṭamādhava and Sāyaṇa. It seems that they have taken the term in its derivative sense, i.e. "not the killer of one's own husband". Griffith, too, translates it as "no slayer of thy husband". But the term *patighnī* has a technical meaning in Lakṣaṇa-Śāstra (i.e. the study of auspicious and inauspicious signs in human body), where *patighnī* means "the mark of a husband killer" (Wilson on *patighnī*: "Lakṣaṇa"). At Pāṇini 3.2.53 *patighnī-pāṇilekhā* means a line on palm indicating that a woman will be disloyal to her husband. Therefore, it may be suggested that the term *ápatighnī* in the context of marriage rituals might indicate that the bride is being asked to be auspicious to her husband, i.e. devoid of any inauspicious sign (*durlakṣaṇahīnā*), or it may even suggest a wife who bears auspicious signs in her body (*sulakṣaṇā*).

Apropos X.86

The original tradition regarding the authorship of *Ṛgveda* X.86, an obscure dialogue hymn ascribed to Indra, Indrāṇī and Vṛṣākapi, must have been lost or even suppressed, which is why tradition has attributed the various *mantra*s to their respective speakers, following the maxim *yasya vākyaṁ sa ṛsiḥ*. Even then, there remains much confusion regarding the ascription of a few verses to particular speakers. Sāyaṇa holds eleven verses, viz. nos. 2-6, 10 and 15-18 as having been spoken by Indrāṇī, while his predecessor Veṅkaṭamādhava attributed verses 1-6, 9, 10, 15, 16 and 18 to her. *Sarvānukramaṇī* refrains from allotting any verses to respective speakers, and merely remarks that the seers are Vṛṣākapi, Indra and Indrāṇī. According to Griffith, the second verse is spoken by Indra, not Indrāṇī, as held by Veṅkaṭamādhava and Sāyaṇa but ascribes also verses 22 and 23 to Indrāṇī. And, in addition to the traditional allotment, Ludwig ascribes also the seventh verse to her.

It has already been mentioned in the earlier chapter that Tilak interprets this hymn in an astronomical background and with its help tries to ascertain the Arctic home of the Aryans. He regards Vṛṣākapi to be the sun near the point of southern zodiac or the sun going down the horizon at the beginning of a long-lasting darkness. Dandekar (1974: 95-111) suggests that in this hymn Indra is spoken of as having lost his virility when a lascivious monkey helps him to get back his manly power with the help of some medicine. He further assumes that here Vṛṣākapi is to be identified with the fertility-god Viṣṇu. The entire hymn according to him refers to Indra's effort to preserve his virility intact. Velankar (1954: 11-15) (also see below in Chapter 4, pp. 178-81) thinks that this hymn portrays Indrāṇī's jealousy for Indra's step-son Vṛṣākapi, her attempt to rouse her husband's jealousy and anger against him, Indrāṇī's wrath against him, as also her clever change of front in the face of discomfiture. Velankar is not in favour of the view that a new Vṛṣākapi cult, an anti-Indra one in nature, is indicated anywhere in this hymn. He thinks that the poem projects Indra's fascination for a poor but sincere sacrificer rather than for a rich worshipper.

Jamison (with Brereton 2014: III.1525 and 1996) considers this hymn an encapsulation of Aśvamedha sacrifice and vv. 16-17 express the central paradox of the Aśvamedha – that the king derives a huge boost in his power from a ritual in which his wife has sex with someone [/something] else, which fits the counter-intuitive statements in those verses.

The first verse of the hymn is of dubious authorship. Sāyaṇa takes it to be Indra's speech, since Vṛṣākapi, who is Indra's relation, has been described as *mátsakhā* (my friend). Veṅkaṭamādhava takes it as coming from Indrāṇī, and ventures to relate a mythical story to this. An animal, a subject of Vṛṣākapi, spoilt the oblation meant for Indrāṇī, and so, out of rage, she spoke this to her husband, who had fathered Vṛṣākapi. Indra, Sāyaṇa thinks, says that "the sacrificers sent by him did not praise him but praised Vṛṣākapi instead; even though my son (*mátsakhā*) Vṛṣākapi enjoyed himself in the sacrifices, I, Indra, am the greatest of all". Griffith's translation is based on Veṅkaṭamādhava's commentary:

> Men have abstained from pouring juice: they count not Indra as a God. Whereat the votary's store my friend Vṛṣākapi hath drunk his fill. Supreme is Indra all over.

The first hemistich in the second verse is explained by Veṅkaṭamādhava and Sāyaṇa as follows: "O Indra, you being extremely moved are rushing towards Vṛṣākapi". Somewhat differently Griffith interprets it as "thou, Indra, needless passest by the ill Vṛṣākapi hath wrought".

The third verse ascribed to Indrāṇī by Veṅkaṭamādhava and Sāyaṇa means, according to them, that,

> O Indra, what good to you has done this animal called Vṛṣākapi that you, like a generous one, are giving prosperous wealth to him at once?

Griffith, however, takes it as Indra's speech towards Indrāṇī, and his translation projects a very different meaning than the one given by Veṅkaṭamādhava and Sāyaṇa to it: "what hath he done to injure thee, this tawny beast Vṛṣākapi, with whom thou art so angry now?", etc.

The word *kapí-* in the fifth verse is taken by Veṅkaṭamādhava and Sāyaṇa as referring to a monkey living in the territory governed by Vṛṣākapi, i.e. a monkey other than Vṛṣākapi himself (if at all he is to be identified as such), viz. the latter's subject. Griffith, however, takes this word as an abbreviated form of Vṛṣākapi himself. Veṅkaṭamādhava and Sāyaṇa interpret the first two lines of this verse thus: "a monkey, a subject of Vṛṣākapi, has spoilt the beautiful oblations prepared for me by the sacrificers". But, Griffith considers it more probable that Vṛṣākapi has assaulted Indrāṇī and inflicted injuries on her person.

Veṅkaṭamādhava and Sāyaṇa accept the seventh stanza as a description of the trembling of Vṛṣākapi's limbs in fear of Indrāṇī's ire, but Griffith after Ludwig thinks that it has been spoken by Indrāṇī to express her indignation at Vṛṣākapi's audacity that made her person quiver in rage.

The expression *avī́rām iva* in the ninth verse has been interpreted by Veṅkaṭamādhava as "as if without a son" (*aputrām iva*), but Griffith takes the word *vīra* to mean the speaker's husband and not the son, translating it as "bereft of hero's love" clarifying it further as: "[one] who has no husband to protect her".

The tenth verse supplies some information of a woman's activities in the days of yore. Veṅkaṭamādhava and Sāyaṇa interpret it as "in ancient times a woman used to attend the sacrifices and other festivities". Griffith guesses that Indrāṇī here meant to say that Vṛṣākapi assaulted her when she was on her way to a festival, which women were accustomed to attend, and that her rank as Indra's consort did not preserve her from insult.

Verses 16-17 apparently appear to be contradictory to each other, in so far as their meanings are concerned, and they seem to be more erotic riddles or puzzle rather than conversations. The two verses might have been applied for some magical rites also, possibly to inculcate virility in men. The traditionalists hold that the sixteenth verse is spoken by the wanton wife while Indra answers her in the following one. Griffith omits these two verses because of the apparent obscenity contained in them. The eighteenth verse, ascribed again to Indrāṇī, suggests, according to Ludwig, that Vṛṣākapi may represent the Moon whose spots are fancifully considered as objects mentioned by Indrāṇī in this stanza.

The final two stanzas are assigned to Indra and Vṛṣākapi respectively by tradition. Though Sāyaṇa thinks that the twenty-second verse could be taken as Indrāṇī's speech, the verse, he strangely interprets it in such a way as would seem unexpected from her:

> O Vṛṣākapi, possessor of the greatest wealth (*paramaiśvaryavān*), come to my house when you are about to leave (*udañceḥ udgāminaḥ santaḥ*), where is that voracious animal, where has he gone, who pleases the people?

Yāska, his predecessor, took the verse in almost identical meaning (*Nir* 13.3). Griffith holds these two concluding stanzas to be spoken by Indrāṇī. The meaning of the twenty-second stanza is for him obscure, while the final stanza also has no apparent connection with the rest of the hymn, i.e. what precedes.

Bergaigne (1878-83: 2.270) holds Vṛṣākapi to be a mythical sacrificer. He further thinks that Vṛṣākapi, Indra's friend, represents *soma* (perhaps because *soma*-plant must be Indra's favourite), and Indrāṇī is prayer incarnate. This hymn symbolizes the myth that Indra is neither satiated with *soma* juice alone nor can he be pleased with mere prayer. He ignores sacrifices as long as the union of these two essential elements of worship remained unaccomplished.

Many scholars hold that the refrain *víśvasmād índra úttara* is a later addition, as it comes at the end of every verse without fitting into the metre. Kosambi (1962: 2.6, 54-55) gives an explanation of this addition; he thinks that this refrain is meant to be chanted by others than the principal characters, presumably by all those who attended the performance.

Apropos of X.95

Ṛgveda X.95 is the famous colloquy of Purūravas and Urvaśī. This much-discussed hymn has a parallel at *Kāṭhaka Saṁhitā* 7.10.3 and *Śatapatha Brāhmaṇa* 11.5.1, probably in its earlier form so far the kernel story is concerned. Though, Jamison and Brereton

(III.1548 f.) consider the Ṛgvedic version earlier. They contend that *Śatapatha Brāhmaṇa* seems to have misunderstood, deliberately or not, several of the crucial verses. A creative misreading of *Ṛgveda* X.95.3 led *Śatapatha Brāhmaṇa* fabricate reasons for Urvaśī's disappearance. It reappears in *Mahābhārata* (1.70.16-22), Purāṇas (*Viṣṇu Purāṇa* 4.6.19, *Vāyu Purāṇa* 2.29) and *Kathāsaritsāgara* (17.4).

Sarvānukramaṇī ascribes nine verses to Purūravas, the son of Ila, and nine verses to Urvaśī, the celestial nymph and the wife of Purūravas. Verses 2, 4-5, 7, 11, 13, 15-16 and 18 are traditionally ascribed to Urvaśī and the rest, to Purūravas. But according to Ludwig, some of the stanzas should be rearranged, in this order: 1-5, 16, 6-9, 11-15 and 10. Kosambi (1962: 2.5, 50-52) thinks that the fourth verse is extra, being neither Urvaśī's speech, nor Purūravas. He also questions the authorship of verse 7, traditionally ascribed to Urvaśī. The ninth verse is also spoken by Urvaśī, holds Kosambi. He further claims that the second half of the fifteenth verse is Purūravas' utterance, not Urvaśī's. According to Rahurkar (1964: 264), it seems that the name of the composer being forgotten, Urvaśī was credited with the authorship of these verses.

The words *vásu* and *váyaḥ* in the fourth verse have been interpreted by Veṅkaṭamādhava and Sāyaṇa as meaning "clothes" and "food" (*vásu vāsakaṁ váyaḥ annam*: Sāyaṇa). Urvaśī says that she used to provide *vasu* and *vayas* to her father-in-law, but Griffith translates them as "life and riches" which is again after Ludwig's suggestion, i.e. "the future grandson".

The word *ávyatyai* in the fifth verse is much disputed. Sāyaṇa, following Veṅkaṭamādhava, interprets it in a rather fanciful way, saying *vyatī-* refers to a woman who gets along with her co-wives, the chance to conjugate with her husband, by turns (*sapatnībhiḥ saha paryāyeṇa patim āgacchati sā vyatī*). One who does not suffer the same fate is *ávyatī-*, i.e. the woman who gets her husband's sole attention. But the word *vyatī-* is found to be used in two different meanings in *Mahābhārata*: "to pass away" or "to elapse". In *Pañcaviṁśa Brāhmaṇa* the word suggests "to take an irregular course", which perhaps inspired the interpretation of Veṅkaṭamādhava and Sāyaṇa. In *Bhagavad-Gītā* it means "to disregard" or "to neglect". Böhtlingk and Roth as well as Monier-Williams explain it as "not longing for copulation". Durga in his commentary on *Nirukta* 3.21 says that the phrase *ávyatyai pṛṇāsi* means "whatever desire I had in my mind, earlier you fulfilled all". Griffith translates this line as "though coldly she received thy fond caresses". Jamison and Brereton (III.1549), too, interpret it as "who did not seek it" [the copulation].

The word *gopī́thyāya* at verse 11 is interpreted by Veṅkaṭamādhava and Sāyaṇa as "to protect the earth". Wilson, Grassmann and Geldner follow Sāyaṇa in this meaning, but Griffith explains it differently, viz. "to drink from earthly milch-kine". The word *sásminn áhan* is taken by the traditional commentators as the short form of *sarvasmin ahani* (everyday). Griffith, however, takes it as "on that day". Sāyaṇa differs from Veṅkaṭamādhava in explaining what *vidúṣī* Urvaśī taught Purūravas; according to him she taught him what *he* should do everyday though Sāyaṇa's predecessor Veṅkaṭamādhava took it as what *she* should do everyday.

In verse 15 *mā́ prá paptaḥ* has been explained by Sāyaṇa as "do not fall down here" (*atraiva patanaṁ mā kārṣīḥ*), but Griffith translates it as "nor vanish".

Griffith thinks that there is a hiatus between the seventeenth and the last, i.e. the eighteenth stanza. In the last stanza Urvaśī abruptly consoles Purūravas calling him *mṛtyúbandhu* (death's friend or whose death is nigh) and tells him that "his offspring will pay oblation to the gods as he himself will rejoice in the heaven". Kosambi (1962: 54) interprets the hymn in a new light; he suggests that the internal evidences of this hymn and the legends regarding the death of Purūravas as preserved in later literature indicate that Purūravas is to be sacrificed after having begotten a son and successor from Urvaśī. He pleads in vain against her determination. Kosambi draws support for his view from the anthropologists to whom this ritual is quite well known as a sequel to some kinds of primitive sacred marriage.

X.107

Ṛgveda X.107 is ascribed to Dakṣiṇā, the daughter of Prajāpati. Literally Dakṣiṇā means the sacrificial fee or the honorarium given to the priests. This guerdon has been personified and eulogized in this hymn. Alternatively the seer is Divya, the descendant of Aṅgiras. The authorship of this hymn is doubtless conjectural as Dakṣiṇā is the honorarium personified.

The first verse has a phrase *víśvaṁ jīváṁ támasaḥ níramoci*. It is explained by Sāyaṇa as "you have freed all creatures from darkness", though his predecessor Veṅkaṭamādhava took *tamasaḥ* to be an imagery and interpreted it as "from the darkness of poverty" (*dāridryatamasaḥ*).

In the third verse the word *kavāríbhyaḥ* has been explained by Veṅkaṭamādhava as "for those who go the wrong way, and who are devoid of religious practices" (*kutsitagāmibhyo 'nācarebhyaḥ*). Sāyaṇa also explains in a similar manner, viz. "for those who do not perform sacrifice" (*kutsitagantṛbhyo 'yaṣṭṛbhyaḥ*). Griffith expresses the hatred contained in this word with "not from the niggards". The word *práyatadakṣiṇāsaḥ* has been explained by the traditional commentators as "those who have given the guerdon" (*sādhubhyaḥ pradīyamānadhanāḥ*: Veṅkaṭamādhava and *dattadakṣiṇāḥ*: Sāyaṇa). But Griffith takes it as "with hands stretched out".[45] The word *avadyabhiyā́* in the same verse is interpreted by Veṅkaṭamādhava as "in fear of any grievous accident" (*upadravabhiyā*), while Sāyaṇa takes it as "in fear of committing a sin" (*pāpabhiyā*). In Griffith's translation it becomes "they dread dishonour".[46]

---

[45] Cf. *prayata* in *Ṛgveda* means "outstretched", Böhtlingk and Roth, s.v.

[46] *avadya-* (dishonour; blamable), cf. *RV* IV.18.5: *avadyám iva mányamānā,* etc.

The phrase *surabhíṁ yónim* in verse 9 is taken by Sāyaṇa as "the cow that produces milk, etc." Griffith, however, does not understand cow for *surabhí-*, which is surely a later association influenced by the Purāṇas, and the word *yóni-* is very often used in the sense of "house" in *Ṛgveda*. Hence Griffith translating the phrase as "fragrant dwelling" is more justified than Sāyaṇa. Though, Jamison and Brereton (III.1572) translate it as "sweet smelling womb". Another phrase in the same verse is *antaḥpéyaṁ súrāyāḥ* which is taken by Sāyaṇa as "supping up" or "drinking of liquor". Veṅkaṭamādhava asserts that "it is the inherent taste of the liquors" (*antaḥsthitaṁ rasaṁ surāyāḥ*). Wilson (1850: 6.378-81) takes it as "deep potation of wine". Griffith translates it as "draught of liquor". The phrase *áhūtāḥ prayánti* in the same verse is variedly interpreted by the commentators. Veṅkaṭamādhava takes it as "the slaves, who come forward in every work without being asked for" (*dāsān ye anāhūtāḥ kāryeṣu pragacchanti*). Sāyaṇa gives a different meaning of the same, viz. "(the enemies) who, due to excessive enthusiasm, come forward to fight even when not challenged" (*ye śatravaḥ ahūtāḥ balādhikyenānāhūyamānāḥ prayanti pramukham āgacchanti*). But Griffith's interpretation is further different, viz. "who, unprovoked, assailed them".

X.108

Ṛgveda X.108 is the famous colloquy of Saramā and the Paṇis. *Sarvānukramaṇī* ascribes the even-numbered verses and the final one to Saramā. This hymn is composed of eleven stanzas of which six are credited to Saramā, the divine bitch, whom Indra sent as his messenger to the Paṇis, who allegedly had stolen Indra's kine and kept them hidden in a distant land.

The third line of the second verse runs thus *atiṣkádo bhiyásā tán na āvat*. Sāyaṇa explains it thus, "in fear that originated from my crossing (the water), the river protected me" (*atiṣkadanād atikramaṇāj jātena bhiyasā bhayena tat nadījalaṁ naḥ . . . mām āvat arakṣat*). Griffith takes it in this way: "This (the appointment of Indra) hath preserved me from the fear of crossing". In both the places the interpreters took *atiṣkádaḥ* to mean "crossing".[47] Another interpretation of the same phrase is also possible, viz. the waters protected me in fear lest I drink them dry (cf. Dharmapal 2003).

Different interpretations are available of a number of words found in the sixth verse. The interpretation of the word *asenyā́* in 6a by Veṅkaṭamādhava is a bit flimsy: "not to be enjoyed by the slave-children" (*asanīyāni dāsaputraiḥ*). The same word is explained by Sāyaṇa as "not fit for an army" (*senārhāṇi na bhavanti*). Wilson (1850: 6.381-84) translates it by, "not in the place of armies", while Griffith explains it as "weak for wounding". The word *aniṣavyā́ḥ* in b has raised much dispute among the commentators. Veṅkaṭamādhava explained it as "not fit to be served, since (the bodies) are devoid of beauty" (*asevitavyāś cāśrīkāḥ*). Sāyaṇa takes *aniṣavyā́ḥ* in a different sense, viz. "not deserving the arrows" (*iṣvarhāṇi na*). Lexicon like Böhtlingk and Roth (s.v.) ascribes the meaning "not to be wounded or killed by arrows" to *aniṣavyā́ḥ*, while Griffith translates it as "arrow-proof". Though Veṅkaṭamādhava indirectly suggests that the word *ádhr̥ṣṭaḥ* in line c means "not touched" (*adhr̥ṣṭaḥ cāyam itaḥ pūrvam*), Sāyaṇa explains it as "not capable of" (*asamarthaḥ*), and Griffith takes it to mean "unmastered". The word *ubhayā́* (both), in the final line is vague in the given context. According to Veṅkaṭamādhava it refers to "both classes of people who are truthful and who are not" (*ubhayān api satyānr̥tayuktān*), but Sāyaṇa takes it as "both of what have been said earlier" (*ubhayavidhān pūrvoktān*). Griffith translates it as "in either case". Veṅkaṭamādhava interprets *ná mr̥ḷāt* in the final line as "does not forgive" (*na kṣamate*), while Sāyaṇa interprets it as "does not sanction happiness" (*na sukhayet*). With so many words interpreted differently by scholars, the meaning of the entire verse becomes uncertain and obscure.

The second line of the verse 10 reads: *índro vidur áṅgirasaś ca ghorā́ḥ*, which according to Veṅkaṭamādhava means:

---

[47] *skand-* (to leap; to jump) — *DhtP*

> *bhavadbhiḥ tathā kr̥te sati indraḥ ca jānāti aṅgirasaś ca ghorāḥ.*
>
> If you do this (i.e. try to allure me with your relationship), Indra and the terrific Aṅgirases will come to know about it.

Sāyaṇa's interpretation is different:

> Indra and the terrific Aṅgirases know this (the brotherhood and sisterhood of yours).

Griffith in his translation follows Sāyaṇa, and so does the translation of Jamison and Brereton (III.1574).

Sāyaṇa after *Sarvānukramaṇī* ascribes the final, i.e. the eleventh stanza to Saramā, but Ludwig holds that Br̥haspati is the speaker here. Griffith thinks the authorship of this verse is uncertain. The second line of this verse is: *úd gā́vo yantu minatī́r r̥téna*. The two words *r̥téna* and *minatī́ḥ* have been variously explained by the commentators. Veṅkaṭamādhava explains it in this way:

> May the cows come up (*ud gacchantu*) from the nether world (*pātālāt*) lowing with water (*r̥tena*).

Sāyaṇa offers more than one explanation of the same line. Once he explains *r̥téna* as "with truth", and *minatī́ḥ* as "destroying (the obstacles)". As a result, the whole sentence might be understood to mean: "May the cows come out destroying with truth the obstruction of the mountain". He interprets it again in a different way: "May the cows who were being arrested by you" (*minatī́ḥ*: *vyatyayena karmaṇi śatr̥. mīyamānā yuṣmābhir bādhyamānās tā gāvaḥ*) come out from the mountain, aided by Br̥haspati and others, with the help of prayer (*r̥téna stutibhiḥ*). Griffith takes *minatī́ḥ* to mean "lowing", after Veṅkaṭamādhava, and translates the line as: "Let the cattle lowing come forth as holy Law (*r̥téna*) commandeth".

X.109

X.109 has been ascribed to Juhū, the wife of *Brahman* alias Br̥haspati. Juhū is a mythical character and the hymn is difficult to fathom, and is perhaps fragmentary. Jamison and Brereton (III.1574) believe that the hymn relates to the much-debated issue in the late *Ṛgveda* about the introduction of the Sacrificer's Wife into ritual performance. A myth is related by Sāyaṇa to this hymn (see before Chapter 1, p. 23 and below Chapter 4, pp. 188-89). The alternative seer for the hymn is Ūrdhvanābha. The word *brahmakilviṣé* at verse 1 is taken as a genitive *tatpuruṣa* compound by Sāyaṇa and has been expounded as "the sin of Brahman (masc., = Brahmā)", but Griffith takes it differently and translates the word as "an outrage on a brahman (= brahmin)" and so do Jamison and Brereton (III.1575) by translating the word as "the offense against the Brahmin".

In the second verse *ahṛṇīyamānaḥ* is explained by Veṅkaṭamādhava as "not being angry" (*akrudhyan*), though the root *hrī-* means "to feel shame" (cf. *DhtP*). Sāyaṇa, however, explains the word as "unabashed, being free from sin" (*pāpāpagamanena alajjamānaḥ san*), while Griffith renders "without reluctance". Commentators differ also in explaining *anvartitā́*. Deriving the word, an adjective to the dual divinities Mitra and Varuṇa, from root *ṛ́-* (to go), Veṅkaṭamādhava paraphrases it with *anugantārau* (the followers). Sāyaṇa, on the other hand, says that *ṛ́-* expresses "hatred", and the word is formed with suffix *-tṛc* attached to the root and means "the approver" (*anu-artitā́*). Griffith also takes this word as adjectival to Mitra and Varuṇa; to quote him: "Mitra and Varuṇa were the inviters".

The second hemistich in the third verse is explained as a figure of speech (i.e. simile) by Sāyaṇa though his predecessor Veṅkaṭamādhava's exposition differs from that. Sāyaṇa says:

> (Juhū) did not reveal herself to the messenger sent to her (*preṣitāya dūtāya tathā na tasthe svātmānaṁ na prakāśayati*) just like a state protected by a kṣatriya is never revealed before the enemies.

But Veṅkaṭamādhava explained it differently, i.e.

> *samarpitāyāṁ tasyāṁ kṣatriyasya indrasya rājyaṁ gupitam abhavat.*
>
> when (the gods) restored her (to her husband) King Indra's state became secured.

Veṅkaṭamādhava further added the reason behind this security, i.e.

> *brāhmaṇasya jāyāṁ devā apaharantīti rāṣṭraṁ kṣubhitam āsit.*
>
> it caused the state's agitation as a brāhmaṇa's wife was stolen by the gods.

Griffith, however, translates this line as "she stayed not for a herald to conduct her". Jamison and Brereton (III.1575) interpret the line as "In this way is the kingship of the ruler protected."

In line 4d, *durdhā́ṁ dadhāti paramé vyoman*, the word *durdhā́m* has been interpreted by Veṅkaṭamādhava as *dausthyām* (difficult to place). Jamison and Brereton, too, follow the suit. But, according to Sāyaṇa 4d means that,

> *tapaḥprabhāvaḥ durdhā́ṁ durdhānam api paramé . . . vyomani uttame sthāne dadhāti vidadhāti khalu.*
>
> the fervor of penance sets in the highest sky even what is difficult to settle.

However, Griffith's translation differs much from those of the ancient commentators, viz. "in the supremest heaven she plants confusion".[48]

The second line in the fifth verse is *sá devā́nāṁ bhavaty ékam áṅgam*. Veṅkaṭamādhava explains *devā́nām* to mean

> *saḥ cāyaṁ bṛhaspatiḥ devānāṁ bhavati mukhyam aṅgam saptāṅgasya rājyasya.*

[48] Cf. the word *durdhā́m* is explained in the context of *ṚV* X.109.4 as "bad order; disarrangement" by Böhtlingk and Roth, s.v.

> this Bṛhaspati forms the principal part of the gods' state consisting of seven parts.

Veṅkaṭamādhava means to say that Bṛhaspati being the chief minister of Indra's court is considered to be the most important part of his kingdom. Sāyaṇa, however, explains it differently, viz. "of sacrifices" and comments that the husband and wife are two parts of a sacrifice and the husband alone forms only one part of it (*jāyāpatī yajñasya dve aṅge khalu*). Griffith translates it more literally as "he is a member of the God's own body".

The sixth verse has been explained by Veṅkaṭamādhava as "the entire state being agitated (Indra) restored the wife to Bṛhaspati for the sake of truth" (*kṣubhite rāṣṭre sarve sambhūya bṛhaspataye satyam anurundhanto jāyāṁ prāyacchan*), but Sāyaṇa prefers the meaning to be "the gods and the mortal kings handed over the wife of brāhmaṇa".

The word *urugāyá* in the final stanza is explained by Veṅkaṭamādhava as well as by Sāyaṇa to mean "with many achievements" (*urukīrtim*: Veṅkaṭamādhava, *bahukīrtim*: Sāyaṇa). Sāyaṇa suggests another meaning for this word, viz. "hymned by many" or "much praised" (*bahubhiḥ stotavyaṁ vā*). Griffith translates the concerned hemistich as:

> They shared the fullness of the earth, and won themselves extended sway.

In *Nirukta* 2.7 the word *urugāyá* is explained in the context of *Ṛgveda* I.154.6. According to Yāska there it means "the loftiest steps of the wide-striding (i.e. of great paces) Viṣṇu". Jamison and Brereton, in the context of *Ṛgveda* X.109.7, explain the word as "wide-ranging (space)".

X.125

The famous Devī or Vāc-Sūkta is ascribed to Vāc, the daughter of Ambhṛṇa. This hymn with eight stanzas is of tremendous importance in the development of *Śabda-Brahman* theory, a doctrine of the Vedāntic philosophy. The seer Vāc, according to many scholars, is conjectural, but as found in the earlier chapter, a feminine vigour is present in almost every stanza of this hymn.

The instrumental plurals in verse 1 are all in the sense of *itthambhāva* (so circumstanced) according to the traditional commentators. But Griffith, Geldner, Jamison and Brereton all take it in the sense of accompaniment (*sahārthe*).

The word *āhanásam*, an adjective of *sómam* in the second verse, is interpreted in the same manner by Veṅkaṭamādhava and Sāyaṇa, viz. "either which is thrashed (by the grinding stones)" (*ā hanyate grāvabhiḥ*: Veṅkaṭamādhava) or "which thrashes (the enemies)" (*śatrūn āhanti*: Veṅkaṭamādhava). But many of the Western interpreters take it as "high swelling". The word *suprāvyè* in the same verse is variously explained by the commentators. Veṅkaṭamādhava takes *av-* in the sense of "to protect", as this meaning is much common in usage, and he explains the word to refer to "him who protects well" (*suṣṭhu prarakṣati iti suprāvīḥ*). But, Sāyaṇa takes it as "for him who has pleased the gods with nice oblation" (*śobhanaṁ havir devānāṁ prāpayitre tarpayitre*), he takes the constituent root of this word, viz. *av-* in the sense of "satisfying", as recorded in the *uṇādi* list. Griffith after Böhtlingk and Roth, s.v. interprets the word as "very zealous".

The word *rā́ṣṭrī* in the third verse is explained by both Veṅkaṭamādhava and Sāyaṇa as the mistress (*īśitrī*: Veṅkaṭamādhava, *īśvarī*: Sāyaṇa), but Griffith takes it more literally, viz. "the Queen". Regarding the meaning of the phrase *bhūri āveśayantīm* most of the translators and interpreters, irrespective of traditional and modern, agree and understand it as "enter into many forms" but Jamison and Brereton (III.1602) considering the undoubted causation in the verb interpret it in a different way: "(I) cause many things to enter (me)." The hemistich concerned thus suggests that not only Vāc is found in many places but also many things enter her. These contrastive, mirrored images are part of her totalizing project.

The verb *úpa kṣiyanti* in the fourth verse has been explained by Sāyaṇa as, "(they) wither away" (*upakṣīṇā saṁsāreṇa hīnā bhavanti*). But according to Veṅkaṭamādhava it means "(they) dwell in (me)" (*mām upa nivasanti*). In Griffith's translation it is "dwell beside me".

Veṅkaṭamādhava paraphrases the word *samádam* at the sixth verse by *kalaham* (quarrel), but Sāyaṇa interprets it to mean something harsher, viz. "the battle" (*samat saṅgrāmaḥ*). Griffith translates the sentence *ahám jánāya samádaṁ kṛṇomi* as "I rouse and order battle for the people".

Veṅkaṭamādhava paraphrases the term *samudré* in verse 7 by *antarikṣe* (in the Ether), but Sāyaṇa takes it as *paramātman* (the Supreme Soul), while according to Griffith it means "in the waters". The commencing line of this verse is *ahám suve pitáram asya mūrdhán*, where Veṅkaṭamādhava takes *pitáram* as *ādityam* (the Sun) and interprets the line as "I send the Sun to the top of this world" (*ahaṁ prerayāmi ādityam asya lokasya mūrdhani*). Sāyaṇa, however, interprets it as

> *pitáraṁ divam ahám suve prasuve . . . asya paramātmanaḥ mūrdhán mūrdhany upari.*
>
> I gave birth to the Heaven on the top of this Supreme Soul.

Griffith comments on the term *pitaram*:

> Heaven or Sky, produced from Vāk [*sic*] identified with Paramātmā, the supreme and universal soul.

The word *ārábhamāṇā* in the final (i.e. the eighth) verse is explained variously by the commentators. Veṅkaṭamādhava says that it means "supporting" (*saṁstambhayanti*), while Sāyaṇa explains it as "producing" (*karaṇarūpeṇa utpādayantī*). Griffith takes it as "hold together" because the constituent root *rábh-* preceded by the prefix *ā́-* means "to clasp" or "to take hold of" in *Ṛgveda*. The phrase *ahám evá vā́taïva prá vāmi* in this verse is explained by Sāyaṇa as *ahám evá pareṇānadhiṣṭhitā svayam eva prá vāmi pravarte. vā́taïva yathā vātaḥ . . . pravāti tad vat.*

I move as wind not being compelled by any one else.

Though his predecessor Veṅkaṭamādhava interpreted the same with a little difference, viz. "I move as quickly as the wind" (*vātaḥ iva śīghraṁ pra gacchāmi*). Griffith's translation does not match with the expositions of either: "I breathe a strong breath like the wind and tempest".

X.127

Ṛgveda X.127, which describes the beauty of the Goddess Night, has been ascribed to Rātri, the daughter of Bharadvāja, the alternative seer being Kuśika Saubhara.

In the second verse the word *urú* is taken by Veṅkaṭamādhava and Sāyaṇa as referring to "the vast atmospheric region" (*urú vistīrṇam antarikṣam*) and Wilson (1850: 6.430-32) follows suit in translating it as "the expanded (firmament)". Griffith, however, translates the word as "the waste". Jamison and Brereton (III.1605) put it as "the broad (midspace)".

The verb *akṛta* with prefix *nír-* in verse 3 has been explained by Veṅkaṭamādhava and Sāyaṇa as "rectifies (with the light)" (*prakāśena saṁskaroti*: Sāyaṇa), but Griffith renders it as "hath set (the dawn her sister) in her place".

In verse 5 *arthínaḥ* is explained by Veṅkaṭamādhava as "sleepy" (*nidrārthinaḥ*) but Sāyaṇa derives the word from root *ṛ́-* (to go), and explains it as meaning "fast-going". Griffith takes it to mean "fain for prey".

A vocative singular *ūrmye*, used to denote the Goddess Night at verse 6, is interpreted by Griffith as "undulating", a word describing the characteristic of night.

The first hemistich of the seventh verse, *úpa mā pépiśat támaḥ kṛṣṇám vyàktam asthita*, is explained by Sāyaṇa as:

> The clinging (*pépiśat*) darkness, black yet bright in its own splendour (*svabhāsā sarvasyāñjakaṁ spaṣṭarūpaṁ vā*) has pervaded me.

Veṅkaṭamādhava's interpretation, despite being almost the same with that of his follower Sāyaṇa's, differs in explaining the meaning of *vyàktam*, explained by him as "lifting particularly" (*viśeṣeṇa uttiṣṭhati*). Griffith translates this hemistich much differently, viz.:

> Clearly hath she come nigh to me who decks the dark with richest hues.

The word *jigyúṣe* in the final stanza means "for the victorious", and Veṅkaṭamādhava thinks that it may refer to any king who is victorious, but Sāyaṇa takes it as *jigyuṣaḥ*, a genitive referring to the seer (*jigyuṣo mama*). Griffith follows Veṅkaṭamādhava's suit in translating *stómaṁ ná jigyúṣe* as "this laud as for a conqueror".

X.134

In *Ṛgveda* X.134 the second hemistich of the sixth and the entire seventh verse are ascribed to Godhā. The hymn has a refrain occurring in the end of every stanza except the seventh, i.e. the final one. The metre of the last stanza is also somewhat different, viz. Paṅkti, as against the Mahāpaṅkti in which the rest are composed. These differences would seem to point to a possibility of its being interpolated.

The tradition of *Bṛhaddevatā* and *Ārṣānukramaṇī* attributes the second hemistich of the sixth verse to Godhā. Sāyaṇa too follows their course. But the difference in metre and the presence of the refrain at the end of the hemistich concerned make it unacceptable that the authorship of this hemistich and that of the following verse should not differ. However, this hemistich ascribed to Godhā exhibits an interesting simile, where the seer is heard to pray to Indra to draw down the branch loaded with desired fruits for the worshippers as a goat does the same with its foremost foot (cf. Griffith and Jamison and Brereton):

pū́rveṇa maghavan padā́jó vayā́ṁ yáthā yamaḥ.

Contrarily Sāyaṇa thinks that the line means:

> As a goat draws a branch with its forefoot, O Maghavan, you, too, control (our) enemies by drawing them down with your power.

The meaning of the verb *ā́ yopayāmasi* is controversial in the context of the seventh verse. Veṅkaṭamādhava explains it as "to mix up the real and unreal" (*āyopanaṁ sadasatoḥ miśraṁam*). Sāyaṇa explains the word as "we will not confuse [anything by not performing it]" (*na kiṁ ca . . . ananuṣṭhānena vimohayāmaḥ*). He derives *yopayāmasi* from the root *yúp-* (to confuse) (*yupu vimohane*). Griffith translates the line concerned as "nor are we ever obstinate".[49] Jamison and Brereton are more justified to have translated the verb as 'confound' (III.1618).

The word *apikakṣébhiḥ loco citato* has been explained by Sāyaṇa as "the middle region of the arms" (*apikakṣo nāma bhāhvor madhyabhāgaḥ*). Veṅkaṭamādhava, however, appears to have grasped the exact, viz. "the shoulders" (*apikakṣaḥ aṁsaḥ*). Griffith takes it as "armpits" (beneath your arms).[50] Jamison and Brereton hold it as "the shoulders".

X.145

Ṛgveda X.145 is ascribed to Indrāṇī, the wife of Indra. This hymn is traditionally titled as "the co-wife's suppression" (*sapatnībādhana-*). The seer is supposed to have uttered this hymn while digging out a herb for arresting the influence of a co-wife over her husband.

The expression *úttānaparṇe* in the second verse is explained by Veṅkaṭamādhava and Sāyaṇa in the sense of "O (herb)

---

[49] Refer *yúp-* (to debar; obstruct; disturb; trouble; confuse; efface; remove; destroy) in *Ṛgveda* and *Śatapatha Brāhmaṇa*: Böhtlingk and Roth, s.v.

[50] Refer *apikakṣá* (the region of the armpits and shoulder blades) in context of *ṚV* X.134.7: Böhtlingk and Roth, s.v.

with leaves facing upward" (*uttānāni ūrdhvamukhāni parṇāni*: Sāyaṇa). Griffith translates it as "with extended leaves". The word *sáhasvatī-* in the same verse is interpreted by Veṅkaṭamādhava as "mighty" (*balavatī-*), while Sāyaṇa takes it to mean "victorious" (*abhibhavanavatī-*).

The phrase *nó asmín ramate jáne* in the fourth verse has been exposed by Veṅkaṭamādhava as:

saṁvaśāt na ca iyam asmin jane ramatām.

May she (the co-wife) not take pleasure in living with this person (viz. my husband).

But, Sāyaṇa takes it in just the opposite sense, viz.

na khalu kā cit asmin jane sapatnyākhye ramate krīḍati.

No one takes pleasure in this person (i.e. the co-wife).

Griffith follows Veṅkaṭamādhava in translating this line, viz. "she takes no pleasure in this man". Jamison and Brereton (III.1631) interpret it as "nor does she rest by this person [= husband]".

Sāyaṇa considers the word *sáhīyasā* in the last verse as an adjective qualifying the pillow which will be used in the magical charm to defeat the co-wife (*abhibhavitṛtareṇa tenopādhānena*). But his predecessor Veṅkaṭamādhava took it as adjectival to the mind (*abhibhāvukena manasā*).

X.151

Ṛgveda X.151 is attributed to Śraddhā Kāmāyanī. An author who is surely conjectural. The hymn praises Śraddhā or Faith (Śraddhā, according to Jamison and Brereton (III.1636) do not refer to 'faith' but 'trust'). The deity and the seer are here identical. Śraddhā is an abstract idea and she is described as *kāmāyanī*: from the family of love.

The phrase *śraddhā́ṁ bhágasya mūrdháni* is interpreted by Veṅkaṭamādhava as "(we tell others) about Śraddhā who is the prime portion of luck" (*śraddhāṁ bhāgadheyasya pradhānāṅge avasthitām*). Sāyaṇa explains it as "(we glorify) Śraddhā (with our praise) who is seated at the prime place of adorable wealth" (*bhajanīyasya dhanasya . . . pradhānabhūte sthāne avasthitām*). Wilson translates *bhágasya mūrdháni* as "(who is seated) on Bhaga's head" (Bhaga: a Sun-god, known for bestowing wealth). Griffith takes it as "height of happiness". Jamison and Brereton translate it as "at the head of good fortune".

3ab runs thus: *yáthā devā́ ásureṣu śraddhā́m ugréṣu cakriré*. Sāyaṇa interprets it in this way: *devāḥ indrādayaḥ asureṣu udgūrṇabaleṣu yathā śraddhāṁ cakrire avaśyam ime hantavyā ity ādarātiśayaṁ kṛtavantaḥ.*

> As the gods made up their mind to kill the mighty demons.

In contradistinction to this, Griffith offers an entirely opposite meaning to Sāyaṇa's: he takes the word *ásura-* in its primitive Indo-Iranian meaning, viz. Dyaus, Varuṇa and some other primeval Aryan gods, who were venerated by Indra and other Indo-Aryan deities of later creation. Hence the above-mentioned hemistich appears in Griffith's translation as:

> Even as the Deities maintained Faith in the mighty Asuras.

The word *úpāsate* in the fourth verse is explained by Sāyaṇa as "(they) pray to (Śraddhā)" (*úpāsate prārthayante*). But Griffith explains it according to its derivative meaning, viz. "draw near to (Faith)".

X.153

Ṛgveda X.153 is ascribed to the mothers of Indra. The hymn consisting of five verses is of dubious authorship. The word *apasyuvaḥ* in the first verse indicates the mothers of Indra. The word being derived from *ápas-*, work, added with a nominal suffix, according to Sāyaṇa, means "women, desirous of working for themselves" (*apaḥ karma ātmana icchantyaḥ*). Griffith translates the word after Sāyaṇa as "The Active Ones" but since *ápas-* also means "water", Griffith adds a cautious note that "the Water-goddesses may be meant". Jamison and Brereton (III.1637) take the word in sense of "the busy women".

The word *vṛṣan* in vocative and nominative singulars has been used in the second verse. Sāyaṇa explains the line concerned to mean:

> *he vṛṣan varṣitaḥ tvaṁ vṛṣed asi kāmānāṁ varṣitai vā bhavasi.*
>
> O bestower, you are indeed the bestower of desired objects.

Wilson takes it as meaning "hero". Griffith renders it by "mighty and strong".

X.154

Ṛgveda X.154 is ascribed to Yamī, the daughter of Vivasvant. The theme of this hymn is "new life" (*bhāvavṛtta*). The authorship might have been artificially attributed to Yamī, considered as the female counterpart of Yama, the king of the world after life.

The first hemistich of the fourth verse, viz. *yé cit pū́rva ṛtasā́pa ṛtā́vāna ṛtāvṛ́dhaḥ* has a parallel in *Ṛgveda* I.179.2 (see below Chapter 6, p. 207). Here the word *ṛtasā́paḥ* is explained by Veṅkaṭamādhava and Sāyaṇa as "those who are in touch with the Law or the fervor or the sacrifice" (*tapaḥspṛśaḥ*: Veṅkaṭamādhava and *ṛtaṁ satyaṁ yajñaṁ vā spṛśantaḥ*: Sāyaṇa). Griffith takes it as "the followers of Law". The word *ṛtāvṛ́dhaḥ* is also interpreted differently by the commentators. Veṅkaṭamādhava takes it as "raised by truth" (*satyena vṛddhāḥ*), while Sāyaṇa takes the word being formed in active voice, viz. "the raiser of truth" (*ṛtasya vardhakāḥ*).

The word *sahásranīthāḥ* in the fifth verse is interpreted by Veṅkaṭamādhava as "those who lead in many ways" (*bahupraṇayanāḥ*), while Sāyaṇa explains it as "those with thousand eyes" (*sahasranayanāḥ*). Griffith ascribes to it a meaning other than those offered by the ancient commentators, viz. "skilled in a thousand ways and means". Jamison and Brereton (III.1638) interpret it as "the poets of a thousand devices".

X.159

Ṛgveda X.159 is ascribed to Śacī, the daughter of Puloman and the wife of Indra, also known as Indrāṇī. The hymn depicts the exultation of a jealous wife who has defeated her co-wives and established her dominance over her husband. However, Wilson conjectures that

> Śacī means also an 'act' and this hymn is metaphorically the praise of Indra's acts.

However, in the five verses of this hymn is heard the joyous exclamation of a wife who has triumphed over her rival wives. The magico-ritualistic purpose of this hymn is same as that of *Ṛgveda* X.145, viz. the suppression of co-wives (*sapatnībādhana*).

Sāyaṇa explains *ketú-* in line 2a as "she who knows everything" (*ketayitrī sarvasya jñātrī:* cf. root *kít-* "to know"). But, Griffith follows Veṅkaṭamādhava taking *ketuḥ* as "banner".

The word *virā́jāni* in the final verse is explained by Sāyaṇa as: "May I glow in splendour" (*viśeṣeṇa rājamānā bhavāni*). Griffith translates it as "I may hold imperial sway over (this Hero and the folk)".

X.189

The last female seer mentioned in the lists of *Bṛhaddevatā* and *Ārṣānukramaṇī* is Sārparājñī attributed with the authorship of *Ṛgveda* X.189. The deity is the seer herself or the Sun according to *Sarvānukramaṇī.*

The spotted bull that is seated before the mother in the east is described in the first verse. Veṅkaṭamādhava and Sāyaṇa equate *mātṛ́* with "the Earth, the mother of all creatures" (*sarvasya bhūtajātasya nirmātrīṁ pṛthivīm*: Sāyaṇa). Griffith, on the other hand, suggests the word represents "the Dawn".

The word *mahiṣáḥ* in the second verse has been interpreted as "the great sun" (*mahān sūryaḥ*) by Veṅkaṭamādhava and Sāyaṇa. Griffith translates the word as "the bull". Jamison and Brereton (III.1660) take the word more literally, i.e. "the buffalo".

3

Socio-Cultural Aspects of the Select Hymns and the World-view of the Women Seers

In order to study the socio-cultural aspects of the select hymns of women seers and their *Weltanschauung* or outlook on the world, it is essential to ascertain the position of women in general in that era, on the evidence gathered from the entire text. It is generally held that women in early Vedic age enjoyed almost equal rights with men. As evidence, the instance of the participation of women in religious and social duties along with their husbands is frequently cited. It is true that women had a prominent role in early Vedic times compared to what she had in later ages, but it is also true that her role in the former age had its limits, and her enjoying equal rights with her husband is but a little exaggeration.

The Ṛgvedic woman of course had the privilege of performing religious duties herself or along with her husband, but it would be better not to ascertain her social status by the religious rights she enjoyed, but to observe her throughout the stages of her life since her birth, or rather even before her birth. Altekar (1938: 3) observes that, the available evidence fails to suggest that the daughter was not as welcome as a son in the early Vedic family. He refers to Geiger's view (in 1885: 53-54), viz. son was preferred to daughter even in the Indo-Iranian age. In the Indo-Aryan society, too, we find the same trend seems to have continued. *Atharvaveda* contains charms and rituals to ensure the birth of a son in preference to that of a daughter (*AV* 3.23; 6.11). Though in an early Upaniṣad we find rituals prescribed for procuring a scholarly daughter (*BṛUp* 4.4.18), it can nevertheless be assumed from the trend of the later social customs that these rituals could never have been as popular as the *puṁsavana*, the rite prescribed for ensuring the birth of a male child. *R̥gveda* itself does not supply much information about the girl child. In the hymns of *R̥gveda* we frequently meet with the earnest desire in general for having heroic sons. It is worthy of note that even the women seers repeatedly prayed to their god to sanction them heroic sons but never or hardly ever wished for a daughter. In the hymn composed by Paulomī Śacī, the boasting of a proud mother to have a reigning daughter, and several heroic sons, is heard (*R̥V* X.159.3). Some scholars suggest that, there was extermination of girl children in Vedic age. They point to the reference of *Taittirīya Saṁhitā* 6.5.10.3, where it is stated that the newborn daughter is placed on the ground, while the son is lifted up.[1] But this statement refers to the inferior position of the girl to that of the boy and not by any means the extermination of the daughter. Zimmer (1879) depending upon a passage in *Kāṭhaka Saṁhitā* (27a) holds that the girl child was exposed to die in the Vedic age, which Böhtlingk attempted to refute.[2]

Though less welcome, the daughter, when born, was not altogether neglected in the Vedic family. They were brought up with care and given education. The later writers of Dharmasūtras inform us of the *upanayana* (initiation ceremony) of the girls in early period.[3] It is also revealed from the Vedic literature[4] that

---

[1] *yádāgrayaṇáḥ sthālyā́ gr̥hṇā́ti vāyavyèna juhoti tásmāt gárbheṇā́vijñātena brahmahā́ 'vabhr̥thám ávayanti párā sthālī́r ásyanty úd vāyavyā̀ni haranti tásmāt stríyāṁ jātā́ṁ párā 'syanty út púmāṁsaṁ haranti* — *TS* 6.5.10.3

[2] At Indra: Chapter 1.

[3] *purākalpe tu nārīṇāṁ | mauñjībandhanam iṣyate |*
adhyāpanaṁ ca vedānāṁ | sāvitrīvacanaṁ tathā ||
— Hārīta and Yama quoted in *Vīramitrodaya*, Saṁskāraprakāśa of Mitramiśra, ed. by Jīvanānanda, Calcutta, 1875, p. 402

[4] Cf. *R̥V* I.173.2cd; V.3.2cd; VIII.31.5, etc.

women had to participate in the religious ceremonies along with their husbands (vide Oldenberg 1912: 1.128), and they needed some sort of education in order to perform that. They were naturally educated in the spiritual and temporal subjects. Upadhyay observes:

> The spiritual side comprised a training in religious lore and perhaps also in the historical tradition and mythology which made them *ṛṣi*s of hymns. — 1941: 174

It was also necessary for girls to attain education in order to get married to suitable husbands. *Atharvaveda* XI.5.18 says:

> A young daughter through the observance of *brahmacarya* acquires youthful husband.

Scholars are not unanimous about the exact nature of *brahmacarya* recommended for girls. Bhattacharya (1987: 31) suggests that this *brahmacarya* is but a ritual (*vrata*) by which maidens obtained good husbands. In Vedic and later literatures *brahmacarya* meant the austerity prescribed for the students while they stayed at their preceptor's house. *Brahman* being a synonym of the Vedas and *brahma-yajña* referring to the study of the Vedas, *brahmacarya* was used to mean the austerity through which they should go while studying the Vedas, and the term *brahmacārin* meant the Vedic student himself.[5] Some maidens attained husbands after the *brahmacarya* while some remained unmarried. The latter generally felt themselves insecure in the society. In the hymns of the female seers, it is often reflected, that a woman without husband or sons was subject to be harassed.[6]

The marriage of the Vedic maiden is depicted in the hymn of Sūryā Sāvitrī in *Ṛgveda* X.85 and in *Atharvaveda* XIV.1-2. Girls were given to marriage in a mature age in Ṛgvedic times, no mention of child marriage is found in the Ṛgvedic literature. Hanns Peter

---

[5] Cf. *ṚV* VII.103.1 has the word *vratacārín* for a "Vedic student"; *AV* XI.5 uses *brahmacārín* to mean the same.

[6] Cf. *ṚV* X.39.6, 86.9.

Schmidt (1987: 1-29) establishes convincingly that girls were given to marriage after they attained puberty in the Ṛgvedic age, though it was also the lookout of the society that as few periods (*ṛtu*) as possible should be missed to ensure a long reproductive period. The *svayaṁvara* (self-chosen) system of marriage prevailed in the Ṛgvedic society. Schmidt (op. cit. 76-109), however, contends that the Veda proper hardly provides an explicit and unambiguous reference to any forms of *svayaṁvara*. The bride is blessed to reign over her in-laws and accompany her husband till old age in *Ṛgveda* X.85.46. The Ṛgvedic Aryans were patriarchal and the husband had the absolute power over his wife and children. Generally the bride brought gifts from her father's house along with her, but it is also mentioned through a simile in *Ṛgveda* I.109.2 that, a man of poor qualities paid plenty of wealth to his in-laws in order to get the bride, *áśravaṁ hí bhūridā́vattarā vāṁ víjāmātur,* etc. In other words, bride price was not unknown to the Vedic Aryans, though it was not appreciated by them as reflected in the expression *víjāmātur* above, as also by such expression as *aśrīrá iva jā́mātā* in *Ṛgveda* VIII.2.20. In later Dharmaśāstras this bride price has been mentioned as a characteristic of *āsura* form of marriage, which was condemned as a reproachable usage in the later Aryan society.

Monogamy was the general trend of the society, though references to polygamy are frequent in *Ṛgveda*.[7] Directly or through similes the polygamous trend of the aristocrats of the society has been revealed in *Ṛgveda*. The royals and the priests had a number of wives. Polyandry, though reflected through some stray similes, can hardly be taken as a social custom of the Vedic people, because all the references to it are made about gods of natural origin, e.g. Sūryā (relating to the rays of the sun or the dawn), Soma (the moon), Aśvins (the twilights appeared in dawn and dusk) or Maruts (the lightning).

Girls had their choice in selecting husbands (cf. *ṚV* X.27.12).

---

[7] Cf. *ṚV* I.62.10, 105.8; VI.18.2, 26.3; X.43.1, etc.

Aśvins are known to have married Sūryā in a chariot race they won (cf. *AiBr* 5.2.17). It appears from the oldest literature of the Indo-Europeans that marriage in primitive society was not always a must for leading a sexual life. Many hymns of *Ṛgveda* indicate men and women mating freely, and living together in the society: "marriage was a later development", observes Thomas (1964: 43), "closely linked with the foundation of political organizations that ensured individual rights through some sort of administrative machinery".

From the testimony of the marriage hymn (i.e. *ṚV* X.85) we gather that the bride was, as she is now, expected to look after the members of her husband's family and do justice to the dependents and cattle (cf. *ṚV* X.85.43-44). She is also asked to take part in *vidáthas* (*ṚV* X.85.26-27), which according to scholars like Müller, Wilson and Griffith were the public assemblies, where the family problems were represented by the housewives and were solved accordingly.

Women went to public sacrifices and war-fields (*ṚV* X.86.10) and general outings. It is understood from the references that women could move about freely in the Ṛgvedic age, but their humiliation had its own place, in such a free society we hear of Indrāṇī digging a plant and practising black magic to get rid of the rival wives (*ṚV* X.145). The agony and insult felt by the wives of the polygamous aristocrats are easily understood in the wrath and rancour against her co-wife expressed in the hymn of Indrāṇī (*ṚV* X.145.3-4).

Women performed sacrificial duties along with their husbands, and no unmarried man was entitled to offer sacrifice as gleaned from the later Sūtra literature. However, in *Ṛgveda* itself women offering oblation to the fire chanting the *mantras* (*ṚV* V.28.1) are found.

In Vedic India, wife was generally regarded as the co-owner of the family property along with her husband as the expression *dampatī* might indicate. The husband, at the time of wedding, appears to have accepted the authority of the wife in household matters (*R̥V* X.85.26). *Taittirīya Saṁhitā*[8] says that the wife was the mistress of the household, and much later Jaimini in his *Pūrvamīmāṁsā-Sūtra* (6.1.16) refers to it for establishing the contention that women could actually own property. *Bṛhadāraṇyaka Upaniṣad* 2.4.3 refers to Yājñavalkya who divided his property between his two wives. The gifts a bride received at the time of marriage were called *pariṇayya* (= *strīdhana* of the later Smṛti literature), over which she had the sole right.

Daughters with brothers did not inherit personal property, as recorded in *R̥gveda* III.31.2:

> A brother should not give any share of his wealth to his sister.

Nirukta 3.6, while explaining this text, says:

> Not to sisters should the legitimate son give the inheritance (*riktha-*). She is made the receptacle of the child of her husband.

Unmarried daughters had the right to stay with their parents, and even brother's family, as they grew old.[9] Verse II.17.7 of *R̥gveda* says that an unmarried daughter could claim her share in her father's property. A daughter having no brother inherited her father's property, despite her being married, but in that case her eldest son was considered as the son of the grandfather from his mother's side (*R̥V* III.31.3), and continued the family line of his maternal grandfather. But *R̥gveda* I.124.7 and *Atharvaveda* I.17.1 suggest that it was difficult for a brotherless daughter to find a groom, as few men would love their first son to be given to their fathers-in-law.

Though the wife was formally the co-owner of her husband's property as long as he was alive, a widow's right to inherit her deceased husband's property remained unrecognized in *R̥gveda*. But in early Vedic times the custom of levirate (*niyoga-*) was a

---

[8] *pátny anvā́rabhate pátnī hí pā́rīṇahyasyéśe pátniyai vā́numataṁ nírvapati yád vái pátnī yajñásya karóti mithunáṁ tád átho pátniyā eváiṣá yajñásyānvārambhó 'navacchittayai.* —*TS* 6.2.1

[9] Cf. *R̥V* I.117.7; II.17.7; X.39.3.

rather common practice, which is why widows without sons were rare. Hence, a vast majority of widows shared their husbands' property[10] — if not directly as their heirs — at least as the guardians of their minor sons, as pointed out by Vishnoi (1987: 17). Remarriage of widows was common in Vedic age, and when remarried, the question of inheriting the deceased husband's property did not arise.

The widows of Ṛgvedic India did not share the same fate as of those in later India. Usually they were remarried to their younger brother-in-law, as has been explicitly referred to in the funeral hymn (*ṚV* X.18). The concerned passages (*ṚV* X.18.7-9) suggest that the new widow was given in marriage to him right at the funeral rite of her dead husband (cf. Upadhyay 1941: 92). In another verse (*ṚV* X.40.2), the sexual relation of a widow with her brother-in-law has been hinted at through a simile.

Macdonell (1898: 165), citing *mantra*s 8-9 of the above hymn, observes:

> Traces even survive which indicate that his widow and his weapons were burnt with the body of the husband.

The first of the above two verses says that the widow of the dead should lie beside his corpse, but the very next verse states that she was lifted by hand by her younger brother-in-law and entered a new life. *Atharvaveda* XVIII.3.1 preserves a custom of widow burning, which it calls an ancient religious duty (*dharmaṁ purāṇam*). Macdonell (1900) remarks that "the evidence of Anthropology shows that this was a very primitive practice widely prevailing at the funeral of military chiefs and it can be proved to go back to the Indo-European age". The Ṛgvedic verse in context, i.e. X.18.7 (cf. especially *ā́ rohantu jánayo yónim ágre*), or *Atharvaveda* XVIII.3.1 for that matter, seems to have alluded to this ancient custom of burning the widow along with the remains of her dead husband. This, however, does not appear to have survived in the Ṛgvedic age

[10] Cf. Ibid I.117.7; II.17.7; X.39.3 (also see Altekar 1938: 250).

as the levirate and remarriage of a widow find frequent mention in the text itself.[11]

Succession to throne was not recommended for the princesses, and ancient Indian history does not furnish instances enough of female sovereigns and administrators. In Vedic literature are found references to a few women participating in political and/ or apolitical wars.[12] Furthermore, in the literature of the Vedas readers also come across to the reference to Śaśīyasī, the queen of King Taranta, who rendered military assistance and presented wealth to Śyāvaśva in order to procure the daughter of King Rathabīti to be his wife.[13] There is only a solitary reference to a woman who styled herself a sovereign queen: *ahám rā́ṣṭrī* (followed by *saṁgámanī vásūnām* "one who amasses riches"), and also mentioned her giving a helping hand to Rudra in his fight against enemies. The speaker is none else than the renowned Vāc, the daughter of Sage Ambhṛṇa and the composer of *Ṛgveda* X.125. But most of the queens met in the Vedic literature are depicted as waiting upon their husbands.[14]

Some of the Ṛgvedic hymns suggest that the society in that age was to some extent permissive,[15] and a woman could approach the man she desired unhesitatingly, still, there are references to women reproached in the Vedic society for their adultery. *Ṛgveda* IV.5.5, X.34.5 and X.40.6 speak, with a note of repulsion, of women who committed adultery. There are mentions of illegitimate children, whose birth was considered sinful, and consequently was hushed up. *Ṛgveda* VIII.46.21 informs of the son of a maiden. In *Ṛgveda* IV.18.5, 8 Aditi, the mother of Indra, is mentioned to have concealed

---

[11] *ṚV* I.116.13, 117.24; VI.62.7; X.39.7, etc.

[12] Viśpalā (*ṚV* I.116.15) and Mudgalānī (X.102.2) fought abreast with their husbands and won the battle.

[13] *ṚV* V.61.5-8, 17-19; *BṛhD* 5.61, 64, 80.

[14] *ṚV* I.62.10, 179.1; VIII.1.34; X.85, 95.

[15] *ṚV* I.126.6,7; IV.18.8; VIII.91; X.10.

the birth of her son, like one would his or her crime.[16]

There are not many references to old women in *Ṛgveda*. Women, as revealed from the hymns like *Ṛgveda* I.179 (verse 1), as also X.39-40, considered their life fruitful when they managed to get married and became mothers of heroic sons. Lopāmudrā, in I.179.1, laments that her youth is worn off and though married, she has not yet enjoyed marital love with her husband. She invites him in passionate words to share the conjugal bliss with her.[17] In *Ṛgveda* X.39-40, the unmarried olden female seer Ghoṣā invokes the Aśvins that they may sanction her a good husband and heroic sons. She longs for the care of a loving husband (cf. *ṚV* X.40.11) and calls herself friendless and looked down upon by her kinsfolk (*ṚV* X.39.6).[18]

The new bride is blessed in the marriage hymn (*ṚV* X.85.36) to accompany her husband till old age. It is easily understood that in the age of *Ṛgveda* when things were decided upon the strength of arms, old people without a next of kin suffered a lot from the insecurities of life and food. The family men were generally looked after by their offspring: there are many references in *Ṛgveda* to the old parents-in-law receiving care and respect from their daughters-in-law.[19] Aged maidens stayed at their fathers' home probably with the families of their brothers. Some of them became *brahmavādinī*s (scholars in the Vedas and lived the life of celibacy).

There are thirty-one hymns in *Ṛgveda*, in which the female seers have contributed.[20] Sikatā and Nīvāvarī, though recorded as seers in *Sarvānukramaṇī,* are not mentioned in *Bṛhaddevatā*. The lists of the female seers found in *Bṛhaddevatā* and *Ārṣānukramaṇī*

---

[16] *avadyám iva mányamānā gúhākar* | *índraṁ mātā́ vīryèṇa nyṛ̀ṣṭam* |
— *ṚV* IV.18.5

[17] *pátnīr vṛ́ṣaṇo jagamyuḥ* — *ṚV* I.179.1.

[18] *ánāpir ájñā asajātyā́matiḥ*.

[19] *ṚV* V.28.1; X.85.46; X.95.4, etc.

[20] See above Chap. 1 p. 35.

do not furnish the names of these two. Further, Indrāṇī and Śacī, though regarded as two individuals by Altekar, seem to be one and the same entity under two separate names, an assumption that finds corroboration in such later texts as the great epics and various Purāṇas. The emotion and the way of expression revealed in both the hymns (i.e. X.145 & 159) are similar in nature. It appears from a close study of these two hymns that the same woman suffering from her co-wife practises sorcery in the former hymn and announces her victory over her rival in the latter.

Readers are informed of another female seer named Mamatā as the author of *Ṛgveda* VI.10.2,[21] but no traditional document is available in support of this view, except the internal evidence of the third line of verse 2 thereof. Here, through a simile, Mamatā is stated as a priest offering oblation to Agni along with beautiful lauds.

As additions to Altekar's list a few other seers also may be assumed to be mundane women on the basis of the internal evidences of the verses ascribed to them: Romaśā (I.126.7), Śaśvatī (VIII.1.34), Apālā (VIII.91), also Yamī Vaivasvatī (X.10) perhaps, Vasukra-patnī (X.28.1), Agastya-svasṛ (X.60.6), Vāc (X.125), Godhā (X.134.6-7), Niṣat and Upaniṣat (the *Ṛgveda Khila*-hymn occurring after *Ṛgveda* I.73, beginning with *prá dhā́rā yantu,* etc.). Of these female seers, Romaśā, Lopāmudrā and Śaśvatī are found in the dialogue hymns conversing with their respective husbands. The question arises here, if the dialogue hymns were really composed by the speakers whom they were attributed to, or they were in fact originally composed by some other poets, who put the dialogues in the lips of the speakers. In the first case, the verses can be considered as having been composed by the female seers themselves, but in the second case it is very likely that a third person, most probably a male poet, composed the entire hymn and imposed his own views on the speakers irrespective of their gender. This probability intensifies when the dialogues, especially in the colloquy of Urvaśī

---

[21] *stómaṁ yám asmai mamáteva śūṣám* (cf. Upadhyay 1941: 177).

and Purūravas (*ṚV* X.95), are critically analysed. Urvaśī is heard as saying thereat:

> There is no (lasting) friendship with womenfolk; their hearts are hearts of hyenas.

Though according to Kosambi (1962: 52), this remark is made by Purūravas and not by Urvaśī, neither the tradition supports this view nor is there any other verse in this hymn where the speakers have mingled their voices. It appears unlikely that in the mid of Urvaśī's speech Purūravas intervened. If it is accepted that this remark was made by Urvaśī, the authorship of the same should be doubted. Urvaśī, herself being a woman, can hardly be expected to make a cynical remark on womenfolk in general.

Apart from the above-mentioned hymns a number of female seers are met with in *Ṛgveda* as mentioned in *Bṛhaddevatā*. They are, however, mostly transcendental in nature and can hardly be regarded as mortals, for example, Aditi (IV.18), Dakṣiṇā (X.107), Rātri (X.127), Śraddhā (X.153), Yamī Vaivasvatī (X.154), Sārparājñī (X.189) and so on. These seers are either mythological transcendental beings or personified ideas, and cannot be treated as the subjects of a socio-cultural study. In spite of that, scattered elements, which render help in ascertaining the socio-cultural position and the world-view of the elite-class women of that age, are available in these hymns. Upadhyay (1941: 3) observes:

> The Ṛgvedic conception of womanhood at its best may well be studied in the goddesses described in this first human literary document, the *Ṛgveda*.

Among such goddesses, Aditi[22] stands first, as she typifies the ideal mother and is called the mother of all gods. But she is the personification of a pure abstraction when such words as "whatever is created and whatever should be created are but Aditi herself" are spoken of her (*ṚV* I.89.10).

---

[22] *ṚV* I.24.1, 43.2, 113.19, 136.3, 162.22, 185.3.

In the select texts Aditi is the seer of a hymn along with her son Indra and the seer Vāmadeva (IV.18). *Bṛhaddevatā* 4.130.2 relates a story to this hymn, which Sāyaṇa has elaborated in the preface of his commentary of this hymn. It is stated there that seer Vāmadeva refused to be born in the usual manner and insisted on coming into the world through another way. Aditi was invoked by his distressed mother, and she came there along with her son Indra to dissuade him from his fatal intention. Griffith, on this point, thinks that this hymn speaks about the birth and infancy of Indra, and his intention to be born through his mother's side. But, the speaker Vyaṁsa, his father, as well as Aditi, his mother or some other person, succeed in dissuading him. Griffith further states that the commentators have erroneously interpreted the hymn as referring to the birth of Vāmadeva.

Any way, the mention of Aditi abandoning her child Indra and the rancour of Indra against his father, announcing himself to be "the destroyer of his own father", make this hymn important for socio-cultural studies.

The next transcendent female seer to be met in *Ṛgveda* is Sūryā (X.85), the daughter of Savitṛ. She is typified as the Aryan bride. Scholars identify her as the light of the sun, which is lent to the moon with which the latter shines (Upadhyay 1941: 20). The marriage of Sūryā with Soma is mentioned at *Atharvaveda* XIV.1-2, *Kauṣītaki Brāhmaṇa* 18.1 and at *Aitareya Brāhmaṇa* 5.2.17. Book 9 of *Ṛgveda* knows her as the Sun's daughter who fetches Soma from the sky (IX.113.3) and purifies him with her hair (IX.1.6). The Sūryā hymn tells that Savitṛ had intended his daughter for Soma, but the Aśvins won the tournament and received her as prize. The same hymn, however, mentions her also as Soma's wife, in which case the Aśvins are her chaperons who convey her to her husband's house.

This hymn, though of dubious authorship, contains some very valuable materials for a study of the socio-cultural aspects of the Vedic Aryans. The Hindu marriage ceremony as described in the hymn still prevails in its basic form in India. A stanza (viz. *ṚV*

X.85.40) which states that Savitṛ first gave her to Soma, then to Viśvāvasu the *gandharva*, who in his turn bestowed her to Agni, who finally handed her over to the mortal bridegroom, has given rise to a controversy regarding the existence of polyandry in Vedic India. Apart from this, this particular hymn supplies information about a number of Aryan customs relating to marriage, such as the father giving gifts to the bride (*ṚV* X.85.13), her occupying an important position in the in-law's house,[23] and so on and so forth.

Indrāṇī of X.86 is obviously a celestial character, but her speech carries a few points which help to understand the social status of the Ṛgvedic women. She says in anger that Vṛṣākapi, whom Indra pampers, insults her as if she is an unprotected woman (i.e. without a husband or son), *avī́rām iva mā́m ayám̐ śarā́rur abhí manyate* (v. 9). Her verses also inform of the social custom, prevalent at that time, of the women going out freely in public festivals. The way in which her husband Indra tried to pacify her rage is also remarkable, light as it throws on the conjugal relation of the time.

*Apsaras*es, a special class of celestial nymphs, are also treated as (quasi-)goddesses in *Ṛgveda*. Among them Urvaśī of X.95 occupies a unique position. Urvaśī is found engaged in a colloquy with her husband Purūravas. Her hymn supplies some sociological information, as, among others:

1. The prevalence also of the contract form of marriage in the Ṛgvedic age. Urvaśī agreed to marry Purūravas on the basis of two conditions, at the breaking of which she could leave her spouse immediately.
2. The high position enjoyed by dancing girls of that time in society. Urvaśī, the nymph of the royal court of Indra, could become a queen.
3. The role a wife played in her in-law's residence. Urvaśī is said to have attended her father-in-law, feeding herself merely on a small quantity of clarified butter.

---

[23] *ṚV* X.85.43-44, 46.

4. Inklings on the conjugal life in that hoary past. In a verse Urvaśī frankly narrates her husband's sexual advances towards her.

Dakṣiṇā of *Ṛgveda* X.107, Rātri of X.127 and Śraddhā of X.151 are nothing but personified abstract concepts or natural phenomena. The hymns attributed to them are fair specimens of Ṛgvedic lyric poetry, but they hardly afford any significant help to socio-cultural studies.

Saramā is the female seer of the much-discussed Saramā–Paṇis dialogue hymn. She is called the "divine bitch" by the commentators. Oldenberg (1890: 51) traces Saramā to the Greek Helena and asserts that the former resembles the Dawn. Indra sent her as his messenger to the Paṇis who had stolen his cows and hid them away. This hymn says that the Paṇis tried to make friendship with her, saying "we will make you our sister" (*svásāraṁ tvā kṛṇavai*, X.108.9), but Saramā refused their purposeful fraternity (v. 10).

The mystic hymn *Ṛgveda* X.109 ascribed to Brahmajāyā Juhū is rather complicated and perhaps contains little socio-cultural element. However, the anecdote related to this hymn, told by the ancient commentators, runs thus: The God *Brahman* or Bṛhaspati abandoned his wife Juhū or Vāc due to his own sin, and the gods restored her to him.[24] Though Juhū is a completely mythical character, her hymn indirectly conveys the message that the desertion of the wife was considered as a husband's sin.

Ṛgveda X.153 is ascribed to the Indramātars, obvious mythological beings. Sāyaṇa, after *Sarvānukramaṇī*, says that these mothers of Indra are the sisters of gods. In the first verse of the hymn it is told that Apasyuvas, swaying about, came near to Indra at his birth and shared his great heroic might. Griffith suggests

[24] In *Mahābhārata* and Purāṇas the wife of Bṛhaspati is Tārā who eloped with King Candra or Soma and was restored to her husband later at the insistance of the gods. (See *Bhāgavata Purāṇa* 1.11, *Viṣṇu Purāṇa* 4.6.5); see also Geldner (1951) and Doniger O'Flaherty (1981).

the term *apasyúvaḥ* denotes the water goddesses (so also Geldner 1951: 384, fn. on verse 1: *Indra's Mütter oder Ammen. Vielleicht die Wasser-göttinnen*). This hymn might probably be connected with the fragment of the story told in *Ṛgveda* IV.18, where Aditi, the mother of Indra, admits that after his birth, she left him in a secret place as if (he was) a sin. The abandoned child was probably brought up by some women who lived near water and eventually were known as the mothers of Indra.

Yamī is the author of *Ṛgveda* X.154. The hymn, dealing with subjects related to death, is addressed to the sacrificers. Different drinks are offered to them in the next world. *Soma, ghṛta* and *madhu* are offered to different personages according to their deeds in the mundane world. On the basis of *Taittirīya Saṁhitā* 3.3.8 (Yama is Agni, Yamī is this earth), Bhattacharji (1978: 93-95) identifies Yamī with Nirṛti, who reigns over decay, disease, dissolution and death, and has also been identified with the earth (*TS* 4.2.5), and observes that they were originally one and the same. Though traditional indices, viz. *Bṛhaddevatā* and *Sarvānukramaṇī*, hold that Yamī Vaivasvatī of *Ṛgveda* X.10 and the seer of *Ṛgveda* X.154 are identical, the humane passion found in the words of Yamī, imploring Yama to make her his consort, as found in X.10, is missing in the latter. *Ṛgveda* X.154 barely contains any material to assert the social position of the seer.

Sārparājñī is the author of *Ṛgveda* X.189. She is also a transcendental woman, as tradition has identified her with Kadrū, the wife of Kaśyapa and the mother of the snakes. Her hymn depicts the glorious activities of the Sun in a metaphorical language. The first stanza, however, strikes a note of motherly feeling by saying that the spotted bull has arrived and set before his mother in the east, and further, is advancing towards his father heaven. The commentators, through the ages, have tried much to bring out the metaphorical meaning hidden in this verse. Though they have explained *pṛ́śniḥ gáuḥ* (the spotted bull) and *mātáraṁ puráḥ* (before mother) in various metaphorical ways, the feminine touch revealed in the simile draws attention.

Similarly, the rivers to which some verses of *Ṛgveda* III.33 are attributed are inanimate objects, but their dialogues with Sage Viśvāmitra are strikingly marked with the same feminine mannerism. The similes used in the above verses often compel the reader to suggest that they were actually composed by some women (cf. especially *ṚV* III.33.10).

In the *khila*-hymns of *Ṛgveda* three more transcendental poetesses, or to say, goddesses are found. They are Śrī, Lākṣā and Medhā, in the order of their occurrence in the text.

Śrī is invoked in a *khila*-hymn which comes after *Ṛgveda* V.87. About the goddess invoked in this hymn, Zimmer (1962: 99) suggests that

> . . . this mother of the world was actually supreme in India long before the arrival of the conquerors from the north.

She finds mention as becoming the protecting goddess of a primarily rice-growing agricultural population at *Śatapatha Brāhmaṇa* 11.4.3.1 as also at *Śāṅkhāyana-Gṛhyasūtra* 2.14.10. Śrī gradually developed into Lakṣmī in later Hindu mythology, considered to be the goddess of prosperity. Though traditionally the concerned hymn is attributed to Śrī herself, the clear distinction between the worshipper and the worshipped manifest in the hymn hardly supports this view. Moreover, internal evidence of this prayer to Goddess Śrī suggests that the seer was probably not a woman (see above Chapter 1). Here the seer prays for worldly desires like fame, wealth, heroic sons, obedient servants and above all the power to master all these coveted objects, which normally were men's, and not women's, pleasures at that period.

Lākṣā is a deity of the herbs, whose glory has been eulogized in the *khila*-hymn coming after *Ṛgveda* X.137. Here too, the seer does not seem to be the deity herself as the welfare of the seer is prayed for from the deity. The tradition, however, attributes the hymn to Lākṣā. There is no other clue in this hymn, which helps one to infer the actual social position of the seer.

The Ṛgvedic society was mainly patriarchal, the father being the master of the family. Though the term *dampatī* recognizes the wife as the co-owner of the household,[25] the ultimate power belonged to the husband (cf. Ramgopal 1959: 439). This is why, after the husband's death the wife's right to inherit the deceased husband's property was ignored (cf. Altekar 1939: 250). The Vedic families in general were joint ones and consequently large. In the marriage hymn the bride is asked to take care of her husband's cattle and servants, in addition to being entrusted with the responsibilities of looking after the entire household including her in-laws (cf. *ṚV* X.85.43-47). The new bride is blessed to give birth to ten heroic sons and is requested to give her husband motherly care (cf. *ṚV* X.85.45). The bride looked after her aged parents-in-law (cf. *ṚV* X.95.4) and showed them due respect. The parents received respect from their offspring in the Vedic society even when they were old and unable to work. The unmarried maidens, however, could not spend the old age in equal comfort. It was necessary for the girls to get married, and to give birth to heroic sons who would ensure their old-age security (cf. *ṚV* X.39-40).

The verse of Vasukra-patnī suggests that in some cases the parents-in-law did not live with the family of their son, as the wife of Vasukra, who had arranged for a sacrifice, lamented over her father-in-law's conspicuous absence (cf. *ṚV* X.28.1).

An Aryan family comprised husband, wife, children, old parents, brothers and sisters. After the death of the father, the eldest son would become the head of the family. Some writers of the Gṛhyasūtras have prescribed that the paternal wealth would go entirely to the eldest son, as it was his duty to look after the other members of the family[26] and to kindle the *gṛhya-agni*, i.e. the

---

[25] *ṚV* V.28.3; X.85.26-27, 36.

[26] Cf. *GauDS* 6.1-3; *ĀpDS* 1.4.146-8.

deified domestic-fire.[27] The elder brother was the chief support of his unmarried sisters, as the term *bhrātr̥*, originating from the root *bhr̥-* (to support; maintain), would seem to suggest. It has cognates in most of the Indo-European languages. That is why the concept of brothers supporting their sisters seems a quite ancient one. A girl without brothers was feared to have gone astray and harassed by gallants. Agastya-svasr̥, the seer of *R̥gveda* X.60.6, is known after her famous brother Agastya. It was difficult for the brotherless maidens to find husbands (vide above Chapter 1), as in that case her first-born son would be counted as her father's son, and would have to continue his maternal grandfather's lineage.

However, the families of the Vedic Aryans were sometimes so large that the food had to be cooked in several kitchens. Gobhila-*Gr̥hyasūtra* and *Khādira-Gr̥hyasūtra* prescribe that in such families the daily *baliharaṇa* ritual should be performed from the food that is prepared in the kitchen of the householder.

According to *Kalpasūtras*, the bond of marriage was irrevocable, the husband and the wife being counted as a single unit. Āpastamba says that one should not abandon his wife if she accompanies him in religious duties and gives birth to his sons.[28] A man who forsakes his wife unjustly is subject to penance.[29] Perhaps this sin of the husband is reflected in Br̥haspati forsaking his wife Juhū, which is termed as *brahmakilviṣá* (*R̥V* X.109.1).

As is but expected, parents used to bring up their children with affection. Bhāradvāja and Āpastamba prescribe that the father, on returning home from a journey, should kiss his sons and daughters affectionately.[30] The family being patriarchal in character, a son was naturally preferred to a daughter in the Vedic society. However, when born, the daughter, too, was brought up with care

---

[27] *GauDS* 28.3.

[28] *ĀpDS* I1.5.11.12: *dharmaprajāsampanne dāre nānyam kurvīta*.

[29] *ĀpDS* 1.10.28, 19-20.

[30] *BhārGS* 1.27, 29.3; *ĀpGS* 6.15.12-13.

and affection, though perhaps in a lesser degree in comparison to that enjoyed by the male child. The daughter was given to marriage when she attained puberty. The marriage hymn suggests that girls were given to marriage at a mature age.[31]

The World of Women in the Ṛgvedic Age

A thorough study of the various phases of the life a woman had to go through will raise some crucial questions and reveal some startling facts.

WERE GIRLS CONDEMNED IN THE ṚGVEDIC FAMILY?

To ascertain the place of women in the household, one must start from that of the daughters in the Aryan families. Though less wanted, the girls, once born, did not suffer the same fate of their Arabian counterparts, many of whom were buried alive till the Prophet declared female infanticide a sin and prohibited this savage superstitious practice.[32] In contradistinction, the Aryan daughters received love and care from their parents.

Aitareya Brāhmaṇa 7.13.8 sums up, as it were, the spirit of the bondage between the family and the wife as well as the daughter in a single sentence[33]: the wife is called the friend and the daughter is a subject to misery as she has to leave the parents at the time of wedding. Some modern scholars, like Bhattacharya (1987: 38) would even unnecessarily go to the length of interpreting the expression *kṛpaṇa-* therein as "the cause of misery". In the present context, however, where the wife is called the friend, and the son the hope of the family,[34] such an adverse comment for the daughter is quite unexpected and hence absurd. Moreover, there are several references in *Ṛgveda* where the affection of the parents

[31] *ṚV* X.85.21-22, 37.

[32] Quran, chap. 18.

[33] *AiBr* 7.13.8c: *sakhā ha jāyā kṛpaṇaṁ hi duhitā.*

[34] *AiBr* 7.13.8d: *jyotir hi putraḥ parame vyoman.*

towards their daughters is poetically expressed. A splendid simile has been drawn to show the relation between the female children and their parents in *Ṛgveda* I.185.5ab, where the Heaven and Earth are stated as two sisters lying on their parents' laps.[35] In another passage the seer Viśvāmitra says that if the parents give birth to both son and daughter, one performs the virtuous duties even as the other receives honour.[36] Here, though the daughter is not said to have any sacrificial right, her respectable position in the family is firmly established and is almost irrefutable. *Ṛgveda* I.123.11ab presents yet another simile, through which the affectionate relation between the mother and the daughter is reflected. It describes Uṣas, as a daughter decorated by her mother, to have uncovered her beautiful physique before the world.[37]

According to the Indian etymologists the word *duhitṛ* (daughter) is derived from *dúh-* (to milk). Having cognates almost in all the major Indo-European languages, the word, if accepted to have derived along the line of the native philologists, may suggest that from a very early date the main task of the Indo-European daughters was to milk the family cattle. Her association with milk and milk products is also revealed in *Ṛgveda* II.3.6d.[38] The daughters of the Vedic family wove clothes and stitched garments (*ṚV* II.32.4), fetched water (*ṚV* VIII.91.1) and offered oblations to gods they invoked (*ṚV* VIII.91.2). It is evident that the daughters were given some education in worldly and spiritual matters. Maidens like Ghoṣā and Apālā composed hymns for their gods. Viśvavārā, though it is not clear whether she was married or not, described herself as offering oblation to the Fire (V.28). Mamatā, the mother of Sage Dīrghatamas, has been appreciated for beautifully singing

---

[35] *saṁgácchamāne yuvatī́ sámaṁ te | svásārā jāmī́ pitrór upásthe |*

[36] *ṚV* III.31.2cd: *yádī mātáro janáyanta váhnim | anyáḥ kartā́ sukṛ́tor anyá ṛndhán |*

[37] *susaṁkāśā́ mātṛ́mṛṣṭeva yóṣāvís tanvàṁ kṛṇuṣe dṛśé kám.*

[38] *sudúghe páyasvatī.*

the sacrificial lores (*ṚV* VI.10.2). *Atharvaveda* mentions that a maiden achieves youthful husband through austerity.[39] It suggests that daughters too, like their brothers, went through the stage of studentship. In all probability female teachers were engaged to teach the girls, since in later literature a few female teachers of the Vedas (as the term Kaṭhī f. would seem to imply) and of the Mīmāṁsā philosophy (like Kāśakṛtsnā) are spoken of.[40]

CHASTITY WAS NOT A NECESSITY FOR ṚGVEDIC WOMEN

In *Ṛgveda*, references to the early Aryan society are often found, and these suggest that it was permissive to some extent. Women were not bound with hard and fast rules to preserve their chastity (cf. Thomas 1964: chap. 2). Most of the verses of the female seers are characterized by the naïvety of their expressions regarding sexual matters. In an umpteen number of similes in *Ṛgveda*, words denoting the male lover (*márya-*) and the paramour (*jārá-*) have been frequently used, besides the term *páti-* for the husband.

Mahābhārata 1.113 also records an early age when marriage had little to do with the sexual freedom of women. King Pāṇḍu, prohibited by a curse to consort with his wives, desired to have sons and requested his wife Kuntī to conjugate with a man other than himself for the sake of progeny. In support of his demand Pāṇḍu alluded to the ancient matrimonial customs of the Aryans. Women, he said, in olden days, were neither confined to their houses, nor were they dependent on their husbands, and yet they were not considered sinful since that was the sanctioned custom of that age.

The hymns of female seers reveal the anxiousness of the Ṛgvedic women to procure heroic husbands and sons.[41] The free mixing between men and women is thereby directly or indirectly

---

39 *AV* XI.5.18: *brahmacáryeṇa kanyā̀ yúvānaṁ vindate pátim.*

40 Cf. *Mahābhāṣya* 4.1.14, 3.155.

41 Cf. *ṚV* VIII.91; X.39-40; the *khila*-hymn ascribed to Niṣat and Upaniṣat.

hinted at. The rituals prescribed in the marriage hymn point to a well-established marriage institution. However, frequent references to *jārá-* (paramour) in *R̥gveda* suggest a frequent violation of the marital bond. Adultery was a very common phenomenon in that age, accepted as natural by the seers. Some Vedic rituals, too, reflect that adultery was not unexpected of the womenfolk. In the Varuṇapraghāsa sacrifice, performed jointly by the husband and the wife, the latter had to confess the number of her paramours by dropping an equal number of the sacrificial grass (*kuśa-*).[42]

In the select verses assigned to the poetesses of *R̥gveda*, the women are often heard asking for sexual union unhesitatingly. Queen Romaśā (I.126.7), the wife of King Svanaya Bhāvayavya, is such a woman. As told earlier, the final couple of verses in *R̥gveda* I.126 are a dialogue between the royal couple, resulting according to *Br̥haddevatā* from Indra's jestful question whether the queen was mature enough to be enjoyed by her husband. In reply Romaśā said that she was hairy all over her body and hence fit to be enjoyed like a wife. This legend, however, of *Br̥haddevatā* does not conform to the textual evidence. A close study suggests that the couplet, where the seventh should have preceded the sixth, constitutes indeed an intimate dialogue between two lovers who can hardly be assumed to be husband and wife (see above Chatpers 1 & 2). The seventh stanza thereat reveals the speakers' unfamiliarity with each other, since the woman had to describe her youth to the man in order to attract him.

The above-mentioned conversation shows that the woman in question had little hesitance or shyness in describing her own youth, as her language hardly cared for a coat of sophistication. Similar stylistics is also discernible in the verses of Lopāmudrā, Śaśvatī, Yamī, Ghoṣā, Indrāṇī and Urvaśī.[43] In the first book of *R̥gveda,* Lopāmudrā, the wife of Agastya the famous seer, prays for a union

---

42 *ŚB* 2.5.2.20: *kéna carasi.*

43 Cf. *R̥V* I.179.1-2; VIII.1.34; X.10.39-40, 86, 95, etc.

with her husband saying that since many years she had been toiling day and night, and now, as old age impairs the beauty of her limbs she should be approached by her ascetic husband to beget progeny. The passionate yet solemn speech of Lopāmudrā is evidently characteristic of women of the elite class of the Ṛgvedic society. At *Ṛgveda* VIII.1.34, Patnī Śaśvatī, who according to *Bṛhaddevatā* was the wife of King Āsaṅga, congratulates her husband on restoration of his manhood which had been lost long since. The language used by the queen indicates that the Ṛgvedic women, despite belonging to the elitist society, did hardly care for sophistication in speech.

PROOF OF INCEST IN ṚGVEDIC AGE

Ṛgveda X.10 bears a document of incest between brother and sister in the early Indo-European age. Yama and Yamī were twins, yet Yamī implored her brother in passionate words to make her his consort. Yama refused her strongly saying that the gods would be offended at such an unnatural meeting, as the sinners never escaped from the ever-watchful spies of the gods (X.10.8). Yamī tried to persuade him by saying that they were consorts even in the mother's womb, and it would not be an offence if they unite again (X.10.5). With Yama rejecting her pleas altogether Yamī lost her calm and started speaking contemptuously to him. The story recurs in *Atharvaveda* XVIII.3.13 with an insignificant variation, where Yama is heard saying that he could not stand the mating of brother and sister. Bhattacharji (1970: 93ff.) gives a socio-historic interpretation of the story. "Socially", she observes, "the hymn may indicate the stage when incest was discouraged or looked down upon for fear of inbreeding. In *Avesta* Yima marries his sister Yimak and produces mankind but is eventually killed by Azi Dahâka for this sin." The abrupt ending of the story both in the Veda and *Avesta* suggests that the original story was combined with the later taboo on incest. The myth of incest between the primitive brother and sister is related to cosmogony myths all over the world, finds Bhattacharji, and incest has been committed there for the sake of creation. This myth of Yama and Yamī was so primitive that the Indo-Iranians could not help including it in their collection of sacred hymns. The social values, however, changed by that time and incest between brother and sister was strictly prohibited. In both the Vedas and *Avesta*, the story appears unfinished yet suggestive that the male partner's aversion to incest prevented the sin from taking place. "Besides the Vedas and *Avesta*", asserts Bhattacharji, "Ovid in his *Metamorphoses* (book 9), giving the story of Byblis and Caunus, has to change the original incest motif, for Byblis, madly in love with her brother Caunus, pursued him through various lands, till at last, worn out with sorrow, she was changed into a fountain." Here, to avoid the tabooed mating the poet took the help of metamorphosis.

Incest played an important role in primitive rituals all over the world to enhance the production of the crops. "Promiscuity must have been the normal sexual relation in very old times", observes Bhattacharji, adding that "with time the social taboo was enforced, consanguinity was considered injurious to the racial stock and sexual union was prohibited between certain prescribed relationships. But the old customs were ritually practised at certain junctures for specific purposes."

The colloquy of Yama–Yamī seems to be composed at a time when the taboo on incest was gradually descending upon the society, yet, when people still remembered the primitive ritual. Upadhyay (1941: 117-22) also supports this view. According to him, Yamī, in order to get Yama fulfil her desire, alludes to an earlier common notion of the people with regard to twins, which sanctioned and praised their marriage, but Yama, who represents a new ethical standard of the society, refutes her plea, and warns her in the name of the watching sentinels of Varuṇa (X.10.8). Yama says:

> Subsequent ages will come when sisters will choose him (a partner) who is not a brother. — v. 10

The statement suggests that Yama stood at the threshold of an age of new moral values. Yāska in *Nirukta* 4.20 explains this stanza in this way: "Surely there will come those future ages, when kinsmen will behave like strangers" (as rendered by Sarup), although Griffith explains the *mantra* differently, and perhaps erroneously:

> Sure there will come succeeding times when brothers and sisters will do acts unmeet for kinsfolk.

Apart from *Ṛgveda* X.10, another passage in the same text (VI.55.5) also suggests that incest was not unknown to the Vedic Aryans. It hints upon such an act between Pūṣan and his sister Uṣas,[44] but both being gods of natural personification, an actual incest, in the literal sense of the term, involving these two deities cannot be accepted as having taken place in reality.

There are even references, mythological though, to paternal incest in the Ṛgvedic literature. *Ṛgveda* X.61.5-7 allude to the story of Prajāpati, who committed a similar crime with his daughter and created the gods. *Ṛgveda* VI.55.5, mentioned above, refers also to incest between Pūṣan and his mother. And, although these most probably are cosmogony-metaphors, what should be kept in mind is that the Ṛgvedic seers could not have drawn such metaphors out of nothing, i.e. unless they had a primary notion thereof, and this notion might have descended to them from the primitive Indo-European society.

THE INSTITUTION OF MARRIAGE

The wedding hymn of *Ṛgveda* (X.85) presupposes that marital institution was well established in the age of *Ṛgveda*. The similarity of marriage customs among the Indo-Aryans, the Parsees, the Romans and other Indo-European peoples goes to suggest that marriage was a well-established institution even in the Indo-European period (cf. Ramgopal 1959: 204). The above hymn is a concrete, illuminating document of the well-developed marriage customs of that age. *Atharvaveda* (XIV.1f.) also gives the details of marriage rituals of the Vedic age. In the Brāhmaṇas and the

[44] *svásur yó jārá ucyáte.*

Upaniṣads, married life is highly praised. *Śatapatha Brāhmaṇa* 5.2.1.10 emphatically declares that a man is incomplete until he finds a wife. The Śrautasūtras would not even permit an unmarried man to perform sacrifices.

The age of marriage for women was their post-puberty period. There is not a single reference to child marriage in *R̥gveda*. *R̥gveda* X.85 gives a vivid description of the wedding of a grown-up bride, viz. Sūryā, which is why it is also popularly known as the Sūryā-Sūkta. The bride is wished to give birth to several sons and to reign over her in-laws, and these cannot be expected from a mere child. Moreover, the speech of the bridegroom in verse 37, which informs of the consummation of the married couple taking place immediately once the marriage ceremony is over, strengthens the assumption of an absence of child marriage. In a number of verses the bride is blessed to be the mistress of the household. Expressions like *jāspatyám* (X.85.23), *gr̥hápatnī* (v. 26 l.c.), *gā́rhapatyāya jāgr̥hi* (v. 27) and so on indicate that this bride was a mature woman and not a minor.

The verses of Ghoṣā testify to the fact that she was left unmarried till old age and *R̥gveda* I.117.7 informs of her getting married to a heroic husband with the help of the Aśvins. Therefore, old-age marriage was not altogether uncommon in the R̥gvedic age. The verses of Apālā and Niṣat as well as Upaniṣat are prayers to gods seeking their assistance in finding them good husbands. As the seers were mature enough to compose hymns, the question of child marriage subsides.

To the R̥gvedic people, marriage not only meant the cohabitation of a man with a single woman, but it also enabled them in performing certain duties jointly. The husband and the wife together formed the nucleus of a family, on whom the aged parents, brothers, sisters and children depended. The married couple alone was empowered to perform sacrificial duties. Satisfying the forefathers (*pitr̥s*) with progeny, they welcomed the strangers by offering them food and drink. They helped the study of the Vedas by giving alms to the Vedic students (*brahmacārins*), and offered food to birds and animals, who keep the balance of the ecosystem. The ideal family life in Vedic India has been expressed in the above-mentioned manner, and reflected in the concept of the *pañca mahāyajñas* (the five great sacrifices) in *Śatapatha Brāhmaṇa* 11.5.6.

Marriage was considered to be the fate or ultimate goal of the womenfolk in Ṛgvedic age. Obviously, some women could not get married, but how passionately they longed for a married life and a caring husband can well be gleaned from the hymns of Ghoṣā (especially *ṚV* X.40.11). An unmarried woman did not receive honour in the society.[45] It is generally accepted by Vedic scholars that there were two types of women in the Ṛgvedic society, one who got married and led a family life and was called *sadyodvāhā*, and the other who remained unmarried, involved herself in the study of the Vedas and sometimes even became a seer, i.e. composer of hymns. The latter came to be known as *brahmavādinī* (speaker of Vedas).[46] But, the interesting point to note is that the hymns of these *brahmavādinī*s, as found in *Ṛgveda*, are often prayers to gods, seeking their assistance in procuring them heroic husbands and sons. There are hymns even by married women, such as Romaśā, Lopāmudrā, Śaśvatī, Sūryā, Indrāṇī, Urvaśī, Agastya-svasṛ, Juhū and Paulomī Śacī. The hymn of Āmbhṛṇī Vāc stands alone in the region of the mundane prayers. In this hymn the seer expresses her sublime experience of being one with the universe, and no prayer for the fulfilment of temporal desires is heard from her. Even in the hymn of Viśvavārā, where the Ṛgvedic woman is heard to be giving oblation to the sacrificial fire in accompaniment with *mantra*s pronounced by her alone, the welfare of the household lordship is prayed for.[47] Ergo, the definitions of *sadyodvāhā* and *brahmavādinī* do often overlap.

---

[45] Cf. *ṚV* X.39.3, 86.9.

[46] Cf. *Vīramitrodaya,* 1875, p. 402.

[47] Cf. *ṚV* V.28.3: *sáṁ jāspatyáṁ suyámam ā́ kṛṇuṣva.*

The Indo-Aryan wife was the co-owner of the household along with her husband, as the term *dampatī* would indicate. It has already been discussed that she had complete sway over her husband's relations and belongings (*R̥V* X.85.43f., 46), and performed her household duties as well. The everyday life of an average Aryan depended so much on his wife that the seer Viśvāmitra says in his hymn: "Wife, O Maghovan, is home and dwelling".[48]

The conjugal life of the R̥gvedic Aryans is often reflected in the verses ascribed to women. If Romaśā is accepted as the wife of the man she converses with, their dialogues show how intensely this couple was sexually attached to each other. The same note also underlies the conversations of Lopāmudrā and Agastya. Śaśvatī, the wife of King Āsaṅga, too, talks to her husband with the same frankness, without any inhibition whatsoever.

The unmarried women of the R̥gvedic age longed primarily for enjoying the conjugal love. Apālā, according to *Br̥haddevatā* 6.99-106, was infected with a cutaneous disease, which made it difficult for her to find a suitor. She was delighted when Indra drank *soma*-juice from her mouth. Commentators, on the basis of this incidence, allude a story to Apālā that she made Indra fall in love with her, and by satisfying him accrued three boons from Indra that cured her disease and helped her find a suitable husband.

Ghoṣā, in her prayer to the Aśvins, prays for a husband and there too, the speaker's intense desire for conjugal pleasure is remarkable (cf. *R̥V* X.40.11).

At the time of wedding, the bridegroom would customarily take hold of the bride's hand and would verbally give vent to his passionate desire of mating with the willing wife (*R̥V* X.85.37).

In the Indra–Indrāṇī–Vr̥ṣākapi hymn, Indrāṇī is proud to declare herself to be the most successful wife, as none but her gives her husband the maximum physical pleasure (*R̥V* X.86.6). The boastful claim of Indrāṇī finds support when it is observed in this

---

[48] *R̥V* III.53.4: *jāyéd astaṁ maghavant séd u yónis.*

hymn that Indra, very submissive to his wife, had to bid farewell to his dear friend Vṛṣākapi (*ṚV* X.86.21) whom Indrāṇī deplored. Here, despite Indra's earnest requests, Indrāṇī did not allow Vṛṣākapi to stay with them. This very Indrāṇī is also the probable composer of *Ṛgveda* X.159, where she claims that her husband is fully under her control. In later ages Indrāṇī became a goddess of Eros, and in *Kāmasūtra* of Vātsyāyana one finds a sexual tip being attributed to her (*Kāmasūtra* 6.6.7, 11). In all probability, her expertise in sexual matters made her a gloriously successful wife in an age when the chieftains and the priests were usually polygamous.

In the hymn of Purūravas and Urvaśī, too, a glimpse of the conjugal relation between couples of that age is available. To eat very little at the in-law's house, to look after the parents-in-law and to please the husband in bed as often as he wished were probably the standard qualities expected from a good wife at that time. In spite of Urvaśī performing all these duties, Purūravas failed to keep his promise. It was a contract marriage, and the contract being violated Urvaśī left her husband at once (X.95.11).

Sex was an important aspect of married life, but the female seers of *Ṛgveda* never complained of any sort of sexual harassment, except dubiously at X.95.5 in the view of some commentators.[49] The Ṛgvedic women seemed to have maintained a proper balance between their basic instinctive urges and the household chores (cf. *ṚV* I.179.2). They had no sky-high ambitions but simply desired to lead a normal family life, with a faithful and caring husband and several heroic sons.

The *Mahābhārata* (1.113) story, as narrated by Pāṇḍu, of the legislative of Śvetaketu restraining women from indulging in extra-marital sexual affairs, indicates that sexual chastity of the wife did not matter much in primitive ages. The wives were expected to remain loyal to their husbands only during the course of their period (*ṛtu-*), since conception was supposed to take place only during a

[49] See before Chapter 2, pp. 87-88.

woman's menstruation, said Śvetaketu. At other times she was free to follow the ancient custom. Thomas (1964: 44), in this regard, thinks that "morality among the ancient Aryans originated from the notions of economic responsibilities and property rights in women and children, and had little to do with sex relations as such".

WOMAN IN HER ROLE AS MOTHER

The housewife was considered to be the best and the foremost preceptor of the children. *Vasiṣṭha-Sūtra* 13.48 asserts that woman is a hundred times superior to man in instructing and elevating a child. *Āpastamba-Śrautasūtra* 1.40.48-49 also make it clear that as the mother performs so many duties for her son, it becomes his duty to serve her constantly even if she is fallen.

PLIGHT OF WOMEN IF AND WHEN THEY LOST THEIR HUSBANDS

The widows of the Ṛgvedic age did not suffer the fate of those of later India. There had probably been no *satī* custom as it flourished later among the Hindus. There is a dubious verse in the whole bulk of *Ṛgveda* which has been advanced as proof of the existence of such a custom in the Ṛgvedic India, but a more satisfactory alternative interpretation has also been offered. *Ṛgveda* X.18.7 refers to non-widows coming forward to anoint the corpse of a dead man before it was consigned to flames. According to Altekar (1938: 117), this verse has been wrongly interpreted as hinting at a practice of the widow's ascent to the funeral pyre along with the corpse of her husband. The last word of the fourth stanza is proved to have been fraudulently changed into *agnéḥ* from *ágre*. If the emendation is not accepted, this verse can even in the wildest possible imagination be claimed to have contained any slightest reference to widow burning.[50]

---

[50] Cf. *ṚV* X.18.7; *AV* 12.2.31, 18.3.57; *TA* 6.10.2:

imā́ nā́rīr avidhavā́ḥ supátnīr | ā́ñjanena sarpíṣā sáṁ viśantu |
anaśrávo 'nāmīvā́ḥ surátnā | ā́ rohantu jánayo yónim ágre ||

But a reference to the widow's accompanying her late husband's body on the funeral pyre, which might reasonably be looked upon as a reminiscence of the custom of widow burning in older days, is available in *Atharvaveda* XVIII.2.1. The *mantra* says that it was still customary for a widow to lie by the side of her dead husband's corpse at the pyre during his last rites. She was asked to come down from there and lead a prosperous life enjoying the bliss of having children and wealth.[51] The verse suggests that the widow's immolating herself had been a primitive custom (*dharmaṁ purāṇam*) of the Aryans, but it went out of vogue in the society of the Vedic Aryans. Widow burning might have been a primitive practice among the Indo-Europeans, as traces of it were found in the civilization of the Gaul's, the Goths, the Norwegians, the Celts, the Slavs and the Thracians. Altekar suggests that *satī* was not current among Aryans who had entered India, and no traces of this practice are to be found down to 400 BCE. The Brāhmaṇical, the Sūtraic as also the Buddhist literatures, Kauṭilya and even the authors of Dharmaśāstras like Manu and Yājñavalkya are silent about this custom. *Mahābhārata*, the major portion of which was composed at about 300 BCE, records a few cases of *satī*. Therefore, following Altekar, conclusion can be drawn that *satī* has never been an early Vedic custom (see below Chapter 4). Upadhyay (1941: 98) thinks that in a military clan like the Vedic Aryans, manpower was most welcome to the people. This need is frequently reflected in their prayers to the gods they invoked. In such a society, women were considered as means of increasing population, which is why the Ṛgvedic people could hardly afford the womenfolk to be wasted after their husbands expire. They preferred utilizing the widows for producing children, rather to burning them alive. Due chiefly to this dire economic need the practices of levirate and remarriage of the widows emerged in the then society.

---

[51] *iyáṁ nā́rī patilokáṁ vṛṇānā́* | *nípadyata úpa tvā martya prétam* | *dhármaṁ purāṇáṁ anupāláyantī* | *tásyai prajā́ṁ dráviṇaṁ cehá dhehi* || —*AV* XVIII.3.1

The system of levirate was current in ancient times among several civilizations all over the planet. The Spartans and the Jews practised it (vide Spencer 1896: 1.661). The Old Testament (Deuteronomy 25.5.10) directs the brother-in-law of a widow to take her to wife. *Gautama-Dharmasūtra* 2.10.27, belonging to a later stratum of the Vedic literature, says that *kulāya hi strī dīyate iti upadiśanti* (woman was given to the family (of the husband)). It can be said that women was generally regarded as property that passed into the husband's family at the time of her marriage. When a person died without leaving a male child behind, it was the duty of his brother to marry his widow or to beget children from her (vide Altekar 1938: 143). The Vedic Aryans, too, followed this ancient custom of levirate. It was quite common for the brother of a dead person to marry the widowed sister-in-law in the Vedic society. A number of references in *R̥gveda* would well go to establish this view. In the funeral hymn (*R̥V* X.18.7), it is said that it was the brother of the dead person who lifted the widow of his brother by hand from the funeral pyre of her deceased husband, and led her towards a new life. It may be of some interest to note that according to Yāska, who was even quoted by Sāyaṇa, the word *deváraa-* (brother-in-law) etymologically meant "the second husband" (*dvitīyo varaḥ*).[52] Though phonetically worthless, this may have some sociological implication reflecting the trend of the contemporary society, at least as understood by two native stalwarts, the first of whom was not very far removed from that age and territory.

In early societies, adopted sons were not as welcome as the sons by levirate. In the list of subsidiary sons, the Dharmasūtras place the son by levirate just after the biological or *aurasa* son in the hierarchy. The Vedic Aryans wanted descendants who would have the family blood running in their veins. If someone died before procreating a son from his wife, it was his brother who fulfilled his deceased brother's duty. An adopted son would bring a different blood in the family, while a son by levirate, produced by the sibling

[52] *Nir* 3.15: *devaraḥ kasmād dvitīyo vara ucyate.*

of the dead man, would possess the family blood. *Mahābhārata* in 1.132.63-64 recommends that a maximum of three sons could be raised by *niyoga*, while the writers of the later Smṛtiśāstras restricted the number to one.

By the side of *niyoga*, widow marriage was also prevalent in the Vedic India. The suggestions of such a remarriage are found in the verses of the funeral hymn. For example, the newly-bereaved wife of a man was remarried to her younger brother-in-law at the funeral rite of the dead husband (cf. *ṚV* X.18.7-9). Altekar (1938: 150-51) has thoroughly probed the issue and concludes that "it is a wrong interpretation of the X.18.8 upon which depends the suggestion; the verse seeks to dissuade the widow from burning herself on her husband's funeral pyre by following archaic *satī* custom, which had gone out of vogue". In Altekar's translation:

> O lady, get up, come back to the world of living; you are lying by the side of a dead person. As far as thy wifehood to thy husband, who had seized thy hand (in marriage), is concerned, you have lived it out completely.

The scholars, inclined to accept the verse as a proposal for remarriage, translate the last line thereof as: "thy wifehood to me, who has seized thy hand and who is thy lover, has now commenced". Sāyaṇa, however, supports the second alternative interpretation.

Atharvaveda furnishes a more concrete proof of widow marriage in IX.5.27-28. A ritual is described there to secure the union of the newly couple in the heaven. The remarrying widow is termed as *punarbhū*, and the marriage is accepted as a normal phenomenon as the seer of the hymn wishes its success. Among the hymns selected for the present study, Ghoṣā at *Ṛgveda* X.40.2 is found to blame the Aśvins for not coming to her. "Like a widow taking her brother-in-law to her bed", complains Ghoṣā with suggestive words, "who compels you to stay with him?".

THE SUBJECTS THAT WOMEN LEARNT

The hymns of the female seers establish firmly that women, at least of the elite class, were imparted with good education, almost at par with men. Women, from their childhood, started studying along with their brothers. Jaimini's *Pūrvamīmāṁsā* 6.1 deals with the equal rights of men and women in performing sacrifices. The *Pūrvamīmāṁsā* (6.1.4-24) presents a debate on the equal rights of men and women of three upper castes to perform sacrifices. Refuting the Pūrvapakṣa, comprising Aitiśāyana and his followers, Jaimini establishes his own view at 6.1.24; i.e. women can only perform those rites that are distinctly laid down for her, as also the "invoking of blessings" and "celibacy"; since she is not equal (to the husband).[53] In this context Śabarasvāmin in his commentary makes it clear that women cannot perform sacrifices equal to men as this performance requires the knowledge of the Vedas which women lack. It seems that Śabara tries to establish that women were not taught the Vedas and therefore could not perform sacrifices on their own.[54] It has already been pointed out that through observing *brahmacarya* (austere studentship), Vedic maidens acquired suitable husbands (*AV* XII.3.18). It is not exactly mentioned in *Ṛgveda* what type of education women received, but from a close scrutiny of the hymns composed by the female seers it can be assumed that they were taught in mythology, liturgy, spiritual matters, folklore, the then current sorceries, fine arts and the arts of warfare.

The hymns of Lopāmudrā, Yamī and Ghoṣā testify to the seers knowledge of mythology, as the seers narrate the happenings of the past, and the heroic deeds of the gods they invoked in the corpus of their hymns. In the hymns composed by Viśvavārā and Apālā, as also in the allusion to Mamatā at *Ṛgveda* VI.10,

---

53 *tasyā yāvad uktam āśīr brahmacaryam atulyatvāt.*
— *Pūrvamīmāṁsā-Sūtra* 6.1.24

54 *atulyā hi strī-puṁsāḥ, yajamānaḥ pumān vidvāṁś ca, patnī strī cāvidyā ca.* —*Śabarasvāmin* on *PMS* 6.1.24

the seers' acquaintance with liturgy is noticed. The hymn of Vāc Āmbhṛṇī is a proof of the high spiritual background of the seer. The concluding triplet of the Apālā-hymn can be looked upon as folklore itself. The final verse deserves a special mention in that it states that Indra drew forth Apālā thrice through the different parts of a chariot, and made her bright-skinned. In addition to this allusion *Śāṭyāyana Brāhmaṇa* records that the skins, cast off thrice by Apālā, became a hedgehog, an alligator and a chameleon, and in that order. This story, no doubt one of the ancient folk tales of the Indo-Europeans, appears in various forms in the Purāṇas and epics of the Indo-Aryans and the Persians, as also in the folk tales of the Slavic countries. The couple of verses ascribed to Romaśā and her husband, too, are considered by Griffith to be a fragment of a now lost popular song, i.e. folklore.

The hymn of Indrāṇī is a fair specimen of the then current sorcery, by which the speaker of the hymn tries to overpower her rival co-wife. Because of the imprecatory nature of this hymn, it has been judiciously declared as an Atharvavedic hymn (*ātharvaṇa*) by the commentators of *Ṛgveda*.

From various references in *Ṛgveda*, it is evident that women danced and sang well in that age. The mention of Uṣas as a dancing damsel (I.92.4) suggests that there were professional dancing women in the society, who kept their breasts unveiled. There are also many references to women singing solo as also in chorus (cf. *ṚV* IX.6.8, 56.3).

WOMEN AT WAR

Viśpalā and Mudgalānī are two famous Ṛgvedic women remembered for their active and successful participation in warfare. Both fought against the enemies of their husbands, and helped them to win the battle (*ṚV* I.116.15 and X.102.2). Their achievement furnishes ample proof that women, at least of the royal class, had good knowledge in the science of warfare. It is revealed from *Ṛgveda* that the Aryan men did not hesitate to hurt the women physically when they challenged them at war, and did them any harm. *Ṛgveda* V.30.9 says that the aboriginal *dāsa*s had a number of women in their army:

> *stríyo hí dāsá ā́yudhāni cakré* ।
> *kíṁ mā karann abalā́ asya sénāḥ* ॥

> The *dāsa*s have taken women for their weapons, what injuries can his feeble army do to me?

Even Indra is heard to have thrown his bolt upon the mother of Vṛtra and killed her as she was engaged in fighting for her son.[55] Again in *Ṛgveda* V.61.7, Sarasvatī, the goddess of speech, has been described as *vṛtraghnī* (slayer of Vṛtra) and is said to have taken part with Indra in his fight against this demon. In the present study, in *Devī-Sūkta* Goddess Āmbhṛṇī Vāc is said to have stretched the bow for Rudra in order to assist him in killing the enemy of *Brahman* or the supreme greatness. In *Taittirīya Brāhmaṇa* an allusion is made to Indrāṇī as the goddess of army.[56] These references, though explained differently by the mystic interpreters of the Vedas, suggest that the tradition of Aryan women of the royal class, taking part in battle along with their husbands, is reflected in the later Aryan society. In *Rāmāyaṇa,* Kaikeyī is said to have accompanied her husband in a battle against the enemies of Indra. In *Mahābhārata*, however, there is no reference to women directly taking part in the historic Kuru–Pāñcāla war.

Weltanschauung of the Female Seers

From an in-depth study of the hymns attributed to the female seers, one may accumulate some notions about their world-view, and what life exactly meant for them. It is evident from the literature of *Ṛgveda* that by no means they had been socially handicapped as the women of India became in the middle age. The Ṛgvedic women

---

[55] *nīcā́vayā abhavad vṛtráputréndro* । *asyā áva vádhar jabhāra* ।
úttarā sū́r ádharaḥ putrá āsīd । *dā́nuḥ śaye sahávatsā ná dhenúḥ* ॥
— *ṚV* I.32.9

[56] Cf. Vishnoi 1987: 9.

could move about freely, and there was no prominent restriction on the free mixing of both sexes. Women were not left aside because of their mere womanhood, because such an attitude towards women was found to have flourished only in the later Indian society. Some critics, depending upon a solitary evidence from *Ṛgveda*, claim that seclusion of women was prevalent in the Ṛgvedic India. *Ṛgveda* I.167.3c refers to the seclusion of one's wife in a simile, but this may only be a stray comment, as in nowhere else in *Ṛgveda* a similar suggestion occurs. Against this view, poignantly stand the references made in the marriage hymn, where the bride has been blessed to look after the household of her husband and to reign over her in-laws. If she be secluded then how would it have been possible for her to look after the cattle and the servants of the family?[57]

Although women in the Ṛgvedic age were free enough to participate in *vidátha*'s,[58] and to go to merry festivities like *samana*'s, their daily life surely was very much different from that of men. The household works were the duties of the womenfolk. Since they were not considered much useful in warfare their main task was to take care of their husbands, children and dependents. Though women of *Ṛgveda* were imparted with the right to participate in sacrificial rites, nowhere in the whole corpus of *Ṛgveda* is there a reference to a woman priest. Viśvavārā is heard of giving oblation to the fire chanting the *mantra*s herself, and Mamatā, mother of the seer Dīrghatamas, was also famous for her beautiful chants. But these isolated references would not suffice to make a case for any general trend of the society.

Women in the Ṛgvedic society in general desired a dependable yet heroic husband and a number of male children, as is the

---

[57] Cf. *ṚV* I.167.3; X.85.26, 27; *AV* VIII.1.6, XIV.1.21; vide Sharma 1959: 64-66ff.

[58] *mimyákṣa yéṣu súdhitā ghṛtā́cī | híraṇyanirṇig úparā ná ṛṣṭíḥ |*
gúhā cáranti mánuṣo ná yóṣa | sabhā́vatī vidathyèva sáṁ vā́k ||
— *ṚV* I.167.3

universal desire of women. Physical pleasure, too, mattered much for them as the verses of the female seers are marked for their ardent longing for sexual pleasure in naïve and unsophisticated language. Their utterances are sometimes so bold and provoking that the later index-makers of *R̥gveda* had no other option but to accept the conversing pairs as husbands and wives. For instances, the speakers of *R̥gveda* I.126.7 or of VIII.1.34 are accepted as the wives of the respective persons whom these verses are addressed to. Though no concrete evidence of their being husbands and wives is available in the texts themselves.

Apart from the above-mentioned basic demands of womenfolk, their wishes to overpower their co-wives are heard in the hymns of Indrāṇī and Paulomī Śacī. In the *khila*-hymn attributed to Śrī, the seer expresses her desire for wealth and fame as well as for sons, which is unique in comparison to the common desires of womenfolk.

The root of the fundamental expectations of the R̥gvedic women or to say of the women of the world in general to get married, and to have a household of their own with a strong yet a loyal husband and a number of offspring, lies perhaps in a feeling of insecurity which they experienced since a very primitive age. Nature has made the female species physically weaker than their male counterparts. It being difficult for her to struggle alone for existence she needed a strong companion to protect herself. Moreover the sexual urge also made man and woman mutually dependent. These primitive necessities gradually gave birth to the institution of marriage, and the origin of individual property, too, played an important part in it. However, with the development of civilization, marriage became indispensable for women, as they felt themselves unprotected and looked down upon by their kinsfolk if they remained single. The lamentation of such an unmarried woman is heard in the hymns of Ghoṣā. The woman needed a home and a husband not to fulfil her present requirements only, but for her future security at an old age as well.

Apart from the desires of mundane life, another note, though very faint, is also heard ringing in the hymns of some of the female seers. The intellectual women of *Ṛgveda*, perhaps, knew a life above the mere temporal necessities. In the colloquy of Purūravas and Urvaśī, Purūravas, crying bitterly at the separation from his wife, begs her to come back to him, but Urvaśī refuses to return to the conjugal life as she flies over the mundane world like a swan. According to Jamison and Brereton (2014: III.1548f) an extraordinary feature of *Ṛgveda* X.95 is that it is uncompromising in its depiction of a resolute and hard-hearted female, unmoved by the abject pleas and emotional blackmail of her former lover who is still in love with her, anxious to return to her carefree life with her fellow *apsaras*es, and happy to abandon her child in order to get free. These modern interpreters go further by commenting that no subsequent version could tolerate the radical portrait of the emotionally detached Urvaśī of *Ṛgveda* where the separation of the former lovers took place in the female's decision.

Arguing along the lines of Aurobindo, Purani (1963: 157-78) accepts Urvaśī to be the light of the supreme consciousness, whom the mortal experiences only once by chance, but never succeeds to retrieve even with many a cries. For this reason he is called the Púrū-ravas (*púru* = many, *ravás* = cry). In the text concerned, Urvaśī consoles Purūravas by advising him not to have faith in a lasting friendship with women, who are cruel hearted by nature. This cynic attitude does not befit a mere courtesan, as Urvaśī is presented to be in later literature, but it suits well a person who has detached herself from the temporary pleasures of conjugal life. This spiritual bend of mind, of a few women at least, is best reflected in the hymn of Āmbhṛṇī Vāc. The seer, who experiences herself as free as the eternally blowing wind, hardly cares for a life partner. On the contrary, she claims that whomsoever she desires, she herself makes him the priest, him alone the mighty and him the seer.

Summing Up

On the whole it transpires that Ṛgvedic women lived a life with less social taboos than their counterparts of the medieval age of India. They were brought up with care and given education. Most of them selected a husband at their own choice and after marriage usually looked after the households of their husbands. Sometimes they worked to support the family, but normally it was the husbands' duty to support their wives. The same tradition survives in the middle-class Indian families even this day. One can without reservations identify Ṛgvedic women, who were not hidden under "purdah" and had their head held high in self-esteem, with the educated middle-class women of modern India. Though there were no restrictions in uninhibited interactions between both the sexes in a permissive society, adultery was nevertheless considered a sin in the Ṛgvedic age. In spite of the frequent mention of extra marital lovers (*jārá-*) and illegitimate children, the society on the whole condemned adulterous people. As a result, an illicit lover in *Ṛgveda* had to seek hidings in darkness, and a mother was compelled to forsake her illegitimate child. So, it can be concluded that the Ṛgvedic society had its value against free sex, though it was a common affair as it is still now in the society. The difference which lies between the Ṛgvedic women and the women of modern India consists in the fact that the former often had to suffer because of co-wives, a suffering which was a curse of a polygamous society. Average people were usually monogamous as can be gleaned from the verses of *Ṛgveda*, but the elite class consisting of the priests and the royal families was generally polygamous. In the Ṛgvedic society elite class women were mostly educated, and it surely was intolerable for those sensitive women to share with other women their husbands' loyalty.

4

Mythological Aspects of the Select Texts

A TREATMENT of the mythological aspects of the select texts requires a preliminary discussion of the general trends in present-day mythological studies.

Myth and Mythology and the Ṛgvedic Context

The word *myth* has been defined in the Micropaedia of the *New Encyclopaedia Britannica* as "a story, usually of unknown origin and at least partially traditional, that ostensibly relates actual events to explain some practice, belief, institution, or natural phenomenon, and that is especially associated with religious rites and beliefs", and *mythology* "denotes both the study of myth and the total corpus of myths in a particular culture or religious tradition". Thus, the study of myths of a particular people or community can provide models for their behaviour, reasoning or institutions. Connections between myths and rituals are frequently seen to exist in most of the communities, but which of the two came first is far from certain. Although there are probably no rituals without accompanying myths, there may exist myths without apparent complementary rituals.

"The importance of studying myth to provide a key to human society is a matter of historical record", says the Macropaedia of the above-mentioned encyclopaedia. The statement more than justifies the necessity of studying the mythological aspects of the literature ascribed to the female seers of *Ṛgveda*, and the myths about them. The term *mythology* denotes both the study of myth, and the body of myths belonging to a particular religious tradition. One of the very ancient literatures of this planet, *Ṛgveda* is considered to be an important storehouse of myths, the study of which has been undertaken by serious scholars since time immemorial. Though the modern approach to mythological studies started with the Romantic movement of the early nineteenth century, various interpretations of myths were offered even earlier. The myths found in *Ṛgveda* have also been studied in the same way.

Trends in Indian Mythological Researches

Two trends of research in the last two centuries had influenced the exploration of Indian mythology: the social anthropological school of E.B. Tylor, Herbert Spencer, Levy Bruhl, Andrew Lang and E. Durkheim, and the Indologists' school of Max Müller, Johann Jakob Meyer and Abel Bergaigne. The first group carried on researches on primitive, tribal people and arrived at totemistic, animistic, manistic, fetishistic, solar, lunar or astral theories of the origin of myths. The second group did their research mainly on the basis of linguistic evidences. In more recent times two trends are again observed in the treatment of Indian mythology, viz. one represented by Sigmund Freud, C.G. Jung, W. Schmidt, J.G. Frazer, Jane Harrison and others, and the other by scholars like Georges Dumézil, Louis Renou, Jan Gonda, Heinrich Zimmer and Ananda Kentish Coomaraswamy. The former group collected their material from primitive and classical cultures, while the second group, primarily consisted of Indologists, depended on the researches of the social anthropologists.

Jung's theory of archetypes was based on his researches mainly following Freud. It says that myths are a projection of the archetypes of human mind, which are buried deep in the collective unconscious. This theory, however, had its difficulty in ignoring the fact that mythological thinking existed side by side with rational thinking. It also underestimates the importance of ritual. Frazer's work showed that primitive beliefs, which gave rise to magic and religion, were based on contiguity and similarity. The ritualistic school of J. Harrison, G. Murray and S.H. Hooke was influenced by Frazer's theory, and made a reassessment of the interrelation of ritual and myth. As a result, it interpreted myth with reference to their relation with corresponding rituals.

As for Indian mythology, a very few scholars of social anthropology brought about their views because of the unavailability of required archaeological evidences. Furthermore, the cultural distance of India with the primitive societies of the world occupied the main array of their research. Müller's philological school of interpretation predominated the study of Indian myths until modern Indologists like Dumézil, Gonda and Renou presented their views. Zimmer and Coomaraswamy were mainly philosophical and idealistic in their approach to myths, and sought a symbolical correlative of myths on metaphysical plane. Mircea Eliade traced common patterns in different mythological systems, and probed into the cultural roots of these patterns. These, together with the inner structural organization, can explain the nature of change, growth and development of the contours and dimension of myths. Eliade's work assumes that myths are projections of vital experiences of a people, or in other words, myths are the only valid medium for externalizing these experiences.

Gods vis-à-vis Mortals

The fundamental attitude of the Ṛgvedic mythopoeic mind is to look upon the gods as mortal-friendly.[1] They are not very far from men, the progenitor of both gods and men being Kaśyapa. Gods would help the mortals who would call them in need. Interestingly enough, the gods shared faults and frailties with their mortal counterparts. Many hymns would suggest that gods were also attributed with human sentiments like anger, jealousy, malice or boastfulness.

The Brāhmaṇas, considered to be a part of the Vedas itself, narrate many stories regarding the origins of various gods and rituals. *Nirukta*, an ancient Indian study of Vedic philology, while

[1] Cf. Choudhuri, 1983.

treating the etymologies of the names of various Vedic gods, refers to the myths about them as well. *Bṛhaddevatā*, a metrical account of the Ṛgvedic gods, is a treasury of myths about gods and seers. The interpreters of *Ṛgveda* down the ages have referred to many myths available at their times. A systematic and scientific approach to understand the Vedic mythology, in order to provide a key to understand the Ṛgvedic society, was started by Indologists of the nineteenth century.

Mythification and Ritual

The history of the interpretation of the Veda demonstrates beyond doubt that the Vedic mythical poetry has been understood at various levels of meaning. Attempts to derive and formulate a precise meaning from the multi-dimensional seeric speech have come down to this day in the form of the vast post-Saṁhitā literature, consisting not only of ritualistic, philosophical, astronomical, grammatical and linguistic texts, but also of the para-mythic historical and legendary texts where the Vedic mythical patterns are recreated. These patterns are to be understood from the various poetic symbols used by the seers. There, too, a mythical poetic symbol is different from a mere rhetorical poetic symbol. The latter provides meanings which are specific and limited in their scope, while the former implies meanings much wider. Yāska, the author of *Nirukta*, says that a poet of vision has love for mythification (*Nir* 10.10.2). In fact, it is through the mythical symbol and structure alone, that a multilevel archetypal meaning is conceived, expressed and conveyed.

As stated above, myth and ritual are very intimately related subjects. The ritual often presents in action an image that is moulded through words in a myth. Ritual and myth are both symbolic, and represent a mode of cognition as also a way of life or a scheme of thought. But in course of time, rituals get fixed while myths may continue to develop further and associate more things than they did previously.

Vedic Mythology

Western scholars like Alfred Hillebrandt, Abel Bergaigne and Arthur Anthony Macdonell treated Vedic mythology as a product of an age and a country, of social and climatic conditions far removed and widely differing from their own. Macdonell observes:

> We have, moreover, here to deal not with direct statements of fact, but with the imaginative creations of poets whose mental attitude towards nature was vastly different from that of the men of today. — 1898: 5

The early stage of thought embedded in this literature is complex enough to deal with, he felt. The character of the poetry in which it is encoded enhanced even further the difficulties experienced by Macdonell.

According to most of the Western scholars, personification of nature in the imagination of several gods was the starting point of the Vedic myths. From this simple stage the secondary stage emerged as soon as a person took the place of a natural force in the imagination. The poetic fancy began to create more things that were not associated with the original creation. For example, Indra, the rain-god as held by the Western scholars, who with his bolt strikes Vṛtra, the cloud that covers the sky, is frequently mentioned in *Ṛgveda*. But, the isolated statement of a poet (*ṚV* I.32.9) that he also struck Vṛtra's mother with his bolt is a later poetic fancy, and is a secondary myth. Another example of secondary myth is the epithet "Vṛtra-slaying" which is appropriately meant for Indra but several times used to denote Soma as well in *Ṛgveda* VI.17.11, as the draught of *soma* juice invigorates Indra in his slaying of Vṛtra, the transfer of attribute being cognizable in this secondary stage of myth-making.

Through mythology the gods and heroes of the Vedic Indians are depicted with their characters and origins, as also with their actions and surroundings. These myths represent the chain of thoughts, the mental conditions and reasoning of the Vedic people. Vedic mythology occupies a very important position in the study of the history of religion as well. Western scholars like Macdonell hold that its oldest source projects an earlier stage in the evolution of beliefs based on the personification and worship of natural phenomena, in comparison to that supplied by any other early literary monuments of the world. The foundation of Vedic mythology comprises the belief, surviving from a remote antiquity, that all the objects and phenomena of nature with which man is surrounded are animate and divine. Everything that impressed the soul with awe and wonder, or was regarded as capable of exercising a good or evil influence on man, might in the Vedic age still become a direct object not only of adoration but of prayer. This lower form of worship, according to Macdonell (1898: 2), however, occupies but a small space in Vedic religion. The true gods of the Veda are glorified human beings, inspired with human motives, emotions and passions, born like men, but immortal. The personified natural phenomena in Vedic mythology are gods like Dyaus (Heaven), Pṛthivī (Earth), Sūrya (Sun), Uṣas (Dawn), whose names represent the double character of natural phenomena and of the persons presiding over them. If the names of the deities are different from that of the physical substrates they represent, they tend to dissociate from the latter, the anthropomorphism being then more developed. Thus the Maruts (Storm-gods) are farther removed from their origin than Vāyu (Wind), though the Vedic poets are still conscious of their connections. The Vedic deities have very few distinguishing features, while many attributes and powers are shared by all alike. The reason behind might be the mutual inclusiveness of the departments of nature they represent. Thus the function of a thunder-god, of the fire-god in his lightning form, and of the storm-god might easily be described in similar language, their main function for the Vedic poets being the discharge of rain.

The characters of some Vedic gods are made up of only a few essential traits combined with a number of other features common to all the gods, such as brilliance, power, beneficence and wisdom.

Thus the section of gods of abstract ideas is created. And among the abstract gods of *Ṛgveda* two classes can be recognized; one class consists of the direct personifications of abstract notions such as desire (*kāma*), intelligence (*medhā*) or faith (*śraddhā*). The other class comprises deities whose names primarily either denote an agent, in the form of a noun derived from a root with the suffix -*tṛ*, such as Dhātṛ (Creator), or designate some attributes, such as Prajāpati (Lord of creatures). The first group is comparatively rare than the second one of abstract gods. The second category does not represent direct abstractions but appears to be derived from an epithet, applied to one or more deities and illustrating a particular aspect of activity or character. In course of time, these epithets got detached from its previous position and finally attained an independent entity. The gods further changed their characters with the passing of time mainly through the impact of non-Vedic population, the result of this cultural and ethnic intermixture being first noticed in the 10th Maṇḍala of *Ṛgveda*, and the process reaches a culmination in the Brāhmaṇas.

A major distinction between the religions of the two periods, i.e. the early Vedic and the later Vedic to Brāhmanical, is that the worship of male gods predominates in the early one, while in the latter the goddesses, too, become powerful. Vedic society being basically patriarchal, the gods dominated the Vedic pantheon more than the goddesses. The goddesses of the *Ṛgveda* are comparatively of minor importance. For example, Uṣas is a minor goddess, and Aditi is much better known because of her sons, and Pṛthivī because of her consort. According to sociologists, in the pre-Vedic Indian society, goddesses were equally and sometimes even more powerful and plentiful in comparison with the gods, as the pre-Vedic excavations show. With the intermingling of the Vedic and non-Vedic people the pantheon of the latter suffered a defeat and went underground. But, with time the pre-Vedic gods gradually regained their prestige, which is why in the Brāhmaṇas a number of mother goddesses pop up. Nirṛti, Śacī, Mīḍhuṣī, Yamī, Ambikā,

Rudrāṇī, Śrī, Lakṣmī, Sarasvatī or Vāc re-emerge as mother goddesses, some of whom were incorporated in the group of 7 or 8 or 9 mother goddesses in the classical Hindu iconography. The goddesses of *Ṛgveda* are mainly found in the 10th Maṇḍala, which is of a later origin.

Mythological Tracks in the Literature of the Ṛgvedic Female Seers

As discussed earlier in the study there are in all thirty-one names of female seers in *Ṛgveda*. But, only seventeen of them can be considered as women of flesh and blood, on whose work a socio-cultural study can be done (see Chapter 3, pp. 114-15). Nevertheless, all the above-listed female seers of whom mythological data are available in the Vedic and subsequent literatures, and the compositions ascribed to them will come under the purview of the mythological study in the present chapter.

ROMAŚĀ

Romaśā is the first name we come across in our select texts. *Bṛhaddevatā* says that she is the wife of King Svanaya Bhāvayavya, and the daughter of Aṅgiras. The dialogue between the husband and wife is contained in the last couplet of *Ṛgveda* I.126. *Bṛhaddevatā* also narrates a different story than the usual love song of the couple. It says that once Indra came to the couple and asked the queen in friendly jest: "Have you hair or have you not, O queen?"[2] In reply the queen addressed him in a childlike manner: "Hug me tight, mighty one". In fact, neither is there any mention of the queen's personal name in the text concerned, nor does *Bṛhaddevatā* give it, the adjective *romaśā́-* (hairy) serving the purpose throughout the Vedic mythology.[3] Griffith has ventured a rational explanation of this couplet in attributing the sixth stanza to Svanaya, and the seventh to his wife Romaśā. He further suggests that these two verses have

---

[2] *romāṇi te santi na santi rājñi* — *BṛhD* 4.2

[3] Cf. Oldenberg 1912: 1.128.

no obvious connection with the foregoing *mantras*, moreover being composed in a separate metre. They look like the fragment of a liberal shepherd's popular love song. The seventh stanza should, it seems, precede the sixth (see before Chapters 1, p. 2 and 3, p. 127).

According to Ludwig the word *yā́durī* in the sixth verse, which is explained by the traditional commentators as an approaching woman[4] and by the philologists as *semen genitale*; *effundens*[5] (Grassmann 1873: s.v.), may actually be the name of a slave girl. Lassen (1836: 2.150) says that the country of Gandhāra, in the statement *gandhā́rīṇām ivāvikā́* (as a ewe of Gandhāras), was situated to the west of the Indus and to the south of the Kophen or Kabul (Vedic Kubhā) River. King Darius in a rock inscription mentions the Ga(n)dāna in association with the Parthians and other races. The name of the country is preserved in that of the modern Kandahar.

The later indigenous researchers of *Ṛgveda*, following the different schools of interpretations, give various explanations of this love song. The mystic school of Aurobindo explains the expression *gandhā́rīṇām* as "of those that hold the light" (vide Purani 1963: 152). Another Indian school translates this stanza attributed to seer Romaśā (vide before, Chapter 1, p. 2).[6] These later explanations, however, may accelerate the rise of yet another phase of myth making, along the line of the observation made beforehand, in view of the continuous process of human mind and civilization.

LOPĀMUDRĀ

The next seer to be taken up is Lopāmudrā, the wife of Agastya the sage. *Bṛhaddevatā* relates this story to the context of the conversation attributed to Lopāmudrā and Agastya. Agastya began, from a desire of secret union, to talk to his wife, the illustrious Lopāmudrā, when

4 *abhikramaṇavatī strī* — Veṅkaṭamādhava.

5 *Flussigheit, ergiessend beim Coitus*, Grassmann 1873, s.v.

6 Sarasvati and Vidyalankar 1977: 3.565.

she had bathed after her courses.[7] Lopāmudrā answered by speaking out her mind in the two stanzas beginning with *pūrvī́r ahám,* etc. (*R̥V* I.179.1-2). Then Agastya, desirous of enjoyment, satisfied her with the two following stanzas of *R̥gveda*, viz. I.179.3-4. The story is further stretched in the hymn itself (*Br̥hD* 4.58f) says that a disciple of the seer, coming to know through sheer austerity the intention of this desiring couple, thought he had committed a sin (*enas*) in listening, sang forth the last two stanzas of the hymn, viz. the fifth and the sixth verses. And then the preceptor and his wife lauding and embracing him kissed him on the head, and smiling, both of them said to him: "You are sinless, son".[8]

Bergaigne (1969: 2.394) is of opinion that the hymn has a mystical meaning. Agastya being identifiable with the celestial Soma, whom Lopāmudrā, representing fervent prayer, succeeds after long labour in drawing down from his secret dwelling place.

Mahābhārata (Vana-Parvan 80.14-24; 81; 83.19-24 and also see Altekar 1938: 6 fn. 4 and Verma 1976) tells the story of Lopāmudrā and Agastya in a different way. It says, Lopāmudrā was the daughter of king of Vidarbha and she was also called Kauṣītaki and Varapradā, whom Agastya solicited as his wife from her father. It further says that Agastya himself created Lopāmudrā, whom he gave to the king of Vidarbha, hence the king was but the foster-father of Lopāmudrā. Once Agastya found his forefathers hanging into a deep abyss. When asked about the reason of their dreadful plight the forefathers said to Agastya that as he had no progeny their family line would soon be destroyed and they would definitely fall into the abyss. Then Agastya created a beautiful girl and kept her with the king of Vidarbha to look after. When the girl grew up Agastya came to solicit her hand from her foster-father, the royal couple very unwillingly gave away their beautiful daughter to the aged sage. Lopāmudrā practised penance with her husband for

---

[7] *Br̥hD* 4.57.

[8] *smitv ainam āhatuś cobhāv anāga asi putraka* — *Br̥hD* 4.60

many years and served him day and night. When Agastya wanted progeny to be born from her she said that without the luxury she was used to in her maidenhood, she would not be able to fulfil the sage's desire, as Eros never finds her way in the clothes of a monk. Agastya went out for begging, and after killing the demon Vātāpi he brought a good fortune for his wife. Lopāmudrā was pleased with the riches and the couple uniting together gave birth to a learned son.

VIPĀŚ AND ŚUTUDRĪ

The next seers are the two rivers in order of appearance in the lists of *Bṛhaddevatā* and *Ārṣānukramaṇī*. Though Vipāś and Śutudrī mentioned at *Ṛgveda* III.33 are excluded from our own list of female seers, the mythical background of their conversation with Sage Viśvāmitra may still be seen at a glance. *Bṛhaddevatā* 4.105-09 deal with the hymn attributed to the rivers and Viśvāmitra. Verse 106 thereat says that the seer accompanying King Sudās as his domestic priest for the sake of sacrifice reached the confluence of the Vipāś and the Śutudrī, and addressed them with "be propitious", etc. It seems that being unable to cross these turbulent rivers, he praised them for their benevolence, and pleased with his lauds, the rivers made themselves calm to enable the seer and his companions travel across.

ADITI

The next female seer according to the lists of *Bṛhaddevatā* and *Ārṣānukramaṇī* is Aditi, the mother of Indra. *Ṛgveda* IV.18 is attributed to Indra, Aditi and the seer Vāmadeva. *Sarvānukramaṇī-Bhāṣya* 4.18 relates a story to this hymn, which Sāyaṇa quotes in his commentary thereon. The great seer Vāmadeva was conscious even in his mother's womb and decided not to be born through the natural passage but through the side of his mother. Aware of his fatal intention, his mother invoked Indra's mother Aditi, who came with her son to the expecting mother. This was when the three, i.e. Aditi, Indra and Vāmadeva, had this conversation.

Bṛhaddevatā 4.130-32, however, offer a different interpretation of this hymn. It says that her, i.e. Aditi's unborn child who refused to be born in the straightforward way was her son Indra, and Aditi, anxious of her own welfare, admonished. Once born, Indra immediately challenged Vāmadeva to fight. The story further goes on to narrate that after Indra had done this violence to him, Vāmadeva engaged him for ten days and nights and vanquished him with might.

The hymn itself is a storehouse of many myths. According to traditional exegesis, the seer from his mother's womb stroke up a conversation with the divine mother and son duo, viz. Aditi and Indra. He said he would not follow the same birth route as all the other gods and mortals had followed so far. In support of his own uniqueness in doing something novel, he put forward Indra's deeds which went against convention, and his account of Indra's deeds exhibits a number of mythological stories which may be summarized as below. Though uninvited there, Indra drank up all the expensive soma extracts which Tvaṣṭṛ had kept for his own sacrifice. This myth has also a parallel at *Taittirīya Saṁhitā* 2.4.12.1. The seer Vāmadeva further describes Indra's misdeeds by elaborating that his mother bore him in her womb for many months and years: Indra thus caused pain to his mother over such a long gestation period. Aditi, unable to listen to Indra's infamy as accounted by Vāmadeva any more, started herself to describe his glorious deeds (*ṚV* IV.18.5cd). She said that Indra as soon as born became the greatest among the born and yet-to-be-born. There was, moreover, really none who could match Indra in valour and glory. As an answer to a supposed question where Indra found his might from, she tried to reason out by saying that, since his mother had known him as sinful as infamy at the time of his birth, she encompassed him with all the powers by means of which Indra, once born, overwhelmed the Heaven and Earth.[9] The greatness of Indra can be heard declared even in the

[9] *áthódasthāt svayám átkam vásāna ā́ ródasī apṛṇāj jā́yamānaḥ*
— *ṚV* IV.18.5cd

song sung by the rivers: the murmur of the flowing rivers lauds that who else than Indra could break upon the cover of the clouds (and let the streams flow)? Had the waters not washed of Indra's sins (of killing Vṛtra, a brāhmaṇa by caste)? How would it have been possible that the sacred "nivid's" (words used in the Marutvatīya Śāstra describing Indra's glory) are uttered for him? My son with this great bolt killed Vṛtra and released the streams (*ṚV* IV.18.6-7). In reply to Aditi's speech, seer Vāmadeva also glorifies Indra. He asserts that by his sheer might Indra performed numerous wonderful acts, like no sooner killing Kuṣavā (a demon woman, according to Sāyaṇa) than he was born, and decapitating Vyaṁsa (also a demon, says Sāyaṇa) with his bolt when the latter hit him at the jaw. As to how Indra could be as strong and invulnerable as to annihilate all his enemies, the seer points only to his mother's good wishes that he be so. Now Aditi concludes her praise for Indra by saying that because of his might all the other gods parry him. At this Indra asks his friend Viṣṇu to become a Vṛtra-slayer, too. The seer again strikes up another glory of Indra by declaring that none else than Indra among the gods could kill his own father by holding his feet whereby his mother was widowed, that none but he could slay the foe, either asleep or awake, and that no god other than him was more benevolent to people.

This hymn comes to an end with a stanza telling another myth about Vāmadeva himself, a myth which was propounded also in later Upaniṣadic literature. It says that the seer was in a disaster, and finding no other way out for living, he cooked the entrails of canine and had to witness his wife humiliated until the Falcon (*śyená*) brought ambrosia for him. According to Ludwig, Bergaigne and Hillebrandt, Indra is the speaker of the stanza, and "the Falcon" alludes to the way in which *soma* was first introduced from heaven. Sāyaṇa explains this as Indra coming swiftly as a falcon.

Though the number of oblations dedicated to Aditi in Vedic ritual is not large, at least a few rites appear to indirectly attach some sort of importance to her. During the twelve *ratnahavis* oblations, offerings are made to Aditi in the dwelling of Mahiṣī:

> Aditi is the earth, and she is the wife of the gods, and the *dakṣiṇā* here is a cow.

On another occasion she is described as the archetype for the housewife. When a girdle is put around the sacrificer's wife, the act is accompanied with the formula *adityai rāsnāsi* (Hillebrandt 1927: 2.63).

Numerous Vedologists throughout ages have dealt with the Goddess Aditi. She occupies an anomalous position in *Ṛgveda*, since though she is not the subject of any complete hymn, her name finds mention about eighty times in its corpus. Cited very rarely alone, she is constantly invoked in association with her sons, the Ādityas. The ambiguity of the name itself would have lead to mystic identifications for "Aditi", as a result of which it was affected by theogonic and cosmogonic speculations found in the later portions of *Ṛgveda*. Thus in *Ṛgveda* X.63.2, gods are said to have been born from Aditi, who has been identified with the boundless sky (*dyáur áditiḥ*) in the very next verse.

In *Atharvaveda* Aditi seems to have been identified with the Earth and this identification is more frequent in *Taittirīya Saṁhitā* and *Śatapatha Brāhmaṇa*. Though in many passages of *Ṛgveda* she is clearly distinguished from Heaven and Earth as in those places she is mentioned separately along with this dual divinity (cf. *ṚV* X.63.10 & c). In *Ṛgveda* I.89.10 Aditi is represented as a personification of the Universal Nature:

> Aditi is the sky, Aditi the air, Aditi the mother and father, and the son, she is all the gods and the five tribes, she is whatever has been born and whatever shall be born. — cf. *KaṭhUp* 4.7

In *Nighaṇṭu* 1.1 the name is given as a synonym of "earth", and in the dual, of "heaven and earth". The name is also added to the lists for the synonyms of *vāc* (speech) and *go* (cow). *Nirukta* 10.4 defines Aditi as the mighty mother of the gods and locates her in the atmospheric region following *Nighaṇṭu* 5.5.

For many of the Western scholars, Aditi had been a favourite subject of dissertation since the nineteenth century. Wallis and Oldenberg are of the opinion that Aditi is a personification of the idea of "freedom from bondage", in contradistinction with Diti "bondage".[10] Müller (1891: 241) thinks that Aditi is the earliest name invented to express the "infinite" as visible to the naked eye, the endless expanse beyond the earth, the clouds and the sky. Roth interpreted Aditi first to mean "inviolability; imperishableness" (cf. *Nir* 4.22), but later he explained her as "eternity". In Böhtlingk and Roth, s.v. he explains her as a personification of the boundlessness of heaven as opposed to the finite earth. Pischel and Geldner (1892: 86) on the other hand suggest that Aditi denotes the earth. Colinet (at Hillebrandt 1927: 2.65f & n.) believes Aditi as the female counterpart of Dyaus. In his doctoral thesis titled *Über die Göttin Aditi* (1876, Breslau), Hillebrandt defined Aditi as "the day-light in its imperishableness".

VIŚVAVĀRĀ

The next seer in this selection is Viśvavārā of seer Atri's family, the seer of *Ṛgveda* V.28. She is rather ignored by the author of *Bṛhaddevatā*, finding mention in the list of the female seers alone. Though she belongs to the rare group of female seers to whom complete hymns are ascribed. Sarasvati and Vidyalankar (1977: 1.220) say that the hymn, which is associated with her name is devoted to the topics of marital happiness and security in life. The word Viśvavārā occurs in the very first stanza, and being interpreted by Dayanand as the lady who chooses or selects the whole universe and symbolizes cosmic light. According to Veṅkaṭamādhava with the sun disappearing Atri generated Dawn, and hence the Dawn, the daughter of Atri, is called Ātreyī Viśvavārā. The fire is kindled at dawn and in the heaven the fervour of dawn resides. The great sun appears in the direction of the dawn, and thus the dawn is to be greeted by all, for which reason it is called Viśvavārā: *viśvaiḥ sarvair varaṇīyā iti*.

---

[10] Wallis 1887; Oldenberg 1896.

Śaśvatī

The next seer is styled as "Śaśvatī Nārī" in the lists of *Bṛhaddevatā* and *Ārṣānukramaṇī*. *Bṛhaddevatā* 6.40 tells that Śaśvatī, the daughter of Aṅgiras, living as his wife, praised her husband, the King Āsaṅga. *Sarvānukramaṇī* clarifies that Āsaṅga, the son of Playoga, was turned into a female due to a divine curse, only to get back his virility later on by practising great penance and as a result of Sage Medhātithi's favour. His wife Śaśvatī, the daughter of Aṅgiras, pleased at his regaining virility praised him with the last verse of *Ṛgveda* VIII.1. Sāyaṇa says in his commentary that grieved at his impotency the wife of Āsaṅga performed great penance for him. As a result of this as also owing to his own penance he got his virility back. During night Śaśvatī noticed the signs of his manhood and overjoyed she extolled him with this verse. The verse exhibits a unique frankness of expression, noticeable also in other passages attributed to female seers of *Ṛgveda*. Sarasvati and Vidyalankar (1977: 1.220) comment that Śaśvatī may not be the historical seer of this verse, but since words have been put into her mouth she has been called an *ṛṣikā* of this verse. Chatterjee (1976: 61) has put forward his views on some other female seers of *Ṛgveda* as well. According to him, it can be reasonably inferred from the hymn of Apālā (*ṚV* VIII.91) that Indra was worshipped by some females, who chose to remain unwedded, as their divine lover or husband (as was the case with the now abolished *devadāsī* system of the recent past, and as some women even in the modern India are found to believe that they are wedded to Lord Kṛṣṇa and prefer to remain single throughout their whole life). It is probably in this background, thinks Chatterjee (1976: 62), that the erotic verse VIII.1.34 is to be explained. As Indra has been lauded in the first twenty-nine verses of this hymn, the pronoun *asya* in verse 34a may also refer to him. That Śaśvatī is not a proper name but denotes "every" is taken for certain by Chatterjee, who also suggests in his hypothesis that the couple of verses at the end of *Ṛgveda* I.126 may be similarly interpreted. In this connection he also reminds the reader of the Purāṇic story of Indra's amours with Ahalyā.

APĀLĀ

Now follows a female seer of the select texts of this study, already discussed at length, viz. Apālā, again of the Atri family, and the composer of *Ṛgveda* VIII.91.1-7. Citing *Śāṭyāyana Brāhmaṇa*, Sāyaṇa narrates an interesting legend about her in the preface of the exegesis of this hymn. It is said that afflicted with a skin disease and repudiated by her husband, Apālā, returned to her father's hermitage to practise hard penances for long seeking the favour of Indra. Intending to make a *soma* offering to the god, once she went to have a bath in the river, and on her way back home found some *soma* which she picked up and ate as she walked. Hearing the noise of the jaws chewing *soma*, Indra mistook it for the sound of the friction of the stones used for pressing *soma*. At once appearing in her front, he inquired from her if there were any stones pounding *soma*. Apālā answered in the negative and told him the truth, at which Indra started turning away from her. Apālā called him back and offered him to drink the *soma*-juice in her mouth cavity. At her insistence, Indra drank the juice from her mouth as she wished for, and could not help falling in love with her. Triumphant at winning his heart, Apālā exclaimed, "I have been repudiated by my husband, and yet Indra comes to me!" Moved, Indra granted her any three boons of her choice. She opted for the following ones: May (1) her father's bald head, (2) barren fields, and (3) the private parts of her own body sprout again. To fulfil her wishes, Indra dragged her first through the wide hole of his chariot, next through the narrower hole of the cart, and finally through the small hole of the yoke. In the process she cast off three skins one after another. The first skin became a hedgehog, the second an alligator and the third a chameleon, and Apālā was graced with a sun-like skin.

Bṛhaddevatā 6.99-107 give a detailed account of the above Apālā hymn. In a delightful-reading narrative style it relates the legend with *Ṛgveda* VIII.91. Somewhat different from the one narrated by Sāyaṇa, the story runs thus: There was once a girl called Apālā, the daughter of Atri, who was suffering from a skin disease.

Indra saw her in the lonely hermitage of her father and fell in her love. Aware of his intention through penance, Apālā went out with a pitcher to fetch water. Having found some *soma* on the way, she praised it (the *soma*), and this incidence is told in the first verse of the hymn. She pressed the plant in her mouth, and thereafter invoked Indra with the second stanza of the hymn, even as the latter sipped it from her mouth. After Indra relished cakes and meal at her place, she praised him with the next three verses. She prayed Indra to make her have abundant hair and faultless limbs and fair skin. Pleased by her praise, Indra passed her first through the carriage aperture, then between the bodies of the cart and in end through the yokes, thrice in all. As a result she became fair-skinned. The rest of this legend is the same as at Sāyaṇa. *Bṛhaddevatā* categorizing the hymn as *aindra* points out that Yāska and Bhāguri accept it as *itihāsa* (story or myth).

Sarasvati and Vidyalankar (1982: 10.3553) derive *apālā́-* from *pā́l-* (to protect), and attributes to the word the meaning "an unmarried girl", lit. "one yet to get protected, i.e. married". However far-fetched the meaning may appear, the term *kanyā̀* in the opening stanza of the hymn suggests that Apālā must have been a maiden, contra Sāyaṇa. Oldenberg (1912: 2.142) rightly points out that the two attributes *patidvíṣaḥ* and *yatī́ḥ* made Sāyaṇa and Veṅkaṭamādhava peculiarly go astray in assuming that Apālā was a married woman. Both the aforesaid words were explained by Sāyaṇa and Veṅkaṭamādhava as "being repudiated by her husband" while Griffith explains the term *patidvíṣaḥ* not as a *bahuvrīhi*, but as a *tatpuruṣa* compound meaning "hostile to the lord". The accentuation however would seem to lend support to Griffith's assumption.

Chatterjee (1976: 61) observes that Sāyaṇa has freely drawn on his imagination in supplementing the statements in *Śāṭyāyana Brāhmaṇa*. The Brāhmanical story is somewhat shorter. Chatterjee strongly believes that Apālā is a maiden, and hence at the end of the hymn she asks for the prosperity of crops in her father's, not any husbands, fields from Indra. Apālā's love relation with Indra is manifest from 4d (*índreṇa saṁgámāmahai*).

Sāyaṇa, Śaunaka and the author of *Śāṭyāyana Brāhmaṇa*, followed recently by Oldenberg and Geldner, have amply brought out the purport of 5d and 6b of the hymn. Chatterjee: o.c., l.c. ingeniously suggests that the desire expressed at these lines for crops and especially for hair below Apālā's waist can be appreciated and gains significance in the present context only by assuming an erotic (or more precisely, erotic-cum-mystic) relation of the speaker with Indra. The first desire is reminiscent of the fertility cult, and the second one expressly refers to her attaining sexual powers. Moreover, Chatterjee: o.c., l.c. points out that in the hymn itself there is, so to say, no reference to any skin disease that Apālā could have had, an inference Śaunaka and Sāyaṇa have dragged in probably from the expression *sū́ryatvacam*. This last word caused a wrong signal for them and provoked them to fancifully imagine that Apālā had had a diseased skin before. Chatterjee also contests Sāyaṇa's explanation (*sarvatra pūjārthe bahuvacanam*) by refuting that the plurals used in verse 4 are actually original singulars converted to honorific plurals. Whatever may be the case, it is proof enough that shows that Apālā was not alone in establishing a relationship of love with Indra, but belonged to a class of women who hated to have husbands, and preferring to remain virgins (i.e. singles) worshipped Indra as their lover instead. The hypothesis (which perhaps could lead to a sort of Immaculate Conception, if at all) may appear probable in view of line 2b and verse 3: Apālā wants the *soma*, and is pressing it with her teeth slowly, albeit very slowly, so as to get enough time to understand her lord fully. It is then during the pressing and flowing of the *soma* in her mouth that she has communion with her divine lover. All this might have given rise to the later Sanskrit, rather Indian, mystic literature.

YAMĪ

Yamī, the daughter of Vivasvant, to whom a few verses of *Ṛgveda*

X.10 are ascribed, is the next female seer from our select texts. *Sarvānukramaṇī* and *Bṛhaddevatā* give almost the same amount of information about this dialogue hymn and its seers. *Sarvānukramaṇī* says that Yamī asked for sexual pleasure from Yama but Yama refused and refuted her pleas.[11] *Bṛhaddevatā* 6.154 says:

> Yama rejects Yamī who solicits him with a view to sexual intercourse: the dialogue, "Hither, indeed", of those two children of Vivasvant is (descriptive of) that.

This hymn ascribed to the two, twin siblings, is remarkable in many aspects. In spite of having many features of lyric poetry it has never been used as a source of classical Indian literature. At the age of the classical poets, the incestual aspect of this hymn, perhaps, was not considered palatable. The great epics and some of the principal Purāṇas, however, contain a number of instances of conjugal relation between brothers and sisters. As, for example, Arjuna married his maternal cousin Subhadrā. Lord Kṛṣṇa, too, wedded Rukmiṇī, a cousin from his mother's side. Many references to such a marriage can be found also in the Buddhist literature (vide Sen 1950). This system gradually became unpopular as the social and moral values with changing time turned against such cases.

Böhtlingk and Roth (s.v.) take Yama and Yamī to be twin brother and sister as their names denote. He accepts them for the first human pair, the originators of the race, as the Hebrew conception closely connected the parents of mankind by making the woman formed from a portion of the man's body. *Bṛhadāraṇyaka Upaniṣad*, too, expresses the same view regarding the origin of woman. Man, says *Bṛhadāraṇyaka Upaniṣad* 1.4.3, being alone in the beginning of the universe, did not find any joy in life. He longed for companion, and dividing himself in two parts he created the husband and the wife. Roth connects this ancient story of origin of mankind to the hymn ascribed to Yama and Yamī, where Yamī says that "even in the

---

[11] . . . *yamī mithunārthaṁ yamaṁ provāca sa tām navamīyugbhir anicchan pratyācaṣṭe.* — *Sarvānukramaṇī* 10.10

womb the creator made us for husband and wife" (v. 5).

Müller (1864: 510) takes Yama as the day and Yamī as the night. In this hymn, the night implores her brother the day to make her his wife, but he refuses. Müller does not seem to accept Yama and Yamī to be the first mortal couple, the Indian version of Adam and Eve, as nowhere in the Veda Yama and Yamī have been mentioned to be the first human pair. Nevertheless, Yama has been mentioned to be the first mortal who has departed to the celestial world after death.[12] But Muir (1870: 5.288), following Müller, refuses to accept Yama as the first mortal, and asserts that such a notion developed only at a later phase of religious thoughts.

Nirṛti is frequently identified with Yamī in the Brāhmaṇas, chiefly because they both are represented as Yama's partners. *Atharvaveda* XVIII.33.14 gives a slightly different version of this hymn. There Yama says that the idea of brother and sister sleeping together is something at which his mind revolts. Also, all the gods will come to know of this heinous crime, and even the sun, opening its eyes, will know this and proclaim the unbrotherly act (*ṚV* X.10.9). Both in *Ṛgveda* and *Atharvaveda*, Yamī argues that since they were together once — in their mother's womb — doing so a second time cannot possibly be wicked.

In *Avesta* Yima marries his sister Yimak and propagates the human race, eventually to be killed by Azi Dahâka for this sin. This version blends the original story together with the later taboo on incest. But what is striking in both the versions, is that the hymn ends abruptly and inconclusively. Bhattacharji (1978: 93ff.) considers this to be significant, the more so, as it is not an isolated version but is related to cosmogony myths all over the world. In other mythologies, too, the incest is found committed for the sake of creation. Bhattacharji also cites the mythologies where the creation of human race is ascribed to androgynous creatures. In Plato, she

---

[12] Cf. Yima the first mortal king mentioned in the Avesta — *Haomo Yašt*, Yasna 9.4.

observes, the idea behind this myth is stated as one half of a soul yearning and searching for the other half. In Ovid's *Metamorphoses*, the pair Byblis and Caunus, a parallel to Yama and Yamī, is found. In Egypt also, the brother and sister duo Osiris and Isis is found, where Osiris corresponds very closely to Yama as the lord of the other world. The Greek pair Deukalion and Pyrrha recreated the human race after its annihilation by deluge. In Japanese mythology also, once the Kami gods and other gods passed away, Izanagi (the male who invites) and Izanami (the female who invites) created an island, as well as other gods and goddesses. Also in Mexican mythology, there is a number of creator gods who are in pairs, and whose names are cognates, like Yama–Yamī's. Eliade (1960: 175) writes on "the absence of hierogamy in archaic religions . . . their supreme beings were androgynies, at once male and female, both Heavenly and Earthly".

According to Bhattacharji, the reason of the abrupt ending of the story in Veda and *Avesta* is that the story was so primitive that it had to be included in the ancient literature, but in order to avoid the inevitable mythological truth, namely their incest, the story remained unfinished. Though unfinished for the later social taboo, the story had its probable ending resulting in incest as it is observed that incest played an important role in primitive rituals to enhance the production of the crops all over the world.

Another hymn, i.e. *Ṛgveda* X.154 is also ascribed to Yamī, the daughter of Vivasvant. The deity or the topic of the hymn is the state of the dead. Sarasvati and Vidyalankar (1977: 1.221) consider Yamī not to be a historical seer, but merely a conjectural name. *Bṛhaddevatā* 8.9 declares this hymn to be evolutional (*bhāvavṛtta*).

WIFE OF VASUKRA

Vasukra-patnī, who has been left out from the lists of *Bṛhaddevatā* and *Ārṣānukramaṇī*, is the seer of *Ṛgveda* X.28.1. But *Bṛhaddevatā* 7.33.30-32 accept her authorship and recognizes her dialogue with Indra. It has been there stated that the daughter-in-law of Indra, seeing the gods had arrived in the sacrifice, but not Śakra, addressed (him) in the third person (*parokṣavat*), saying: "My father-in-law has not come, [but] should he come, he would eat grain and would drink *soma*". The bolt-bearer on hearing this speech of hers, came that very moment, and standing on the northern alter (*uttarā vedī*), said aloud: "He bellowing loud, etc.".[13] *Sarvānukramaṇī* along the line of *Bṛhaddevatā* says that Vasukra is the son of Indra, and hence his wife is Indra's daughter-in-law. According to the legend, her father-in-law Indra was present in disguise at her sacrifice, but she, not recognizing him, complained that all other gods have come to attend her sacrifice, but Indra, her father-in-law is not come. To convince her that he has actually come, Indra and Vasukra had a dialogue which is contained in the following verses of the same hymn.

Sarasvati and Vidyalankar (1977: 1.221) hold Vasukra and his wife both to be conjectural seers. This hymn comprising twelve stanzas in addition to the first verse is of mystic character according to them.

GHOṢĀ

Ghoṣā, said to be the daughter of seer Kakṣīvant, is the next female seer to have two complete hymns to her credit. *Ṛgveda* X.39-40 are ascribed to her having Aśvins the twin celestial physicians as their deities. *Bṛhaddevatā* 7.41-47 narrate an account of Ghoṣā: An evil disease disfigured Ghoṣā. In the days of old she remained in her father's house for sixty years. She fell into great grief (thinking):

> In vain I have reached old age, having no son or husband. I (will) therefore resort to the lords of Light (*śubhaspatī*). Since my father, by propitiating them, obtained youth, long life, health, power and poison for killing all beings. I, his daughter, (would obtain) beauty and good fortune, if to me also were revealed formulae with which the Aśvins shall be praised by me.

---

[13] *sá róruvat* — *ṚV* X.28.2 (tr. Macdonell).

Even as she was brooding in this way, she saw the two hymns "Your encircling, etc." and "Where goes the chariot, etc." The two divine Aśvins, being praised, were pleased. Entering her organ (*bhaga*), they rendered her ageless, free from disease and beautiful (*subhagā*). They gave her a husband and Sage Suhastya as her son.

In her hymns, Ghoṣā praises the twin gods with references to their glorious deeds in the past. Thus, the hymns ascribed to Ghoṣā work as a secondary source of myths in *R̥gveda*. The third stanza of *R̥gveda* X.39 expresses the desire that as the twin gods had been the saviours of those who were starving, were of low origins (*apamásya*) and were blind and weak, they may in the same way grant a husband to Ghoṣā, who is getting old in her father's house. Moreover, they also cured persons with broken bones (*rutásya* "of the man with broken bones", Griffith, but *r̥tásya* "of the sacrifice = *yajñasya*", Sāyaṇa). The fourth verse of the same hymn mentions that the Aśvins changed the ageing Sage Cyavana to a youth, as a carpenter mends an old chariot to move again, and saved Bhujyu, the son of Tugra, from the sea. These deeds of theirs are praised aloud in all soma sacrifices. The seventh stanza thereof records many other deeds of the Aśvins. It says that they took Śundhyuva, the daughter of Purumitra, to Sage Vimada by chariot (cf. *R̥V* I.116.1). They also came to Vadhrimatī who having lost her arm in a war invoked them, there being also a similar reference to their providing her with a golden arm (cf. *R̥V* I.116.13). The present verse says that the twin gods gave noble offspring (*súṣuti* = *suprasavaṁ śobhanam aiśvaryaṁ vā*, Sāyaṇa) to this *púrandhi* (= *bahuprajñāyai*, Sāyaṇa but "to this happy wife", Griffith). The next verse mentions that they transformed the ageing Sage Kali into a youth again (cf. *R̥V* I.112.15). They rescued Sage Vandana, who in grief of separation from his wife, fell into a well (cf. *R̥V* I.112.5). They also made King Khela's wife Viśpalā walk, when she lost her leg in a battle with the enemies (cf. *R̥V* I.116.15). The following verse records further noble deeds of the Aśvins. They saved Sage Rebha who was kept in a cave by the *asura*s and was dying (cf. *ṚV* I.116.24), made the blazing fire low down for the sake of Sage Atri and cooled it down by pouring rains (cf. *ṚV* I.116.8), and also freed Sage Saptavadhri from the wooden chest in which he had been held captive by King Aśvamedha for some offence (cf. *ṚV* V.78.5). The tenth verse extols another deed of the Aśvins that has no other counter-reference in *Ṛgveda*: as well as nine other horses, they gave King Pedu a white horse, which was a sure conqueror of enemies in war, carried its friend very swiftly and brought pleasure to mankind as a pricey property. The thirteenth stanza mentions that the twin gods rushed towards mountains in their victorious chariot, while a counter-reference in *Ṛgveda* VI.62.7 gives the rest of the story, adding that they rushed there in the winning chariot as they had heard the call from Vadhrimatī. The same stanza narrates as well another deed of theirs, viz. they made an old cow milking again for the sake of Śayu (cf. *ṚV* I.118.8), in addition to yet another when they saved a sparrow from the mouth of a wolf that was about to swallow it up (cf. *ṚV* I.117.16).

The following hymn ascribed to the same seer, i.e. *Ṛgveda* X.40 has also some references to the deeds of the Aśvins. Most of which are repetitions of those mentioned in the previous hymn. One or two new myths, however, can be gleaned therein. The sixth verse mentions such two myths. In the first one hears of the Aśvins to have mounted the chariot to reach the sacrificer, just like Kutsa, who had been praising them. The rest of the story is supplemented in *Ṛgveda* IV.16.11, which tells that along with the Aśvins, Kutsa and Indra also mounted the chariot together. The sixth verse, with a cross-reference in *Ṛgveda* I.119.9, records that the Aśvins also filled the mouth of the bees with honey.[14] The seventh verse again centres round some other myths related to the dual divinities, by repeating that they came in rescue of Bhujyu, the son of Tugra, from the sea, that they came also to rescue King Vaśa who had been nearly defeated by his enemies armed with elephant power,

---

[14] *yuvór ha mákṣā páry aśvinā mádhvāsā́ bharata* — *ṚV* X.40.6cb.

and lastly that they rescued Atri, too, from a blazing fire (cf. *R̥V* VIII.5.25).

Macdonell and Keith (1910: 1.251) would like to term Ghoṣā as a protégée of the Aśvins in these two R̥gvedic passages. She is mentioned as a probable recipient of a husband, who is perhaps named in another passage as Arjuna,[15] though Macdonell and Keith hold that this is not likely. The reference to a skin disease as mentioned by Sāyaṇa is considered in the later tradition of *Br̥haddevatā* to be the cause of her remaining unwed, but Macdonell and Keith think that this view is untenable. According to Sāyaṇa, her son Suhastya is alluded to in an obscure verse of *R̥gveda* (I.120.5). Oldenberg (1912), however, sees here a reference to Ghoṣā herself. Suhastya is apparently invented from *R̥gveda* X.41.3, probably assisted by the fact that Vadhrimatī was given a son Hiraṇyahasta, by the Aśvins at *R̥gveda* I.117.24. But, Pischel and Geldner (1889, 1892: 1.4, 2.92) think that the word *ghóṣe* is not a noun at all, but a verb form.

AGASTYA'S SISTER

The next female seer to be met is Agastya-svasr̥, who has been accredited with *R̥gveda* X.60.6. *R̥gveda* X.60 is according to the *Sarvānukramaṇī* a heterogeneous hymn, as the first five and the last six verses are ascribed to the seers called Bandhus of the family of Gopāyana.

Br̥haddevatā 7.82-95 narrate a story as the background of *R̥gveda* X.57-59. It says that there were four brothers named Bandhu, Subandhu, Śrutabandhu and Viprabandhu, all priests of King Asamāti of the Ikṣvāku clan. For some reason, the king fired them and appointed two crafty priests, Kirāta and Ākuli by name,[16] whom he considered the best ones. These two priests, in the guise of pigeons, went against the Gopāyanas and fell upon Subandhu

---

15 *R̥V* I.122.5; see Oldenberg 1912: 1.123.

16 Kilāta in *ŚPBr* 1.1.4.14.

with their crafty power and magical art (*yoga*). When Subandhu swooned and fell from the pain of their attack, they plucked his spirit and returned to the king. At this, the other three Bandhu brothers composed these hymns to bring Subandhu back to life.

In continuation, the Bandhu brothers showered their praises on King Asamāti in the first four verses of *Ṛgveda* X.60, wherefore Asamāti is considered to be the deity thereof. The following verse invokes Indra, wishing the king's welfare. In the sixth verse, the mother of the Bandhus herself praised the king. Legends have it that the king, thus praised and ashamed, went to the Gopāyanas. The next five verses are the invocation of Subandhu to life and the last one is his resuscitation (vide Wilson 1850: 6.192). Griffith, however, refuses to accept any connection whatsoever of the first six stanzas of *Ṛgveda* X.60 with the following six stanzas.

The indices of *Ṛgveda* do not preserve the name of the poetess to whom *Ṛgveda* X.60.6 is ascribed. She was known only after her famous brother and sons. In the single verse comprising only twelve words, the sister of Agastya is heard as praising King Asamāti, whose enmity had taken one of her son's life away. Here, she glorifies his charity to her sons. The verse shows that the sister did not forget to mention the name of her illustrious brother in order to impress the king, so that he might forgive her offspring who were related to Agastya as well. It may be in passing mentioned that Sarasvati and Vidyalankar (1984: 12.4255) interpret the phrase *agástyasya nádbhyaḥ* as "for conducting the faculties of faultless chariot of body".

SŪRYĀ

Ṛgveda X.85 is a celebrated hymn ascribed to Sūryā Sāvitrī, i.e. the daughter of Savitṛ. In this hymn Sūryā describes her marriage with Soma, most of the verses the Hindus recite till date while marrying. *Nirukta* 12.9 considers the hymn as having a link with the following Indra–Indrāṇī–Vṛṣākapi hymn, viz. *Ṛgveda* X.86. Yāska ventures to propound that the origin and nature of Sūryā

(Sūrya's wife according to him) is provided in the next hymn and that Vr̥ṣākapi is none but Sūrya himself.

Going to discuss the Sūryā hymn, *Br̥haddevatā* 7.119-40 hold Sūryā as Vivasvant's spouse who is praised as Vr̥ṣākapāyī and is called Uṣas. Having divided herself into three, this Uṣas goes to the Lord of rays (Gopati = Sūryā). Uṣas before sunrise, comments *Br̥haddevatā,* she becomes Sūryā at midday, and at sunset she goes down in the form of Vr̥ṣākapāyī. According to *Br̥haddevatā* the first stanza of *R̥gveda* X.85 projects Sūryā as connected with *satyá, sū́rya, r̥tá* and *sóma*, but with the following three stanzas (2-4) *sóma* has been spoken of as a plant. One may, however, be tempted, if at all, to accept Śaunaka's contentions only with reservations, as it is clear from verse 3 that the seer hardly means the plant called *sóma*, but has in mind but the divine pleasure called *sóma*, whom nobody can devour but whom only the seekers after the highest Truth (*brahmā́ṇa*s) know. Coming back to *Br̥haddevatā*, it asserts that by the term *sóma* the fifth stanza clearly denotes the moon.

As regards the deities of the hymn, viz. the Aśvins, *Br̥haddevatā* presents the then current views that they are traditionally held to be (1) the sun and the moon, (2) or *prāṇa,* i.e. outward breath and *apāna,* i.e. downward breath (or rather, as in the view of some modern scholars, inhalation and exhalation), or again (3) day and night, or even (4) the two worlds, viz. heaven and earth (*rodasī*). All these alternative possibilities regarding their true identity have their seeds in the texts themselves, since there these dual divinities, pervading the world with light and moisture, fare each separately, to the south and to the north.

Hillebrandt (1927: 2.25) states that the complete synonymy between Uṣas and Sūryā implies that Sūryā is one and the same as Uṣas also at *R̥gveda* X.85. Some scholars viewed Sūryā here as the solar woman, this hymn standing as a glorification of the marriage between the sun and *soma,* i.e. the moon. Hillebrandt, however, is against this interpretation, because the Indian linguistic usages, where the sun is always masculine, would then go against such an assumption. He prefers to take Sūryā as the daughter of the Sun-god, as she is called Sāvitrī at *Atharvaveda* VI.82.2, XIV.2.30, *Aitareya Brāhmaṇa* 5.7.1 and passim. The marriage dealt within this hymn can only be that between dawn and the moon, a marriage that took place possibly on the first full-moon day in the New Year or in spring, when the marriage procession of Sūryā started. Macdonell (1898: 125) wisely thinks that the most likely interpretation seems to be the one which identifies Saraṇyu with the sun maiden, i.e. Sūryā or the dawn, i.e. Uṣas.[17] Incidentally, he points out that the wife of the Aśvins is once in *Ṛgveda*, viz. in X.85.8 called Aśvinī (= Sūryā). In this connection, be it remembered that Sūryā is said to have married, apart from Soma (cf. *ṚV* X.85.9), also the Aśvins (ibid.).

Hillebrandt saw some reasons to defy this oft-mentioned relationship of Soma to the daughter of Sūryā. He quotes three verses from *Ṛgveda* to establish his view, IX.1.6, 72.3 & 113.3. Of these, the first and the last speak of the daughter of Sūrya in terms of a monthly relation with Soma, but the rest refers to the Sūryā whom Soma married. On the authority of *Ṛgveda* IX.113.1, Hillebrandt tries to explore the possibilities of explaining Sūryā in the light of a motherly relation with Soma, because in the rainy season, when Parjanya, a rain-god, is mentioned as mating with her, the *soma* plant grows, Sūryā and Parjanya clearly making a pair thereat. On the other hand, *Atharvaveda* X.10.6 declares that the wife of Parjanya is Vaśā, who is doubtless to be identified with Pṛśni, otherwise the wife of Rudra and the mother of the Maruts. Pṛśni is in her turn identical with the *apsarā́ yóṣā*, who, according to *Ṛgveda* X.123.5 carries *sóma* "in the highest heaven", exactly as the *sū́ryasya duhitā́* is said to be doing at *Ṛgveda* IX.1.6. Hillebrandt concludes that the daughter of the Sun is Vaśā or Pṛśni or *apsarás*, i.e. the same *yóṣā* (woman) who, according to another version of the myth found at *Ṛgveda* III.48.2, pours, like the mother of Indra,

---

[17] Macdonell 1898: 51; Kaegi 1886: n. 148; cf. Weber 1862: 178-89; Bergaigne 1969: 2.486; Pischel and Geldner 1889: 13-29; Oldenberg 1896: 241.

for him the *soma* in her father's (i.e. the Sun's) abode.

Hillebrandt thinks that this daughter of the Sun-god to whom the rainy season belongs should be carefully distinguished from Uṣas whose bridegroom Soma is in the renowned marriage hymn, i.e. *Ṛgveda* X.85. "*Sū́ryasya* 'the shining one'," says Hillebrandt, "cannot be identical with Pṛśni, the other daughter of Sūryā. It is obvious that the shining one is a counterpart of Pṛśni who rules over the rainy season, and thus denotes the bright season, i.e. autumn or spring. Just as the day and night are his wives, so are the two halves of the year like his unequal daughters."

Though of dubious mythological origin, Sūryā in the Ṛgvedic marriage hymn is considered to be the typical Aryan bride. Some scholars explain her as the light of the sun, which is lent to the moon (Soma), by means of which the latter can shine. This is poetically expressed as Sūryā's marriage to Soma in this hymn. The sun, where the light "Sūryā" is generated and has her abode, is conceived as her father, and the moon, Soma, her husband. A marriage is arranged between Sūryā and Soma in which the Aśvins (*ṚV* X.85.9), the twin gods of the morning and evening twilight, representing the transition of the sun's light, play the bestmen and carry the bride in their chariot to her groom (ibid. and *ṚV* X.85.26).

In another passage the gods are said to have given Pūṣan to Sūryā (*ṚV* VI.58.4). The Aśvins themselves are mentioned very commonly as Sūryā's husbands. They are called her two husbands (*pátī*)[18] whom she chose (*ávṛṇīta*) (*ṚV* VII.69.4). Sūryā the maiden (*ṚV* V.73.5) mounted their chariot or opted for it (*ṚV* VIII.8.10). The Aśvins possess her "as their own" (*ṚV* VII.68.3) and carry her away in their chariot (*ṚV* VIII.29.8). She is consequently styled as Aśvinī (*ṚV* V.46.8).

Ṛgveda X.85.40-41 say that Savitṛ gave her first to Soma, and then to Viśvāvasu the Gandharva, who again gave her to Agni, and finally Agni handed her over to her groom. It has been already found

[18] *ṚV* IV.43.6; cf. *ṚV* I.119.5.

that at *Ṛgveda* VI.58.4 Pūṣan is mentioned as Sūryā's bridegroom. *Kauṣītaki Brahmaṇa* 18.1 deals with Sūryā's wedding at some length:

> Now when Savitṛ gave Sūryā to Soma the king, he made over to his daughter (whether she was Prajāpati's or his own) on her marriage these thousand verses which were in possession of the (above-mentioned) deities. They said, "Let us run a race for this thousand", they ran the race and the Aśvins were victorious by means of the donkey.

The nucleus of this story is found in *Aitareya Brāhmaṇa* 5.2.17: "The Aśvins won the tournament and married Sūryā." In mythologies of several people the sun's marriage to the moon is a common myth and this would tend to make Sūryā the sun maiden, for she was intended for Soma and according to certain myths was actually married to him.

Scholars differ regarding the identity of Sūryā as a distinct personality. E.H. Meyer (1883: 2.673) holds Sūryā as a cloud goddess. Many scholars regard her as dawn, as we have already seen, identifying her with Uṣas, and interpret her marriage with the Aśvins as the proximity of the morning and the evening stars to dawn and dusk. As Hillebrandt identifies Sūryā with Uṣas, Mannhardt supports his view. Oldenberg suggests that Sūryā is the sun maiden, a suggestion which has its support in the very old concepts of the feminine sun: Die Sonne (the sun) is in feminine gender in German. The feminine sun is celebrated in many old Teutonic myths and also in the fairy tales told by the Grimm brothers. Campbell (1968: 213) writes:

> The motif of the sun as a goddess instead of a god is a rare and precious survival from an archaic, apparently once widely defused, mythological context. The great maternal divinity of South Arabia is the feminine sun Ilat. Through Siberia as well as in North America scattered stories survive of a female sun.

In this context, Bhattacharji (1978: 224-25) offers some more valuable references to the concept of feminine sun from mythologies of different countries. "The Japanese Sun-goddess Amataresu is another example. The sun is mild and pleasant in Siberia, North America and Northern Europe and hence the tendency of the mythopoeic mind to imagine it as a maiden who bestows mild warmth is quite understandable" suggests Bhattacharji, this may have given birth to the conception of Sūryā. According to her the transformation of a god into a goddess is quite common in mythology, thus Sūrya and Sūryā might have appeared as the mutually convertible forms of the sun. The conversion was made only to give stress upon some characteristics of the sun, where the masculine form suggested the power and brilliance of the sun while warmth, charm and mildness were emphasized by the feminine form.

Regarding the marriage of Sūryā respectively with Soma, the Aśvins, Viśvāvasu, the Gandharva and Agni, Bhattacharji comments that the marriage hymn occurring in the much later tenth book of *Ṛgveda* may well bear the signs of a mixed product of Aryan and non-Aryan factors. Hence it may be so that though the Soma–Sūryā or Aśvinau–Sūryā pair was of Indo-European origin, the claims of the Gandharva or Agni being wedded to Sūryā appeared at a later stage. The hierogamy of the sun and the moon is a very common myth found almost all over the world. Gods corresponding to the Aśvins are married to goddesses of the Sūryā-type also in other Indo-European mythologies. Sūryā in the Sūryā-hymn was desired by Savitṛ her father for Soma. Later, however, the Aśvins obtained her. This story has a parallel in the Greco-Roman mythology (cf. J.G. Frazer's footnote on p. 312, Loeb edn of Ovid's *Fasti*):

> Castor and Pollux, sons of Tyndareus carried off Phoebe and Hilaria, daughters of Leucippus, betrothed to Idas and Lynceus.

The twin brothers with Sūryā on their chariot also constitute a familiar image. The horse-taming Castor and the prize-winning Polydeukes, desiring to be Helen's husbands, had her on their chariot, tells the Greek mythology. Bhattacharji finds parallels of this trio in the triad of Kṛṣṇa, Balarāma and Subhadrā (*Padma Purāṇa,* Utkalakhaṇḍa 19.11-17, 45-46), and the image of the Aśvins with Sūryā between them on their chariot offers a striking resemblance therein.

Jaiminīya Brāhmaṇa, however, narrates a rather remarkable anecdote about Sūryā's marriage. Prajāpati wanted to marry off his daughter Uṣas with Bṛhaspati, when the gods competed in a tournament, the Aśvins won her. Here, Uṣas takes the place of Sūryā, and Bṛhaspati, that of Soma (1.257).

INDRĀṆĪ

The next woman seer in our list is Indrāṇī, to whom a few verses of *Ṛgveda* X.86 are ascribed. *Bṛhaddevatā* 7.141 does not say much about Indrāṇī. Indra's wife is several times referred to in *Ṛgveda*.[19] Her name is Indrāṇī in this hymn (*ṚV* X.86.11-12), in which she is represented as conversing with Indra. This name occurs in some other passages enumerating the goddesses.[20] *Śatapatha Brāhmaṇa* 14.2.1.8. expressly states Indrāṇī to be Indra's wife, while *Aitareya Brāhmaṇa* 3.22.7 mentions Prāsahā and Senā as his wives. Nevertheless, these last two are identical with Indrāṇī.[21] Pischel (1892: 5.2) thinks, rather curiously, that Śacī is the proper name of Indra's wife in *Ṛgveda* as well as in the post-Vedic literature. *Atharvaveda* VII.38.2 speaks of an *asura* female who drew Indra down from among the gods and *Kāṭhaka Saṁhitā* 15.3.479 states that Indra enamoured of a *dānavī* named Vilisteṅgā and went to live with her among the *asuras*, assuming the form of a female among females and of a male among males.

Macdonell (1898: 64) suggests that the myth of Indra and Vṛṣākapi seems to have no general significance but it is simply the invention of a later poet of *Ṛgveda*. The details of this myth are

---

[19] E.g. *ṚV* I.82.5-6; III.53.46; X.86.9-10 and so on.

[20] *ṚV* I.22.12; II.32.8; V.46.8.

[21] *TBr* 2.4.2.7-8; *MS* 3.8.4, 4.12.1.

given somewhat obscurely in *R̥gveda* X.86. The hymn speaks of a dispute between Indra and his wife Indrāṇī on the monkey Vr̥ṣākapi, whom Indra favoured but Indrāṇī despised, as he had damaged her property. Vr̥ṣākapi was soundly thrashed and he escaped only to return when conciliation took place between the couple. According to Bradke (1892: 465), this story is a satire which is presented under the names of Indra and Indrāṇī, but intended to mean a chieftain and his wife (vide also Oldenberg 1890: 172-74).

The hymn, which is a dialogue between Indra and his wife over some offence of Vr̥ṣākapi, occurs in the 10th Maṇḍala of *R̥gveda*, reproduced in the 20th book of *Atharvaveda* (hymn no. 126). The story runs as follows. Vr̥ṣākapi, a favourite of Indra, offended Indrāṇī for which she was extremely angry, and she tried to rouse Indra's anger against him and threatened to punish him herself, unless Indra moved in the matter.

European scholars are not unanimous regarding the meaning or significance of this hymn. Like Macdonell, many have taken Vr̥ṣākapi to mean "a monkey" or more precisely, "strong ape or male ape" (*Mannaffe*). According to Bergaigne (1969: 2.270ff), Vr̥ṣākapi was a mystic sacrificer. Geldner (1951: 2.23) took this hymn as a humorous description of the domestic life of the gods. Griffith remarks that Vr̥ṣākapi, literally "the strong ape" or "the male ape", appears to be a sort of intermediate between a demi-god and a demon, but it is not easy to determine his exact character. Griffith further comments following *Nirukta* and *Br̥haddevatā* 2.67 that Vr̥ṣākapi may be the setting sun as well, and he who draws up vapour and irrigates with mist. Tilak in his *Orion* (chap. 7) ventured to propose an astronomical interpretation of the myth.

Br̥haddevatā 7.141 & 2.67, however, following *Nirukta* 12.9.27 suggest that Vr̥ṣākapi is none but the Sūrya himself. Sāyaṇa explains him as Indra because he pours showers of desired objects and can go wherever he wishes, like Indra does. Elsewhere, however, Sāyaṇa and his predecessor Veṅkaṭamādhava considered Vr̥ṣākapi as the son of Indra.

Indra's wife in the Vedic period was Indrāṇī, who stayed at home (*ṚV* III.53.6). *Taittirīya Saṁhitā* 1.7.13 says that Indrāṇī was much above the other women and is to be considered as being originated along with her husband, which is why her husband Indra would never die of old age. Bhattacharji (1978: 270) considers this remark to be a reference to Indra's solar and hence immortal character, or it may refer to Indra's inexhaustible youthfulness and vigour.

It has already been pointed out that *Aitareya Brāhmaṇa* 3.22 called Indra's wife Prāsahā. She was his beloved and the chief queen (*vāvātā*). She is also called Senā (army) by *Aitareya Brāhmaṇa* 3.2 and *Gopatha Brāhmaṇa* (*uttara-bhāga*) 2.9. Her father-in-law (i.e. Indra's father) was Ka (i.e. Prajāpati). *Taittirīya Brāhmaṇa* 3.2.4.20 calls her Śrī, who is in later literature came to be known as Lakṣmī and is held to be Viṣṇu's wife. Bhattacharji finds no wonder in it, as Viṣṇu was Indra's mythological heir (cf. Indra vis-à-vis Upendra).

At *Ṛgveda* V.37.3 Indra's wife wants her husband to go to sacrifices but desires also to accompany him herself. In the present hymn, viz. *Ṛgveda* X.86, Indrāṇī is a vigorous personality equalling Hera, the wife of the lord of gods Zeus, in Greek mythology.

Curiously, Sītā occurs as Indra's wife at *Ṛgveda* VIII.21.3. Bhattacharji (1978: 271) considers this to be justified because Sītā corresponds to Indra's character as fertility-god, as he is called *úrvarāpati* (lord of the fertile field) in the same passage. Rāma, the epic heir of Indra, had Sītā for his wife.

Jaiminīya Brāhmaṇa 1.363 mentions an episode where Indra stole Aiśakṛta Sitibāhu's *soma* in the shape of a monkey. Bhattacharji considers *Ṛgveda* X.86 to be the first literary reference into monkey worship in Indian religion, still prevailing in northern India. The Vṛṣākapi hymn belongs to the tenth book of *Ṛgveda*, which according to Bhattacharji (1978: 276) shows that non-Aryan elements of the population were already making their impact felt in religion, social institutions and other spheres of culture, and Aryans were also moving towards the south-eastern part of the country from Punjab, and were probably settled in the present Uttarakhand, an old seat of monkey worship. Hence, the sudden intrusion of the monkey cult was a major pre-Aryan influence which the Vedic Indians had to fight against, but eventually had to compromise with. Bhattacharji thinks that Indrāṇī's resentment for Vṛṣākapi in *Ṛgveda* X.86 contains this apathy of the Aryans towards the monkey cult, a cult that mingled with the solar cult of Indra, Viṣṇu and their incarnations. Thus Arjuna, the solar hero (of Indra origin) of *Mahābhārata* was Kapidhvaja, "with the monkey-emblem", and Rāma, the solar hero of *Rāmāyaṇa*, won his battle against the *rākṣasa*s with the help of monkeys. The Vṛṣākapi hymn carries the refrain to emphasize the supremacy of Indra in order to resist the advent of monkey cult. Chatterji (1962) says that the name Hanumat (*hanumant-* = monkey) is probably derived from Tamil *an-manti* (male monkey), which Bhattacharji considers a literal synonym of Vṛṣākapi (*vṛṣa-* = male and *kapi-* = monkey). Thus the revulsion of the Vedic Aryans towards the pre-Aryan monkey cult has been recorded in the hymn through Indrāṇī's protests against Vṛṣākapi's admission.

Indrāṇī is also the independent *ṛṣi* of a powerful hymn, viz. *Ṛgveda* X.145, a jealous wife's spell which she utters while digging out a herb for arresting the influence of an ascendant wife over her husband Indra. Another hymn, viz. *Ṛgveda* X.159, is also probably ascribed to Indrāṇī, this time under the name of Śacī Paulomī, very probably her another name (vide Pischel and Geldner 1889: 2.52). This hymn records her triumph over her other co-wives, probably as a result of the efficacy of the herb which she refers to in the earlier hymn, X.145.

URVAŚĪ

Urvaśī is a celestial nymph to whom, along with King Purūravas, the dialogue hymn, *Ṛgveda* X.95, is ascribed. *Bṛhaddevatā* 7.146-54 give an account of the mythological background of this colloquy. It says that in the days of yore the nymph dwelt with the royal-seer

Purūravas. Having made a contract with Purūravas, Urvaśī lived in wedlock with him. Jealous of Purūravas' cohabitation with her and his (as also *Brahman*'s) passion for her as if he were Indra, the latter, intending separate the couple, asked the bolt at his side: "Destroy, O Bolt, the alliance of these two, if you wish to do me a favour". The Bolt agreed, and destroyed their alliance with its craft. Bereft of her, the king wandered about, distracted as it were. As he wandered, he saw in a lake the beautiful Urvaśī, as it seemed, surrounded by five beautiful maidens, her friends, at her side. He pleaded her to come back to him, but she sorrowfully replied: "You cannot now have me here, but will obtain me again in heaven". *Bṛhaddevatā* 7.153 thinks that this reciprocal narrative is a story, though it also records the view of Yāska, who considers it to be a dialogue as it is in connection with a summons (*āhvāna*).

Śatapatha Brāhmaṇa 11.5.1 supplies a yet older version of this legend (cf. Macdonell 1904: 2.291), informs as it of Urvaśī's taking the form of a swan, the archetype of an ur-Indo-European myth (cf. Bhattacharji 1987: 125-27). In this account, Urvaśī the nymph desired Purūravas, the son of Ila, agreeing to live with him on condition that she should never see him naked, as this was distasteful for a woman of her sensitivity and nobility. This celestial light called Urvaśī stayed with him, who impregnated her, when the *gandharva*s thought that she should not live with a human being anymore and wanted her back. They hatched a plan and stole one of her two rams which were fastened to her bed. At this, she cried out saying:

> I am as helpless as a female can be without a husband and anybody to help, that the ram, which is like my son, is being stolen.

The *gandharva*s having filched the second ram, the nymph repeated her lamentations, at which Purūravas sprang up from his bed to recover the rams, without having the time to dress up. At that very moment the *gandharva*s flashed lightning on him, and seeing him naked, Urvaśī at once disappeared. Wandering in her pursuit afterwards, Purūravas found her swimming with other nymphs in the forms of swans in a lotus lake near Kurukṣetra. She recognized him to be the human being she had lived with in the past, and called him and stroke up a conversation, in reply to which Purūravas uttered the opening verse *hayé jā́ye,* etc. of *R̥gveda* X.95.

Sāyaṇa has quoted also the legend given in the commentary of Ṣaḍguruśiṣya. In a lucid narrative style it says that Mitra and Varuṇa were initiated for a sacrifice, but seeing Urvaśī they became lustful and ejaculated in a pitcher (the semen eventually, as we know from other sources, gave birth to Agastya and Vasiṣṭha). Angry at this, the dual divinity cursed Urvaśī that she would be enjoyed by a human being in the earth. On the other hand, King Ila along with the sons of Manu, went a hunting and entered the forest on his horse in the area where Śiva was having sex with his consort Pārvatī. Śiva having previously vouched that whichever male would enter the forest would be transformed into a female, King Ila became a woman and he begged Śiva for the restoration of his virility. Śiva advised him to appease Pārvatī to fulfil his wish. The goddess granted him virility after six months of womanhood. And, during his "womanhood" once Budha, the son of Soma, was charmed with Ilā, i.e. female Ila's beauty and mated with her. As a consequence, Purūravas was born of Ilā. Purūravas was the king of Pratiṣṭhānapura and Urvaśī fell in love with him. She made a contract with him that if she saw him naked other than in bed she would vanish as she came, and the two rams that were like her sons should never be separated from her. Four years had passed when one night the gods stole two rams of Urvaśī. In the commotion the king rose up without his clothes on, and when he was returning after retrieving them, the gods revealed his nudity to Urvaśī by sending a flash of lightning. The contract being violated Urvaśī went to the heaven back. Then the king madly searched for her everywhere, to at last find her at the beach of the Mānasa Lake, where she was playing with other nymphs. Purūravas desired to be reunited with her and begged Urvaśī to come back, whereat she asked him to go back.

Hillebrandt (1927: 2.25) thinks that Urvaśī defies a definite mythological interpretation, since she enters the realm of fables among the *apsaras*es without possessing any individual characteristics.

The followers of Aurobindo's mystic interpretation of the Vedas like Purani (1963: 157-78) would take Urvaśī as the divine light or the "wide enjoyment" (*uru-* = wide, *vaś-* = to enjoy; shine) or "infinite delight", and Purūravas denotes "the many voiced human being crying aloud for satisfying his desires" (*puru-* = many, *ravas-* = voice). Urvaśī, the divine delight, came to Purūravas, a man seeking for ordinary human pleasures. Purūravas got hold of the heavenly delight once but failed to recognize it and consequently it forsook him.

DAKṢIṆĀ

Dakṣiṇā Prājāpatyā is most probably a conjectural seer, whom *Ṛgveda* X.107 is ascribed to. The hymn has, however, been ascribed to seer Divya of the Aṅgiras family. Here, either the honorarium (*dákṣiṇā*) offered to the priests or the institutors of sacrifice who offer the honorarium is/are praised with this hymn. As Dakṣiṇā is praised in this hymn, she is the deity thereof. *Bṛhaddevatā* 8.22 offers still another alternative in saying that with the hymn beginning with *āvír abhūt,* etc. Dakṣiṇā Prājāpatyā praised herself. Purāṇas say that Dakṣiṇā is the daughter of Ruci and Ākūti, and was the consort of Suyajña, an *avatāra* of Hari, having twelve sons known as the Tuṣita gods (Yamas) of the period of Svayambhuva Manu.

SARAMĀ

Ṛgveda X.108 is ascribed to Saramā and the Paṇis. Sāyaṇa after *Sarvānukramaṇī* calls Saramā *devaśunī* (a divine bitch), and narrates a story in this connection. The army of the demon Vala, who were called the Paṇis, stole the cattle of Bṛhaspati, who sent Saramā, the divine bitch, to find out the cattle. Having crossed the great river she reached the abode of Vala and found the cattle kept in a secret place. Aware of the situation the Paṇis tried to make friendship with her through conversation (i.e. the dialogue contained in *Ṛgveda* X.108).

Bṛhaddevatā 7.30-35, however, have a somewhat different story to tell in this connection. It says that though Saramā had crossed the River Rasā, and reached where the Paṇis hid the cattle, she rejected the offer of the Paṇis' fraternity and a share of the cows, but was tempted to drink the milk of the hidden cattle. When she returned to Indra, being under the influence of the demons' milk, she replied negatively when asked by Indra about the cattle's whereabouts. Indra struck her with his foot in anger. Then throwing the milk out, she went trembling with fear, back again to the Paṇis. Indra, on his chariot, by the track of her steps, went and smote the Paṇis and brought back the cows.

The Ṛgvedic text, viz. X.108.5, however, does not explicitly call Saramā a bitch. It rather says that Saramā, the messenger of Indra, seeks from the Paṇis the kine they have carried away. They threaten her with battle and tell her about their sharp weapons. But, she was not to be bullied and said:

> Your words cannot wound, O Paṇis! even if your wicked bodies be arrow-proof. —*ṚV* X.108.6

The Paṇis change their attitude and say:

> We shall make you our sister, don't go back. We shall give you a share of the cattle, O blessed one! —*ṚV* X.108.9

Stubborn, she refuses to yield to sentiments:

> I care neither for brotherhood nor for sisterhood. —*ṚV* X.108.10

The expression *subhage* in the fifth verse meaning "O blessed one!" with the root word *bhaga* (bliss or grace), is usually applied to a goddess. It is also applied courteously to a woman, as at *Ṛgveda* X.10.10. This root word was later used in terms like *bhagavant*, a name for the divine person. At *Yajurveda* 11.20, in a new combination, viz. *bhaginī-*, the word is applied to a goddess meaning the blissful or the gracious one.

Oldenberg considers Saramā to be the dawn. In his view, *Ṛgveda* speaks of the Goddess Saramā, a female dog, who takes the ruddy cows of the gods to their concealment when stolen. Her sons, who also have canine shapes and appear to play the part of genii of sleep and death, bear the matronym *sārameya-*. It was thought that the Greek Hermes and Hermeias had been discovered in this context, as the guide of souls into the realm of death, the dream-sending god of sleep. The root *sár-* (to hurry) in Saramā as in Saraṇyu, both wives of Vivasvant, seemed to conduct the mythological interpreter into the realm of the agitated atmosphere, just as in the case of Erinys. Saramā, "the hurrying one", is to be explained as the wind. In the natural symbolism of the myth, the dog-form of the goddess and her canine children seem to correspond to the speed of the wind.

Oldenberg (1890 (1962): 51), however, does not think that the wind is the only thing in nature that fleets, and keeping in mind the retrieving of treasure of ruddy cows lost in the darkness, Saramā could well mean the morning blush, the dawn. To support this view, Oldenberg considers the resemblance of her name with that of Helena. In that case, the story of the Iliad is found again in one of the standing themes of the Veda-hymns, thinks he: the siege of Troy would be but a repetition of the daily siege by the martial forces of the sun, of the entrenchments of night, where the treasures of light are locked up.

Hillebrandt, too, holds Saramā to resemble the Dawn. The general character of the verses attributed to Saramā has an undeniable similarity with those of the Uṣas hymn, viz. *Ṛgveda* V.45.7-8. There, she is not any more the messenger of Indra, but appears in connection with the cattle which she finds or helps to find. In her task she was helped by Bṛhaspati and the Aṅgirases. Exactly as Saramā has been said to tread *ṛtásya pathā́*, the Dawns are also in a similar manner called *ṛtásya devī́ḥ* (*ṚV* IV.51.8) and *ṛtájātasatyāḥ* (*ṚV* IV.51.7). As the Navagva Aṅgirases (a term which, as Sāyaṇa understands it, would also include the Daśagvas) and Bṛhaspati take part in the opening of the cowshed in the present hymn (*ṚV* X.108.11), so also, in another Saramā-hymn, *Ṛgveda* V.45, Bṛhaspati, Soma, the stones and the wise *ṛṣis* are likewise closely connected. The second half of verse 7 mentions Saramā with these words:

ṛtáṁ yatī́ sarámā gā́ avindad ।
víśvāni satyā́ṅgirāś cakāra ॥

And, the eighth verse begins with a hint which can surely be applied to the above-mentioned Saramā:

víśve asyā́ vyúṣi mā́hināyāḥ ।
sáṁ yád góbhir áṅgiraso návanta ॥

On the basis of their above-mentioned common traits, Hillebrandt prefers to conclude that Saramā is a synonym of Uṣas. Her character as the mother of the Sārameyas can well be explained once she is taken to represent the Dawn goddess. Bloomfield interpreted the two Sārameyas as the sun and the moon. Hillebrandt suggests that if Bloomfield's interpretation is correct, then Saramā, the mother of the two Sārameyas, would be a mythological synonym for Uṣas, the mother of the sun and the moon. Hillebrandt, too, like Oldenberg, holds that the names of Saramā, as also of Vivasvant's wife Saraṇyu who abandons the twins and has the same colour as that of the Uṣas, are mythological synonyms, and they are not different from Uṣas. In this understanding, Saramā and Saraṇyu would only be linguistic synonyms, except for the fact that the latter is not a mere adjective, which is also probable. The Aśvins, and the Sārameyas who faded out in Vedic mythology, would be mythological synonyms as well.

It may be added to justify Hillebrandt's suggestion that Yama, the son of Vivasvant, is stated to have as his two Sārameyas watchful loyal companions, who may well be conceived of as his mythological step brothers, i.e. the sons of Saraṇyu alias Saramā by Vivasvant. In passing it may be mentioned that the Aurobindo school considers Saramā to represent some intellectual faculty of human mind, a consideration miles apart from the previous interpretations.

The Paṇis, suggests Hillebrandt, were a tribe hostile to the *soma*-pressing Aryans. It was the raids of these Paṇis in particular that the poets of the book of the Bhāradvājas had in mind. In the Saramā-hymn (*ṚV* X.108), they have been transformed into demons and were given a berth in the world of saga, and the poet sees them in the remote distance on the other side of the River Rasā.

JUHŪ

Juhū, the wife of *Brahman* (masc.), has *Ṛgveda* X.109 to her credit. The alternative seer of this hymn is Ūrdhvanābha, the son of *Brahman* himself. Sāyaṇa relates a story with this hymn. Juhū, otherwise known also as Vāc, is the wife of *Brahman*. Since Bṛhaspati is known as Vācaspati (the lord of Vāc or "speech"), it is quite understandable that Bṛhaspati is the husband of Juhū. Once Bṛhaspati's sin (*kilviṣa-*) resulted in Juhū's ill luck, as her husband forsook her. Gods like the Ādityas and others then consulted together, and erasing her sins restored Juhū to Bṛhaspati (see before Chapter 3, p. 119 fn.). This story, according to Wilson, is "a curious and not very intelligible legend", and his view appears to be justified because it is rather unintelligible and at places obscure to a modern mind: why should the husband's sin result in the wife's ill fate, and why should her sinning husband forsake her for a sin not hers? Unfortunately without going into any detail, *Bṛhaddevatā* 8.36 merely mentions that Brahmajāyā Juhū sang this hymn addressing the All-gods.

The mystic interpreters consider *Ṛgveda* X.109 to be one of the finest mystic hymns. In ritualistic applications, the word *juhū́-* stands for "a sacrificial ladle". The hymn in concern, according to them, consists of a symbolic description of the Atharvavedic priest *Brahman*'s function in respect to this mystic Juhū (cf. Sarasvati and Vidyalankar 1977: 1.222).

Verses 2-3 and 5-6 explicitly dwell on the incidence of handing over of Juhū by the gods to her husband, an incidence that resembles the handing over by Soma, Agni and other gods of the bride Sūryā at *Ṛgveda* X.85.41. Here too, in their turns Soma, Varuṇa, Mitra and Agni, the gods, human beings and the kings who keep their promises passed on Juhū to her spouse, Bṛhaspati.

VĀC

Vāc, the daughter of Ambhṛṇa, is the seer who is accredited with the authorship of *Ṛgveda* X.125.

The hymn being a renowned one and having a tremendous impact on the non-dualistic doctrine of the later Vedānta philosophy as well as on the theory of *Śabda-Brahman* is considered by some scholars as ascribed to a conjectural poet. Popularly known as Devī-Sūkta, it forms the basis of *Bāṣkala-Mantropaniṣad* and *Saptaśatī* or *Caṇḍī* of later period. *Bṛhaddevatā* 2.87 & 8.43 mention Vāc Āmbhṛṇī to be its seer but no legend attached to her is to be found there. Macdonell and other Western scholars like Weber and Oldenberg consider her to be the personified Speech, who describes herself in this hymn as accompanying all the gods and performing numerous deeds on their behalf. About herself, she declares that her origin is in the waters, the sea, and she encompasses all beings. In *Ṛgveda* VIII.100.10-11 she is mentioned as divine and as lording over the gods (*devī́:* VIII.100.11, *rā́ṣṭrī devā́nām:* VIII.100.10).[22]

Nirukta 2.17 mentions Vāc as "the thunder" or Mādhyamikā Vāc, "the voice of the middle region". According to Macdonell the above-mentioned terminology of the commentators of *Nirukta* may have been the starting point of the personification of the Speech.

Vāc is considered *Śabda-Brahman* of the later times pervading the entire universe and accompanying all the gods. She is the primeval energy of the universe, the feminine counterpart of the

---

[22] Also see Macdonell 1898: 124; Weber 1865: 473; Oldenberg 1885: 58-59.

creating and annihilating god. Radhakrishnan (1923: 487) considers her hymn to have made the basis of Śāktism in India. He interprets her as "the energy drawing forth from *paramātman* the whole universe from *ākāśa* downwords". Here he identifies the conception of Vāc with the universal soul, and with the later conception of Śiva, whose inseparable half is Śakti. The goddess through this hymn establishes emphatically her important position in the governance of the universe. She is conceived as the guiding feminine principle in the scheme of creation, and no god's work can be accomplished without his innately wedded Śakti.

Looking back to the Ṛgvedic Vāc, one finds another hymn addressed to Speech at *Ṛgveda* X.71. Some scholars think that this is the hymn that gave birth to the theory of *Śabda-Brahman*.

Thomas (1964: 88) thinks that the idea of Speech as accompanying and supporting all the gods, and reaching wherever the magic power of *Brahman* extended, bears a resemblance to the Word of God as personified in the Wisdom of Solomon in Old Testament, 18.15ff; and to the Logos of Philo in Greek mythology, though the idea of Vāc did not mount up to the same development in Cosmogonic doctrine.

Perusing world mythology, parallels of Vāc can be found at several places. The Greeks recognized the warning of a god in the voice of thunder. They worshipped it as Ossa Dios Aggelos (the word Messenger of Zeus), whom only the wise could understand. The Romans worshipped it as Goddess Fama. In Indian mythology Indra adores it as "the Voice in the cloud". As Vāc Āmbhṛṇī, who on one hand issues from the waters and from the forehead of the father, and on the other throws deadly arrows against the foe of *Brahman*, so the word from above is either a weapon that kills, or a revelation that teaches (vide Darmesteter 1880).

Chatterji (1945) has tried to establish that the development of Vāc of *Ṛgveda* as an active female divine power, bestowing grace to mortals, through the Brāhmaṇic period was more and more like that of the Greek Logos. He tries to establish that during this period Truthful Word came to be considered as God. Along the lines of Hopkins, Chatterji traces the growth of the conception of Logos beginning with Heraclitus, to be passed on to the Stoics and to be adopted by Philo, eventually to become a prominent feature of Neo-Platonism and to appear again in the Gospel of St. John. He concludes after Hopkins that Heraclitus might have received the idea of Logos from the contemporary philosophers of the East, if not directly, at least indirectly.

Hopkins says that as in ancient Greece and Rome, in early Babylonian religion also the Word was exalted, through the influences of a higher religion, as a great cosmic divine agency, sometimes personified.

Mainly basing her arguments upon the Brāhmaṇical statement (*TBr* 1.3.8.4; *TS* 3.7.6.3) "Bṛhaspati is the god's *brāhmaṇa* (priest)", Bhattacharji (1978: 318), on the other hand, thinks that Bṛhaspati is rather the concept which resembles the creative word, Logos. She, however, observes that this "word" is, in Indian mythology, the sacrificial formula that calls forth the cosmos out of chaos. It is this word, finds Bhattacharji, which is Vāc, the *mānasakanyā* of *Brahman*, who came out of the latter's head (i.e. thought). With her he committed incest and procreated, which is why this was the creative word. Bṛhaspati as the potent power behind the sacrificial formula is the lord of this word; he is Vācaspati (*TBr* 1.7.4.7; 2.6.19.2), the *hotṛ* of the ten *hotṛ* priests (i.e. the best among them).

Hillebrandt, however, thought that the origin of the feminine gender on the grammatical side was alone responsible for the position which Vāc, Purandhi, etc. held as goddesses, being feminine in gender. According to him, the conception of many goddesses is connected with certain general notions which caused the division into masculine and feminine genders. The mighty aspects of nature resulted in conceiving male gods like Agni, Rudra, the Parjanyas and others, while their benign and mild counterparts became the female goddesses.

RĀTRI

In the texts selected for the present study, Bharadvāja's daughter Rātri is the next female seer, to whom *Ṛgveda* X.127 is ascribed. It should nevertheless be mentioned that though *Bṛhaddevatā* 2.82 and 8.44 take her as the sole seer of the above hymn, for the same the *Sarvānukramaṇī* alternatively suggests also the name of Kuśika, the son of Sobhari. In all probabilities, Rātri, the night, is a conjectural poetess praising herself as the Goddess of Night. Rātri and Uṣas, night and the dawn, are two sisters, daughters of heaven both, just as the Aśvins are brothers. Rātri in this beautifully crafted lyric poem is not conceived as dark but as the bright star-lit night. She shines manifold with her starry eyes. Decked with all splendours, she fills the valleys and heights and dispels the darkness with light. When night approaches, men retire to their home as birds do to their nests. The night is prayed for driving away the wolves and thieves, to guide her worshippers to safety.

Macdonell (2000: 124) supposes that Night probably became a goddess by way of antithesis to Dawn, being invoked with her in several verses as a dual divinity. Hillebrandt, again, considers Rātri as belonging to the class of feminine deities like Pṛthivī, Sūryā, Uṣas, Paurṇamāsī and Amāvasyā, whose conceptions are based on ground reality, therefore on concrete foundations.

GODHĀ

Not much is known of Godhā, whom the second hemistich of *Ṛgveda* X.134.6 and the seventh verse of the same are attributed to. Sāyaṇa speaks of her as a *brahmavādinī*. Unlike in the cases of other seers, tradition is completely silent about her parentage, lineage or relations. *Bṛhaddevatā* 2.82 mentions Godhā as a mere female seer. Nevertheless, from an internal estimation of the hymn it appears that the seventh stanza is an interpolation to the previous six stanzas, of which except the last hemistich are ascribed to Māndhātṛ, the son of Yuvanāśva. In the forgoing verses Indra is invoked, while *Bṛhaddevatā* holds that the seventh verse invokes the All-gods (i.e.

Viśvedevāḥ). It is also worth noticeable that *Sarvānukramaṇī* says nothing about the change of deity in the last verse. The first line of the verse ascribed to Godhā appears in *Sāmaveda* 1.2.2.4.2 with some variants.

Godhā(ḥ) in masculine plural number is attested in *Mahābhārata* 6.9.42 as the name of a people. In *Ṛgveda* the word Godhā is found at X.28.10-11, where it means "a sinew" and again at VIII.69.9 it stands for "a chord". But, the name of the seer at X.134 may perhaps be treated as a woman of the Godha people, who took up the religion of the Vedas and composed prayers for its deities, but was not considered to be at par with the Vedic poetesses, as is testified by the fact that the parentage of this seer is neither mentioned nor preserved in the tradition.

5

Liturgical Peculiarities of the Select Texts

Sāyaṇa in his commentary on *Ṛgveda* gave almost every possible sacrificial application of all the hymns and individual verses, mainly following the instructions of the Brāhmaṇas, Āraṇyakas, Śrautasūtras as well as Gṛhyasūtras. What follows is primarily based on his references, so far as the *viniyoga*s of the particular hymns and verses are concerned. In addition, the relevant sources of the particular applications will also be treated through the device of cross-referencing in the ritualistic texts and Sāyaṇa's commentary, and in the order of the hymns and verses as arranged in *Ṛgveda* at that.

I.126.7

Regarding the application of *Ṛgveda* I.126.7, Sāyaṇa says *ukto viniyogaḥ* meaning that its application is to be found in *prātar-anuvāka* and *āśvina-śastra*, where many hymns in general are read out from *Ṛgveda*. In *prātar-anuvāka*, a part of the *soma* sacrifice, at least 100 hymns are read out by the *ṛtvij*s (priests) till the first call of bird is heard. The day in which the juice of the *soma* plant is extracted and offered to gods is called the *sutyā-dina*. In the last half of the night of *sutyā-dina* the priests read the morning litany, i.e. at least 100 hymns in all the seven Vedic metres for the gods Agni, Uṣas and Aśvins (cf. *ĀśvŚrS* 4.13). If the first birdcall is not heard even after reading the prescribed hymns, the *ṛtvij*s recite any other hymns from *Ṛgveda*, of their choice. Similarly in *āśvina-śastra*, a part of the *atirātra* variety of *soma* sacrifice, at least, if not more,

100 hymns are read by the *ṛtvij*s till sunrise. Even if reading after the prescribed hymns there is still time left for sunrise, the *ṛtvij*s recite any other hymns of their choice from *Ṛgveda* (cf. *ĀśvŚrS* 6.5). The hymns and the verses of *Ṛgveda*, which have no other apparent applications, can be used at these two places. Whenever Sāyaṇa says *ukto viniyogaḥ* or *gato viniyogaḥ* for any hymn or verse, he only means the above applications.

I.179

Regarding the application of *Ṛgveda* I.179, Sāyaṇa says: *viśeṣaviniyogo laiṅgikaḥ* whereby he means that the special application of this hymn should be performed in accordance with the indication found in itself. This dialogue hymn of Agastya and Lopāmudrā has Eros or Rati as its deity as the dialogues reveal the sexual relationship of a man with his wife. No revered source of sacrificial paraphernalia gives any hints on its special application, but Sāyaṇa from the Mīmāṁsaka point of view keeps open the possibilities of its *viniyoga* considering the *liṅga-pramāṇa* (authority of symbol) contained therein.

III.33

Ṛgveda III.33 also has no apparent special application in the Śrauta or Gṛhya rites, and hence Sāyaṇa says: *sūktaviniyogo laiṅgikaḥ*. It is a dialogue hymn ascribed to the seer Viśvāmitra and the two rivers, Vipāś and Śutudrī. Here Viśvāmitra praises the two rivers that they may lower themselves so as to help him cross over. The hymn, according to Sāyaṇa, may have special *viniyoga* depending upon the *liṅga* or internal evidence of it.

IV.18

Sāyaṇa did not mention any *viniyoga* for *Ṛgveda* IV.18, which suggests that its application is to be found in *prātar-anuvāka* and *āśvina-śastra* among other Ṛgvedic hymns in general.

V.28

For *Ṛgveda* V.28 Sāyaṇa says that the sacrificial application of the entire hymn depends on its internal evidence: *sūktaviniyogo laiṅgikaḥ*. But, three verses at least of this hymn have several individual applications (*ṛg-* or *mantra-viniyoga*). The third verse of this hymn is applied as the *yājyā* verse in the *sviṣṭakṛt* of the Pavitreṣṭi. *Āśvalāyana-Śrautasūtra* 2.12.11 says about the *iṣṭi* that

> *saiṣā saṁvatsaram atipravāsataḥ*
>
> One should perform this rite when he has been staying in a foreign land more than a year.

Sviṣṭakṛt is an inclusive part of an *iṣṭi* type of sacrifice. It is performed just after the principal offering of an *iṣṭi* sacrifice. *Yājyā* is a verse that is read at the time of offering oblation to the sacrificial fire. *Ṛgveda* V.28.3 is read as the *yājyā* verse of the *sviṣṭakṛt* rite in the Pavitreṣṭi. This verse has another special application, in being read as the *yājyā* of the *sviṣṭakṛt* rite in the *sākamedha parvan* of the Cāturmāsya sacrifice. Cāturmāsya is a year-long sacrifice performed in four parts (*parvan*s) and *sākamedha* is a part thereof. In the *sākamedha parvan* of Cāturmāsya, an *iṣṭi* is performed in the morning of the full-moon day for the gods Krīḍin Maruts, this *iṣṭi* is called *krīḍineṣṭi* (cf. *ĀśvŚrS* 12.29). In the *sviṣṭakṛt* rite thereat, V.28.3 is applied as the *yājyā* verse (cf. *ĀśvŚrS* 2.12.22).

The fifth and the sixth verses of the same hymn, i.e. V.28, are applied in the Darśapūrṇamāsa rite among the *sāmidhenī* verses. Darśapūrṇamāsa is a very important sacrifice and is considered as the model of all the *iṣṭi* sacrifices. In the first phase of this rite, the sacrificial fire is kindled in a prescribed ritual called *agnyādhāna*, during which fifteen verses called the *sāmidhenī*s are read out. Thus *Ṛgveda* V.28.5-6 are two *sāmidhenī* verses.

VIII.1.34

The next verse by a female seer, namely the wife Śaśvatī, is *Ṛgveda* VIII.1.34. The hymn is quite long, with thirty-four verses. Some ritualistic applications are prescribed for a number of verses of this hymn, but neither the entire hymn nor the last verse thereof (the one ascribed to a wife named Śaśvatī) has been prescribed for any specified application. Hence, this verse having Eros or Rati as its theme has no apparent *viniyoga*.

VIII.91

The famous hymn of Apālā, viz. *Ṛgveda* VIII.91 has not been used in any special rite, cf. Sāyaṇa: *viniyogo laiṅgikaḥ* (the ritual application depends on the inherent evidence [of the hymn]).

X.10.39-40

For *Ṛgveda* X.10 also, Sāyaṇa has *gato viniyogaḥ*, meaning that the application of this hymn is to be found in the *prātar-anuvāka* and the *āśvina-śastra*, and it has not been applied specially in any rite whatsoever. This dialogue hymn of Yama and Yamī also has Eros or Rati as its theme.

Āśvalāyana-Śrautasūtra 4.15.2 prescribes an application for the two hymns ascribed to Ghoṣā, viz. *Ṛgveda* X.39-40. It says that both the hymns are read in the Āśvina-Kratu of *prātar-anuvāka* among the *jāgata* hymns. As mentioned above, the hymns in *prātar-anuvāka* are read for the deities Agni, Uṣas and Aśvins, and the cluster of hymns read out for the Aśvins is called Āśvina-Kratu. As it is imperative to read hymns in all the seven major Vedic metres, the Jagatī metre with forty-eight syllables also finds a place here, and the hymns composed in Jagatī are called the *jāgata* hymns. The metre of *Ṛgveda* X.39-40 being Jagatī, they are included here.

X.85

The next hymn ascribed to a female seer is *Ṛgveda* X.85 which describes the marriage of Sūryā Sāvitrī. On the ritualistic application of the hymn in its entirety, Sāyaṇa has: *sūktaviniyogo laiṅgikaḥ*. Many isolated verses of this hymn, however, find several separate applications in both the Śrauta and the Gṛhya rites. A use is prescribed for the nineteenth verse of the hymn in *Āśvalāyana-Śrautasūtra* 9.8, which recommends it to be read as the *yājyā* verse in the Cāndramasīṣṭi of the Atimūrti type of *soma-yāga*, performed on a single day. If anyone wants to perform the Atimūrti rite, he is enjoined to perform first the two *iṣṭi* rites named Saurī and Cāndramasī for a month (o.c., 9.8.1). Cāndramasī should be performed in the light fortnight while the other takes place in the dark half of the month (cf. *ĀśvŚrS* 9.8.3).

The twenty-fourth verse of the Sūryā-hymn is applied in the *patnī-saṁyāja* part of the Darśapūrṇamāsa sacrifice. A chain of rites is performed in a sacrifice, and Darśapūrṇamāsa is the model of all the sacrifices of the *iṣṭi* class. In this sacrifice, prior to the principal offering occurs a number of rites, while some are performed thereafter. *Śaṁyuvāka* is such an inclusive rite that comes a little later than the main offering, while after *śaṁyuvāka* is performed the *patnī-saṁyāja*. A girdle of *mauñjī* grass that was tied to the waist of the *yajamāna*'s wife at the beginning of the sacrifice is untied during this *patnī-saṁyāja* in accompaniment of X.85.24. Either the *hotṛ* priest or the *adhvaryu*, while untying it, utters this verse (cf. *ĀśvŚrS* 1.11.3).[1] *Kātyāyana-Śrautasūtra* 3.8.2, however, differs a little and enjoins that the wife herself has to untie the girth.

The Sūryā hymn plays a significant role in the nuptial rite, a Gṛhya ceremony. *Āpastamba-Gṛhyasūtra* 1.7.1f. says that in the nuptial rite customs widely vary according to the practices current among various peoples of various localities, but *Āpastamba-Gṛhyasūtra* prescribes only those customs and rites which are common to all. Nearly the entire Sūryā-hymn is relevant in the nuptial rite. *Ṛgveda* III.22.3c states that the father should recite *sūryāyai bhāvavṛttam* in order that his daughter may procure a suitable husband. This was, therefore, probably a regular designation of the eight stanzas, i.e. *Ṛgveda* X.85.6-13, in the Brāhmaṇa-style (cf.

[1] See also the exegesis of Nārāyaṇa on it.

Bṛhd 7.123).[2] At the time of wedding, to the west of the nuptial fire are placed a stone slab (*dṛṣad*) and a grinding stone (*upalā*), while to its north-east a pot full of water is kept, where the groom, touching the bride, offers an oblation to the fire. If the bridegroom desires that only male children be born to him, he should, after the offering, face the west and holding the thumb of the bride, who is sitting facing the east, should utter the thirty-sixth verse of the hymn. If he is desirous of having female children only, he should utter the same verse this time holding the bride's other fingers (excluding the thumb). If he wishes for both male and female children he should utter the same verse while, however, holding the hairy portion of her hand including the thumb (cf. *ĀpGS* 1.7.3-5). The principal offering (*homa*) being over the *lājahoma* (whey-offering) and the *saptapadī-gamana* (taking seven steps [together]) are performed, which legitimizes the marriage. The newly-wed bride should spend the night in the house of such an aged *brāhmaṇa* woman with her spouse and offspring alive.

At the time of starting for the in-laws' house, the bride is led to mount the cart by her husband while uttering X.85.26 (cf. *ĀpGS* 8.1.8). On the way whenever they come across sacred places, trees and four-point crossings, the groom is to murmur silently (*japet*) the thirty-second verse of the hymn (cf. *ĀpGS* 1.8.6). Whenever on the way, curious people will gaze at the bride from their abodes, the groom should look back at the spectators at home silently muttering the verse X.85.33 (cf. *ĀpGS* 1.8.7). When they reach the groom's place, he should enter the bride his home, while uttering the twenty-seventh verse of the Sūryā-hymn (cf. *ĀpGS* 1.8.8). Having established at home the nuptial fire he has carried along from the nuptial fireplace, he sits the bride on a bullock's skin to the west of the fire. Thereafter the groom while touching her should offer oblation to the fire reciting four verses, viz. X.85.43-46. When the oblation is over, with the utterance of the forty-seventh

[2] Cf. Meyer, *Ṛgvidhāna*, pp. 9 and 28, also see *BṛhD* 7.123 (the *Bṛhaddevatā* attributed to Śaunaka, part II, by Macdonell).

verse the groom is enjoined to eat one portion of the curd, i.e. the oblation, and offer the remaining portion to the bride. According to another opinion, he should smear the remnant of the oblation on both their chests (cf. *ĀpGS* 1.8.9). The newly-wed couple should observe austerity (*brahmacarya*) for three or twelve nights and on completion of the *vrata* (austerity) the groom should give away the bride's wedding garment to a person who knows the Sūryā-hymn (cf. *ĀpGS* 1.8.13).

X.86

As stated earlier, *Ṛgveda* X.86 is a dialogue hymn ascribed to Indra, Indrāṇī and Vṛṣākapi. It is read out by *brāhmaṇācchaṁsin*, an assistant of the *hotṛ* priest in the fourth day of the Pṛṣṭhya-ṣaḍaha, a variety of *soma* sacrifice to be performed through six days. The hymn is recited in the same manner of the *hotṛ*'s recitation of the first verse of the *ājya-śastra* (cf. *AiBr* 30.3 and *ĀśvSrS* 8.3.4). *Āśvalāyana-Śrautasūtra* 8.3.5 says that though *Ṛgveda* X.86 is read out in the manner of the first *mantra* of *ājya-śastra* allotted to the *hotṛ* priest, this hymn should be read in Paṅkti metre and not in the metre of that particular *mantra* of the *ājya-śastra*.

In another application, *brāhmaṇācchaṁsin* recites X.86 in Paṅkti metre in the *śilpa-śāstra* on the sixth day of the Pṛṣṭhya-ṣaḍaha (cf. *ĀśvŚrS* 8.4.6, 9), an application also attested at *Aitareya Brāhmaṇa* 30.3.

X.95, 107-09, 127

Regarding the next five hymns ascribed to women seers, viz. X.95, 107-09 and 125, Sāyaṇa says *gato viniyogaḥ*, and so these may be applied in *prātar-anuvāka* and *āśvina-śastra*.

Aitareya Āraṇyaka 3.2 prescribes an application for X.127. It first describes a number of *ariṣṭa*s (signs) to be taken as signalling an imminent death, some of which are perceived when one is awake, and some in dreams. The *ariṣṭa*s seen in dream, ten in number, are as follows:

1. a man with dark complexion and black teeth beating the person in concern,
2. a boar hitting him,
3. a monkey mounting on him,
4. a wind blowing him away,
5. a person eating gold and throwing it out,
6. he himself licking honey,
7. he himself eating a lotus stalk,
8. a person holding a red lotus,
9. he himself being carried by a donkey or a boar, and
10. a black cow with a black calf being led towards south by a man wearing a garland of red flowers.

Aitareya Āraṇyaka prescribes that if a man dreams anything from the above-mentioned list, he must keep a fast, prepare some *caru* (rice cooked in milk), offer it with each verse of the Rātri-Sūkta, i.e. *Ṛgveda* X.127 and feed brāhmaṇas with rice, and this will help him out of the impending danger (cf. *AiBr* 3.2.4).[3]

X.134

Sāyaṇa again has *gataḥ sūktaviniyogaḥ* on the application of the entire *Ṛgveda* X.134, but he does mention a specific *viniyoga* for the two *tṛca*s (triads), i.e. three consecutive verses, of this hymn. In the *catur-viṁśa* sacrifice of the *mādhyandina-savana* (the midday oblation of *soma* juice), *acchāvāka*, an assistant of the *hotṛ* priest, recites ten pairs of *stotriya-anurūpa* verses, among which X.134.1-3 are read as the fifth *stotriya-tṛca*, its pairing *anurūpa-tṛca* being the next verses 4-6 of the same hymn (cf. *ĀśvŚrS* 8.4.4). Thus, the second half of verse 6, ascribed to the female seer Godhā, manages somehow to find a ritualistic use, but, the following seventh verse, ascribed to her, is ignored and has not been allotted a separate application.

---

[3] Also see the commentary of Sāyaṇa thereat.

On the ritualistic application of the next hymn ascribed to a woman seer, viz. *Ṛgveda* X.145, Sāyaṇa has referred to *Āpastamba-Gṛhyasūtra* 9.5.8 prescription. If a woman wants to get rid of her co-wife, she may perform a rite in which a herb called *pāṭhā* is mainly used. With the first verse of X.145 the herb is dug out, while the verses following are rubricated to rouse the potential magical power in the herb (*abhimantrayet*). Thereafter, the wife ties up the hidden herb in her hand, and in accompaniment with the final verse embraces her husband in such a way as the herb comes in touch with him.

X.151

On the application of the next hymn ascribed to a female seer, viz. X.151, Sāyaṇa says: *laiṅgiko viniyogaḥ*, meaning that this hymn of Śraddhā Kāmāyanī may be used in certain rituals depending on its internal evidences.

X.153

The next hymn dealt within this dissertation is X.153 by the mothers of Indra. It is recited by the *maitrā-Varuṇa* alias *praśāstṛ*, an assistant of the *hotṛ*, as the *yājyā* verse in the second phase (*paryāya*) of the *atirātra*, a variety of the *soma* sacrifice (cf. *ĀśvŚrS* 6.4.10). In *atirātra*, three phases are held in the night, in each of which all the four assistants of the *hotṛ* priest recite one *śastra* (i.e. a group of hymns prescribed for being read in rituals) each. Thus, four *śastra*s are read out in each *paryāya*, these being preceded by four *stotra*s (i.e. a group of hymns prescribed to be sung in rituals).

This hymn is also read in the *brahma-śāstra* of *prātaḥ-savana* in the *mahā-vrata*. This last is a special day in the Gavām-ayana sacrifice. The rite is performed almost throughout a whole year (361 days, to be exact). It is divided in three parts. The first part is called *pūrva-pakṣa*, the second one *viṣuva* and the final one, *uttara-pakṣa*. *Pūrva-pakṣa* is performed over 180 days, while the intermediate 181st day is termed *viṣuva*, after which *uttara-pakṣa* goes on during the next 180 days. Both *pūrva-* and *uttara-pakṣa*s are considered to have six months comprising thirty days (6 × 30 = 180). In *pūrva-pakṣa* the first month has thirty-two days, but the next four months all have thirty days each, while the sixth month has only twenty-eight days. In *uttara-pakṣa*, however, all the six months have equally thirty days. In *pūrva-pakṣa*, the *iṣṭi*-rites are performed in a prescribed order. After the expiry of the first 180 days, comes the *viṣuva* day, the prime day in the Gavām-ayana. After the *viṣuva* day, the *uttara-pakṣa* begins. Here, the rites for the coming six months follow just the reverse order of the *iṣṭi*s held in *pūrva-pakṣa*. In the seventh month of *uttara-pakṣa* the opposite order of *pūrva-pakṣa* is followed up to the twenty-eighth day of the month. The twenty-ninth day is called *mahā-vrata*, as important in the Gavām-ayana as the *viṣuva* day. In it prevails the model Agniṣṭoma pattern of *soma* sacrifice, where all the *stotra*s have twenty-five *stoma*s (i.e. the song sung by the Sāmavedic priests in a *tṛca* by repeating its three verses, the complete song including the repeated ones). During the sacrifice, a gross deviation from the model sacrifice is observed in that, on the *mahā-vrata* day in *prātaḥ-savana* (i.e. the morning sacrifice performed with extracted *soma* juice) is read in addition also the *brahma-śāstra*, where *Ṛgveda* X.153 finds an application.

X.154

The next hymn ascribed to a woman seer is X.154 by Yamī Vaivasvatī. This hymn is applied in the funeral rites of an initiated *yajamāna*. If an initiated *yajamāna* dies during the *satra* or in the *ekāha* variety of the *soma* sacrifice, performed on a single day, the priests have to perform some prescribed funeral rites. The day the *yajamāna* expires, his corpse is burnt outside of the sacrificial pyre (*vedi*) in the southern direction. On return from the funeral, the priests complete the scheduled rites of that day. In next morning the regular rites are performed but with some restrictions. *Śastra, anuvacana, abhiṣṭavana* and *saṁstava*s are not repeated as usually they are, and the *abhihiṁkāra* is also omitted, contrary to the regular practice. On this day, the *ṛtvij*s go to the funerary place through the *tīrtha* (i.e. the place at the north-eastern direction of the pyre through which the priests enter) before taking the *graha*s (i.e. the utensils used to offer the *soma* juice), and circumambulate the funeral place thrice anti-clockwise. Then, they sit at four sides of the funeral place. Once they have all taken their seats, the priests of *Sāmaveda* sing the *tṛca* (consecutive three verses): *ā́yáṁ gáuḥ,* etc., i.e. *Ṛgveda* X.154.1-3, in *upāṁśu-svara* (i.e. a silent note). After their singing, the *hotṛ* takes three rounds of the funeral place anti-clockwise, chanting the very *tṛca* (cf. *ĀśvŚrS* 6.10.16-17), and along with this triad chants the *yāmi-mantra*s (i.e. verses seen by Yama) as prescribed in *Āśvalāyana-Śrautasūtra* 6.10.19-20. Of the twenty prescribed hymns in this ritual, X.154 is the penultimate one. Having uttered this *śastra*, the *hotṛ* places the pot containing the bones of the *yajamāna* on the seat where he used to sit before his death. Sāyaṇa prescribes an individual application for the first verse of this hymn. It is read out at the time of *brahma-yajña* (i.e. the recital of the Vedas in general).

X.189

Ṛgveda X.189 ascribed to Sārparājñī is chanted in the *mānasa-graha* of the *avivākya* day (cf. *ĀśvŚrS* 6.10.16-17 and 8.13). In the *satra*-type of *soma* sacrifice Daśarātra is a variety, where the tenth day is called the *avivākya*. It is a special day in comparison with the preceding nine days. On this occasion no *ṛtvij* speaks about anything done or uttered by their other counterparts, and hence the day is appropriately called *avivākya*. On this day, after the *patnī-saṁyāja*, *udgātṛ*s, the priests belonging to *Sāmaveda*, enter the *sado-maṇḍapa* (i.e. the sacrificial place), and sings in *mānasa-stotra* (i.e. they sing in their mind and not vocally) in the *tṛca Ṛgveda* X.189.1-3 (cf. *SV-Utt* 1376-78). When the *hotṛ* priest assumes that the song (*stotra*) of the *udgātṛ*s is complete, he makes the *āhava* (i.e. he calls out the *adhvaryu* priest as "*adhvaryo*") in *madhyama-svara* (i.e. the middle tone), and the *adhvaryu* makes the *pratigara* (i.e. he replies with "*ho* *hotaḥ*"). Then, the *hotṛ* reads out the *tṛca* X.189.1-3 in an *upāṁśu* note (i.e. as already told, silently moving his lips) (cf. *ĀśvŚrS* 7.13.3-6). *Aitareya Brāhmaṇa* 24.4 also mentions this application of *Ṛgveda* X.189.1-3.

The Hymn Ascribed to Niṣat and Upaniṣat

The *khila*-hymn ascribed to Niṣat and Upaniṣat beginning with *prá dhā́rā yantu mádhuno ghṛtásya,* etc. has the following application according to *Āpastamba-Gṛhyasūtra* 3.12.14. The twelfth part of the third chapter of *Āpastamba-Gṛhyasūtra* discusses the rites to be performed for the welfare of a king going to put on armours for a battle. When the king is preparing for a war, the royal priest dresses him up with armour and other weapons (cf. *ĀpGS* 3.12.1). After giving the king his armour, bow and quiver with *mantra*s chanted by himself and by the king, the priest chants *mantra*s when the chariot starts moving towards the desired direction. At this juncture, he chants *mantra*s for the steeds as well. The king should remain gazing at his arrows even as the priest chants *mantra*s over the missiles. When the king puts on his gloves to protect his hands from injuries caused by his bow-string, the priest chants a *mantra*. And, when the king is being carried away in a chariot, the priest gets on to the chariot and makes the king utter two hymns, viz. *Ṛgveda* X.174 and VIII.101.3-4 (cf. *ĀpGS* 3.12.1-12). Then, the priest glances at the king uttering three hymns, viz. *Ṛgveda* X.103, 152 and the Sauparṇa-Sūkta, i.e. *prá dhā́rā yantu,* etc.[4]

---

[4] *ApGS* 3.12.13, 3.9.14; *AiBr* 6.25.7, 8.10.4.

6

Literary Appreciation of the Select Texts and the Poetic Imageries Therein

As has already been discussed, among the twenty-seven R̥gvedic women seers enlisted at *Br̥haddevatā* 2.82-84 and *Ārṣānukramaṇī* 10.100-02, as also the four others not found in them, seventeen alone can be accepted as women in flesh and blood who can be brought under the purview of a socio-cultural study.[1] But, for a critical appreciation of the literary aspects of the writings ascribed to female seers in general, the compositions of some female seers other than the selected fourteen also deserve a close study. Though the authorship is dubious in many such cases, the way of expression is common in some of the verses ascribed to both the groups. The use of poetic imageries is more frequent in the section of compositions with doubtful authorship. Any way, an attempt may be made to evaluate the poetic aspects of all potential verses ascribed to the female seers.

Chief Elements of Oral Poetry Found in the Select Texts

R̥gveda represents a very ancient form of oral literature. Its hymns were composed and transmitted through generations orally for an undetermined long period. Since some characteristic features distinguish the oral literature from the literature in writing, one cannot be oblivious of the importance of these characteristics while attempting an appreciation of the literary aspects of the select texts. *R̥gveda* as oral literature is marked by repetitions,

---

[1] See above p. 35.

refrains, alliterations, assonance and other mnemonic devices that add flavour to its poetic character as well. Broadly following Bhattacharji (1984: 83), several motives are found to have worked in introducing these devices, such as:

(a) To make the prayer more effective in magical content, in particular to create a sort of hypnotic word-magic, effective to produce the community's awe and response to it.

(b) To memorize the hymns easily for recitation.

(c) To enhance the poetic beauty of the compositions in order to make them more appealing to the gods.

(d) To meet the requirements of metres, etc.

The select texts of the female seers are not devoid of the chief oral characteristics of *R̥gveda*, and the above-mentioned motives influenced their outcome.

An estimate of the relevant texts may at the outset be made from the viewpoint of its repetitive characteristic. In the dialogue hymn of Lopāmudrā and Agastya in the first book of *R̥gveda*, a phrase in the Triṣṭubh metre, *yé cid dhí pū́rva r̥tasā́pa* (I.179.2a), has a counterpart in Anuṣṭubh *yé cit pū́rva r̥tasā́pa* (X.154.4d) which occurs also in *Atharvaveda* (XVIII.2.15a). This suggests that the seer of I.179.2 may have borrowed the phrase from the older poets and only inserted the monosyllabic indeclinable *hí* to suit her own metre or, the case may have also been just the opposite.

In connection with this hymn, it may be noted, interestingly, that Agastya is the composer of a bunch of hymns from *R̥gveda* I.165-190, and he often repeats the same phrases whenever theme and metre would agree. The line *vidyā́m eṣā́m vr̥jánaṁ jīrádānuṁ* has been repeated in eighteen hymns among the twenty-six hymns of Agastya, but curiously not in the dialogue hymn of Lopāmudrā and Agastya, i.e. I.179, though the hymns immediately preceding and following it incorporate the repetition, and everywhere the line is placed at the end of the concluding verses of the hymns concerned.[2] Its theme being rather uncommon, *Ṛgveda* I.179 shares almost no repetition with the other twenty-five hymns of Agastya within the above periphery in *Ṛgveda*. But, the second verse of I.179 has a parallel in the hymn of Yamī Vaivasvatī: *yé cit pū́rva ṛtasā́pa ṛtā́vāna ṛtāvṛ́dhaḥ* (X.154.4). These two verses from two different female seers have nothing in common as regards their themes, yet they sound very similar. The first and the tenth books of *Ṛgveda* being of later origin in contradistinction to the rest of it, it is difficult to assert who borrowed from whom. It may also be possible that both the composers coined the popular phrase from the earlier poets, as the case might be in *Ṛgveda* III.4.11; VII.2.11 and/or X.70.11, with a minor change to suit their own verses.

The last line of verse 5 of *Ṛgveda* IV.18, ascribed to Aditi, runs in the praise of Indra. The expression *ā́ ródasī apṛṇād jā́yamānaḥ* thereat finds a parallel at X.45.6b, where the same phrase is said of Agni.

In *Ṛgveda* V.28.3, a verse attributed to Viśvavārā, a female seer of Atri's family, the phrase *sáṁ jāspatyáṁ suyámam ā́ kṛṇuṣva* is found to have a counterpart at X.85.23, this also from another female seer, Sūryā, the daughter of Savitṛ (cf. *sáṁ jāspatyáṁ suyámam astu devāḥ* at line d). Both the verses in question have the same metre, Triṣṭubh, with only the verb being changed in the latter.

Interesting from various points of view, another hymn, *Ṛgveda* VIII.91 ascribed to Apālā, another female seer of Atri's family, carries some internal repetitions. This hymn runs in the way a folk tale runs, and as folk tales often repeat the same words or same expressions to retain the continuity of the storyline, this hymn of Apālā also has a typical story-telling characteristic of folklore. In the very first verse, the phrase *sunavai tvā* has been repeated in the concluding two lines to give a swing to the metre:

kanyā̀ vā́r avāyatī́ | *sómam ápi srutā́vidat* ||

---

[2] Cf. *ṚV* I.165.15d, 166.15d, 167.11d, 168.10d, 169.8d and so on for the repetition of a single phrase.

ástaṁ bháranty abravīd। *índrāya* ***sunavai tvā*** ।। *śakrā́ya* ***sunavai tvā*** ।।

The Āstāra-Paṅkti metre of the present verse should normally have a syllabic distribution like 8/8/12/12, as it is found in the next verse, i.e. VIII.91.2, and not like what is found: 7/8/10/11. An emendation by splitting the semi-vowels at a (in *kanyā̀*) and at c (in *bháranty abravīt*) would make the metre read in this way: 8/8/11/11. Dropping one syllable each at lines c and d leads to a metrical charm. Again, in the third verse cd runs thus:

śánair iva śanakáir ivén । ***drāyendo*** *pári srava* ।।

Here *śánaiḥ* (slowly) and *śanakáiḥ* (quickly) are antonyms but the alliteration sounds like a repetition giving the Anuṣṭubh metre a rhythmic undulation.

The indeclinable *kuvít* is repeated four times in a single Anuṣṭubh verse, viz. VIII.91.4, to maintain the repetitive character of the hymn. The final verse concludes a folk tale very precisely, but it does not fail to repeat the word *khé* thrice in its short span of the Anuṣṭubh metre, and even when the verse is short of three syllables than the usual thirty-two syllables of the Anuṣṭubh.

In the tenth book of *R̥gveda*, repetition occurs in some of the verses ascribed to women seers. In X.10, the famous Yama–Yamī hymn, a number of repetitions from other passages of *R̥gveda* are found. *R̥gveda* X.10.2b is a descriptive line (*sálakṣmā yád víṣurūpā bhávāti*) repeated by Havirdhāna Āṅgirasa in a following hymn to Agni, viz. X.12, at 6b. According to Bloomfield (1916: 464), in the first instance, i.e. X.10.2, the line in question appears in natural connection with the verse, while in the second instance it is unintelligible, certainly enigmatic and secondary. Grassmann (1873, s.v.) also supported this view. Another clause in the same verse, i.e. *R̥gveda* X.10.2c, is *mahásputrā́so ásurasya vīrā́ḥ*, having a close resemblance with *divásputrā́so asurasya vīrā́ḥ* by Ayāsya Āṅgirasa (*R̥V* X.67.2b). Both the clauses may have been derived from an earlier composition of Viśvāmitra, viz. *divásputrā́so ásurasya vīrā́ḥ* (*ṚV* III.53.7b).

The fifth verse of the same hymn (*ṚV* X.10) has a phrase in line b: *devás tvā́ṣṭā savitā́ viśvárūpaḥ*. This seems to have been borrowed from a verse of Prajāpati Vaiśvāmitra (*ṚV* III.55.19a). In the former verse, the following line c *nákir asya prá minā́nti vratā́ni* has prominent similarity with the line *nákiṣ ṭa etā́ vratā́ minānti* from a hymn to Agni by Parāśara Śāktya (*ṚV* I.69.7a), probably a later poet. In the Yama–Yamī hymn, 6b (*ká iṁ dadarśa ká ihá prá vocat*) was probably influenced by *kó addhā́ veda ká ihá prá vocat* of Prajāpati Vaiśvāmitra (*ṚV* III.54.5a). This latter again probably inspired the composition of *kó addhā́ veda,* etc. at *Ṛgveda* X.129.6a by Parameṣṭhin, where the poet preferred the original root *víd-* to *dṛ́ś-* used by the composer of *Ṛgveda* X.10.

The prayer to Ādityas by Gṛtsamada or Kūrma Gārtsamada (*ṚV* II.27.7c), *bṛhán mitrásya váruṇasya śárma*, was probably transformed into *bṛhán mitrásya váruṇasya dhā́ma* at *Ṛgveda* X.10.6c. Here, only the last word *śárma* of the original phrase was replaced with the synonymous *dhā́ma*, but the idea remained unaffected. In the tenth verse of *Ṛgveda* X.10, line a, *ā́ ghā tā́ gacchān úttarā yugā́ni*, has a counterpart at *Ṛgveda* III.33.8, *ā́ yát te ghóṣān úttarā yugā́ni*, again a composition of Viśvāmitra. The entire Yama–Yamī hymn has, however, only one internal repetition: in the final couple of verses, i.e. verses 13 and 14, the beautiful imagery *pári ṣvajāte líbujeva vṛkṣám* "embrace (the man) as a creeper [clings to] a tree" is repeated twice, in 13d and 14b, to augment the poetic beauty.

Ṛgveda X.39-40 are ascribed to Ghoṣā, the daughter of Kakṣīvant. At X.39, 4d invokes the twin gods Aśvins: *víśvét tā́ vāṁ sávaneṣu pravā́cya*. A reading very close to this is found at *Ṛgveda* I.51.13d: *víśvét tā́ te sávaneṣu pravā́cya*, where, however, Indra is the deity being invoked. Hence, only the numbers of the pronoun *yuṣmad* differ in these two passages, and nothing more and nothing less.

The marriage hymn, i.e. *R̥gveda* X.85, ascribed to Sūryā, the daughter of Savitr̥, has a phrase at line c of its eighteenth verse: *víśvāny anyó bhúvanābhi cáṣṭe*, which has parallels with insignificant variations in many verses scattered passim in *R̥gveda*. These include *abhí yó víśvā bhúvanāni cáṣṭe* (*R̥V* VII.61.1c) and in Kutsa Āṅgirasa's *abhi víśvāni bhúvanāni cáṣṭe* (*R̥V* I.108.1b), where only one syllable from *R̥gveda* X.85.18c is missing. The older composition of Gr̥tsamada, too, has two almost similar phrase blocs, one in *víśvāny aryó bhúvanā jajāna* (*R̥V* II.35.2d) and the other in *víśvāny anyó bhúvanā jajā́na* (*R̥V* II.40.5a). All the above-mentioned parallels were sung to different gods in the background of the cosmogonic myths. This fact may suggest that this word-combination was inherited from a common source (vide Sikdar Datta 1999: 117).

The earlier composition *prá no muñcátaṁ váruṇasya pā́śāt* (*R̥V* VI.74.4c) has a very close parallel in *prá tvā muñcāmi váruṇasya pā́śāt* at *R̥gveda* X.85.24a. The verb in dual number in the prior composition was replaced by its singular form to suit the purpose of the latter. The famous refrain *jī́vema śarádaḥ śatám* of *R̥gveda* VII.66.16c was borrowed with a change of person in the verb in *jī́vāti śarádaḥ śatám* (*R̥V* X.85.39d).

There are more cases of resemblance in the celebrated marriage hymn. The phrase-structure *víśvam ā́yur vyàśnutam* of X.85.42b has close similarity with *víśvam ā́yur vyàśnutaḥ* of VIII.31.8b, and with *víśvam ā́yur vyàśnavat* of I.93.3d. The mode of blessings perhaps had such a particular phrase pattern.

Again in *R̥gveda* X.85, where the bride is blessed to be pleasant towards the biped and quadruped members of her in-laws' family, the phrase *śáṁ no bhava dvipáde śáṁ cátuṣpade* is repeated in the final lines of both verses 43-44. This is again perhaps borrowed from an older composition *śáṁ no bhūtaṁ dvipáde śáṁ cátuṣpade* (*R̥V* VI.74.1d). In the earlier composition, the deities were Soma and Rudra, and hence the dual of the verb has been substituted by a singular in the marriage hymn. In another verse of the tenth book of *Ṛgveda*, the above-mentioned phrase bloc surfaces again with a change in the verb *śáṁ no astu dvipáde śáṁ cátuṣpade* (*ṚV* X.165.1d).

Some internal repetitions may also be observed in this hymn. The word *samrā́jñī* has been repeated for four times in verse 46, and the prefix *sám* has been repeated for five times in a single verse, the last one in this hymn, X.85.47.

Ṛgveda X.107 is attributed to Dakṣiṇā, the daughter of Prajāpati. Here, the term *dákṣiṇā* is repeated five times in verse 7, while in verse 9, the word *jigyuḥ* is repeated four times.

Ṛgveda X.108 is a dialogue between Saramā and the Paṇis. In this hymn also, internally, the phrase *katháṁ rasā́yā ataraḥ páyāṁsi* at 1d has been nearly repeated at 2d: *táthā rasā́yā ataraṁ páyāṁsi*. The phrase *góbhir áśvebhir vásubhir nyṛ̀ṣṭaḥ* at verse 7 exhibits a parallel at *Ṛgveda* VII.90.6b: *góbhir áśvebhir vásubhir híraṇyaiḥ*.

The spiritual (*ādhyātma*) hymns of *Ṛgveda* are in major part accumulated in its tenth book. They share some common features, of which repetition is an important one. These hymns, viz. the hymns to Viśvakarman (*ṚV* X.82), Vāc (*ṚV* X.125) and Hiraṇyagarbha (*ṚV* X.121) have some internal repetitions, presenting in addition a few thematic similarities. A phrase found in the hymn of Vāc, the daughter of Ambhṛṇa, *paró divā́ pará enā́ pṛthivyā̀* (*ṚV* X.125.8c), corresponds to 5a of *Ṛgveda* X.82. Some internal repetitions characterize these spiritual verses, e.g. the word *viśvátaḥ* is found used no less than four times in a single verse, viz. *Ṛgveda* X.81.3, to emphasize the all-pervasiveness of God. Similarly, in *Ṛgveda* X.121 *kásmai devā́ya havíṣā vidhema* is the refrain in all the verses except the last one, doubtless a later addition. In the hymn of Vāc too, one finds that each and every verse begins with the pronoun *ahám* or its inflected form. They frequent the entire hymn to establish the supremacy of the self, i.e. of the seer herself.

The second hemistich of verse 6 of *Ṛgveda* X.134 and the whole verse 7 are ascribed to Godhā. The third and fourth lines of verse 6 carry the refrain of the previous five verses of the hymn, viz. *devī́ jánitry ajījanad bhadrā́ jánitry ajījanat*. Verse 7 of the same hymn is devoid of the aforesaid refrain, but it has an internal repetition of the indeclinable *náki*.

R̥gveda X.145, ascribed to Indrāṇī, has a repetitive application of various inflected forms of the word *úttarā*, as in *úttarāham úttara úttaréd úttarābhyaḥ* (*R̥V* X.145.3ab).

R̥gveda X.154, attributed to Yamī, the daughter of Vivasvant, has a refrain in the final line of four verses of the total five verses it comprises, viz. *tā́ṁś cid evā́pi gacchatāt*.

R̥gveda X.159, attributed to Śacī, the daughter of Puloman, has an entire verse, the fourth one, which corresponds to that of Abhivarta Āṅgirasa with a single change at line d, i.e. *asapatnā́* in place of *asapatnáḥ* in *R̥gveda* X.174.4d. The verse of Śacī runs thus:

yénéndro havíṣā kr̥tvy। *ábhavad dyumny ùttamáḥ*।।
idáṁ tád akri devā। *asapatnā́ kílābhuvam*।। —*R̥V* X.159.4

A Survey of the Figures of Speech Used in the Select Texts

The poetic figures of the select texts may be examined from the view of traditional Sanskrit poetics. In the first verse of the very first hymn in the select texts, attributed to Romaśā (*R̥V* I.126.7), line a presents an alliteration (*anuprāsa*) of the sound *p*, viz. *úpopa me párā mr̥̄́śa*, and line b bears the alliterative use of the sound *m* as well as of dentals like *th*, *d* and *n*, viz. *mā́ me dabhrā́ṇi manyathāḥ*. An alliterated *m* may also be found at line c: *sárvāhám asmi romaśā́*. The final line of the verse has a splendid simile (*upamā*) in *gandhā́rīṇām ivāvikā́*, where the poet compares herself as mature and full of hair as a ewe of Gandhāra. Though the poet is known as Romaśā even in the indices of the *R̥gveda*, the epithet "hairy" (*romaśā́*) is used as her name, which most likely is not her distinctive appellation.

Alliteration again appears in the next verse of our select texts. In

Ṛgveda I.179.1 of Lopāmudrā, *pāda* a has ***ś****arádaḥ* ***ś****a****ś****ramāṇā́*, with a prominent alliteration of *ś*, while line b has a repetitive sequence of *ṣ* and *s* (*doṣā́ vá****s****tor u****ṣ****á****s****o,* etc.). Again, in this verse commencing with *pūrvī́r ahám,* etc. a spontaneous description, regarded as a figure of speech in Sanskrit poetics (*svabhāvokti*), can be detected, describes as it the course of action and the physical appearance of the speaker in a beautiful lyrical way.[3] The second verse of the hymn has an alliteration of *s* in line a, *yé cid dhí pū́rva ṛta****s****ā́pa* *ā́****s****ant* ***s****ākám,* etc. where a note of paronomasia (*yamaka*) is heard in *sāpa* and *sāka.*[4] It may be remembered (vide Ghosh 1998: 31) that in the Sanskrit language *p* and *k* sounds are interchangeable; cf. e.g. *takman-* for **tapman-*, etc. The same figure of speech is hinted also in *Ṛgveda* X.134.7, a verse attributed to another female seer, Godhā, where at line c, *pakṣébhir apikakṣébhir*, etc. *pakṣébhir* and *kakṣébhir* can be treated as offering an instance of paronomasia on the aforesaid ground.

A fine example of alliteration of the *n*-sound is heard in the third hymn of our select texts by female seers, viz. *Ṛgveda* III.33, where such lines as 8d are witnessed: *mā́* ***no ní*** *kaḥ puruṣatrā́* ***n****ámaste*. The tenth verse of the hymn has again an alliterative use of *n* at cd: ***n****í te* ***n****aṁsai pipyā****n*** *éva yóṣā/ máryāyeva ka****n****yà śaśvacái te*. The metaphorical simile (*rūpaka*-based *upamā*) in this stanza is worth noticing: the rivers bend down (for Viśvāmitra) as the milking mother does (to her child), or does a maiden, to give her man a hug.

In the present study, the next verse worthy of mention for its poetic brilliance is *Ṛgveda* IV.18.6 attributed to Aditi. It commences with *etā́ arṣanty alalābhávanti,* etc. and means: "these gurgling rivers, who, soared up, are proceeding, making various sounds. Ask them what they are saying, and who broke the cloud, the barrier of waters." The lucidity (*prasāda-guṇa* or *artha-vaimalya*) is probably

---

[3] *svabhāvoktir durūhārthasvakriyārūpavarṇanam* — *SD* 10.92

[4] *saty arthe pṛthag arthāyāḥ svaravyañjanasaṁhateḥ* |
krameṇa tenaivāvṛttir yamakaṁ vinigadyate || — *SD* 10.8

the key ingredient to the beauty of this verse. Moreover, the power of imagination in hearing many mutterings in the gurgling noise of the inanimate rivers enhances its poetic charm.

The next piece of poetry is *Ṛgveda* V.28 in our selection. Viśvavārā, the daughter of Atri, is credited with its authorship. This six-verse hymn has *sámiddha* or *samidhyá* in all its verses save at nos. 3 and 6. The words, however, may be considered to be the "catch-word" of the hymn, a conception propounded much later by the Sanskrit poeticians. Clusters of sounds like *dhy*, *ddh* and *dhv* occur in profusion in the fourth, fifth and sixth verses of this hymn.[5] The third verse of this hymn is a fair specimen of the above-mentioned *svabhāvokti* figure of speech for its lyrical description:

ágne śárdha mahaté sáubhagāya ।
táva dyumnā́ny uttamā́ni santu ॥

sáṁ jāspatyáṁ suyámam ā́ kṛṇuṣva ।
śatrūyatā́m ábhi tiṣṭhā máhāṁsi ॥

O Agni, show yourself off for the sake of great good fortune. Let your brilliance be very high. Let our united household be easy to control. Surmount the great powers of those who act as our rivals.
— Jamison and Brereton (2014: II.690)

The fourth stanza of the same hymn has an alliteration of *dh* in line d: *sám a**dh**varéṣv i**dh**yase*; which almost onomatopoeically expresses the sound of growing flames (cp. the adverbial use of "*dhak dhak*" in Bengali or "*dhū dhū*" in Hindi to modify the act of burning).

Apālā, the daughter of Atri, has to her credit the hymn VIII.91 of *Ṛgveda*. Alliteration of the sound-cluster *nd* is to be heard in the final foot of the third verse: *í**nd**rāye**nd**o pári srava*. Again, at 4abc, alliterations of *k*, *v*, *t* and *r* are attested:

kuvíc* chá*kat* *kuvít* *kárat । ***kuvín* no *vá*syasas *kárat*** ॥
kuvít* pa*t*idvíṣo ya*tī́r । . . .

[5] Cf. *Harṣacaritam*, the introductory verse.

Ṛgveda X.10 is ascribed to the twin siblings, Yama and Yamī, the son and daughter of Vivasvant. Being a dialogue hymn it possesses a rather free flow of expression. The verses ascribed to Yamī have some poetic qualities worth mentioning. Verse 1 has an alliterated *dh* at cd:

> *pitúr nápātam ā́ da**dh**īta ve**dh**ā́* ।
> *á**dh**i kṣámi pratarā́ṁ dī́**dh**yānaḥ* ।।

Verse 3 of the same hymn offers a *luptopamā* (simile with a dropped part) according to Sāyaṇa. Clarifying, he quotes that at line d, *jányuḥ pátis tanvàm ā́ viviśyāḥ*, where *jányuḥ* means "*like* the procreator".[6]

Verse 7 has alliterations of *y* and *m* at line a, viz. ***y**a**m**ásya **m**ā **y**a**m**yàṁ kā́**m**a,* etc. The third and fourth lines together present two similes, viz. at c *jāyéva pátye tanvàṁ riricyām* (like a wife to her husband I will expose my physique [to you]), and at d *ví cid vṛ́héva ráthyeva cakrā́* (we will move forward in many ways as the two wheels of a chariot draw it forward).

Verse 9 has *vṛttyānuprāsa* of *y* and *m*, as well as a *śrutyānuprāsa* of *y* and *j* in the final foot: ***y**a**m**ī́r **y**a**m**ásya bibhṛyād ájāmi*, where *yamī* and *jāmi* are examples of *śrutyānuprāsa* as *y* and *j* both palatals sound alike in Indian tradition.[7]

Yamaka is to be found in verse 13, where line a reads thus: ***bató batā**si yama,* etc. Here, the first *bataḥ* means "weak" ('jerk' — Jamison and Brereton 2014: III.1383) while the second *bata* is an interjection exclaiming pity. A chain of simile (*mālopamā*) is witnessed in cd:

> *anyā́ kíla tvā́ṁ kakṣyèva yuktáṁ* ।
> *pári ṣvajāte líbujeva vṛkṣám* ।।
>
> Other woman clings to you as the girth (to a horse), [and] embraces you deeply like a creeper a tree.

---

[6] *janyuḥ iti luptopamā etat. Janyur iva* — Sāyaṇa

[7] Vide *jakārayakārayor ekatra sthāne tālāv uccāryatvāt sādṛśyam* — *SD,* chap. 10

Ṛgveda X.39-40 are ascribed to Ghoṣā. In the first hymn is found a number of poetic figures as listed below. In verse 6, line b reads: *putrā́yeva pitárā máhyaṁ śikṣatam* which may be understood either as "give me treasures, as parents give to their son" (cf. *śikṣataṁ dhanaṁ dattam:* Sāyaṇa), or alternatively as "teach me in the same way the parents teach their son".

Verse 10 offers a plenty of alliterations, e.g. the alliteration of the sound-cluster *śv* at line a, viz. *yuváṁ **śv**etáṁ pedáve '**śv**inā́**śv**am.* A *yamaka* in the word *nava* is witnessed at line b: ***navá**bhir vā́jair **nava**tī́ ca vājínam.* At c, an alliterated *d* is found in ***dad**athur **d**rāvayátsakham,* etc. An alliteration of *bh* is heard in the final line, viz., ***bh**ágaṁ ná nṛ́**bh**yo hávyaṁ mayo**bh**úvam.*

In verse 14 of the same hymn a sequence of similes is found to call it *mālopamā* (a chain of similes): *bhṛ́gavo ná rátham* in line b, *yóṣaṇām ná márye* in line c, and *nítyaṁ ná sūnúṁ tánayaṁ dádhānāḥ* in line d. The verse, in its entirety, means:

> O Aśvins, I sing this prayer for you, just in the way the Bhṛgus chiselled a chariot. We have clasped it to ourselves like a dashing youth a maiden, holding it close like our own son who continues our lineage. —tr. of cd.: Jamison and Brereton, op. cit. p. 1441

In *Ṛgveda* X.40.1, a *yamaka* can faintly be come across in line a, *rátham̐ yā́ntaṁ **kúha kó ha** vām,* where *kúha* and *kó ha* sound almost similar, in spite of the vocalic difference between the high vowel *u* and the mid mean *o* and semasiological difference between *kúha* and *kó ha*. A chain of similes is attested also in the second verse of the same hymn, at cd, which reads:

> *kó vāṁ śayutrā́ vidháveva deváraṁ* ।
> *máryaṁ ná yóṣā kṛṇute sadhásthā ā́* ।।
>
> Who takes you to bed, like a widow her brother-in-law, or to a rendezvous like a maiden a dashing youth? —tr. op. cit. p. 1443

In verse 3, alliteration of the sound-sequence *jar* appears in line a (*prātár **jar**ethe **jar**aṇéva kā́payā*), while a simile is found in line d:

rājaputréva sávanā́va gacchathaḥ

You two reach the *soma*-sacrifice, like a prince [= princes].

The fourth verse of this hymn has again a simile in line a:

yuvā́ṁ mṛgéva vāraṇā́ mṛgaṇyávaḥ

You two are sought after like the elephants (sought after by hunters).

Another simile is attested in verse 6 at lines cd:

yuvór ha mákṣā páry aśvinā mádhv+ ।
āsā́ bharata niṣkṛtáṁ ná yóṣaṇā ।।

The bee holds the honey of you two encircled with her mouth, O Aśvins, as a young woman (holds) a tryst (within her mouth) [= keeps quiet about it]. — tr. op. cit., p. 1444

Readers come across yet another simile at 9c, where the expression *nivanéva síndhavaḥ* suggests that "the rivers flow for him as if into a valley (the herbs and plants have grown in plenty for the young husband)". Verses 10-11 exhibit *svabhāvokti* in describing the poet's desire lyrically.

In *Ṛgveda* X.60.6, a verse ascribed to Agastya-svasṛ, a repeated sequence of alliterated *n* and *r* is heard in lines c and d: *paṇī́n **n**y **à**k**r**amī**r** abhí víśvā**n** rāja**n** **n**a**r**ādhásaḥ.*

The famous marriage hymn of *Ṛgveda*, X.85, attributed to Sūryā, is full of metaphors which add to its lyrical charm. Wonderful metaphors are strewn all over the six verses (6-8, 10-12) which describe Sūryā's journey to her consort's home, to express the intense desire of the bride to get to her groom's abode. Verse 6 says that the *ráibhī* hymns were Sūryā's companions who were to accompany her in her husband's abode, the *nārāśaṁsī́* hymns were the maids to serve her there, and her beautiful garment was purified (or decorated, as Sāyaṇa) by the *gā́thā*s. The seventh verse tells that when Sūryā went to her husband, her thought was the cushion of her car (cf. *cíttiḥ devatā:* Sāyaṇa), her eyes were their own anointment, while heaven and the earth were the interior part (*kóśa-*) of her carriage. Using other similes, the eighth verse says that the *stómas* were the crossbars of the pole (*pratidháyaḥ*) of her chariot, and the Kurī́ra metre formed its pillow (*opaśáḥ*).[8] In the tenth verse it is said that when Sūryā went to her husband's abode, her mind was the chariot, and the heaven formed its canopy (*dyáur āsīd utá cchadíḥ*). With the aid of yet other chariot-related similes, 11cd says that

> All ears were thy two chariot-wheels, and the heavenly path became the road for your chariot.

The twelfth verse describes the spirit-fashioned car of Sūryā (vide Griffith):

> Two wheels were the two ears of Sūryā (eager to hear the attributes of her husband), the axis was the wind ("Breath was hammered in as the axle" — Jamison and Brereton op. cit. p. 1522), and Sūryā rode the spirit-fashioned chariot (*áno manasmáyam*) while going to her husband.

A beautiful metaphor is found in the eighteenth verse:

> *pūrvāparáṁ carato māyáyaitáu* ।
> *śíśū krīdantau pári yāto adhvarám* ॥
>
> These two (sun and the moon) play like two children running one after the other, as they go round and round in sacrifice.

Verse 20 describes the real chariot which was to carry Sūryā to the abode of her spouse; owing to its lyrical description, it may be considered as a fair specimen of *svabhāvokti*:

> *sukiṁśukáṁ śalmalíṁ viśvárūpaṁ* ।
> *híraṇyavarṇaṁ suvṛ́taṁ sucakrám* ॥
>
> *ā́ roha sūrye amṛ́tasya lokáṁ* ।
> *syonáṁ pátye vahatúṁ kṛṇuṣva* ॥
>
> O Sūryā, step into the chariot which is decked with beautiful

---

[8] Chowdhury (1931: 62-65) has, however, conclusively proved that the word means "the circular sliced-bamboo rim".

kiṁśuká flowers, which is made of *śālmali* wood,[9] which is beautiful in every aspect (*viśvárūpam*), which is adorned with the colour of gold, which is well covered (or smooth going: *suṣṭhuvartanam*, as Sāyaṇa), and which has good wheels, [and] do make your wedding procession a comfortable place for your husband.

— tr. of d according to Jamison and Brereton, op. cit., p. 1523

In *Ṛgveda* X.86, a dialogue hymn ascribed to Indra, Indrāṇī and Vṛṣākapi, two verses, viz. the sixteenth and the following, are ascribed to Indrāṇī. These are apparently totally contradictory in meaning to each other, and many scholars think that their meanings are also obscured by the guise of obscenity. Though later rhetoricians like Mammaṭa Bhaṭṭa or Viśvanātha Kavirāja could not regard it as a figure of speech, ancient poeticians of India did accept puzzle (*prahelikā*) as a kind of *śabdālaṁkāra*, which might be attested also in this couple of verses.

Lyrical way of expression makes *Ṛgveda* X.95, the famous dialogue hymn of Purūravas and Urvaśī, an excellent piece of literature. In the second verse thereof is found a number of figures of speech, cf.:

kím etā́ vācā́ kṛṇavā távāhám ।
prā́kramiṣam uṣásām agriyéva ॥

púrūravaḥ púnar ástaṁ párehi ।
durāpanā́ vā́taïvāhám asmi ॥

What we will do with these talks, [since] like the first dawn I have left you behind! Hence O Purūravas, go home back, like wind I cannot be attained (by you).

Here in line b *utprekṣā* is noticed, as there is an acute similarity between the first dawn and the speaker in both of their leaving others behind.[10] The same figure of speech occurs at d, where Urvaśī

[9] "The silk-cotton tree" Böhtlingk and Roth, s.v.

[10] Cf. *bhavet sambhāvanotprekṣā prakṛtasya parātmanā* — *SD*, chap. 10

compares her inaccessibility with that of the wind. And, in line c, alliterations of *p* and *r* are evident: ***púrū**r**avaḥ* ***púnar*** *ástaṁ* ***pár**ehi*. A rather complex figure of speech, *kāvyaliṅga* is used in verse 15, where the cause stated in line c has been explained in line d:[11]

> No [lasting] friendship can be possible with women, [because] their hearts are [the hearts] of hyenas.

> *ná vái stráiṇāni sakhyā́ni santi* ।
> *sālāvṛkā́ṇāṁ hṛ́dayāny etā́* ।।

In *Ṛgveda* X.107, a hymn ascribed to Dakṣiṇā, the following figures of speech are discernible. In verse 4, *yamaka* is to be found in line b, *nṛ**cákṣa**sas té abhí* ***cakṣa****te havíḥ*, where two *cakṣa*-clusters sound identical but have different meanings. While the first *cakṣa* has no particular meaning, as the compound *nṛcákṣas* as a single unit refers to a person who watches over the human beings, the second *cakṣa* is part of a verb implying "to know" or "to see". *Yamaka* is again attested in verse 5, where the similarity of vowel-consonant sequence but dissimilarity in meaning in *grāma* and *grame* of line b (*dákṣiṇāvān* ***grāma****ṇír á****gram e****ti*) makes it an example thereof. In verse 10cd, two similes are chained together to describe the beauty of the donor's house, viz.

> *bhojásyedáṁ puṣkaríṇīva véśma* ।
> *páriṣkṛtaṁ devamānéva citrám* ।।

> This house of the donor is decorated like a pool and is beautiful like a divine car.[12] (This dwelling of the benefactor is like a lotus-pond, adorned and shimmering like the palaces of the gods — Jamison and Brereton, op. cit., p. 1572)

An alliterated *d* adds to the beauty of verse 4 of *Ṛgveda* X.108, ascribed to Saramā, where lines a and b reads:

> *nā́háṁ táṁ veda dábhyaṁ dábhat sá* ।
> *yásyedáṁ dūtī́r ásaraṁ parākā́t* ।।

---

[11] Cf. *hetor vākyapadārthatve kāvyaliṅgaṁ nigadyate* — *SD*, l.c.

[12] *devamānam iva devayānam iva* — Sāyaṇa

Utprekṣā is found in the third verse of *Ṛgveda* X.109, attributed to Juhū, in which the act of non-revealing by the speaker has been compared to that of a state run by a kṣatriya at lines cd:

> *ná dūtā́ya prahyè tastha eṣā́* ।
> *táthā rāṣṭrám̐ gupitám̐ kṣatríyasya* ॥
>
> As a state protected by a kṣatriya does not reveal (its secrets) before an ambassador (sent by another king), she (Juhū) did not reveal herself before the gods' messengers.

Ascribed to Vāc, *Ṛgveda* X.125 offers a nice specimen of *utprekṣā* in its final, the eighth verse, where the speaker says "It is I who flow like the wind" (*ahám evá vā́taïva prá vāmi*): the flow of wind is the *upamāna* or *para* which has acute similarity with the unbound continuous movement of the speaker, the *upameya* or *prakṛta* in this instance.

Ṛgveda X.127 is a beautiful lyrical hymn addressed to the night goddess, ascribed to Rātri, the daughter of Bharadvāja. In its very first verse, the star-lit night appears to the poetess as a goddess graced with all splendours, watching intensely with her innumerable eyes (of stars). *Svabhāvokti*, with a suggestion of metaphor, in imagining the starry night as a deity with thousand eyes, brings a rare charm to this verse. In the fourth verse, line c conceives the home-seeking people at the approach of night as birds trying to find shelter on trees: *vṛkṣé ná vasatím̐ váyaḥ*: this may be considered as an example of the figure of speech called *dṛṣṭānta*, where a resemblance between two things having the same characteristics is established as if by mirror-reflection.[13] In lyrically expressing the world of men and animals resting at night, the fifth verse stands as an instance of the *svabhāvokti*:

> *ní grā́māso avikṣata* ।
> *ní padvánto ní pakṣíṇaḥ* ।
> *ní śyenā́saś cid arthínaḥ* ॥

---

[13] *bimbānubimbatvabhāvaḥ* and *dṛṣṭāntas tu sadharmasya vastunaḥ pratibimbanam* — *SD*, chap. 10

All men, all animals with legs, all birds with wings and even the fast moving eagles also take rest (at night).

The last line of verse 7 has a simile in saying "O Uṣas, dispel (darkness) like debts" (*úṣa ṛṇéva yātaya*), where the darkness of night has been compared with debts which make life of men miserably dark like night. Simile is witnessed also in the final and eighth verse of the hymn, at line a: *úpa te gā́ ivā́karam* (I approach you like a cow).

Godhā is said to have authored *Ṛgveda* X.134.6cd & 7, whereat 7c a *yamaka* or *vṛttyānuprāsa* is to be found in the juxtaposition of words like *pakṣébhir* and *kakṣébhir*.[14]

Ṛgveda X.145, ascribed to Indrāṇī, is called a *sapatnībādhana* hymn, applied as it was to cast a spell on the husband to drive away the influence of the woman's co-wives on him. A number of repetitions of similar sounding words, to fit in its magical contents and to charge it with magic potency, are found in this hymn. Rhetorically considered, these may be looked upon as instances of *yamaka* as well. At 3ab, *úttarā* is the catchword to work magic for the speaker, which is why it has been repeated in various senses no less than four times in the mere span of fourteen syllables:

***úttarā**hám **uttára** | **úttaré**d **úttarā**bhyaḥ* |

Similarly, *párā* in two allied but somewhat distinguished meanings is repeated twice at 4c: ***párām** eva **parā**vátam* "(I will drive my co-wife to) the farthest of the farther lands". Again, in the fifth verse the catchword is *sáha*, used in various forms to serve a certain magical purpose, viz.:

*ahám asmi **sáha**mānā́* | *-tha tvám asi **sāsahíḥ*** |
*ubhé **sáha**svatī bhūtvī́* | *sapátnī me **sahā**vahai* ||

This use of *sáha* continues to *pāda*s a and b of the next verse as well:

*úpa te 'dhāṁ **sáha**mānām* | *abhí tvādhāṁ **sáhīyasā*** |

---

[14] See earlier rhetoric discussion on *ṚV* I.179.2, p. 214.

Glimpse of the very familiar cow-and-calf simile appears at cd of the same verse: *mā́m ánu prá te máno* | *vatsáṁ gáur iva dhāvatu* (Let your mind rush after me as the cow does to its calf), even as another simile is to be seen in line e: *pathā́ vā́r iva dhāvatu* (as the water rushes to its course). Both the similes in the single verse intend to qualify the same *upameya* (i.e. your mind towards me), making this a case of *mālopamā*.

Ṛgveda X.153, ascribed to the Mothers of Indra, has, at 2c, a *lāṭānuprāsa*, where the word and its meaning remain the same but their import alone differs:[15]

tváṁ ***vṛṣan vṛ́ṣéd*** *asi*

O Vṛṣan (rain-maker)! you are indeed the bestower of desires.

This figure of speech reappears at 4ab of the next hymn, of Yamī, this time the sound-cluster being that of *ṛta*: *yé cit pū́rva* ***ṛta****sā́pa* ***ṛtā́****vāna* ***ṛtā****vṛ́dhaḥ*, and at 5a of X.159, ascribed to Śacī Paulomī: ***asapatnā́ sapatna****ghnī́,* etc. An *utprekṣa* is also attested in the second hemistich of the latter verse:

ā́ vṛkṣam anyā́sāṁ várco |
rā́dho ástheyasām iva ||

I have ripped of the lustre of the other women, like the gifts of the feckless [enemies].[16] — tr. Jamison and Brereton, op. cit., p. 1642

In the *khila*-hymn II.6.5, addressed and ascribed to Goddess Śrī, a *svabhāvokti* is found. This hymn beautifully describes Śrī (Lakṣmī) as all-golden, with a gold-and-silver garland around her neck, magnanimous and shining with her own brilliance, in whom gods take delight. To cite an example:

híraṇyavarṇāṁ háriṇīṁ | *súvarṇarajatasrajām* |
cándrāṁ híraṇmayīṁ lákṣmīṁ | *jā́tavedo mām ā́ vaha* ||

---

15 *śabdārthayoḥ paunaruktyaṁ bhede tātparyamātrataḥ*
— *SD*, chap. 10

16 *ástheyasām iva asthiratarāṇāṁ satrūṇāṁ yathā* — Sāyaṇa

Imageries Found in the Select Texts

Though the modern term "imagery" is not much older than a century or so, its use was frequent in ancient literature. The Imagist movement in the beginning of the twentieth century was a creation of the French "symbolist" poets. With the increasing importance of psychology in literary appreciation, imagery came into limelight. To understand the imageries projected in the select hymns ascribed to female poets of *R̥gveda*, this terminological expression with all its significances should be understood properly.

WHAT IS IMAGERY?

A glossary of literary terms (Abrams 1993: 86) defines "imagery" as follows:

> This term is one of the most common in modern criticism, and one of the most variable in meaning. Its applications range all the ways from "mental pictures" which, it is sometimes claimed, are experienced by the reader of a poem, to the totality of the components which make up a poem.

Elsewhere (Baldic 1990: 106) it has been defined as

> a rather vague critical term covering those uses of language in a literary work that evoke sense-impressions by literal or figurative reference to perceptible or "concrete" objects, scenes, action or argument or exposition.

Yet another source (Preminger et al. 1974) explains:

> In literary usage, imagery refers to images produced in the mind by language, whose words and statements may refer either to experiences which could produce physical perceptions were the reader actually to have those experiences, or to the sense-impressions themselves.

All these definitions lead to consider imagery as a picture-like representation of the poetic thought or experience, a picture which might be different from the original subject in question but is somehow related to it due to a similarity of appearance or to the sentiment associated with it. Imagery not only pasteurizes the experience of the poet, it also enables the reader to know the bend of the poet's mind. T.E. Hume, Ezra Pound and other poets of their group contributed much in establishing the definition of poetic imagery through their "imagist credo". The conscious use of imagery took place in poetry only after its concept was defined in the twentieth century. The term has often been applied particularly to the figurative language used in a literary work, especially to its metaphors and similes. Images suggesting further meanings and associations, in ways that go beyond the fairly simple identifications of metaphor and simile, are often called symbols.

Imagery is used in three discriminable senses to give poetry a concrete shape, as opposed to the abstract. These are as follows:

1. Imagery (i.e. "images" taken collectively) is used to signify all the objects and qualities of sense perception referred to in a literary work, whether by literal description, by allusion, or in the vehicles (the secondary references) of its similes and metaphors. The term "image" is not only meant to give a visual reproduction of the object referred to, but also of the qualities that are auditory, tactile, thermal, olfactory, gustatory and kinesthetic according to the psychologists.
2. Imagery is used, more narrowly to signify only descriptions of visible objects and scenes, especially if the description is vivid and particularized. Here, imagery may be identified with what is called *svabhāvokti alaṁkāra* in Sanskrit rhetorics. A good example of *svabhāvokti* always builds up a visual image of the object being described, e.g. in one of Rabindranath Tagore's poems (from Sahaj Pāṭh):

   chāẏār ghom 'ṭā mukhe ṭāni। āche āmāder pāṛākhāni।
   dighi tār mājh 'khān 'ṭite,। tāl 'ban tāri cāri bhite।

   bā̃kā ek saru gali beye। jal nite āse jato meye।
   bā̃ś gāch jhũke jhũke paṛe। jhuru jhuru pātāguli naṛe। …

A charming description of the shady village with its lake surrounded by palm trees, girls oft to fill water coming through the bending of a narrow lane, the trembling of the sleek leaves of stooping bamboos produce a picturesque image in the reader's mind.

3. In recent usage, imagery most commonly signifies "figurative language" specially the secondary references (vehicles) of metaphor and similes. After 1930s, critics, mostly the new critics[17] gave much stress than their predecessors on imagery, holding it to be the essential component in poetry and a major factor in poetic meaning, structure and effect.

In fact, whatsoever importance was given to the simile before twentieth century could well be applied to imagery also. To Aristotle or Vāmana, the term "imagery" was not known, but their discussion on metaphor or simile might go for imagery as well. Even after the Imagist movement the tendency of not discriminating imagery and simile/metaphor is still prevalent. The reason behind this indiscrimination is that the bases of both simile metaphor and imagery stand on the similarity of two objects or events in their appearances or in sentiments associated with them. A simile or a metaphor evolves to imagery when it gives an image, rich in suggestion of the poet's individual or personal feelings.

So far so good, in holding that imagery is a picture-like expression, the essence of which is simile, but it goes far beyond the mere similarity between two objects. Imagery creates a suggestive image which may not be even experienced by the reader before, e.g. when it is said that camel is the only means of transport in desert, it does not give birth to any picture in the hearer's mind, but when one describes camel as the ship of the desert, it certainly becomes an image suggesting the endless desert looking like an ocean, and the slow movement of the camel over it as that of a lone cargo ship. Again, when Tagore says:

---

[17] J.C. Ransom, Cleanth Brooks, Allen Tate and others.

tomār kharga ā̃dhār-mahiṣe dukhānā karila kāṭiyā ।
— from "Suprabhāt", *Sāmayik Patra*

The image of the bright dawn as a flashing sword slashing the monstrous darkness (a dark buffalo) at once comes to one's mind. This is precisely why a critic commented:

> The image must not be conceived as a material copy or thing but merely as the content of a thought in which attention is centred on sensory quality of some sort. — Downey 1929

IMAGERY TURNING INTO "SYMBOL" OR "LEITMOTIF"

A frequently repeated image in a literary work gradually becomes a symbol or leitmotif of that particular piece of literature, the recurrence of which usually indicates or supports a theme. Leitmotif, a German term meaning "the leading motif" comes from the arena of music criticism, where it was first used to describe the repeated musical themes or phrases used to denote certain characters or ideas in opera. In ancient literatures, like in that of *Ṛgveda*, such leitmotifs are often found met with. In the hymn of Sūryā, *Ṛgveda* X.85, the image of a chariot is repeatedly mentioned which would carry Sūryā, the bride, to her groom's house. There it has become a symbol of the earnest desire of the bride to reach her husband's abode *fast*.

Motif is also a literary aspect evolving from repeated imagery in a particular sequence, in many different literary works, folk tales or myths. A motif is a conspicuous element, such as a type of incident, device, reference or formula, which occurs frequently in literary works. Thus the motif of a chariot comes umpteen times in the hymns of Ghoṣā for the Aśvins, viz. *Ṛgveda* X.39-40. But, critics prefer to call it leitmotif when it occurs in a single work. According to them, the term motif is more appropriate in respect of a class of literature. Of speaking as a whole, the Ṛgvedic literature is strewn with the motifs of cow, the cow and calf pair, the man and woman pair, the paramour, and so on so forth.

THE HOW OF ṚGVEDIC IMAGERY

This apparently novel concept of imagery was well familiar to the Ṛgvedic poets. A comparison of the imagery of *Ṛgveda* with that of the classical Sanskrit literature reveals that these two streams of poetry do not belong to the same literary genre. According to Sastri (1948: 152ff.) some of the common concepts present in the mainstay of classical Sanskrit literature are absent in the Ṛgvedic poetry, e.g. the common comparison of the Himalayas in classical Sanskrit is found only once in the bulk of *Ṛgveda* (X.121.4a). The Ganges or lotus or the cool southern breeze, the emotional moon-lit night and the facts relating to cupid are absolutely unknown to *Ṛgveda*. The Ṛgvedic imagery adopts the images taken from rearing of cattle, lowing of the cows and bulls, gods and music, milk and butter, sword and skin, shipping and gold, women and angels, and so on.

The Ṛgvedic poet perceived beauty in his surroundings and in his fellow beings. As a result of this feeling, his imagery is familiar, simple, unexpected and elevated. Women and unmarried girls yielded a fruitful and lovely imagery, as they are very often seen to recur fondly. The effeminate, ascetic and pessimistic mood of the later literature is not the flavour of the *mantra* literature.

As Bergaigne (1881) pointed out, the rhetoric of the Veda is in reality a bizarre one, which seems to shock even to this day the most authoritative interpreters of *Ṛgveda*. This justifies the unexpected nature of the Ṛgvedic imagery, e.g. when Soma is figured as a lover but is suddenly imagined as a hawk or a horse with wings — unexpected, since the imagery was not by then moulded by the cliché. In this way, the Ṛgvedic poet mixes up many ideas and presents a very original imagery which is complex in nature.

The most part of the Vedic literature is not ornamental in character, as they were possibly close to colloquial speech-style of that age, but quite a major part of the Ṛgvedic poetry contains good image. Bhattacharji (1984: 93) finds the imagery in ancient India not merely decorative but also functional, i.e. "magical in intent". Bhattacharji divides simile into three principal categories:

viz. (1) spontaneously poetic; (2) intentionally decorative; and (3) frankly magical. In *Ṛgveda Saṁhitā*, purely decorative similes are rarely found, with the poetic and magical ones prevailing there, and they are often not mutually exclusive.

The similes found in *Ṛgveda* can be classified in six heads on the basis of their chief characteristics:

1. Inanimate nature, viz. rivers, lakes, trees, creepers, etc.
2. The animal world with familiar correspondences of traits and characteristics.
3. Human relationships such as parental, conjugal or that pertaining to siblings and so on.
4. Various professions of the people of the age.
5. Objects from everyday life.
6. Cosmic objects and incidents.

The common man's empirical world is latent in the poet's Aesthetic Universe, to make it explicit, the poet takes to imagery. Through the facts of mundane life, the poet implies their inner significance. Selecting the known facts, the poet transmutes them to bring out their inner spiritual character. Imagery does perform this function in general, and so does the Ṛgvedic imagery in particular.

The Ṛgvedic poet chose his imagery from the most common-place things and affairs. He poeticized the mundane material and presented it in a new and fresh form. A good portion of the Ṛg-vedic poetry bears evidence to the fact that the ancient poets had eyes keen and acute enough to penetrate into the subtleties and complexities of the simple, and they could enhance the charm of their poetry with its flavour. This simplicity has attributed to the freshness and innocence breathing throughout the entire range of imagery of the Ṛgvedic poetry. The Ṛgvedic imageries are generally characterized by their basis of solid irrefutable facts of existence, rather than through fanciful recreations.

AN ESTIMATE OF INDIVIDUAL IMAGERIES IN THE LITERATURE OF THE ṚGVEDIC WOMEN SEERS

Going through the literature ascribed to women seers in *Ṛgveda*, the connoisseur relishes occasional glimpses of imagery, a discussion of which may now be attempted to find out if they possess the aforesaid six broad characteristics of simile or not.

Inanimate Nature

The inanimate nature unfolds itself in the imagery used by Yamī in X.10.13d: *líbujeva vṛkṣám*, where she accuses her brother Yama for allowing women, but not her to embrace him in a way a creeper clings to a tree. Here the image is visual-cum-tactual, since the tight grip of the creeper clenching a tree can be felt by the reader.

Urvaśī in *Ṛgveda* X.95.2 and Vāc in X.125.8 identify themselves with the wind, in two different contexts, though: the former expresses her inaccessibility through the image of wind (*durāpanā́ vā́ta ivāhám asmi*), while the latter feels herself identical with the eternally-flowing wind (*ahám evá vā́ta-iva prá vāmi*), in which case the image is of kinesthetic category.

The starry night is imagined by poetess Rātri as a goddess looking upon the earth with her innumerable eyes in *Ṛgveda* X.127.1 (*rā́trī vyakhyad āyatī́ | purutrā́ devy àkṣábhiḥ*).

The Animal World

The animate world of animals has also been exploited to create imagery, as a verse ascribed to Romaśā (*ṚV* I.126.7) would show:

> *úpopa me párā mṛśa | mā́ me dabhrā́ṇi manyathā |*
> *sárvāhám asmi romaśā́ | gandhā́rīṇām ivāvikā́ ||*

> Come close to me, give me a deep embrace, I am hairy all over my physique — like a little ewe of the Gandhāris.

Here the hairiness of the speaker compared to that of a ewe gives not only visual but a tactile image as well, as it imbibes an invitation for a tight hug. Elsewhere (at *ṚV* III.33.1), Vipāś and Śutudrī, two rivers, swiftly move like two contending mares with loosened rein, and like two bright cows that lick their calves:

gā́v eva śubhré mātárā rihāṇé । *vípāṭ chutudrī́ páyasā javete* ।

In *Ṛgveda* X.39.13, a verse ascribed to Ghoṣā, the Aśvins are told to have freed the quail from the jaws of the wolf:

vṛ́kasya cid vártikām antárāsyād ।
yuvám̐ śácībhir grasitā́m amuñcatam ॥[18]

Yāska believed that the wolf was none other than the bright Sun. This is a frequent image, and the quail stands for the dawn swallowed by the dark night. At *Ṛgveda* X.40.4, yet another verse ascribed to Ghoṣā, the speaker's intensity in seeking the Aśvins with oblations is projected as hunters chasing two wild animals: *yuvā́m̐ mṛgéva vāraṇā́,* etc. The animal world has been observed closely to take into account the patience and tenacity of a hunter seeking elephants. In the sixth verse of this hymn, it is said that the bee bears the honey of the Aśvins in its mouth, as the maid carries it purified in her hand, as a lady resorts her secret rendezvous with her lover:

yuvór ha mákṣā páry aśvinā mádhv ।
āsā́ bharata niṣkṛtám̐ ná yóṣaṇā ॥

In *Ṛgveda* X.95.15 Urvaśī the celestial nymph is heard addressing her mortal ex-husband Purūravas:

ná vái stráiṇāni sakhyā́ni santi ।
sālāvṛkā́ṇām hṛ́dayāny etā́ ॥

> There is no friendship with women; their hearts are like the hearts of hyenas.

Though the dictionaries are not very sure of the exact meaning of *sālāvṛká-*,[19] it nevertheless has the image of an animal never appreciated for its all-out loyal services, and one never knows

---

18 Cf. also *ṚV* I.112.8, 116.14, 117.16.

19 "House-wolf?" Böhtlingk and Roth (s.v.) are unsure about it, it also suggests "a kind of wolf or hyena or jackal or similar animal".

when the apparently benign beast will snatch its prey. This passage creates an image of womenfolk in general, prone to suddenly break the hearts of their suitors.

In *R̥gveda* X.127.4, Rātri the seer compares her home-seeking kinsmen at night with birds whose abode is the trees: *vr̥kṣé ná vasatiím̐ váyaḥ*. In its eighth verse is found another animal imagery where the speaker uses the bovine simile: "I approach you as one approaches the cows" (*úpa te gā́ ivā́karam*, whereat approaching a cow for the desired milk worked in the poet's mind, in view of which her prayer seems justified in anticipating the deity she is speaking to, to fulfil her desire for certain, just like the cow fills up one's vessel with her milk). This favourite cow image is again met within the second hemistich of *R̥gveda* X.145.6, where the seer Indrāṇī prays for an undivided attention of her husband with

> *mā́m ánu prá te máno* | *vatsám̐ gáur iva dhāvatu* |

> Let your mind rush after me as the cow does for its calf.

The urge and focused attention of the milking cow for its calf inspired the poet to seek a similar attitude to herself from her husband. In *R̥gveda* X.189.1, seer Sārparājñī describes the advancing sun in the east as a speckled cow sitting before its mother and approaching its father in the heaven

> *ā́yám̐ gáuḥ pŕ̥śnir akramīd* |
> *ásadan mātáram̐ puráḥ* |
> *pitáram̐ ca prayánt svàḥ* ||

Human Relationships

Various human relationships are reflected through imagery as well in the select texts. Rivers Vipāś and Śutudrī in *R̥gveda* III.33.10 agree to bend down for Viśvāmitra, as a feeding mother bends for her baby and a maiden to her man to embrace him. In *R̥gveda* X.39.6, seer Ghoṣā prays to her gods, the Aśvins, to teach her in the way parents teach their son, while in the very next hymn, she accuses them for not coming to her but visiting others, and likens them with a widow's brother-in-law who goes to her bed, and with a man who lives together with a woman (*ṚV* X.40.2).

Objects from Everyday Life

Objects from day-to-day life frequent the imageries of *Ṛgveda*, and our select texts are also no exception. The chariot image is favourite of seer Sūryā Sāvitrī when she beautifully describes the journey of a bride to her husband's place, as is evident from *Ṛgveda* X.85.7. There Sūryā says that when she left for her husband, the sky and the earth together were her chariot, her mind was its seat and sight, the unguent for her eyes — all this, expressed through unique metaphors, imparts to this hymn a rare lyrical touch.[20] In *Ṛgveda* X.40.9, a verse by Ghoṣā, the rapid growth of the plants are imagined as rivers flowing into a valley (*nivanéva síndhavaḥ*), while in X.107.10, a verse ascribed to Dakṣiṇā, the beautiful house of a donor is compared to a well-maintained lotus-pool.[21]

Cosmic Objects and Events

A cosmic imagery reveals itself in *Ṛgveda* VIII.91.7, a verse ascribed to Apālā, where the seer says that by pulling Apālā forth thrice through a cart, a wagon and a yoke respectively, Indra gave her a flawless skin as radiant as the sun. In Sūryā's hymn, the second verse declares that the moon has his place in the lap of the stars (*átho nákṣatrāṇām eṣā́m upásthe sóma ā́hitaḥ*), while the fifth says that Soma shapes the years (*sámānāṁ mā́sa ā́kṛtiḥ*), where the poetess further envisions the sun and the moon as two playing children running *after each other*, since the cosmic phenomena of the rise of the sun and of the moon never coincide (cf. *ṚV* X.85.18).

It transpires from the discussions above that nearly every type of imagery attested in the writings of the male seers in *Ṛgveda* is also conspicuous in the hymns ascribed therein to the female seers,

---

[20] *ṚV* X.85.8, 10-12.

[21] See above p. 221.

except the one relating to the occupations and professions of the Ṛgvedic people, which may be explained away with reference to the meagre amount of women's poetry surviving in the present text. The poetesses of *Ṛgveda* cannot at least be accused of lacking in imagery in their poetry.

CITRAKALPA

Judging by its second definition, which almost equates imagery with *svabhāvokti alaṁkāra* of the Indian rhetoricians, there is plenty of it in our select texts (see earlier in this chapter).[22] The term *citrakalpa* for "imagery" in Indian poetics can be expounded as "images created through mere words" instead of "images oriented from simile".[23]

Thus, the prayer embodied in Viśvavārā's verse (V.28.3: *ágne śárdha mahaté sáubhagāya* | *táva dyumnā́ny uttamā́ni santu* "O Fire, light up for great fortune; let your flames be the highest") brings up a clear visual image of the sacrificial fire, kindled up in high flames as if indicating the rising fortune of the sacrificer. Again, the verse of Apālā (*ṚV* VIII.91.1) is a fair specimen of *citrakalpa*, gives as it a picture-like description of a maiden, off to fill up her water pitcher, who finds *soma* on her way back home and decides to press it for her god, Indra:

> *kanyā̀ vā́r avāyatī́* | *sómam ápi srutā́vidat* |
> *ástaṁ bháranty abravīd* | *índrāya sunavai tvā* |
> *śakrā́ya sunavai tvā* ||

Again, in the hymn addressed to Night (*ṚV* X.127), seer Rātri brings forth a picturesque description of the nocturnal world, with all the creatures including human beings, animals and birds asleep, in verse 5:

---

[22] See above pp. 214, 215, 219, 222, 234 and c.

[23] *citrasya kalpaḥ nirmāṇam iti citra-kalpaḥ* or *citrasya kalpaṁ tulyam iti*.

ní grā́māso avikṣata ।
ní padvánto ní pakṣíṇaḥ ।
ní śyenā́saś cid arthínaḥ ।।

All these are examples of imagery, if imagery is considered as picture made by words, i.e. vision presented through words.

IMAGERIES OF FEMALE SEERS VIS-À-VIS THOSE OF SOME MALE SEERS

The imageries found in *Ṛgveda* come under six broad categories, as already discussed. A parallel can be drawn from the poetry of some male seers, where similar types of imageries already met within the poetry ascribed to female seers, can be found.

From the animal world a number of images are drawn. Particularly, cow had a distinct place in the Ṛgvedic imagery, as already discussed subject to the verse of Rātri (*ṚV* X.127.8), where the seer approaches her god as she would approach a cow for the desired milk (*úpa te gā́ ivā́karam*), and again subject to the verse of Indrāṇī, in which the speaker prays for the undivided attention of her husband as the cow rushes to its calf (*ṚV* X.145.6), or subject to X.189.1 where Sārparājñī imagines the sun in the east as a spotted cow sitting before its mother. These expressions can be favourably compared with the following compositions, of some of the male seers, randomly selected where the cow is the common source of vivid images attested therein. For example, in *Ṛgveda* I.32, a hymn ascribed to Hiraṇyastūpa of Āṅgirasa family, one finds the expression *vāśrā́ -iva dhenávaḥ* (like the cows to their calves) (*ṚV* I.32.2), or in the ninth verse of the same hymn we find a similar imagery in *sahávatsā ná dhenúḥ* (like a cow with its calf). Seer Asita or Devala Kāśyapa describes the inspired poets' call to Indra like mother cows' call to their calf: *gā́vo vatsáṁ ná mātáraḥ* (*ṚV* IX.12.2b).

The images drawn from the human relationships mainly centre on the relationship between a man and wife, or simply between a man and a woman. This man–woman relationship has already been observed in the verses of Vipāś and Śutudrī, and of Ghoṣā.[24] Imagery akin to this is detected in a verse of Kutsa Āṅgirasa (*ṚV* I.115.2: *máryo ná yóṣām abhyèti paścā́t* "following as a youth a woman"). And again, in Nodhā Gautama's verse (*ṚV* IX.93.2c: *máryo ná yóṣām abhí niṣkṛtáṁ yán* "like a youth going to a maiden at the trysting place"). Again, at IX.96.23b Pratardana Daivodāsi describes the *soma* juice rushing towards the vat like an illicit lover hastening towards his woman: *priyā́ṁ ná jāró abhígīta índuḥ*. In a verse of Vācya Vaiśvāmitra (or Prajāpati), a similar image unfurls itself: *sáraj-jāró ná yóṣaṇām* (as a paramour runs to his woman) (*ṚV* IX.101.14). The words of Vipāś and Śutudrī are repeated almost verbatim in a verse of Kavaṣa Ailuṣa (*ṚV* X.30.6):

> *evédyū́ne yuvatáyo namanta yádīm uśánn uśatī́r ety ácchā*
>
> (Waters flow towards the *soma*), just in the way young women accede to a young man, when he goes to them who are as eager as him.[25]

As for images drawn from the inanimate nature, parallels are found in the literatures of both male and female seers. At *Ṛgveda* X.40.4 Ghoṣā likens the rapid growth of herbs with the flow of the river course into a valley. A similar image unfolds itself at VI.24.6ab, a verse of Bārhaspatya Bharadvāja.

> *ví tvád ā́po ná párvatasya pṛṣṭhā́d* |
> *ukthébhir indrānayanta yajñáiḥ* |
>
> Like waters coming down in torrents from the back of a mountain, they proceeded forth from you along with solemn words and sacrifices, Indra.
>
> — line b tr. Jamison and Brereton 2014: II.807

At X.127.1 the starry Night has been visualized by Rātri Bhāradvājī as a goddess, graced with all her beauties, beholding the world beneath with innumerable eyes, while at X.68.11 Ayāsya Āṅgirasa

---

[24] *ṚV* X.39.14, 40.6.

[25] Cf. *ṚV* III.33.10: *ní te naṁsai . . . máryāyeva kanyā̀ śaśvacái te*.

visions the nocturnal sky as decorated by the ancestors with the luminaries in the way people deck out a black horse with pearls, cf.:

> *abhí śyāvám̐ ná kṛ́śanebhir áśvam̐* ।
> *nákṣatrebhiḥ pitáro dyā́m apim̐śan* ।

The above study, though brief, unmistakably proves that there was parity in the poetic bend of mind in *Ṛgveda* irrespective of the gender of the poets. Seers from both sexes drew images for their poetry from their surroundings, from the relationships they were acquainted within their society, and last but not the least, from the early fund of poetry they had inherited. The Ṛgvedic images, outcome of an intimate and direct observation of life, are characterized by their naïvety, and the poetry of both sexes of poets reflects a unique freshness. Images used in the poetry did not serve mere decorative purpose, but they were believed to have a ritualistic efficacy, too, if not in the dawn of civilization, at least in a little later age. Poetry by neither sex lacked the above-mentioned characteristics, and as a result the poetry ascribed to the female seers can hardly be discriminated from that ascribed to their male counterparts, at least on the basis of poetic imagery.

7

A Study of the Language and Stylistics of the Text

THE language of *Ṛgveda* in general is not the same throughout the whole text, as it belongs to different periods. The bulk of the Ṛgvedic hymns was composed during a considerable length of time. A linguistic analysis of the corpus would doubtless point to the fact that books 1 and 10 thereof are of later origin, while more archaic compositions are preserved in the family books, viz. 2-7. The compositions ascribed to the female seers are mostly found in the tenth book, whereas of the rest only two appear in the first book, and six in books 3-5, 8 and 9.

In what follows, some hymns and a few verses from some other, ascribed to female seers, which somehow share a common place in their vigorous expression of desires, emotions and earnestness, are selected for a syntactic analysis. Renou (1965: 230-34) noticed a peculiarity of the Vedic syntax: since a word in *Ṛgveda* is quite autonomous and contains almost all the grammatical information, the word-order in a sentence is altogether free, with a few exceptions related to the positions of short enclitics or proclitics. According to him, the Vedic *mantra* is characterized rather by juxtaposition than by the syntactic organization.[1] What Speijer spoke about Sanskrit in his monumental work (in 1886), viz. "like all languages, that possess a rich store of inflections, Sanskrit affords a comparatively great freedom as to the order of words in the sentence", applies equally to the Vedic. Lowe (2015: 37-39) has estimated different

---

[1] Quoted by Tatyana J. Elizarenkova: 1995.

modes of research on Vedic constituent order. Viti (2010: 54) has shown the possible ordering of S(ubject), V(erb) and O(bject) in the *Ṛgveda*. Her analysis tends to prove that the more prominent elements of a sentence occur further leftward in the clause. Lowe further elaborates that it is often assumed that despite the apparent freedom of constituent order there was nevertheless an 'unmarked' or 'canonical' word order in Ṛgvedic Sanskrit, viz. SOV. Recent researchers like Hock (2013) contend that this type of sentence pattern may be held responsible for the deaccentuation of finite verb in main clauses.

In this chapter the higher constituents, viz. the subject (S), the object (O) and the verb (V), of the sentences constituting the select verses of women seers will be primarily observed. To understand the predominant sentence pattern in the literature of the women poets, various kinds of sentences need to be sorted out. A brief comparison of the orders of the higher constituents (HC) in the poetry ascribed to female seers with those of the male seers has to be made as well. A short comparative study will be done on the HC orders in the negative sentences randomly selected from the poetry ascribed to both groups of seers. A similar study of the interrogative sentences will also follow. All analysed data will be briefed in concerned charts followed by graphs showing the frequency of the HC orders in literature ascribed to both groups of seers. The present study broadly follows the apparatus and methodology as presented at Das Gupta and Manoharan (1990).

Analysis IA: A Study of the HC Orders in Select Verses of the Female Seers

(To determine the word-order of select verses following abbreviations have been used: Abl = ablativc, Acc = accusative, Adj = adjective, Acl = adjective clause, Adv = adverb, Advcl = adverb clause, con = conjunctive, Dat = dative, Indcl = indeclinable, Inf = infinite, Instr = instrumental, IP = interrogative particle, IPr = interrogative pronoun, Loc = locative, Neg = negative, NP = noun phrase, Num = numeral, Pass = passive, Ptcpl = participle, Poss = possessive, pre = prefix, Pro = pronoun, Voc = vocative)

The first verse in our selection ascribed to Romaśā (*R̥V* I.126.7) and the preceding verse ascribed to Svanaya are considered by Griffith as fragments of a liberal shepherd's love-song, as these two are incongruous to what precedes in the same hymn. This verse of Romaśā has the following sentence structure:

1. *úpopa me párā mr̥śa* | *mā́ me dabhrā́ṇi manyathā* |
   sárvāhám asmi romaśā́ | *gandhā́rīṇām ivāvikā́* ||

The word order is as follows

O pre V | Neg O AdjO V |
Adj_1S S V Adj_2S | Poss Indcl S ||

Here S is dropped in line a as also in line b. Line c has an intransitive verb; hence O is absent there. Line d acts as the predicate to line c or it can be taken as an Acl qualifying the nominal *romaśā́* in line c. The HC orders in these three sentences constituting the verse are as follows:

(i) OV

(ii) (Neg) OV

(iii) SV

2. *R̥gveda* I.179.1-2 are ascribed to Lopāmudrā, and the first verse runs thus:

pūrvī́r ahám̐ śarádaḥ śaśramāṇā́ |
doṣā́ vástor uṣáso jaráyantīḥ |
mināti śríyam̐ jarimā́ tanū́nām |
ápy ū nú pátnīr vŕ̥ṣaṇo jagamyuḥ ||

The word order is as follows:

Adj_1Acc_1 S Acc_1 Ptcpl | Acc_2 Acc_3 Adj_2Acc_1 |
V O S | Poss Indcl Indcl Indcl O S V ||

In line a, the participle *śaśramāṇā́* is counted as a verb. There are three sentences in this verse; the first sentence comprises three accusatives, which all indicate duration of time (*vyāpti*). The second sentence starts in line c and continues till the middle of line d. The order of the HCs is:

(i) S(V)

(ii) VOS

(iii) OSV

3. The second verse of Lopāmudrā runs thus:

yé cid dhí pū́rva ṛtasā́pa ā́sant |
sākám devébhir ávadan-n ṛtā́ni |
té cid ávāsur nahy ántam āpúḥ |
sám u nú pátnīr vṛ́ṣabhir jagamyuḥ ||

The word order is as follows:

SPro Indcl Indcl Adj_1S Adj_2S V | Indcl Instr V O |
S(Pro) Indcl V Indcl O V | pre Indcl Indcl S Instr V ||

The verse has one complex sentence in active voice and one simple sentence in passive. The complex sentence runs through lines a, b and c; line c is the noun phrase which itself is a compound sentence with a dropped conjunctive. Line b is an Acl qualifying the S in line a, and line a is another Acl qualifying the NP in line c. Line d is a simple sentence in passive voice; here the V *jagamyuḥ* corresponds to *pátnīḥ*: hence it is S and *vṛ́ṣabhiḥ* is instrumental, but according to the Sanskrit grammarians[2] *pátnīḥ* is O and *vṛ́ṣabhiḥ* is S. The HC orders in both sentences are as follows:

(i) SV, VO, (SV,OV)

(ii) SV

4. An entire hymn ascribed to Viśvavārā (V.28) is selected here for a syntactic analysis. This hymn consists of six verses, of which the first runs as:

---

[2] Vide *abhihite tu karmaṇi*: Vidyasagar; *kartṛkaraṇayos tṛtīyā:* Pāṇ. 2.3.18.

sámiddho agnír diví śocír aśret।
pratyáṅ-ṅ uṣásam urviyā́ ví bhāti।
éti prā́cī viśvávārā námobhir।
devā́ṁ īḻānā havíṣā ghṛtā́cī॥

The word order is:

Adj$_1$S S Loc O V। Adj$_2$S O Adv pre V।
V Adj$_1$S S Instr$_1$। O Adj$_2$S Instr$_2$ Instr$_3$॥

There is a dispute among the interpreters regarding the nature of the word *viśvavārā*. According to some it is a proper noun, while others hold it to be an adjective (see before pp. 56-57). Lines a and b make a compound sentence with a dropped con, while lines c and d make a simple sentence. The HC orders are:

(i) SOV, OV
(ii) VSO

5. The second verse of this hymn goes thus:

samidhyámāno amṛ́tasya rājasi।
havíṣkṛṇvántaṁ sacase svastáye।
víśvaṁ sá dhatte dráviṇaṁ yám ínva।
syā́tithyám agne ní ca dhatta ít puráḥ॥

The word order is:

AdjS O V। O V Adv।
AdjO S V O ProO V। O Voc Indcl Indcl V Indcl Indcl॥

There are four simple sentences in four lines respectively. The HC orders are as follows:

(i) SOV
(ii) OV
(ii) SVO
(iv) OV

6. The third verse is as follows:

ágne śárdha mahaté sáubhagāya |
táva dyumnā́ny uttamā́ni santu |
sáṁ jāspatyáṁ suyámam ā́ kr̥ṇuṣva |
śatruyatā́m abhí tiṣṭhā máhāṁsi ||

The word order is:

Voc V Adv Adv | Poss S AdjS V |
pre_1 O AdjO pre_2 V | Poss pre V O ||

Here too, there are four simple sentences in four lines respectively. In line c two prefixes adjoin a single verb. The HC orders are as follows:

(i) (Voc) V
(ii) SV
(iii) OV
(iv) VO

7. The fourth verse is:

sámiddhasya prámahasó | *'gne vánde táva śríyam* |
vr̥ṣabhó dyumnávā̃ asi | *sám adhvaréṣv idhyase* ||

The word order is:

Adj_1Poss Adj_2Poss | Voc V Poss O |
S AdjS V | pre Loc V ||

In this verse lines a and b contain a simple sentence, lines c and d are also simple sentences. The HC orders are as follows:

(i) (Voc) VO
(ii) SV
(iii) V

8. The fifth verse of this hymn runs thus:

sámiddho agna āhuta | *devā́n yakṣi svadhvara* |
tváṁ hí havyavā́ḷ asi ||

The word order is:

> Adj_1 Voc Voc Adj_2 Voc | O V Adj_3 Voc |
> S Indcl AdjS V ||

There is one simple sentence running through lines a and b, while another simple sentence occurs in line c. The HC orders are as follows:

(i) (Voc) OV

(ii) SV

9. The final verse runs thus:

> *ā́ juhotā duvasyátā* | *'gníṁ prayaty àdhvaré* |
> *vr̥ṇīdhváṁ havyavā́hanam* ||

The word order is:

> pre V V | O AdjLoc Loc |
> V O ||

There is a compound sentence with a dropped conjunctive in lines a and b. Line c has one simple sentence. The HC orders are as follows:

(i) VVO

(ii) VO

10. The next verse selected for a syntactic analysis is *R̥gveda* VIII.1.34, ascribed to Śaśvatī. The verse runs as follows:

> *ánv asya sthūráṁ dadr̥śe purástād* |
> *anasthá ūrúr avarámbamāṇaḥ* |
> *śáśvatī nā́ry abhicákṣyāha* |
> *súbhadram arya bhójanaṁ bibharṣi* ||

The word order is as follows:

> pre Poss S V(Pass) Indcl | S AdjS Ptcpl(V) |
> S AdjS pre V_1 V_2 | AdjO Voc O V ||

Here, line a has a passive simple sentence, while the sentence in line b has no verb but a Ptcpl *avarámbamāṇaḥ* functioning as a verb. Line c has an infinite verb (V_1) and a finite verb (V_2), which should be counted together as a compound verb. Line d has a simple sentence. The HC orders are as follows:

(i) SV (Pass)

(ii) S(V)

(iii) SV_1V_2

(iv) (Voc) OV

11. The entire hymn VIII.91 ascribed to Apālā is selected here for a syntactic analysis, since this hymn stands out in many aspects, as already discussed in previous chapters (see before in Chapters 1-3). The hymn consists of seven verses. The first verse reads thus:

kanyā̀ vā́r avāyatī́ | *sómam ápi srutā́vidat* |
ástaṁ bháranty abravīd | *índrāya sunavai tvā* |
śakrā́ya sunavai tvā ||

The word order is:

S O Ptcpl(V) | O Indcl Loc V |
O SAdj V | Dat V O | Dat V O ||

Here, line a has a Ptcpl *avāyatī́* acting as a verb to which *vār* is O. Line b can be considered as the predicate of line a. Similarly, lines d and e are the predicates of line c. In line c, *bhárantī* is actually an adjective to *kanyā̀* in line a, but in this sentence it takes the position of S. The HC orders are as follows:

(i) SO (V)

(ii) OV

(iii) OSV

(iv) VO

(v) VO

12. The second verse runs thus:

asáu yá éṣi vīrakó | *gr̥háṁgr̥haṁ vicā́kaśat* |
imáṁ jámbhasutaṁ piba | *dhānā́vantaṁ karambhíṇam* |
apūpávantam ukthínam ||

The word order is:

S Pro V Adj_1S । O Adj_2S ।
O Adj_1O V । Adj_2O Adj_3O । Adj_4O Adj_5O ॥

There are two simple sentences occurring respectively in the first and second hemistich of the verse. The HC orders are as follows:

(i) SVO

(ii) OV

13. The third verse runs thus:

ā́ caná tvā cikitsāmó । *'dhi caná tvā némasi* ।
śánair iva śanakáir ivén- । *drāyendo pári srava* ॥

The word order is:

pre Indcl O V । pre Indcl O (Neg) V ।
Indcl(Adv) Indcl Indcl Indcl । Dat Voc pre V ॥

There are two simple sentences occurring respectively in lines a and b, while another simple sentence is contained in lines c and d. The HC orders are:

(i) OV

(ii) O (Neg) V

(iii) (Voc) V

14. The fourth verse has a number of interrogative sentences, and as such it will be discussed below in a relevant place. The fifth verse of the Apālā-hymn runs thus:

imā́ni trī́ṇi viṣṭápā । *tā́nīndra ví rohaya* ।
śíras tatásyorvárām । *ā́d idáṁ ma úpodáre* ॥

The word order is:

Pro(Adj_1) Num(Adj_2) O । Pro(O) Voc pre V ।
O Poss AdjO । Indcl O Poss Loc ॥

In this verse a complex sentence runs through lines a and b, the NP occurring in line b and line a being the Acl qualifying the NP.

Sāyaṇa, however, considers line a to be a simple sentence with a suggested verb *santi*; line b is also another simple sentence according to him. Lines c and d have no verbs but the verb *ví rohaya* in line b is to be understood in both the sentences.

The HC orders are as follows:

(i) O(Acl) (Voc) V

(ii) OO

15. The sixth verse is:

asáu ca yā́ na urvárād । *imā́ṁ tanvàṁ máma* ।
átho tatásya yác chíraḥ । *sárvā tā́ romaśā́ kṛdhi* ।।

The word order is:

S Indcl (con) S Neg $AdjS_2$ Indcl (Acl) । Pro S Poss (Acl) ।
Indcl Poss Pro(S) S (Acl) । O Pro(O) AdjO V (NP) ।।

This verse has a rather complicated and incoherent sentence structure. A complex sentence runs through the four lines. The NP occurs in the fourth line, i.e. line d, and all the three Acls in lines a, b and c are devoid of any verb, *asti* or so being understood in each clause. The HC order is:

(i) S (Acl) S (Acl) S (Acl) OV

16. The seventh verse is:

khé ráthasya khé 'nasaḥ । *khé yugásya śatakrato* ।
apālā́m indra tríṣ pūtvy । *ákṛṇoḥ sū́ryatvacam* ।।

The word order is as follows:

Loc Poss Loc Poss । Loc Poss Voc ।
O S Num Inf । V O ।।

A simple sentence runs through the four lines. The O *apālā́m* in line c corresponds to the infinite verb *pūtvī́*, and line d is the predicate of the sentence. The HC order is:

(i) OS Inf VO

17. Coming to the tenth book, where most of the dialogue hymns are accumulated, the first female seer to meet is Yamī Vaivasvatī. *Ṛgveda* X.10 is a conversation between Yamī and his brother Yama. This hymn being interesting in many ways, a verse therefrom is being analysed here. Verse 7 goes thus:

> *yamásya mā yamyàṁ kā́ma*। *ā́gant samāné yónau sahaśéyyāya*।
> *jāyéva pátye tanvàṁ riricyāṁ*। *ví cid vṝhéva ráthyeva cakrā́*।।

The word order is:

> Poss Pro(O) O S V। Adj(Loc) Loc Dat।
> S Indcl Dat (comparison) O V। pre Indcl V AdjS Indcl S (comparison)।।

A simple sentence runs through lines a and b, while another simple sentence occurs in line c where a comparison is made, and a similar sentence occurs in line d. The HC orders are:

(i) OSV
(ii) SOV
(iii) VS

18. *Ṛgveda* X.39-40 are ascribed to Ghoṣā. One verse from the former and two verses from the latter may be selected for a syntactic study. The sixth verse of X.39 reads:

> *iyáṁ vām ahve śṛṇutáṁ me aśvinā*। *putrā́yeva pitárā máhyaṁ śikṣatam*।
> *ánāpir ájñā asajātyā́matiḥ*। *purā́ tásyā abhíśaster áva spṛtam*।।

The word order is:

> S O V V Poss Voc। Dat Indcl S (comparison) Dat V।
> Adj$_1$S Adj$_2$S Adj$_3$S Adj$_4$S। Indcl Pro(Abl) Abl pre V।।

There are five short sentences in the four lines of this verse. The fourth sentence found in line c has dropped S and V; the suggested

S is *ahám* and the V, *asmi*. In the fifth sentence the S and O are dropped, and are suggested to be *tvám* and *mā́m* respectively. The HC orders of the five sentences are as follows:

(i) SOV

(ii) V (voc)

(iii) SV

(iv) —

(v) V

19. The fourteenth verse of the same hymn is:

etáṁ vāṁ stómam aśvināv akarmā́ | *takṣāma bhṛ́gavo ná rátham* |
nyàmṛkṣāma yóṣaṇāṁ ná márye | *nítyaṁ ná sūnúṁ tánayaṁ dádhānāḥ* ||

The word order is:

Pro(O) Poss O Voc V | V S Indcl O (comparison) |
pre V O Indcl Dat (comparison) | Indcl Indcl O AdjO Ptcpl (V) ||

Here line a has a simple sentence, line b has a dropped S, viz. *vayám* corresponding to V *atakṣāma*, and the rest is a comparison. Similarly, line c has a comparison and the dropped S is again *vayám* corresponding to V *nyàmṛkṣāma*. Line d has a participle *dádhānāḥ* acting as the V of the sentence. The HC orders are as follows:

(i) OV

(ii) V (SO)

(iii) V(O)

(iv) OV(Ptcpl)

20. *Ṛgveda* X.86 is the famous dialogue hymn of Indra, Indrāṇī and Vṛṣākapi. The ninth verse ascribed to Indrāṇī runs thus:

avī́rām iva mā́m ayáṁ | *śarā́rur abhí manyate* |

utā̃hám asmi vīríṇīn- I *drapatnī marútsakhā* I
víśvasmād índra úttaraḥ II

The word order is:

AdjO Indcl O Pro(S) I S pre V I
Indcl S V Adj_1S I Adj_2S Adj_3S II Abl I S AdjS

Here apart from the refrain in line d, which is a simple sentence, two more simple sentences occur respectively in the first and second hemistich of the verse. The HC orders are:

(i) OSV

(ii) SV

21. *R̥gveda* X.95 is the famous colloquy of Purūravas and Urvaśī. The fifth verse ascribed to Urvaśī runs thus:

tríḥ sma mā̃hnaḥ śnathayo vaitaséno- I *tá sma mé 'vyatyai pr̥ṇāsi* I
púrūravó 'nu te kétam āyaṁ I *rā̃jā me vīra tanvàs tádāsīḥ* II

The word order is:

Num Indcl O Poss V Instr I Indcl (con) Indcl Dat AdjDat V I
Voc pre Poss O V I S Poss Voc Poss Indcl V II

In this verse a compound sentence runs through lines a and b, while two simple sentences occur in lines c and d respectively. The HC orders are:

(i) OV (con) V

(ii) (Voc) OV

(iii) SV

22. *R̥gveda* X.125 ascribed to Vāc is famous for its unique expression of self-realization. The final verse, viz. the eighth, may be selected for analysis. The verse is as follows:

ahám evá vā̃ta-iva prá vāmyā I *rábhamāṇā bhúvanāni víśvā* I
paró divā̃ pará enā pr̥thivyai I *tā̃vatī mahinā̃ sáṁ babhūva* II

The word order is:

> S Indcl Poss Indcl pre V I Ptcpl(Inf) O AdjO I
> Indcl Instr Indcl Pro(Instr) Instr I AdjS Instr pre V I I

Here lines a and b constitute a simple sentence where the Ptcpl *ārábhamāṇā* acts as an infinite verb, and the O *bhúvanāni* corresponds to it. The adjective *etā́vatī* in line d qualifies the S *ahám* in line a, but being a separate sentence the second hemistich has *etā́vatī* as its S. The HC orders are:

(i) SV (Inf) O

(ii) SV

23. *Ṛgveda* X.145 expresses the vigorous rancour of a co-wife, viz. Indrāṇī. The sixth verse goes as:

> *úpa te 'dhāṁ sáhamānām* I *abhí tvādhāṁ sáhīyasā* I
> *mā́m ánu prá te máno* I *vatsáṁ gáur iva dhāvatu* I
> *pathā́ vā́r iva dhāvatu* I I

The word order is:

> Pre Poss V O I pre O V Instr I
> O Indcl pre Poss S/ <u>O S Indcl</u> (comparison) V I <u>Instr S Indcl</u>
> (comparison) V I I

Here, lines c, d and e have a compound sentence running through. In lines d and e two comparisons are drawn; hence, *gáur* and *vā́r* are the subjects of the concerned sentences respectively. The HC orders are:

(i) VO

(ii) OV

(iii) OS, OSV, SV

24. The next verse is selected from X.189 ascribed to Sārparājñī. The first verse runs thus:

> *ā́yaṁ gáuḥ pṛ́śnir akramīd* I *ásadan mātáraṁ puráḥ* I
> *pitáraṁ ca prayánt svàḥ* I I

The word order is:

pre Pro S AdjS V। V O Indcl।
O Indcl (con) Ptcpl(V) Loc॥

Here, the Indcl *svàḥ* in line c has been described by Sāyaṇa as the adjective of S *gáuḥ* in line a. The HC orders are:

(i) SV

(ii) VO

(iii) O (con) V(Ptcpl)

The HC orders of the sentences consisting the verses discussed so far are depicted in a chart given in the next page; the serial numbers given to the verses will show in the chart. Another chart is attached to this basic data to present the frequency of the HC orders occurring in the sentences of the select verses. The following page will graphically show the frequency distribution of the HC orders found there.

A Study of the HC Order in Select Verses of Female Seers

Sl. No.	*Female Seers*	*Sl. No.*	*Female Seers*	*Sl. No.*	*Female Seers*	*Frequency*
1	OV	13	OV	1	VOS	1
	(Neg) OV		O (Neg) V	2	VO	6
	SV		(Voc) V	3	V(Voc) O	1
2	S(V)	14	O(Acl) (Voc) V	4	V(SO)	1
	VOS		OO	5	V(O)	1
	OSV	15	S (Acl) S (Acl) S (Acl) OV	6	VVO	1
3	SV, VO (SV,OV),	16	OS Inf VO	7	V (Voc)	1
	SV	17	OSV	8	V	2
4	SOV, OV		SOV	9	SVO	2
	VSO		VS	10	SV, VO (SV, OV)	1
5	SOV	18	SOV	11	SV (Pass)	1
	OV		V (Voc)	12	SV (NP) V (Acl)	1
	SVO		SV	13	SV (NP) V (Acl)	1
	OV		—	14	SV (Inf) O	1
6	(Voc) V		V	15	SV	10
	SV	19	OV	16	SOV, OV	1
	OV		V(SO)	17	SOV (NP) OV	1
	VO		V(O)	18	SOV	3
7	(Voc) VO		OV (Ptcpl)	19	SO (V)	1
	SV	20	OSV	20	S_1VS_2	1
	V		SV	21	S(V)	2
8	(Voc) OV	21	OV (Con) V	22	(Neg) OV	1
	SV		(Voc) OV	23	SV_1V_2	1
9	VVO		SV	24	S (Acl) S (Acl) S (Acl) OV	1
	VO	22	SV (Inf) O	25	S	2
10	SV (Pass)		SV	26	O (con) V(Ptcpl)	1
	S(V)	23	VO	27	OV(Acl)OV(NP)	1
	SV_1V_2		OV	28	OV (Con) V	1
	(Voc) OV		OS, OSV, SV	29	OV	10
11	SO (V)	24	SV	30	OSV	4
	OV		VO	31	OS, OSV, SV	1
	OSV		O (con) V (Ptcpl)	32	OS Inf VO	1
	VO			33	OO	1
	VO			34	O_1O_2V	1
12	SVO			35	O(Acl) (Voc) V	1
	OV			36	O(Acl) (Voc) V	1
				37	O (Neg) V	1
				38	—	1
				39	(Voc) VO	1
				40	(Voc) V	2
				41	(Voc) OV	3
				42	VSO	1

Frequency distribution is shown graphically in the next page.

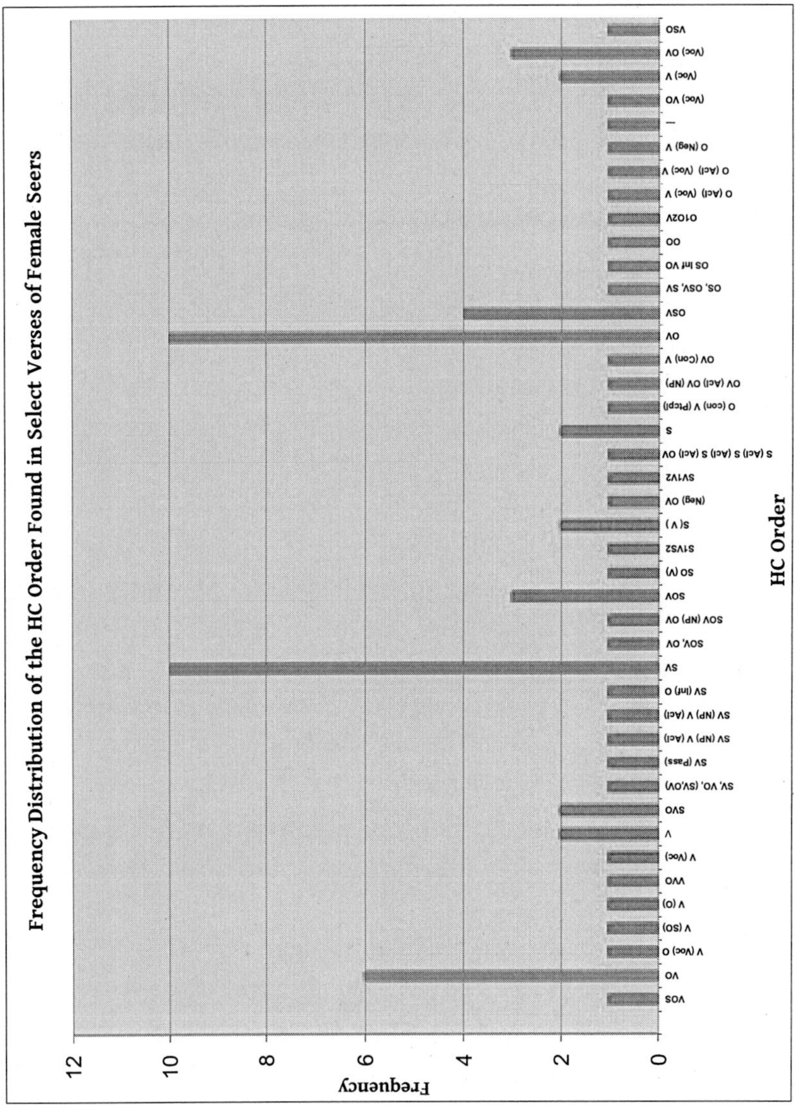
Frequency Distribution of the HC Order Found in Select Verses of Female Seers
Frequency
12
10
8
6
4
2
0
HC Order
VOS
VO
V (Voc) O
V (SO)
V (O)
VVO
V (Voc)
V
SVO
SV, VO, (SV,OV)
SV (Pass)
SV (NP) V (AcI)
SV (NP) V (AcI)
SV (Inf) O
SV
SOV, OV
SOV (NP) OV
SOV
SO (V)
S1VS2
S(V)
(Neg) OV
SV1V2
S (AcI) S (AcI) S (AcI) OV
S
O (con) V (Ptcpl)
OV (AcI) OV (NP)
OV (Con) V
OV
OSV
OS, OSV, SV
OS Inf VO
OO
O1O2V
O (AcI) (Voc) V
O (AcI) (Voc) V
O (Neg) V
—
(Voc) VO
(Voc) V
(Voc) OV
VSO

Analysis IB: A Brief Study of the HC Orders in Select Verses of Male and Female Seers

SELECT VERSES OF SOME MALE SEERS

Eight verses have been selected from hymns ascribed to some of the male seers of *Ṛgveda* for a syntactic analysis. There, too, six verses occur in those dialogue hymns where female seers are seen as co-poets. The verses selected are:

1. I.126.6 of Svanaya Bhāvayavya, the verse following which is spoken by Romaśā.
2. From I.179, a dialogue hymn of Agastya and Lopāmudrā, the fourth verse ascribed to Agastya has been selected.
3. From IV.18, a dialogue hymn of Indra–Aditi–Vāmadeva, the fourth verse ascribed to Vāmadeva is chosen.
4. V.28 is ascribed to Viśvavārā, very near to which is V.22 ascribed to a male poet named Viśvasāma Ātreya of Viśvavārā's parental Atri family. The fourth verse of this latter hymn is selected.
5. VIII.91 is the famous hymn ascribed to Apālā, the preceding hymn, i.e. VIII.90, is ascribed to two male seers, Nṛmedha and Puruṣamedha of the Aṅgiras family. The opening verse of this hymn is selected here.
6. X.86 is a dialogue hymn of Indra, Indrāṇī and Vṛṣākapi, the twelfth verse of which, ascribed to Indra, has been chosen here.
7. The famous colloquy of Purūravas and Urvaśī is X.95; the first verse ascribed to Purūravas is being analysed here.
8. Finally, from X.108, a dialogue between Saramā and the Paṇis, the ninth verse ascribed to the Paṇis has schematized.

1. The verse I.126.6 runs as follows:

ā́gadhitā párigadhitā | *yā́ kaśī́kéva jáṅgahe* |
dádāti máhyaṁ yā́durī | *yā́śūnāṁ bhojyā̀ śatā́* ||

The word order is:

> Adj_1S Adj_2S । S(Pro) S Indcl (comparison) V ।
> V Dat S । Poss AdjS O ।।

Two simple sentences occur in the two hemistichs of the verse. The HC orders are:

(i) SV

(ii) VSO

2. The next verse is I.179.4, which runs thus:

> *nadásya mā rudhatáḥ kā́ma ā́gann* । *itá ā́jāto amútaḥ kútaś cit* ।
> *lópāmudrā vŕ̥ṣaṇaṁ nī́ riṇāti* । *dhī́ram ádhīrā dhayati śvasántam* ।।

The word order is:

> Poss O AdjPoss S pre V ।
> Indcl(Abl) Ptcpl Indcl Indcl IP(Abl) Indcl ।
> S O Pre V ।
> O S V AdjO ।।

There are four simple sentences in the four lines of the verse. The HC orders are as follows:

(i) OSV

(ii) V (Ptcpl)

(iii) SOV

(iv) OSV

3. The third verse is IV.18.4. It reads:

> *kíṁ sá ŕ̥dhak kr̥ṇavad yáṁ sahásraṁ* । *māsó jabhā́ra śarádaś ca pūrvī́ḥ* ।
> *nahī́ nv asya pratimā́nam ásty an-* । *tár jātéṣūtá yé jánitvāḥ* ।।

The word order is:

> IP S O V O_1 $AdjO_2$ । O_2 V O_3 Indcl $AdjO_3$ ।

Neg Indcl Indcl Poss S V | Indcl Loc Indcl Loc AdjLoc ||

There is one interrogation in line a and a negation in line c. There are three sentences in the verse. The HC orders are as follows:

(i) (IP)SOV

(ii) $O_1O_2VO_3$

(iii) (Neg) SV

4. The fourth verse is V.22.4. It runs as:

ágne cikiddhy àsyá na | idáṁ vácaḥ sahasya |
táṁ tvā suśipra dampate | stómair vardhanty átrayo |
gīrbhíḥ śumbhanty átrayaḥ ||

The word order is:

Voc V Poss Poss | Pro(O) O Voc |
Pro(O) O Voc Voc | Instr V S | Instr V S ||

There are three simple sentences in this verse. The HC orders are:

(i) (Voc) VO

(ii) OVS

(iii) VS

5. The fifth verse is VIII.90.1. It runs as follows:

ā́ no víśvāsu hávya | índraḥ samátsu bhūṣatu |
úpa bráhmāṇi sávanāni vṛtrahā́ | paramajyā́ ṛ́cīṣamaḥ ||

The word order is:

Pre Poss Loc AdjS | S Loc V |
pre AdjO O S | Adj_1S Adj_2S ||

There are two simple sentences running through the verse. The second sentence has a dropped V. The HC orders are:

(i) SV

(ii) OS

6. The sixth verse is X.86.12. It is as follows:

nā́hám indrāṇi rārana ǀ *sákhyur vr̥ṣā́kaper r̥té* ǀ
yásyedám ápyaṁ havíḥ ǀ *priyáṁ devéṣu gácchati* ǀǀ
víśvasmād etc.

The word order is:

(Neg) S Voc V ǀ Poss Poss Indcl ǀ
Poss Pro(S) Adj_1S S ǀ Adj_2S OV ǀǀ

There are two simple sentences in this verse. Of which the former is a negative sentence. The HC orders are as follows:

(i) (Neg) SV

(ii) SOV

7. The seventh verse is X.95.1. It runs as:

hayé jā́ye mánasā tíṣṭha ghore ǀ *vácāṁsi miśrā́ kr̥ṇavāvahai nú* ǀ
ná nau mántrā ánuditāsa eté ǀ *máyaskaran páratare canā́han* ǀǀ

The word order is:

Voc Voc Instr V Voc ǀ O AdjO V Indcl ǀ
Neg Poss S AdjS Pro(S) ǀ O V AdjLoc Indcl Loc ǀǀ

There are three simple sentences in this verse. The third one is a negative sentence. The HC orders are:

(i) (Voc) V

(ii) OV

(iii) (Neg) SOV

8. The last verse to be analysed is X.108.9. It is as follows:

evā́ ca tváṁ sarama ājagántha ǀ *prábādhitā sáhasā dáivyena* ǀ
svásāraṁ tvā kr̥ṇavai mā́ púnar gā ǀ *ápa te gávāṁ subhage bhajāma* ǀǀ

The word order is:

Indcl Indcl S Voc pre V ǀ AdjS Indcl Instr ǀ
O_1 O_2 V Neg Indcl V ǀ pre O Poss Voc V ǀǀ

There is one simple sentence running through lines a and b, and three short simple sentences occur in lines c and d. The third sentence is a negative one. The HC orders of these are as follows:

(i) SV

(ii) O_1O_2 V

(iii) (Neg) V

(iv) O(Voc) V

SELECT VERSES OF FEMALE SEERS

Eight verses from the literature of female seers in *Ṛgveda* are selected for comparing on the basis of syntactic structure with those of the male seers. The verses of female seers selected are as follows:

1. The verse of Romaśā, viz. I.126.7, is the first one in the select group.
2. I.179.2 ascribed to Lopāmudrā comes next.
3. The third one is IV.18.5 ascribed to Aditi.
4. To be followed by V.28.3 of Viśvavārā.
5. The fifth one is VIII.91.2 of Apālā.
6. The sixth is X.86.9 ascribed to Indrāṇī.
7. The penultimate one is X.95.5 of Urvaśī.
8. The final one is X.108.10 ascribed to Saramā.

Among these eight verses the syntactic structures of six have already been analysed; only the HC orders of these verses are given below serially. Only IV.18.5 and X.108.10 will be quoted and analysed syntactically.

1. Verse of Romaśā (I.126.7 see p. 241):

(i) OV

(ii) (Neg) OV

(iii) SV

2. Verse of Lopāmudrā (I.179.2 see p. 242):

(i) SV, VO, (SV, OV)

(ii) SV

3. Verse of Aditi (IV.18.5):

avadyám iva mányamānā gúhākar | *índraṁ mātā́ vīryèṇā nyṟ̥ṣṭam* |
áthódasthāt svayám átkam vásāna | *ā́ ródasī apṟ̥ṇāj jā́yamānaḥ* ||

The word order is:

O Indcl Ptcpl(Inf) Loc V | O S Instr AdjO |
Indcl pre V S O Ptcpl | pre O V AdjS ||

There are three simple sentences running through the verse. The word *mányamānā* in line a is a Ptcpl acting as an infinite verb, and *avadyám iva* is O to it. The Ptcpl in line c is actually an AdjS having *átkam* as its O. The HC orders are as follows:

(i) OV(Ptcpl) VOS

(ii) VSO

(iii) OVS

4. Verse of Viśvavārā (V.28.3 see pp. 243-44):

(i) (Voc) V

(ii) SV

(iii) OV

(iv) VO

5. Verse of Apālā (VIII.91.2 see pp. 246-47):

(i) SVO

(ii) OV

6. Verse of Indrāṇī (X.86.9 see pp. 250-51):

(i) OSV

(ii) SV

7. Verse of Urvaśī (X.95.5 see p. 251):

(i) OV (Con) V

(ii) (Voc) OV

(iii) SV

8. Verse of Saramā (X.108.10):

nā́hám̐ veda bhrātṛtvám̐ nó svasṛtvám | *índro vidur áṅgirasaś ca ghorā́ḥ* |
gókāmā me acchadayan yád ā́yam | *ápāta ita paṇayo várīyaḥ* ||

The word order is:

Neg S V O Neg O | S_1V S_2 Indcl (con) AdjS_2 |
S Poss V (NP) Indcl V (Acl) | pre Indcl V Voc O ||

There are two compound sentences in lines a and b respectively, in both cases a single verb has been used. Line c is a complex sentence, where *gókāmā . . . acchadayan* is the NP and *yád ā́yam* is the Acl. The HC orders are:

(i) (Neg) SVO, (Neg)O

(ii) S_1VS_2

(iii) SV(NP) V (Acl)

(iv) V(Voc) O

The HC orders found in the select literature ascribed to male and female seers are diagrammed separately in the next page. Two other diagrams show the frequency of the HC orders in the basic data. The page following presents two graphs showing the frequency distribution of the HC orders in the select verses ascribed to both groups of seers.

A Study of the HC Orders in Select Verses of Male and Female Seers

Sl. No.	*Male Seers*	*Sl. No.*	*Count*	*Frequency*	*Sl. No.*	*Female Seers*	*Sl. No.*	*Count*	*Frequency*
1	SV	1	SV	3	1	OV	1	OV	3
	VSO	2	VSO	1		(Neg) OV	2	(Neg) OV	1
2	OSV	3	OSV	2		SV	3	SV	5
	V (Ptpcl)	4	V (Ptpcl)	1	2	SV, VO (SV, OV)	4	SV, VO (SV, OV)	1
	SOV	5	SOV	2		SV	5	OV (Ptcpl) VOS	1
	OSV	6	(IP) SOV	1	3	OV (Ptcpl) VOS	6	VSO	1
3	(IP) SOV	7	$O_1O_2VO_3$	1		VSO	7	OVS	1
	$O_1O_2VO_3$	8	(Neg) SV	1		OVS	8	(Voc) V	1
	(Neg) SV	9	(Voc) VO	1	4	(Voc) V	9	VO	1
4	(Voc) VO	10	OVS	1		SV	10	SVO	1
	OVS	11	VS	1		OV	11	OSV	1
	VS	12	OS	1		VO	12	OV (Con) V	1
5	SV	13	(Voc) V	1	5	SVO	13	(Voc) OV	1
	OS	14	OV	1		OV	14	(Neg) SVO, (Neg) O	1
6	(Neg) SV	15	(Neg) SOV	1	6	OSV	15	S_1VS_2	1
	SOV	16	O_1O_2V	1		SV	16	SV (NP) V (Acl)	1
7	(Voc) V	17	(Neg) V	1	7	OV (Con) V	17	V(Voc) O	1
	OV	18	O(Voc) V	1		(Voc) OV			
	(Neg) SOV					SV			
8	SV				8	(Neg) SVO, (Neg) O			
	O_1O_2V					S_1VS_2			
	(Neg) V					SV (NP) V (Acl)			
	O (Voc) V					V(Voc) O			

Frequency distribution is shown graphically in the following pages.

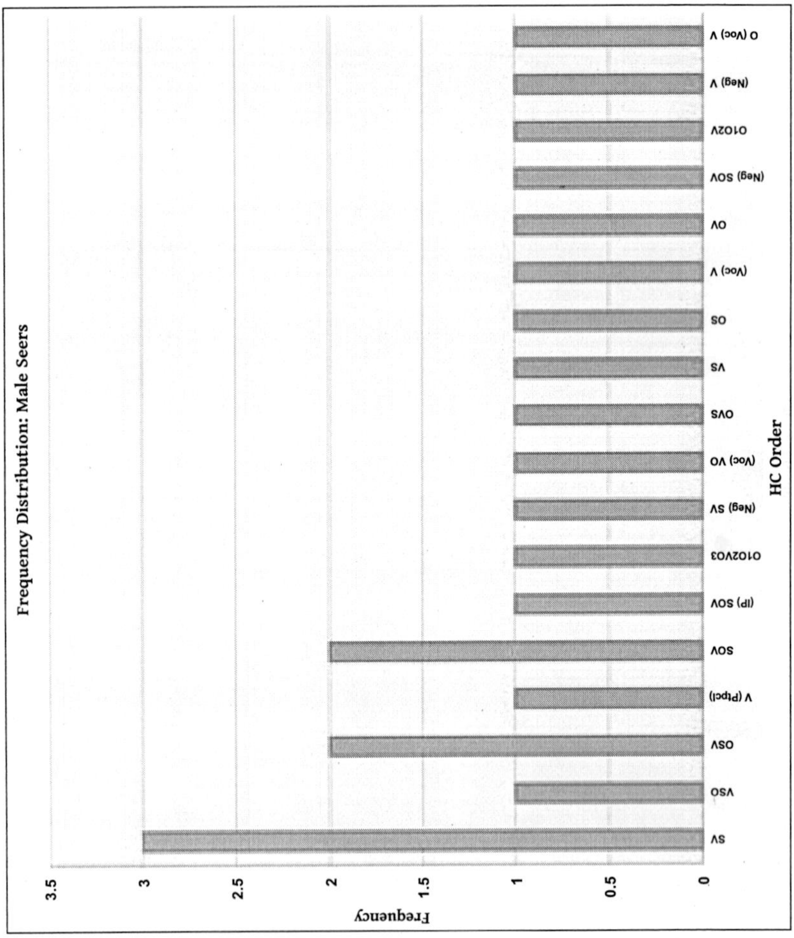
Frequency Distribution: Male Seers
Frequency
3.5
3
2.5
2
1.5
1
0.5
0
SV
VSO
OSV
V (Ptpcl)
SOV
(IP) SOV
O1O2VO3
(Neg) SV
(Voc) VO
OVS
VS
OS
(Voc) V
OV
(Neg) SOV
O1O2V
(Neg) V
O (Voc) V
HC Order

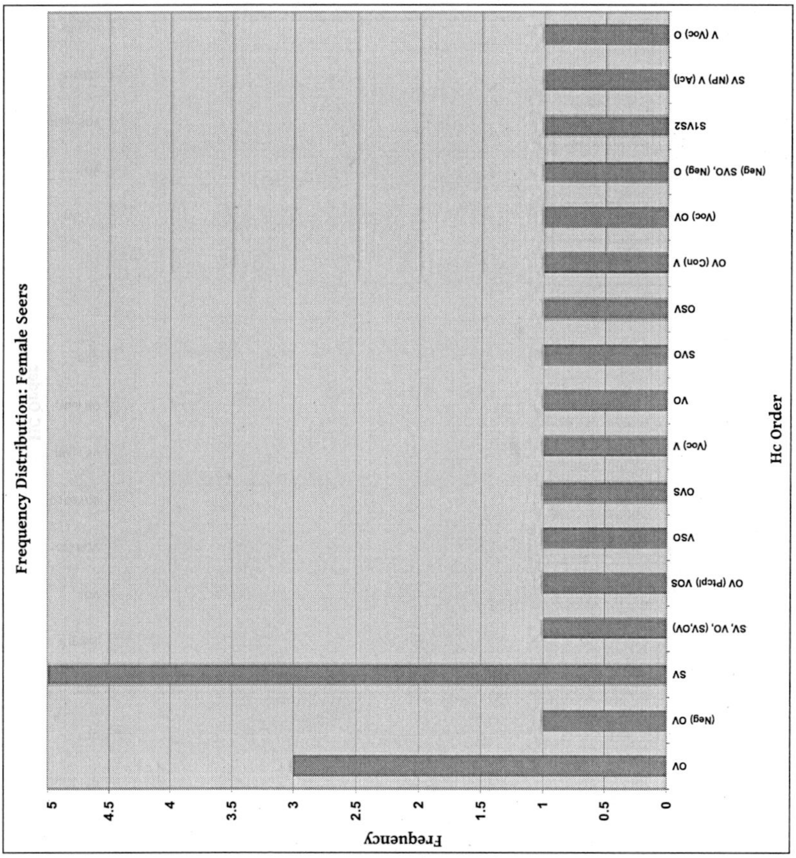
Frequency Distribution: Female Seers
Frequency
Hc Order
0
0.5
1
1.5
2
2.5
3
3.5
4
4.5
5
OV
(Neg) OV
SV
SV, VO, (SV,OV)
OV (Ptcpl) VOS
VSO
OVS
(Voc) V
VO
SVO
OSV
OV (Con) V
(Voc) OV
(Neg) SVO, (Neg) O
S1VS2
SV (NP) V (AcI)
V (Voc) O

Analysis II: A Study of the Negative Sentences in Verses Ascribed to Male and Female Seers

SELECT VERSES OF MALE SEERS

Eight verses with negative sentences are randomly selected from the hymns ascribed to male seers in *Ṛgveda*. They are being analysed here syntactically.

1. Verse of Kutsa Āṅgirasa (I.109.3):

mā́ cchedma raśmī́r íti nā́dhamānāḥ | *pitṝṇā́ṁ śaktī́r anuyácchamānāḥ* |
indrāgníbhyāṁ káṁ vṛ́ṣaṇo madanti | *tā́ hy ádrī dhiṣáṇāyā upásthe* ||

The word order is:

Neg V O Indcl (Advcl) Ptcpl(Adj_1S) | Poss O Ptcpl(Adj_2S) |
Instr O S V (NP) | S Indcl AdjS Poss pre V ||

Here, a complex sentence runs through the first three lines of the verse, *mā́ … íti* is the adverbial clause modifying the verb *madanti* in the NP. A simple sentence occurs in line d. The HC orders are as follows:

(i) (Neg) VO (Advcl) $Ptcpl_1$ O $Ptcpl_2$ OSV (NP)

(ii) SV

2. Verse of Gṛtsamada (II.18.8):

ná ma índreṇa sakhyáṁ ví yoṣad | *asmábhyam asya dákṣiṇā duhītā* |
úpa jyéṣṭhe várūthe gábhastau | *prāyéprāye jigīvā́ṁsaḥ syāma* ||

The word order is:

Neg Poss Instr S pre V | Dat Poss S V |
pre Adj_1Loc Adj_2Loc Loc | Indcl(Loc) S(Ptcpl) V ||

There are three simple sentences in this verse. The Ptcpl *jigīvā́ṁsaḥ* in line d acts as the S of the sentence. The HC orders are:

(i) (Neg) SV

(ii) SV

(iii) SV

3. Verse of Vāmadeva Gautama (IV.30.1):

nákir indra tvád úttaro | *ná jyā́yā̃ asti vṛtrahan* |
nákir evā́ yáthā tvám ||

The word order is:

Neg Voc Abl S_1 | Neg S_2 V Voc |
Neg Indcl Indcl S ||

Two negative sentences run through the verse. The first one is a compound sentence with a dropped conjunctive and the V *asti* solely acts for the two sentences. The HC orders are as follows:

(i) (Neg) S_1 (Neg) S_2 V

(ii) (Neg) S

4. Verse of Śaṁyur Bārhaspatya (VI.44.11):

mā́ jásvane vṛṣabha no rarīthā | *mā́ te revátaḥ sakhyé riṣāma* |
pūrvī́ṣ ṭa indra niṣṣídho jáneṣu | *jahy ásuṣvīn prá vṛhā́ pṛṇataḥ* ||

The word order is:

Neg Dat Voc O V | Neg Poss Poss Loc V |
AdjS Poss Voc S Loc | V O, pre V O ||

There are four simple sentences in this verse two of which are negatives and two positives. The HC orders are:

(i) (Neg) OV

(ii) (Neg) V

(iii) SVO

(iv) VO

5. Verse of Viśvamanā Vaiyaśva (VIII.23.15):

ná tásya māyáyā caná | *ripúr īśīta mártyaḥ* |
yó agnáye dadā́śa | *havyádātibhiḥ* ||

The word order is:

Neg Poss(O) Instr Indcl | S V AdjS ||
S Dat V Instr ||

There are two sentences in this verse. One is negative and the other is positive. The HC orders are as follows:

(i) (Neg) (O) SV

(ii) SV

6. Verse of Yama Vaivasvata (X.10.8):

ná tiṣṭhanti ná ní miṣanty eté | *devā́nāṁ spáśa ihá yé cáranti* |
anyéna mád āhano yāhi tū́yaṁ | *téna ví vr̥ha ráthyeva cakrā́* ||

The word order is:

Neg V Neg pre V S | Poss S Indcl(Loc) Pro(S) V |
Instr Abl Voc V Indcl | Instr pre V AdjS Indcl S (comparison) ||

There are three sentences in this verse. The first one is a negative complex sentence, of which line a has the NP and the Acl occurs in line b. Next two lines have one simple sentence each. The HC orders are:

(i) (Neg) V (Neg) V S (NP) SV (Acl)

(ii) (Voc) V

(iii) VS

7. Verse of Aindra Vasukra (X.27.3):

nāháṁ táṁ veda yá íti brávīty- | *ádevayūnt samáraṇe jaghanvā́n* |
yadā́vā́khyat samáraṇam ŕ̥dhāvad | *ā́d íd dha me vr̥ṣabhā́ prá bruvanti* ||

The word order is:

Neg S O V (NP) S Indcl V। O Loc Adj(Ptcpl)।
Indcl(Loc) V O Adj। Indcl Indcl Indcl Poss O pre V॥

There are three sentences in the verse. The first one is a negative complex sentence, where *nā́hám̐ … veda* is the NP and *yá … jaghanvā́n* is the Acl. The Ptcpl *jaghanvā́n* in line b acts as the verb. In the last sentence *vr̥ṣabhā́* is O according to Sāyaṇa, when it may also be counted as the S of the sentence. The HC orders are:

(i) (Neg) SOV (NP) SVOV (Ptcpl) (Acl)
(ii) VO
(iii) OV

8. Verse of Nābhānediṣṭha Mānava (X.62.9):

ná tám aśnoti káś caná। divá-iva sā́nv ārábham।
sāvarṇyásya dákṣiṇā। ví síndhur iva paprathe॥

The word order is:

Neg O V_2 S Indcl। Poss Indcl S (comparison) Inf(V_1)।
Poss S। pre S Indcl (comparison) V॥

The verse has two sentences, of which the first is a negative simple sentence, where *ārábham* is an infinite verb. The HC orders are:

(i) (Neg) OV_2SV_1
(ii) SV

SELECT VERSES OF FEMALE SEERS

Eight verses are selected from the literature ascribed to female seers for a study of the negative sentences contained therein. They are as follows:

1. Verse of Apālā Ātreyī (VIII.91.3):

This verse is already analysed in analysis IA (see p. 247), only the HC orders are given below:

(i) OV
(ii) O (Neg) V

(iii) (Voc) V

2. Verse of Ghoṣā Kākṣīvatī (X.40.11):

ná tásya vidma tád u ṣú prá vocata | *yúvā ha yád yuvatyā́ḥ kṣéti yóniṣu* |
priyósriyasya vṛṣabhásya retíno | *gṛháṁ gamemā́śvinā tád uśmasi* ||

The word order is:

Neg Poss V O Indcl pre_1 pre_2 V | S Indcl Indcl Poss V Loc |
Poss Poss Poss | OV Voc O V ||

There are two complex sentences running through lines ab and cd respectively. In the first sentence the NP is *tád u ṣú prá vocata*, and *na tásya vidma* as also *yúvā … yóniṣu* are the two Acls qualifying the NP. In the second case the NP occurs at the end of line d, viz. *tád uśmasi* and the rest is the Acl. The HC orders are as follows:

(i) (Neg)V(Acl) OV(NP)SV(Acl)

(ii) OV(Acl) OV(NP)

3. Verse of Indrāṇī (X.86.6):

ná mát strī́ subhasáttarā | *ná suyā́śutarā bhuvat* | *ná mát práticyavīyasī* |
ná sákthy údyamīyasī | *víśvasmād índra úttaraḥ* ||

The word order is:

Neg Abl S Adj_1S | Neg Adj_2S V |
Neg Abl Adj_3S | Neg O Adj_4S | Abl S AdjS ||

The verse has four negative simple sentences. The sentence in line a has S but V is lacking there. The HC orders are:

(i) (Neg) S

(ii) (Neg) SV

(iii) (Neg) S

(iv) (Neg) OS

(v) S

4. Another verse of Indrāṇī (X.86.16):

ná séśe yásya rámbate । *'ntarā sakthyā̀ kápr̥t* ।
séd īśe yásya romaśám । *niṣedúṣo vijŕ̥mbhate* ।। *víśvasmād* etc.

The word order is:

Neg S V Poss V । Indcl Poss S ।
S Indcl V Poss S । Poss V ।। Abl etc.

This verse has two complex sentences, wherein line a *ná séśe* is the NP while the rest of the first hemistich is the Acl. Similarly, in line c *séd īśe* is the NP, and the rest excluding the refrain *víśvasmād,* etc. is the Acl. The HC orders are:

(i) (Neg) SV (NP) VS (Acl)

(ii) SV (NP) SV (Acl)

5. Verse of Urvaśī (X.95.15):

púrūravo mā́ mr̥thā mā́ prá papto । *mā́ tvā vŕ̥kāso áśivāsa u kṣan* ।
nā́ vái stráiṇāni sakhyā́ni santi । *sālāvr̥kā́ṇāṁ hŕ̥dayāny etā́* ।।

The word order is:

Voc Neg Indcl Neg pre Ptcpl(V) । Neg O S AdjS Indcl V ।
Neg Indcl AdjS S V । Poss AdjS Pro(S) ।।

Here, the simple sentence in line d has an understood V. The HC orders are:

(i) (Neg) V(Ptcpl)

(ii) (Neg) OSV

(iii) (Neg) SV

(iv) S

6. Verse of Saramā (X.108.4):

nā́háṁ táṁ veda dábhyaṁ dábhat sá । *yásyedáṁ dūtī́r asaraṁ parākā́t* ।

ná táṁ gūhanti sraváto gabhīrā́ । *hatā́ índreṇa paṇayaḥ śayadhve* ।।

The word order is:

Neg S O V AdjO V S । Poss O S V Abl ।
Neg O V AdjS S । Adj Instr Voc V ।।

There are three simple sentences and one complex sentence in the verse, viz. *dábhat sáḥ . . . parākā́t*, where *dábhat sáḥ* is the NP and the rest is Acl. The orders of the HCs are:

(i) (Neg) SOV

(ii) V S (NP) OSV (Acl)

(iii) (Neg) OVS

(iv) (Voc) V

7. Another verse of Saramā (X.108.10):

This verse is already analysed in Analysis IB (see p. 262), and hence only the HC orders are given here:

(i) (Neg) SVO, (Neg) O

(ii) S_1VS_2

(iii) SV(NP) V(Acl)

(iv) V(Voc)O

8. Verse of Godhā (X.134.7):

nákir devā minīmasi । *nákir ā́ yopayāmasi* ।
mantraśrútyaṁ carāmasi । *pakṣébhir apikakṣébhir* ।
atrābhí sáṁ rabhāmahe ।।

The word order is:

Neg O V । Neg pre V ।
OV । Instr Instr । Indcl pre_1 pre_2 V ।।

There are three short simple sentences in lines a, b and c respectively. The HC orders are:

(i) (Neg) OV

(ii) (Neg) V

(iii) OV

(iv) V

From all these 16 verses ascribed to both groups of seers only the negative sentences are picked out to estimate the syntactic patterns in the charts appearing in the next page. What follows shows the frequency of the negative sentence patterns in the verses of both groups of seers in a table, shaded separately.

A Study of the HC Orders in Negative Sentences in Select Verses of Male and Female Seers

Sl. No.	*Male Seers*	*Count*	*Freq.*	*Sl. No.*	*Female Seers*
1	(Neg) VO (Advcl) Ptcpl$_1$	***Male Seers***		1	O (Neg)V
	O Ptpcl$_2$ OSV (NP)	(Neg) VO (Advcl) Ptcpl$_1$		2	(Neg) V (Acl) OV (NP)
2	(Neg) SV	O Ptpcl$_2$ OSV (NP)	1		SV(Acl)
3	(Neg) S$_1$ (Neg) S$_2$ V	(Neg) SV	1	3	(Neg) S
	(Neg) S	(Neg) S$_1$ (Neg) S$_2$ V	1		(Neg) SV
4	(Neg) OV	(Neg) S	1		(Neg) S
	(Neg) V	(Neg) OV	1		(Neg) OS
5	(Neg) OSV	(Neg) V	1	4	(Neg) SV (NP) VS (Acl)
6	(Neg) V (Neg) VS	(Neg) OSV	1	5	(Neg) V (Ptcpl)
	(NP) SV (Acl)	(Neg) V (Neg) VS			(Neg) OSV
7	(Neg) SOV (NP)	(NP) SV (Acl)	1		(Neg) SV
	SVOV (Ptcpl) (Acl)	(Neg) SOV (NP)		6	(Neg) SOV
8	(Neg) OV$_2$SV$_1$	SVOV (Ptcpl) (Acl)	1		(Neg) OVS
		(Neg) OV$_2$SV$_1$	1	7	(Neg) SVO, (Neg) O
				8	(Neg) OV
		Female Seers			(Neg) V
		O (Neg)V	1		
		(Neg)V(Acl) OV (NP)			
		SV(Acl)	1		
		(Neg) S	2		
		(Neg) SV	2		
		(Neg) OS	1		
		(Neg) SV (NP) VS (Acl)	1		
		(Neg) V (Ptcpl)	1		
		(Neg) OSV	1		
		(Neg) SOV	1		
		(Neg) OVS	1		
		(Neg) SVO, (Neg) O	1		
		(Neg) OV	1		
		(Neg) V	1		

Frequency distribution is shown graphically in the following pages.

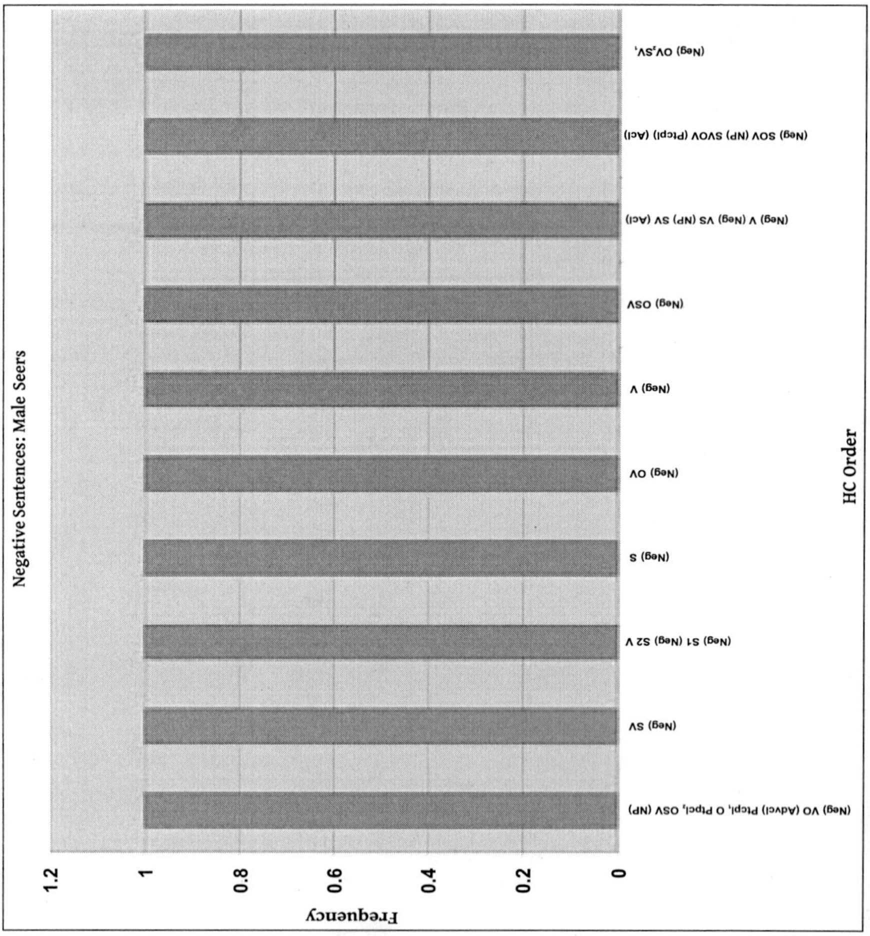
Negative Sentences: Male Seers
Frequency
HC Order
0
0.2
0.4
0.6
0.8
1
1.2
(Neg) VO (Advcl) Ptcpl, O Ptpcl, OSV (NP)
(Neg) SV
(Neg) S1 (Neg) S2 V
(Neg) S
(Neg) OV
(Neg) V
(Neg) OSV
(Neg) V (Neg) VS (NP) SV (AcI)
(Neg) SOV (NP) SVOV (Ptcpl) (AcI)
(Neg) OV,SV,

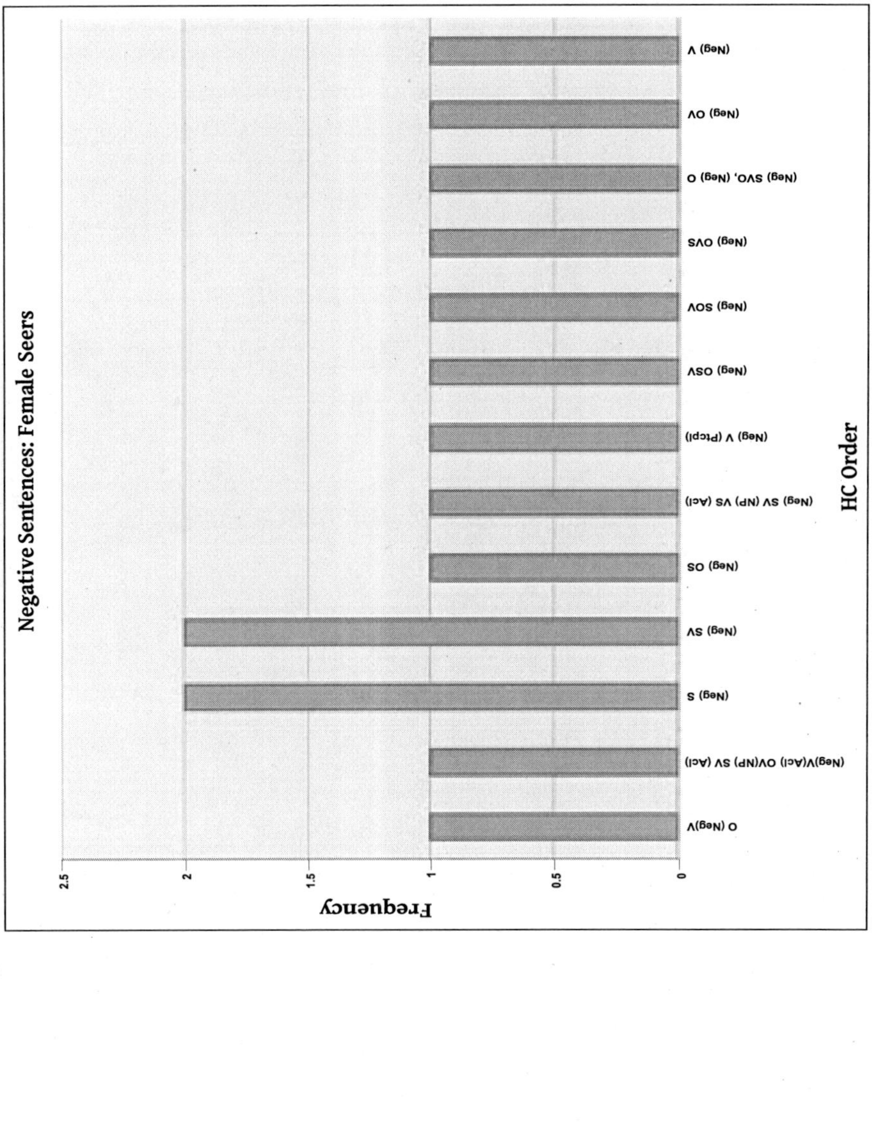
Negative Sentences: Female Seers
Frequency
2.5
2
1.5
1
0.5
0
O (Neg)V
(Neg)V(AcI) OV(NP) SV (AcI)
(Neg) S
(Neg) SV
(Neg) OS
(Neg) SV (NP) VS (AcI)
(Neg) V (Ptcpl)
(Neg) OSV
(Neg) SOV
(Neg) OVS
(Neg) SVO, (Neg) O
(Neg) OV
(Neg) V
HC Order

Analysis III: A Study of the Interrogative Sentences in Verses of Male and Female Seers

SELECT VERSES OF MALE SEERS

A few verses with a number of interrogative sentences ascribed to male seers are selected at random (since such sentences occur profusely in the verses of Paura Ātreya, I was somewhat compelled to pick up no less than three verses of his alone), which are now being syntactically analysed. They are as follows:

1. Verse of Paura Ātreya (V.74.1):

kū́ṣṭho devāv aśvinā । *'dyā́ divó manāvasū* ।
tác chravatho vṛṣanvasū । *átrir vām ā́ vivāsati* ।।

The word order is:

IP(Loc) V Voc Voc । Indcl Abl Voc ।
Indcl V Voc । S O pre V ।।

There are three sentences in this verse, the first of which is an interrogative sentence running through lines a and b. The HC orders are:

(i) IPV (Voc)
(ii) V (Voc)
(iii) SOV

2. Another verse of Paura Ātreya (V.74.2):

kúha tyā́ kúha nú śrutā́ । *diví devā́ nā́satyā* ।
kásmin-n ā́ yatatho jáne । *kó vāṁ nadī́nāṁ sácā* ।।

The word order is:

IP(Loc) Pro(S) IP(Loc) Indcl Loc । Loc AdjS S ।
IPr(Loc) Indcl V Loc । IPr(S) O Poss Indcl ।।

Among the four sentences constituting the verse all are interrogatives. The HC orders are:

(i) IPS

(ii) IPS

(iii) IPrV

(iv) IPr (S)O

3. The third verse of the same hymn by Paura Ātreya (V.74.3):

káṁ yāthaḥ káṁ ha gacchathaḥ । *kám ácchā yuñjāthe rátham* ।
kásya bráhmāṇi raṇyatho । *vayáṁ vām uśmasīṣṭáye* ।।

The word order is:

IPr(O) V IPr(O) Indcl V । IPr(O_2) Indcl V O_1 ।
IPr (Poss) O V । Pro(S) O V Dat ।।

There are five sentences in the four lines of this verse, and four of them are interrogatives. The HC orders are:

(i) IPr(O) V

(ii) IPr(O) V

(iii) IPr(O_2) VO_1

(iv) IPr OV

(v) SOV

4. Verse of Medhātithi and Medhātithi Kāṇva (VIII.1.7):

kvèyatha kvéd asi । *purutrā́ cid dhí te mánaḥ* ।
álarṣi yudhma khajakr̥t purandara । *prá gāyatrā́ agāsiṣuḥ* ।।

The word order is:

IP(Loc) V IP(Loc) Indcl V । Loc Indcl Indcl Poss S ।
V Voc Voc Voc । pre S V ।।

There are five simple sentences in this verse, of which two are interrogatives. The HC orders are:

(i) IPV

(ii) IPV

(iii) S

(iv) V (Voc)

(v) SV

5. Verse of Pragātha Kāṇva (VIII.64.8):

kásya svit sávanaṁ vṛ́ṣā | *jujuṣvā̆ áva gacchati* |
índraṁ ká u svid ā́ cake ||

The word order is:

IPr(Poss) Indcl O Voc | AdjVoc pre V |
O IPr(S) Indcl Indcl pre V ||

There are two sentences in this verse and both of which are interrogatives. The HC orders are:

(i) IPr O (Voc) V

(ii) OIPr(S) V

6. Verse of Gopavana Ātreya (VIII.73.4):

kúha sthaḥ kúha jagmathuḥ | *kúha śyenéva petathuḥ* |
ánti ṣád bhūtu vām ávaḥ ||

The word order is:

IP(Loc) V IP(Loc) V | IP(Loc) S Indcl (comparison) V |
Indcl AdjS(Ptcpl) V Poss Indcl ||

There are four sentences in this verse, where three are interrogatives. The HC orders are:

(i) IPV

(ii) IPV

(iii) IP(S) V

(iv) VS

SELECT VERSES OF FEMALE SEERS

A few interrogative sentences are found in the verses of X.40 ascribed to Ghoṣā and X.85 ascribed to Sūryā, as also one in a verse ascribed to Apālā, viz. VIII.91.4. They are as follows:

1. Verse of Ghoṣā (X.40.1):

ráthaṁ yā́ntaṁ kúha kó ha vāṁ narā | *práti dyumántaṁ suvitā́ya bhūṣati* |
prātaryā́vāṇaṁ vibhvàṁ viśéviśe | *vástorvastor váhamānaṁ dhiyā́ śámi* ||

The word order is:

O Adj_1O IP(Loc) IPr(S) Indcl Poss Voc | pre Adj_2O Dat V |
Adj_3O Adj_4O Loc | Loc Adj_5O Instr Loc ||

There is one long simple sentence running through the four lines of the verse. The HC order is as follows:

(i) O IP IPr(S) (Voc) V

2. The second verse of Ghoṣā (X.40.2):

kúha svid doṣā́ kúha vástor aśvínā | *kúhābhipitvám karataḥ kúhoṣatuḥ* |
kó vāṁ śayutrā́ vidháveva devắraṁ | *máryaṁ ná yóṣā kr̥ṇute sadhástha ā́* ||

The word order is:

IP(Loc) Indcl Loc IP(Loc) Loc Voc | IP(Loc) O V IP(Loc) V |
IPr(S) O <u>Loc S Indcl O</u> (comparison) | <u>O Indcl S</u> (comparison) V Loc pre ||

A repetitive use of IP *kúha* is found in the first hemistich of the verse. The HC orders are:

(i) IP IP IP OV

(ii) IPV

(iii) IPr(S) O (SO) (OS) V

3. The third verse of Ghoṣā (X.40.3):

prātár jarethe jaraṇéva kā́payā | *vástorvastor yajatā́ gacchatho gr̥hám* |
kásya dhvasrā́ bhaváthaḥ kásya vā narā | *rājaputréva sávanā́va gacchathaḥ* ||

The word order is:

Indcl(Loc) V Instr Indcl (comparison) Instr | Loc S V O |
IPr(Poss) S V IPr(Poss) Indcl (con) Voc | S Indcl
(comparison) O pre V ||

Four simple sentences appear in the last hemistich. The HC orders are:

(i) V

(ii) SVO

(iii) IPr SV

(iv) IPr Voc (S) OV

4. Another verse of Ghoṣā, l.c. (X.40.14):

kvà svid adyá katamā́sv aśvínā vikṣú | dasrā́ mādayete śubháspátī |
ká īṁ ní yeme katamásya jagmatur | víprasya vā yájamānasya vā gṛhám ||

The word order is:

IP(Loc) Indcl Indcl (Loc) IP(Loc) Voc Loc | Voc V Voc |
IPr(S) O pre V IP(Poss) V | Poss Indcl Poss Indcl O ||

Three interrogative sentences appear in the four lines of this verse. The HC orders are:

(i) IP IP (Voc) V

(ii) IPr(S) OV

(iii) IP VO

5. Verse of Sūryā (X.85.15):

yád áyātaṁ śubhaspatī | vareyáṁ sūryā́m úpa |
kváikaṁ cakráṁ vām āsīt | kvà dveṣṭrā́ya tasthathuḥ ||

The word order is:

Indcl V Voc | AdjO O pre |
IP(Loc) Num(AdjS) S Poss V | IP(Loc) Dat V ||

There are three simple sentences in this verse, the last two of which are interrogatives. The HC orders are:

(i) V (Voc) O

(ii) IP SV

(iii) IPV

6. Verse of Apālā (VIII.91.4):

kuvíc chákat kuvít kárat । *kuvín no vásyasas kárat* ।
kuvít patidvíṣo yatī́r । *índreṇa saṁgámāmahai* ।।

The word order is:

IP V IP V । IP O AdjO V ।
IP AdjS S । Instr pre V ।।

Here, line a has two sentences, where the interrogative particle *kuvit* occurs four times. Hence, four interrogative sentences are found in the short span of three lines of this verse. The HC orders are as given below:

(i) IPV

(ii) IPV

(iii) IP OV

(iv) IP SV

From all these twelve verses of both groups of seers, only the interrogative sentences are picked out to estimate the syntactic pattern. The HC orders of the interrogative sentences appear serially in two charts in the next page along with two frequency charts for both groups of seers. The frequency distribution of the HC orders will be shown in tabular format and graphically in the following pages.

A Study of the HC Orders in Interrogative Sentences in Select Verses of Male and Female Seers

Sl. No.	*Male Seers*	*Count*	*Freq.*	*Sl. No.*	*Female Seers*
1	IPV (Voc)	*Male Seers*		1	O IP IPr(S) (Voc) V
2	IPS	IPV (Voc)	1	2	IP IP IP OV
	IPS	IPS	2		IPV
	IPr V	Ipr V	1		IPr(S) O (SO) (OS) V
	IPr(S)O	IPr(S) O	1	3	IPr SV
3	IPr(O) V	IPr(O) V	2		IPr Voc(S) OV
	IPr(O) V	IPr (O_2) VO_1	1	4	IP IP (Voc) (V)
	Ipr(O_2) VO_1	IPr OV	1		IPr(S) OV
	IPr OV	IPV	4		IP VO
4	IPV	IPr O (Voc) V	1	5	IP SV
	IPV	O IPr(S) V	1		IPV
5	IPr O (Voc) V	IP(S) V	1	6	IPV
	O IPr(S) V				IPV
6	IPV	*Female Seers*			IP OV
	IPV	O IPr(S)(Voc)V	1		IP SV
	IP(S) V	IP IP IP OV	1		
		IPV	4		
		IPr(S) O (SO) (OS) V	1		
		IPr SV	1		
		IPr Voc(S) OV	1		
		IP IP (Voc) V	1		
		IPr(S) OV	1		
		IP VO	1		
		IP SV	2		
		IP OV	1		

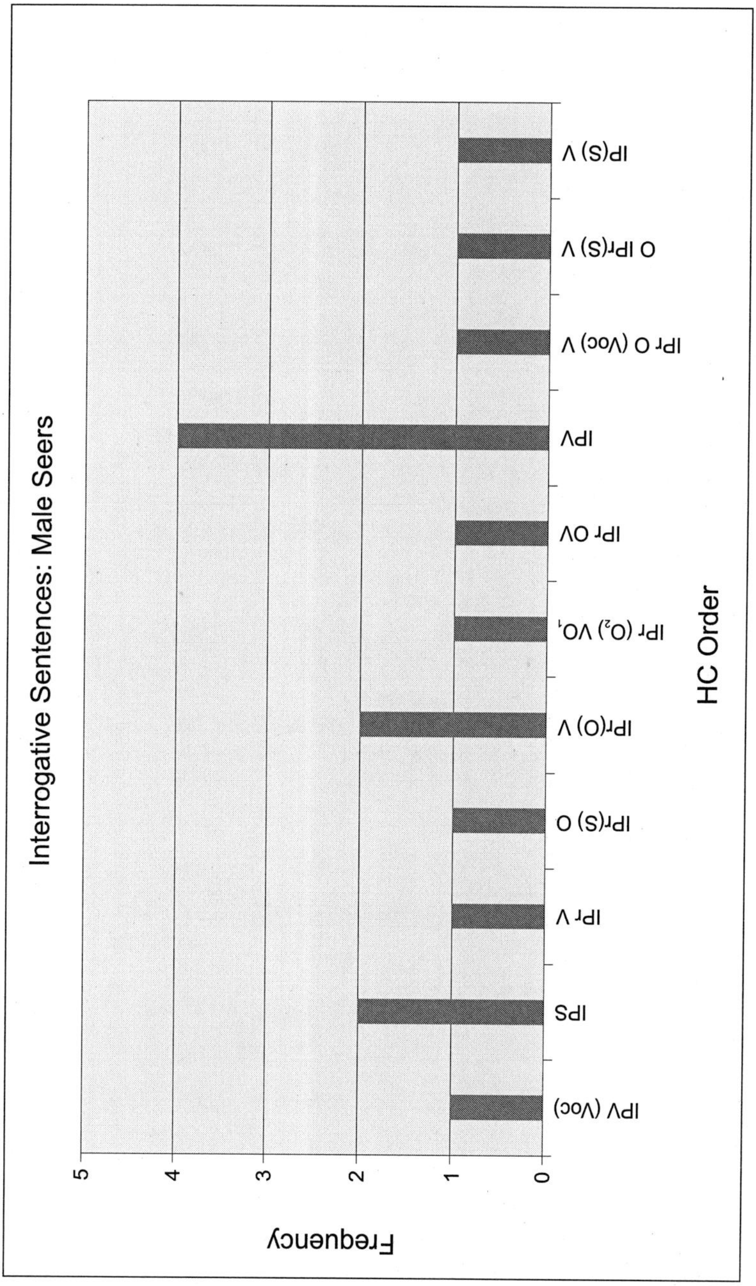
Interrogative Sentences: Male Seers
Frequency
0
1
2
3
4
5
IPV (Voc)
IPS
IPr V
IPr(S) O
IPr(O) V
IPr (O2) VO,
IPr OV
IPV
IPr O (Voc) V
O IPr(S) V
IP(S) V
HC Order

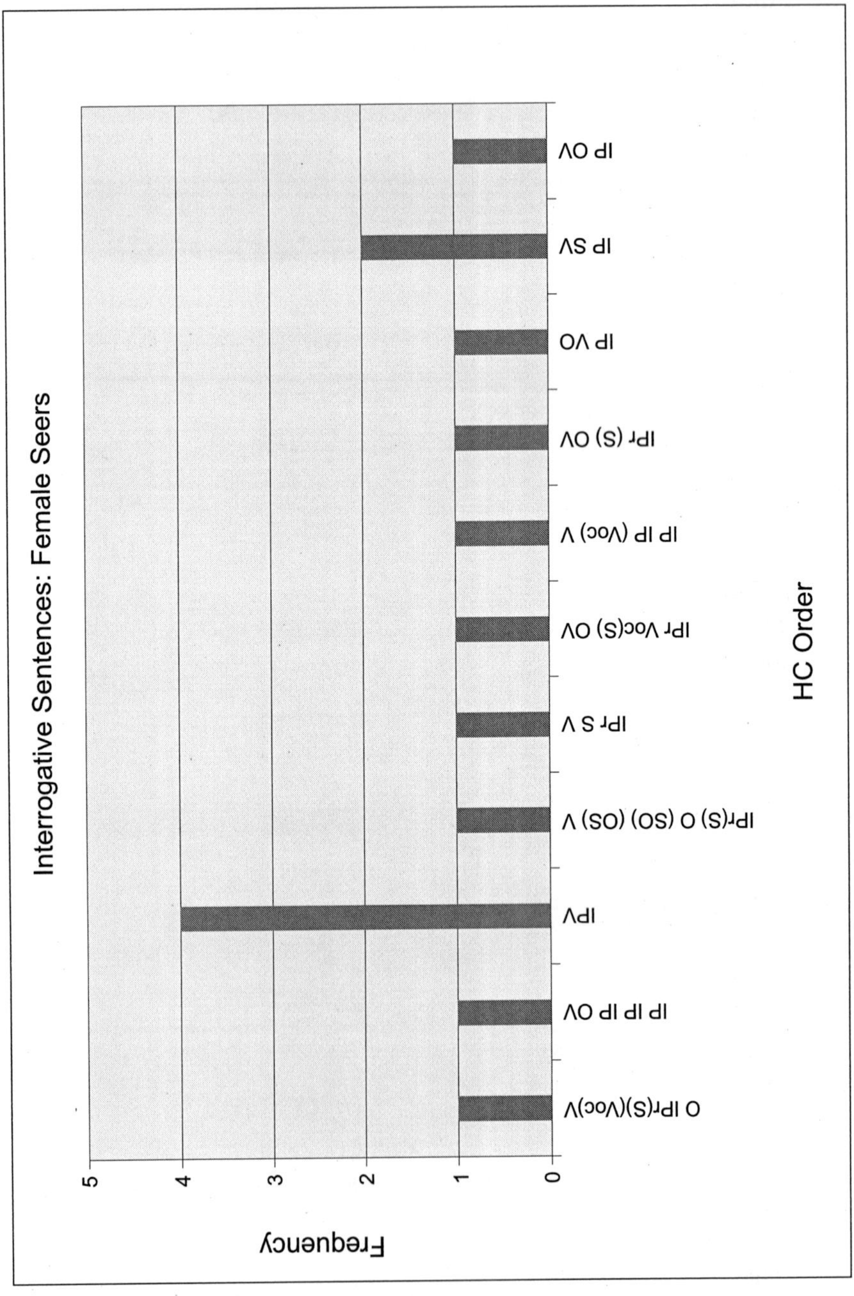
Interrogative Sentences: Female Seers
Frequency
0
1
2
3
4
5
IP OV
IP SV
IP VO
IPr (S) OV
IP IP (Voc) V
IPr Voc(S) OV
IPr S V
IPr(S) O (SO) (OS) V
IPV
IP IP IP OV
O IPr(S)(Voc)V
HC Order

Findings from the Above Analyses

From the above analyses, though based on a very limited data, some interesting information can be gathered. For example, from Analysis IA it appears that the predominant sentence patterns in the literature of the female seers were Object–Verb and Subject–Verb. These two patterns stand out 70 per cent more than other combinations. Next to these two come Object–Subject–Verb and Subject–Object–Verb patterns, though trailing much behind.

From Analysis IB the predominant sentence pattern seems to be the Subject–Verb one in literatures ascribed to both male and female seers, while the Object–Verb combination frequents the literature of female seers more than that of their male counterparts. The OSV and SOV combinations are also found in almost the same ratio as they were found in Analysis IA.

Analysis II reveals an interesting trend in the Negative sentence patterns in the literature ascribed to both groups of seers. It suggests that the males were more innovative in telling "no" than their female counterparts. From the data, though scanty, it is observed that not a single pattern of the negative sentences has been repeated in the randomly selected verses of the male poets. Contrarily, even in this limited scope of study at least two patterns of the same are repeated in the verses by female poets.

Analysis III suggests that female poets were more inquisitive, given to their innovative ways of questioning. As this study shows, only two patterns are repeated among the eleven patterns selected from the verses of the female seers. In contradistinction, male seers have repeated almost 38 per cent patterns in questioning, i.e. out of eight patterns selected from the verses of the male seers, three patterns find repetitions.

It may not be proper to come to a conclusion on the basis of such a limited data about the general trends of the language style in literature of both groups of seers. Still, random selection often projects a close picture of the general trend, and hence, the above findings may have some significance in inciting a more thorough study of the same.

8

Epilogue

In view of the account given at Chapter 1 (see p. 35), it can be presumed that there were at least seventeen female seers who were of this earth and soil. Consequently, in the hymns composed by them, their desire, happiness, sorrow and triumph have been faithfully reflected. Altekar (1962) opines that although some of the women seers of *Ṛgveda* may have been mythical personages, internal evidence shows that some others like Lopāmudrā, Viśvavārā, Apālā, Sikatā, Nīvāvarī and Ghoṣā were the women in flesh and blood, who once lived in the "Hindu" society. He further goes on arguing that the authors of *Ṛgveda* X.145 and 159 are undoubtedly women, though it may be questioned if their real names were Indrāṇī and Śacī, as recorded by tradition. As a sequel to Altekar's view, a thorough examination of the hymns concerned has compelled us to arrive at a conclusion that Romaśā, Śaśvatī, Vasukra-patnī, Agastya-svasṛ, Vāc, Godhā, Niṣat and Upaniṣat, and to some extent also Yamī of X.10 were indeed women of this soil. Their hymns contain a lot of materials for estimating the position of the poetesses in ancient Indian civilization.

The findings of this study establish that on no account the female seers of *Ṛgveda* were lagging behind their male counterparts. Interpreters of the traditional school as well as of the Western school did discuss the hymns and verses ascribed to women poets with an equal importance they attached to the writings of the male poets. A detailed analysis of the expositions of the select texts by both the traditional and modern schools of interpretation, respectively of the East and the West, shows that the literature ascribed to the fair sex was extensively treated by the commentators, and they did not discriminate between the literatures of men and women only on account of their genders.

It is generally believed that women in the early Vedic age enjoyed equal rights with men. In support of this view, the participation of women in religious and social duties along with their husbands is frequently referred to. The study based on the socio-cultural perspective of the select hymns suggest that though women indeed had a prominent role in early Vedic times compared to the one she possessed in later ages, it is also true that her role in the earlier age had also its limits, and her enjoying equal rights with her husband is but a little exaggeration based on hallucination. A thorough study proves that the Ṛgvedic women lived a life with less social bindings than the one women of the middle age lived. They were brought up with care and given education, and most of them selected a husband at their own choice, after marriage usually looking after the households of their husbands. Sometimes they did work to support the family, but generally it was the husband's responsibility to support their wives. The same tradition continued in the middle-class Indian families down to this day. Today, we can identify the Ṛgvedic women, who were not hidden under "purdah" and whose head was held high in self-respect, with the educated middle-class women of modern India. Physical pleasure also mattered much for them, and the verses of the female seers are remarkable for the longing for sexual pleasure in a quite naïve and unsophisticated language.

Chapter 4 of this study ventured to discuss the personal traits of all the female seers and their compositions on the solid basis of the mythological data available in the Vedic and subsequent literatures. This reveals that the origins of a number of female seers go back to the Indo-European age, and in course of time many human characters were transcreated into mythical beings. Characters such as Aditi, as Indra's mother, was originally probably a woman in flesh and blood, but in course of time this simple stage passed on to the next secondary stage that emerged as soon as the person concerned was in the collective consciousness of imagination awarded a place in the natural phenomena. Even afterwards, poetic fancy went on creating many more attributes, which had not been associated with the primary concept.

Chapter 5 of this dissertation attempts to establish that the hymns and verses of female seers were as important in ritualistic application as those of the male seers had been. Hymns like *Ṛgveda* X.85, 127, 153 and 154 find vital applications in both the Śrauta and Gṛhya rites. In the age of the Brāhmaṇas, the importance of the *mantras* was determined by their efficacy in various rituals and sacrifices. Even from this point of view, too, *mantras* ascribed to women seers were nearly at par with those authored by their male counterparts.

A literary analysis of the select texts, with special emphasis on the poetic imageries found therein, has been done in the sixth chapter of this study. This tends to show that there was parity in the poetic bend of mind in *Ṛgveda* irrespective of the genders of the seers. Poets from both sexes collected images for their poetry from their surroundings, from the relationships they found in their society, and from the early fund of poetry they inherited. The Ṛgvedic images, born of close and direct observations of life, are characterized by their freshness and naivety. Images used in the poetry did not serve a mere decorative purpose, but they were believed to have a ritualistic efficacy as well. Poetry by neither sex lacked the above-mentioned characteristics, since it would not be fair to discriminate the poetry of female seers from that of their male counterparts, at least on the ground of poetic imagery.

The syntactic analysis of the verses of female poets brings forward some interesting traits in the seventh chapter of this study. A modest comparative study of the sentence-patterns in the literature ascribed to both sex of seers shows that the female seers were more innovative in structuring interrogative sentences than their male counterparts, whereas the male seers were keen in telling "no" in every possible way because the negative sentence patterns are hardly repeated in their literature. Similar charts may well be used in a wider scope to determine sentence patterns in the literature of *Ṛgveda* as a whole.

Bibliography

Abrams, M.H., 1993, *A Glossary of Literary Terms*, 6th Indian edn, Bangalore: Prism Books.

Altekar, Anant Sadashiv, 1959 (repr. 1962), *The Position of Women in Hindu Civilization: From Prehistoric Times to the Present Day*, 2rd edn, Delhi: Motilal Banarsidass.

Apte, Vasudeo Govind, ed., 1926, *Taittirīyāraṇyakam*, Poona: Anandasrama.

Aufrecht, Theodor, 1858, "Die Sage von Affe", *Indische Studien,* 4: 1ff.

Baldick, Chris, 1990, *The Concise Oxford Dictionary of Literary Terms*, New York: Oxford University Press.

Bergaigne, Abel, 1878-83 (1969), *La Religion Védique d'pres les Hymnes du Rigveda*, 3 vols., Paris, tr. V.G. Paranjape, Poona: Aryasamskrti Prakasana.

———, 1881, "Quelques observations sur les figures de rhétorique dans le Rig-veda", *Mémoires de la Société de Linguistique de Paris,* 4: 96ff.

Bhattacharya, [Bhattacharji] Sukumari, 1394, BE (1987), *Prācīn Bhārat*: Samāj o Sāhitya (Bengali) (*Ancient India*: *Society and Literature*), Kalikātā: Ananda Publishers.

Bhattacharji, Sukumari, 1978, *The Indian Theogony: A Comparative Study of Indian Mythology from the Vedas to the Purāṇas*, Corrected Indian edn, Calcutta: Firma KLM (1st publ. Cambridge University Press, London, 1970).

———, 1984, *Literature in the Vedic Age*, vol. 1, Calcutta: Firma KLM.

Bloomfield, Maurice, 1906, *A Vedic Concordance*, Cambridge, MA: Harvard Oriental Series, vol. 10, Indian repr., 1964, Delhi: Motilal Banarsidass.

———, 1916, *Ṛigveda Repetitions*, Cambridge, Massachusetts, Harvard Oriental Series, vol. 24.

Böhtlingk, Otto and Rudolf Roth, 1852-75, *Sanskrit-Wörterbuch*, 7 Theile, St. Petersburg, 1st Indian edn, 1990, Delhi: Motilal Banarsidass.

Bradke, P. von, 1892, "Ein lustiges Wagenrennen in Altindien", *Zeitschrift der Deutschen Morgenländischen Gesellschaft,* 46: 445ff.

Brereton, Joel P., 2013, "The Ṛgvedic Ghoṣā Hymns and the Atirātra", in *Beyond Hatti: A Tribute to Gary Beckman*, ed. Billie Jean Collins and Piotr Michalowski, pp. 45-61. Atlanta, GA: Lockwood Press.

Campbell, Joseph, 1968, *The Hero with a Thousand Faces*, 2nd edn, New York: Princeton University Press.

Charpentier, Jarl, 1920, *Die Suparṇasage: Untersuchungen zur altindischen Literatur-und Sagengeschichte*, Uppsala-Leipzig: Otto Harrassowitz.

Chatterjee, Kshetres Chandra, 1976, *Studies in Vedic and Indo-Iranian Religion and Literature*, vol. 1, Varanasi: Bhāratīya Vidyā Prakāśana.

Chatterji, Kshitis Chandra,1945, *Devī-sūkta*, Calcutta: University of Calcutta.

Chatterji, Suniti Kumar, 1962, *Indianism and the Indian Synthesis*, Calcutta: University of Calcutta.

Chattopadhyay, Amar Kumar, 2001, *Ṛgvedīya Gṛhyasūtra* (Bengali) (*Ṛgvedic Gṛhyasūtras*), Kalikātā (Kolkata): Sanskrit Pustak Bhandar

———, 2002, *Āśvalāyana-Śrautasūtra* (Bengali), Kalikātā (Kolkata): The Asiatic Society.

Choudhuri, Usha, 1983, *Vedic Mythopoeia: An Approach to Religion, Myth and Poetry*, Delhi: Nag Publishers.

Chowdhury, Tarapada, 1931, "On the Interpretation of Some Doubtful Words in the Atharva-Veda", *Journal of the Bihar and Orissa Research Society,* 17.1 ([January-] March 19[30-]31): 25-100 (also separately publ., with the same pagination).

Cowell, Edward Byles, 1866, *Introduction to H.H. Wilson's Translation of Ṛig-Veda-Sanhitā: A Collection of Ancient Hindu Hymns …*, vol. 5, London: N. Trübner & Co.

Dandekar, Ramchandra Narayan, 1974, "Viṣṇu in the Veda", in *Mm. Dr.*

P.V. Kane Commemoration Monograph, ed. S.N. Gajendragadkar, University of Bombay, pp. 95-111.

Darmesteter, James, tr., 1880, *Zend Avesta*, Oxford, Sacred Books of the East, no. 4.

Das, Abinas Chandra, 1927, *R̥gvedic India*, rev. 2nd edn, Calcutta: R. Cambray & Co. (1st publ. 1920).

Das, Rahul Peter, 1987, "On the Identification of a Vedic Plant", in *Studies on Indian Medical History*, ed. Gerrit Jan Meulenbeld and Dominik Wujastyk, Groningen Oriental Studies vol. 2, Groningen, pp. 19-42.

Das Gupta, Dipankar and S. Manoharan, 1990, "Sentence Structure in Some Indian Languages", in *Linguistic Traits across Language Boundaries: A Report of All India Linguistic Traits Survey*, ed. Shree Krishan, Calcutta: Anthropological Survey of India.

Dharmapal, Gauri, 1996, *Beder Bhāṣā o Chanda* (Bengali) (*The Language and Metres of the Veda*), Kolkata: West Bengal State Book Board.

———, 2003, *Puronotun Beder Kabitā* (Bengali) (*The Ever New Poetry of the Veda*), Kolkata: Ritam.

Doniger O'Flaherty, Wendy, 1981, *The Rig-veda: An Anthology*, Harmondsworth, UK: Penguin Books (Kindle Edition).

Downey, June E., 1929, *Creative Imagination*, London: Routledge and Trench: Trubner & Co.

Eliade, Mircea, 1960, *Myths, Dreams and Mysteries*, New York: Columbia University and Harper & Brothers.

Elizarenkova, Tatyana J., 1995, *Language and Style of the Vedic R̥ṣis*, Albany, NY: State University of New York.

Geiger, Wilhelm, 1885, *Civilization of the Eastern Iranians in Ancient Times: With an Introduction to Avestan Religion*, tr. from German by Darab Dastur Peshotan Sanjana, London: Henry Frowde Amen Corner, E.C.

Geldner, Karl Friedrich, 1951, *Der Rig-veda: aus dem Sanskrit ins Deutsche übersetzt und mit einem laufenden Kommentar versehen*, Teil 1, Cambridge (MA), London, Wiesbaden: Harvard Oriental Series, vol. 33.

Ghosh, Abhijit, 2000, *Non-Aryan Linguistic Elements in the Atharva Veda*: A Study of Some Words of Austric Origin, Calcutta: Sanskrit Pustak Bhandar.

Glasenapp, Helmuth von, 1961, *Die Literaturen Indiens*, Stuttgart: Alfred Kröner.

Gonda, Jan, 1975, *Vedic Literature* (*Saṁhitās and Brāhmaṇas*), A History of Indian Literature, vol. I, Fasc. I, Wiesbaden: Otto Harrassowitz.

Grassmann, Hermann, 1873, *Wörterbuch zum Rig-Veda*, Leipzig: Brockhaus.

———, 1877, *Rig-veda: übersetzt und mit kritischen und erlaüternden Anmerkungen versehen*, 2 Theilen, Leipzig: Brockhaus.

Griffith, Ralph Thomas Hotchkin, 1896-97, *The Hymns of the Rigveda,* tr. with a popular commentary, 2 vols., Benares: E.J. Lazarus & Co. (1st publ. 1889-92 in 4 vols.).

Griffiths, Arlo, 2009, *The Paippalāda Saṁhitā of the Atharvaveda, Kāṇḍas 6 and 7: A New Edition with Translation and Commentary*. Gronigue: Egbert Forsten (Groningen Oriental Studies XXII), LXXXVI+540 p.

Hillebrandt, Alfred, 1927, *Vedische Mythologie*, 2 vols., Breslau, tr. S.R. Sarma, Delhi: Motilal Banarsidass, 1980.

Hock, Hans Henrich, 2013, "Proto-Indo-European Verb-finality: Reconstruction, Typology, Validation", *Journal of Historical Lingustics*, 3(1): 49-76.

Indra, 1955, *The Status of Women in Ancient India*, 2nd edn, Delhi: Motilal Banarsidass.

Jamison, Stephanie W., 1996, *Sacrificed Wife / Sacrificer's Wife: Women, Ritual and Hospitality in Ancient India,* New York: Oxford University Press.

Jamison, Stephanie W. and Joel P. Brereton (tr.), 2014, *The Rigveda: The Earliest Poetry of India,* 3 vols., South Asia Research Series, ed. Martha Selby, a publication series by University of Texas South Asia Institute and Oxford University Press, New York: Oxford University Press (Kindle edition).

Jha Sharma, Mukunda, ed., 1989, *Niruktam* (with a commentary after the

Ṛjvartha-vyākhyā of Durgācārya, in Sanskrit), Delhi: Chowkhamba Sanskrit Pratishthan.

Kashikar, Chintamani Ganesh, 1962, *Śrautakoṣa*, vol. 1, pt. 2, Poona: Vaidika Saṁśodhana Maṇḍala.

Kaegi, Adolf, 1880, *Der Rigveda*, 2nd edn (first publ. 1978-79 in 2 pts.). Authorized tr. with additions to the notes by R. Arrowsmith, Madison: Wisconsin, 1886.

Kosambi, Damodar Dharmanand, 1962, *Myth and Reality*, Bombay: Popular Prakashan.

Lanman, Charles Rockwell, 1889, *A Sanskrit Reader: With Vocabulary and Notes*, 2nd edn, Boston: Ginn, Heath (1st publ. 1884: vols. 1, 2; 1889: vol. 3).

Lassen, Christian, 1836, *Die Altpersischen Keilinschriften von Persepolis: Entzifferung des Alphabets und Erklaerung des Inhalts*, Bonn: Eduard Weber.

Lowe, John J., 2015, *Participles in Rigvedic Sanskrit: The Syntax and Semantics of Adjectival Verb Forms,* Oxford: Oxford University Press (Kindle edition).

Ludwig, Alfred, 1876, *Der Rigveda: oder die heiligen Hymnen der Brāhmana, zum ersten Male vollständig ins Deutsche übersetzt mit Kommentar und Einleitung*, 2 Bde, Prag: Tempsky.

Macdonell, Arthur Anthony, 1897, *Vedic Mythology*, Strassburg (New Delhi: Munshiram Manoharlal, 2000).

———, 1900, *A History of Sanskrit Literature*, London: William Heinemann.

———, ed. and tr., 1904, *The Bṛhad-devatā Attributed to Śaunaka: A Summary of the Deities and Myths of the Rig-veda*, 2 pts., Cambridge, MA: Harvard Oriental Series, vols. 5 & 6.

———, 1910, *Vedic Grammar*, Strassburg: K.J. Trübner & Co.

Macdonell, Arthur Anthony and Arthur Berriedale Keith, 1912, *Vedic Index of Names and Subjects*, 2 vols., London: Johan Murray.

Mayrhofer, Manfred, 1996, *Etymologisches Wörterbuch des Altindoarischen*, Erster Teil: Ältere Sprache, 2 Bde, Heidelberg: C. Winter.

Meyer, Elad Hugo, 1883, *Indogermanische Mythen*, Bd. 1: Gandharven-Kentauren, Berlin: Ferd Dümmlers Verlagsbuchhandlung.

Monier-Williams, Monier, 1899, *A Sanskrit-English Dictionary*, new edn, greatly enlarged and improved with the collaboration of E. Leumann, C. Cappeller and other scholars, Oxford: Clarendon Press (1st publ. 1872).

Muir, John, 1870, *Original Sanskrit Texts*, vol. 5, London and Edinburgh: Trübner & Co.

Müller, Friedrich Max, 1864, *Lectures on the Science of Language*, 2nd series, London: Longman.

———, 1877, *The Hymns of the Ṛig-veda in the Saṁhitā and Pada Texts*, 2 vols., Koeln: Trübner.

———, 1891, *Vedic Hymns*, Oxford, Sacred Books of the East, vol. 32.

Oldenberg, Hermann, 1885, "Ākhyānahymnen im Ṛgveda", *Zeitschrift der deutschen morgenländischen Gesellschaft,* 39: 52ff.

———, 1896, *Ancient India: Its Language and Religions*, Chicago: The Open Court Publishing Co. (originally publ. in 1890 in German in Deutshe Rundeschau of Berlin).

———, 1912, *Rigveda. Textkritische und exegetische Noten*, 2 Bde, Berlin: Weidmann.

———, 1917, *Zur Geschichte der altindischen Prosa: mit besonderer Berücksichtigung der prosaisch-poetischen Erzählung*, Berlin: Weidmann.

Pischel, Richard and Karl Friedrich Geldner, 1889/1892, *Vedische Studien*, vol. 1, vol. 2 pt. 1, Stuttgart.

Preminger Alex, ed. (associate eds.: Frank J. Warnke and O.B. Hardison, Jr.), 1974, *Princeton Encyclopedia of Poetry and Poetics*, enlarged edn, Princeton: Princeton University Press.

Purani, A.B., 1963, *Studies in Vedic Interpretation: On the Lines of Sri Aurobindo*, Varanasi: Chowkhamba Sanskrit Series Office.

Radhakrishnan, S., 1923, *Indian Philosophy*, vol. 1, Centenary edn, 1989, London: Oxford University Press.

Raghu Vira and Lokesh Chandra, 1954, *Jaiminīya Brāhmaṇa of Sāmaveda*, Nagpur: Lokesh Chandra.

Rahurkar, V.G., 1964, *The Seers of the Ṛgveda*, Poona: University of Poona.

———, 1969, "The Ṛṣikās (Female Seers) of the Ṛgveda", in *Professor R.N. Dandekar Felicitation Volume*, ed. G.V. Devasthali, Bombay (= *Indian Antiquary*, 3rd series, vol. 3), pp. 41-55.

Ramgopal, 1959, *India of Vedic Kalpasūtras*, Delhi: National Publishing House, (2nd edn, Delhi: Motilal Banarsidass, 1983).

Renou, Luis, 1965, "Remarqués générales sur la phrase védique" in *Symbolae linguisticae in honorem Georgi Kuryłowicz, Wrocław-Warszawa-Kraków, Zaklad narodowy imienia Ossoliŋskich, Wydawnictwo Polskiej Akademii Nauk.*

Roth, Rudolf, 1850, "Die Sage von Dschemschid", *ZDMG*, 4: 417ff.

Sarasvati, Svami Satya Prakash and Satyakam Vidyalankar, 1977, 1982, 1984, *Ṛg-veda Saṁhitā*, vols. 1, 3, 10, 12, New Delhi: Veda Pratishthan.

Sarup, Lakshman, 1967, *The Nighaṇṭu and the Nirukta*, repr. Delhi: Motilal Banarsidass (1st publ. Oxford and Lahore 1920-27 in 4 vols. under various titles).

Sastri, P.S., 1948, "Imagery of Ṛigveda", *Annals of the Bhandarkar Oriental Research Institute,* 29: 152-96.

Sehgal, S.R., 1960, *Śāṅkhāyana-Gṛhyasūtra*, New Delhi: Munshiram Manoharlal.

Sen, Kṣitimohan, 1950, *Prācīn Bhārate Nārī* (Bengali) (*Women in Ancient India*), Śāntiniketan: Visva-Bharati Gabeshana Prakashan Samiti.

Sharma, Ram Sharan, 1959, *Aspects of Political Ideas and Institutions in Ancient India*, Delhi: Motilal Banarsidass.

Sharma, Tripat, 1987, *Women in Ancient India*, New Delhi: Ess Ess Publications.

Shastri, Chinnaswami, ed., 1928, *Āpastambagṛhyasūtra* (with two commentaries: *Anukūlā* of Haradatta Miśra and *Tātparyadarśana* of Sudarśanācārya), Varanasi.

Shastri, Chinnaswami and Pattabhiram Shastri, eds., 1937, *Śatapathabrāhmaṇa*, pt. 1, Varanasi.

Shastri, S.R. Rao, 1954, *Women in the Vedic Age*, Bombay: Bharatiya Vidya Bhavan.

Schmidt, Hanns Peter, 1987, *Some Women's Rites and Rights in the Veda*, Poona: Bhandarkar Oriental Research Institute.

Sikdar Datta, Nilanjana, 1999, *The Ṛgveda as Oral Literature*, New Delhi: Harman Publishing House.

Sontakke, Narayana Sharma and Chintamani Ganesh Kasikar et al., eds., 1933-51, *Ṛgveda Saṁhitā*, 5 vols., Poona: Vaidika Saṁśodhana Maṇḍala.

Speijer, Jacob Samuel, 1886, *Sanskrit Syntax*, Leiden: E.J. Brill.

Spencer, Herbert, 1896, *Principles of Sociology*, London: Williams and Norgate.

Thomas, Paul, 1964, *Indian Women through the Ages*, New York: Asia Publishing House.

Tilak, Bal Gangadhar, 1903, *The Arctic Home in the Vedas*, Poona (repr. Poona City: Tilak Bros, 1925).

Upadhyay, Bhagwat Saran, 1941, *Women in Ṛgveda: Indian Women through the Ages*, Benares (2nd edn, New Delhi: S. Chand & Co., 1974).

Velankar, Hari Damodar, 1954, "Hymns to Indra in Maṇḍala X", *Journal of the University of Bombay,* 23.2: 11-15.

Verma, Hari Narain, 1976, *Indian Women through the Ages* (a Dictionary), New Delhi: Great Indian Publishers.

Vidyasagar, Iswar Chandra, 1918, *Vyākaraṇa-Kaumudī*, Kalikātā (Kolkata).

Vishnoi, Savita, 1987, *Economic Status of Women in Ancient India*, Meerut: Kusumanjali Prakashan.

Viśvabandhu, ed., 1965-66, *Ṛg-veda with the Padapāṭha and the Available Portions of the Bhāṣyas by Skandasvāmin and Udgītha, the Vyākhyā by Veṅkaṭa-Mādhava and Mudgala's Vṛtti Based on Sāyaṇa-bhāṣya*, 8 vols., Hoshiarpur: Vishveshvaranand Vedic Research Institute.

Viti, Carlotta, 2010, "The Information Structure of OVS in Vedic", in *Diachronic Studies on Information Structure: Language Acquisition and Change*, eds. Gisella Ferraresi and Rosemarie Lühr, Berlin: De Gruyter, pp. 37-62.

Wallis, Henry White, 1887, *Cosmology of the Ṛigveda*, London: Williams & Norgate.

Weber, Albrecht, 1862, "Vedische Hochzeitsprüche", *Indische Studien,* 5: 177ff.

———, 1865, "Vāc und logos", *Indische Studien,* 9: 473ff.

———, 1876, *Akademische Vorlesungen über Indische Literaturgeschichte*, 2nd edn, Berlin (first publ. 1853. References are to the English tr. of the 2nd edn by John Mann and Theodor Zachariae, sanctioned by the author: *The History of Indian Literature*, London 1878, 4th edn, 1904, popular re-issue 1914).

Wilson, Horace Hayman, 1850, *Rig-Veda Sanhita*, 6 vols., Oxford.

Winternitz, Moritz, 1905, *Geschichte der Indischen Literatur*, vol. 1, pt. 1, Prague (References are to the only authorised English tr. by S. Ketkar, revised by the author: *A History of Indian Literature*, vol. 1, pt. 1, University of Calcutta, 1927, 3rd edn, 1962).

Zimmer, Heinrich, 1879, *Altindisches Leben: die Cultur der vedischen Arier nach den Saṁhitā dargestellt*, 3 Bde., Berlin.

Zimmer, Heinrich Robert, 1946/1962 *Myths and Symbols in Indian Art and Civilization*, Harper and Brothers edn, 1962.

Index of English Terms

ablative 240
Abrams 225
accusative 240, 242
active voice 242
Adam 166
adjective 240, 243, 252
adjective clause 240
adultery 113, 127, 145
adverb 240
adverbial clause 240, 266
Agastya's sister 1, 76, 171
Aggelos, O.D. 190
alliterated 216, 218
alliteration 207
alliterative 214
alludes 129-30
Altekar A.S. 35, 106, 112, 115, 122, 135-38, 155, 286
anthropomorphism 151
archetype 21
Aristotle 227
assonance 207
Aufrecht, T. 34, 62
Aurobindo 21, 40, 144, 184, 187
Avesta 128-29, 166-67
Azi Dahâka 128, 166
Babylonian religion 191
Baldic 225
Beas 47
Bergaigne, A. 3, 19, 44, 46, 86, 147, 150, 155, 158, 174, 179, 229
Bharatas 53-54
Bhattacaharji, S. 120, 128-29, 166-67, 176-77, 180-82, 191, 207, 229
Bhattacharya, S. 21, 108, 124
black magic 110
Bloomfield, M. 187, 209
Böthlingk, A. von 69-71, 81, 88-89, 91, 94, 96, 100, 107, 160, 165, 220, 232
Bradke, P. von 179
Brereton, Joel P. 2, 6-7, 12-13, 29, 39-40, 44-46, 54-55, 57, 59, 61-62, 66-70, 72-76, 80-81, 83, 86, 88, 90, 92-96, 98-105, 144, 215-17, 219, 221, 224, 237
bride price 109
Brooks, C. 227
brother-in-law 112, 137-38, 217, 234
Bruhl, L. 147
Buddhist literature 12, 136, 165
Byblis 167

Campbell, J. 176
Castor 177
catch-word 215, 223
Caunus 129, 167
celestial 44, 46, 118, 182
celibacy 46, 114
Celts 136
chariot-centric metaphor 69
chariot-related similes 219
Charpentier, J. 33
chastity 134
Chatterjee, K.C. 161, 163-64
Chatterji, K.C. 24, 181, 190-91
Choudhuri, Usha 148
Chowdhury, T. 77-78, 219
colloquial 59, 68, 86, 90, 118, 129, 144, 181
    speech style 229
colloquy of Purūravas and Urvaśī 20, 86, 251, 256
complex sentence 247-48, 262, 268, 270-72
compound sentence 243, 251-52, 262, 267
conjugal 144, 230
    bliss 114
    life 133
    pleasure 45
    relation 118-19, 134, 165
conjugate 63
conjunctive 240, 242, 245, 267
consort 63-64, 85, 152, 183-84, 218
contract from of marriage 118
Coomaraswamy, A.K. 147-48
co-owner 110-11, 122, 133
cosmogonic 211
cosmogony 27, 130, 166
cosmos 30
courtesan 144
Cowell, E.B. 62
co-wife 27-28, 30-31, 87, 100-01, 110, 115, 140, 143, 145, 181, 223, 252

Dandekar, R.N. 61, 83
Darius 154
Darmesteter, J. 24, 190
Das, A.C. 23
Das, R.P. 27
Das Gupta, D. 240
dative 240
daughter 106-08, 111, 123-25, 130, 153-54, 161-62, 169, 172, 174, 176, 192, 198
daughter-in-law 67
Dawn 57, 104, 119, 160, 186-87, 192
Dayanand 6, 40, 160
Dayananda 49
Deukalion 167
Dharmapal, G. 91
dialogue hymn 3, 115, 119, 181, 195, 197, 200, 207, 216, 220, 249-50, 256
Doniger O'Flaherty, Wendy 119
Downey, J. 228
Dumézil, G. 147-48
Durkneim, E. 147
Dyaus 102, 151, 160

Earth 65, 77, 104, 125,
Eliade, M. 148, 167
Elizarenkova, Tatyana J. 239
Encyclopaedia Britannica 146

Erinys, 186
equal rights 106, 139, 287
Eros 43, 134, 156, 195, 197
erotic 85
esoteric 27
Ethos 12
Eve 166

father-in-law 67, 87, 118, 180
female infanticide 124
fertility 19, 75, 164, 180
five rivers 48
folklore 208
folktale 140, 208, 228
foster-father 155
fraternity 119
Frazer, J.G. 147-48, 177
free-sex 145
Freud, S. 147
funeral
    hymn 112, 137
    rite 112, 203

Gauls 136
Geiger, W. 106
Geldner, K.F. 7, 42, 44, 46, 49, 52-53, 57-58, 60-62, 64, 66-67, 71, 73, 76, 79-80, 88, 96, 119-20, 160, 164, 171, 174, 179, 181
Ghosh, A. 19, 61, 78, 214
Gonda, J. 147-48
Goths 136
Graham 204
Grassmann, H. 60, 74-75, 82, 88, 154, 209
Greco-Roman mythology 177
Greek mythology 177, 180, 190
gṛhya rites 195, 197-98, 288
Griffith, R.T.H. 2-6, 10, 12-13, 15-17, 19, 28-29, 39-40, 43, 45, 48, 50-53, 55, 57-67, 69-105, 110, 117
Griffiths, A. 34
Grimm 176
guerdon 89

Haoma Yašt 166
Harrison, J. 147-48
HC (Higher Constituents) 240-53, 256-62, 267, 269-84
Heaven 65, 70, 77, 88, 120, 125, 138, 173, 238
Hebrew 12, 165
Helen 177
Helena 118, 186
Hera 180
Hermeias 186
Hermes 186
heterogeneous hymn 16
hiatus 88
Hilaria 177
Hillebrandt, A. 150, 158-60, 173-76, 184, 186-88, 191-92
Hindu nuptial ritual 76
Hock, H.H. 240
Homer, E. 63
honorarium 21, 89, 184
Hooke, S.S. 148
Hopkins, W. 191
household 133-34, 143
Hume, T.E. 226
husband 60, 62, 64, 66, 74-76, 78,

82, 84-85, 87, 94-95, 100-01, 104, 106, 108-15, 117, 119, 121-28, 139-43, 145, 153, 155, 161-66, 168-69, 171, 175, 177, 180, 182, 188-89, 198, 202, 216, 218-20, 223, 228, 233-34, 236

Idas 177

Iliad 186

imageries of *Ṛgveda* 229, 234

imagery 77

Imagist
- credo 226
- movement 225, 227

incest 128-30

Indeclinable 240

Indo-European 21, 110, 136, 140

Indo-Aryan society 106

Indo-Aryans 130, 133, 140

Indo-European
- age 112, 128, 287
- daughters 125,
- languages 123, 125,
- mythologies 177, 182
- origin 177
- peoples 130
- period 130
- society 130

Indo-Iranian 102, 106, 129

Indologist 147-49

infinite 240

instrumental 240, 242

interrogative 240, 277-78, 281
- particle 240, 281
- pronoun 240
- sentences 247, 276, 278, 281

Isis 167

Izanami 167

Izanagi 167

Jamison, S.W. 2, 6-7, 12-13, 29, 39-40, 44-46, 54-55, 57, 59, 61-62, 66-70, 72-76, 80-81, 83, 86, 88, 90, 92-96, 98-105, 144, 215-17, 219, 221, 224, 237

Japanese mythology 167

Jews 137

Jung, C.G. 147

Kaegi, A. 174

Kandahar 154

Kashikar 33

Keith, A.B. 171

Kopnen/Kabul 154

Kosambi, D.D. 86-88, 116

Lang, A. 147

Lanmann, C.R. 75, 79

Lassen, C. 154

Leitmotif 228

leprosy 73

Leucippus 177

liturgy 139

locative 240

Logos 190-91

Lowe, J. 239-40

Ludwig, A. 41, 60, 81, 83, 85, 87, 92, 154, 158

Lynceus 177

lyric 34

lyricism 15

Macdonell, A.A. 5, 7, 27, 36, 43, 59,

112, 150-51, 168, 171, 174, 178-79, 182, 189, 192, 199
Macropaedia 146
magic 223
magical 223, 229-30
man-woman relationship 236
mannerism 27
manhood 128
Mannhardt, W. 176
Manoharan, S. 240
Mantra literature 229
marriage 75, 79, 124
 ceremony 82, 117
 hymn 17, 110, 114, 122, 124, 142, 175, 177, 211, 218
 institution 131
 life 46
 mantra 76
married
 couple 58
 life 75
 woman 60
maxim 82
Maxmüller, F.M. 147
metaphor 69, 77, 130, 218-19, 222, 226-27
metaphorical language 120
Mexican mythology 167
Meyer, J.J. 147, 176
Micropaedia 146
middle-class 145
Mills, L.H. 24
mnemonic device 207
Monkey-cult 181
monogamy 109
Moon 85
motif 129
Muir 13, 74, 166
Müller, F.M. 13, 34, 110, 147-48, 160, 166
Murray, G. 148
mythology 146-51, 153, 177, 187, 190

negative 240, 259-60, 266-68
 complex sentence 269
 sentence 269, 273, 285, 288
 simple sentence 269-70
Night 98, 235, 237
nominal 241
noose 79
Norwegian 136
noun phrase 241
numeral 241
nymph 20-21, 87, 118, 182-83

object-subject-verb 285
object-verb 285
oblation 65, 96, 125, 142, 158, 232
Oldenberg, H. 108, 153, 160, 163-64, 171, 174, 176, 179, 186-87, 189
oral literature 206
Orion 179
Osiris 167
Ovid 129, 167, 177

paramour 127, 228
Parthians 154
participle 241
passive 241-42, 245
 voice 242
patriarchal 109
Paul, T. 110, 126, 135, 190

Pedu 170
permissive 113, 145
Phobe 177
phrase bloc 212
Pischel, R. 160, 171, 174, 178, 181
Plato 166
poetess 17, 60, 68, 193
poetic 213-14, 217
    imagery 26, 238
    images 288
Pollux 177
polyandry 18, 82, 109
polygamy 109
polygamic 28
possessive 241
Pound, E. 226
Preminger 225
progeny 19, 63-64, 126, 128, 155-56
promiscuity 129
puberty 109, 124, 131
Purani, A.B. 21, 144, 154, 184
Pyrrha 167

queen 96, 127
Quran 124

Radhakrishnan, S. 190
Rahurkar, V.G. 87
Ramgopal 122, 130
Ransom, J.C. 227
refrain 207
remarriage of widow 112-13
rendezvous 74, 217, 232
Renou, L. 147-48, 239
repetition 206, 208, 210, 212-13, 223
Ṛgvedic
    imageries 230, 236
    poetry 230
rhetoric 229
riddle 85
rival-wives 28, 31
Roman 130
Roth, R. Von 12-13, 69-71, 81, 88-89, 91, 94, 96, 100, 160, 165, 220, 232

sacrifice 65, 70, 73, 75, 79, 83-86, 95, 103, 110, 120, 122, 127, 139, 156-57, 168-69, 180, 183-84, 194, 196, 198, 200-204, 218-19
sacrificial
    fee 89
    pyre 203
Sacrificer's Wife 93
Sahaj Pāṭh 226
Śaktism 190
Sarasvati, Svami S.P. 3, 6, 8, 10, 15, 19, 24, 29, 32, 40, 49, 51, 141, 154, 160-61, 163, 167-68, 172, 188
Sarup, L. 12, 53, 78, 130
Sastri 229
satī custom 135
Schmidt, H.P. 10, 109
Schmidt, W. 11, 147
Seig 7
Sen, Kshitimohan 12, 18, 165
sentiment 226
sex relation 135
sexual
    harassment 134
    pleasure 143
    relation 129

union 66, 129
Sharma, R.S. 142
Sikdar Datta, N. 211
simile 125, 142, 216, 218-19, 223, 226-27, 230, 233, 235
simple sentence 243, 247-52, 257-61, 266, 268, 271-72, 277, 279-81
six broad characteristics of simile 231
Slavic 140
Slavs 136
social
anthropologist 147
position 30
socio cultural study 22
Son 106-08, 111-12, 114, 117, 122-26, 130, 134-35, 137-38, 141, 152, 156-59, 161, 169-70, 172, 182-83, 192, 233
Spartan 137
speech 25, 56, 189-90, 213, 220
Speijer, J.S. 39
Spencer, H. 137, 147
spiritual 140
śrauta and *gṛhya* rights 195, 197, 288
Subject-Verb 285
Sun 31-32, 51, 57, 61, 65, 83, 97, 104-05, 117, 120, 162, 177, 232, 234
Sun God 61, 70, 78, 174-75
Sutlej 47
symbolist 225
syntactic analysis 239, 245-46

taboo 129
Tagore, R. 226-27
Tate, A. 227
Tatyana, J. Elizarenkova 239
Teutonic 176
The Arctic home of the Aryans 19, 83
The Old Testament 137
Thracians 136
Tilak, B.G. 19, 83, 179
tournament 178
twin
gods 68
sibling 216
Tylor, E.B. 147
Tyndareus 177
unmarried 10, 108, 111, 114, 131
Upadhyay, B.S. 108, 112, 115-17, 129, 136
Vedānta philosophy 96, 189
Vedic syntax 239
Velenkar, H.D. 83
Veṅkaṭamādhava 3, 5-6, 10, 15, 19, 41, 43, 46, 49, 52-53, 55-62, 68, 70-74, 76-85, 87-101, 103-05, 154, 160, 163, 179
Verma, H.N. 155
Vidyalankar, S. 3, 6, 8, 10, 15, 24, 29, 32, 40, 49, 51, 154, 160-61, 163, 167-68, 172, 188
Vidyasagar 242
virility 83
Vishnoi, S. 112, 141
Viti, C. 240
vocative 241, 243

Wallis, H.W. 25, 160
warfare 139-40
war-field 110
Water-goddesses 29

Weber, A. 81, 174, 189
Weltanschauung 106, 141
widow 112
    marriage 138
wife of Vasukra 1, 67, 167
Williams, M.M. 88
Wilson, H.H. 12, 23, 28-30, 32, 51-53, 55, 66, 74, 77, 79-82, 88, 91, 98, 102, 104, 110, 172, 188
womanhood 142, 183
womenfolk 56, 136, 142-43, 233

Yima 13, 128, 166
Yimak 128, 166

Zeus 180
Zimmer, H. 107
Zimmer, H.R. 121, 147-48

Index of Sanskrit Terms

Agastya 3-4, 16-17, 42-46, 76, 123, 127, 154-56, 172, 183, 195, 207-08, 256

Agastya-svasṛ 11, 16, 35, 76, 115, 123, 171, 218, 286,

Agni 5, 7, 18, 31, 58, 78, 82, 115, 118, 120, 175, 177, 189, 191, 194, 197, 208-10, 215

Agniṣṭoma 203

agnyādhāna 196

Aṅgiras 8, 22, 59, 89, 153, 184

Aṅgirases 92, 186

acchāvāka 201

ajāmi 66

atimūrti 198

atirātra 194, 202

Atri 5-9, 56-57, 60, 256

Atri Saṁhitā 18

Atharvaveda 27, 79, 106, 108, 111-12, 117, 126, 128, 130, 136, 138, 159, 166, 174, 178-79, 207

Aditi 1, 4-5, 29, 54-55, 113, 116-17, 120, 152, 156-60, 214, 256, 260-61, 287

adhvaryu 198, 204

Anukramaṇī 92

Anukramaṇī-Bhāsya 4-5, 54-55, 156

anuprāsa 213

Anumati 34

Anuṣṭubh 17, 40, 207-09

anuvacana 203

apatighnī 82

Apasyuvaḥ 29, 119-20

apāna 173

Apālā 1, 8-10, 27, 35, 60-62, 115, 125, 131, 133, 139-40, 161-64, 197, 208, 215, 234-35, 246-47, 256, 260-61, 269, 278, 281, 286

apsaras 118, 144, 174, 184

abhimantrayet 202

Abhivarta Āṅgirasa 213

abhiṣṭavana 203

Abhihiṁkāra 203

amājura 14

amāvasyā 192

Ambhṛṇa 95, 113, 189, 212

Ayāsya Āṅgirasa 209, 237

ariṣṭa 200

Arjuna 12, 165, 171, 181

avivākya 204

aśvamedha 83, 170

Aśvinī 174-75

Aśvins 10, 13-15, 33, 68-70, 109-10, 114, 117, 131, 133, 138, 168-71, 173-78, 187, 192, 194, 197, 228, 232-33

Asamāti 16, 171-72

Asita 236
asura 102, 169, 178
Ahalyā 161
Ahi 50-51
Ākuli 16, 171
Ākūti 184
Āṅgirasa 236
Āṅgirasī 8
ājya-śastra 200
Ātreyī 56-57
Ātreyī Uṣā 6
Ātharvaṇa 140
Āditya 159, 188, 210
ādhyātma 212
Āpastamba 123
Āpastamba-Gṛhyasūtra 27, 198, 202, 205
Āpastamba- Śrautasūtra 135
Āprī sūkta (hymn) 6
Āmbhṛnī 23, 25, 31
Āraṇyaka 194
Ārṣānukramanī 1, 4, 67, 99, 107, 114, 156, 161, 167, 206
Āśvalāyana-Gṛhyasūtra 33
Āśvalāyana-śrautaśutra 196-98, 200, 204
āśvina-kratu 197
āśvina-śastra 16
Āsaṅga 7-8, 59, 128
āsura 109
Āstāra-paṅkti 209
āhava 204

Ikṣvāku 16, 171
itihāsa 10, 163
Indra 4-5, 8-10, 16, 19-20, 22, 26, 29, 32, 34, 38, 47-48, 50-51, 53-56, 61-62, 67, 82-84, 86, 90-92, 94-95, 99-100, 102, 104, 107, 113, 117-20, 133-34, 140-41, 150, 153, 156-58, 161-64, 167-68, 170, 172, 174, 178-82, 185-86, 200, 202, 208, 210, 220, 224, 234-36, 250, 287
Indramātar 1, 29, 119
Indrāṇī 1, 19-20, 27-28, 30, 35, 54, 82-86, 100, 104, 110, 115, 118, 127, 132-34, 141, 143, 178-81, 200, 213, 220, 223, 233, 236, 250, 252, 256, 260-61, 270-71, 286
Indra-Indrāṇī-Vṛṣākapi 18, 133, 172
Ila 20, 87, 182
Ilā 183
iṣṭi 196, 198, 203

uttara pakṣa 202-03
utprekṣā 220, 222
udgātṛ 204
udgītha 14, 69-74
upanayana 107
Upaniṣat 33, 35, 115, 126, 131, 205, 286
Upaniṣad 1, 27, 106
upapada tatpuruṣa 62
upamā 213-14
upamāna 222
upameya 222, 224
upalā 199
upāṁśu-svara 204
Upendra 180
Urvarāpati 180
Urvaśī 1, 20-21, 86-88, 115-16, 118-

19, 127, 132, 134, 144, 181-84, 220, 231-32, 251, 260, 262, 271
Uvaṭa 31
Uṣas 6, 57, 125, 130, 140, 151, 173-76, 178, 186-87, 192, 194, 197, 223

Ūrdhvanābha 23, 93, 188

Ṛgvidhāna 35, 199
Ṛgveda Saṁhitā 11, 207, 230
ṛta 30, 173
ṛtu 109, 134
ṛtvij 194-95, 204
ṛṣi 181
ṛṣikā 8, 11, 24, 35, 161

ekāha 203

Aitareya Āraṇyaka 200-01
Aitareya Brāhmaṇa 33, 117, 124, 174, 176, 178, 180, 200, 205
Aitiśāyana 139
Aindra Vasukra 268
Aiśakṛta Sitibāhu 180

Ka 180
Kakṣīvant 2, 13-14, 37-40, 68, 168, 210
Kaṭha Upaniṣad 159
Kaṭhi 126
Kaṇva 8, 59
Kathāsaritsāgara 21, 87
Kadrū 31, 120
Kali 169
Kalpasūtra 123
Kavaṣa Ailuṣa 237
Kaśyapa 31, 120, 148
Kāma 28
kāma 152
Kāṭhaka Saṁhitā 20, 86, 107, 178
Kātyāyana 43
Kātyāyana-Śrautasūtra 198
Kāmasūtra 134
Kāśakṛtsnā 126
kiṁśuka 78, 220
Kirāta 16, 171
Kutsa 170, 211, 237, 266
Kuntī 126
Kubhā 154
Kurīra 219
Kurukṣetra 183
Kuru-Pāñcāla 141
kuśa 127
Kuśika 25, 98, 192
Kuṣavā 158
Kuhū 19
Kūrma Gārtsamada 210
kṛpaṇa 124
Kṛṣṇa 12, 161, 165, 178
Kaikeyī 141
Kośa 77, 219
Kauṭilya 136
Kauṣītaki 155
Kauṣītaki Brāhmaṇa 117, 176
Khādira-Gṛhyasūtra 123
khila 33-35, 115, 121, 126, 143, 205, 224
Khilānukramaṇī 33
Khela 169
Krīḍin Marut 196

krīḍineṣṭi 196
kṣatriya 93, 222

gato viniyoga 195, 197, 200
Gandhāra 39, 154, 213
Gandhārī 231
gandharva 18, 20, 64, 82, 118, 175, 177, 182
Gavām-ayana 202-03
gāthā 218
Gāyatrī 17
gārhapatitvāya 80
Gṛtsamada 210-11, 266
gṛhapati 80
gṛhapatnī 131
Gṛhyasūtra 194
Gobhila- Gṛhyasūtra 42, 123
Gobhilīya-Gṛhyasūtra-Pariśiṣṭa 18
Godhā 1, 11, 26, 35, 99, 115, 192-93, 201, 212, 214, 223, 272, 286
Gopatha Brāhmaṇa 180
Gopavana Ātreya 278
Gopāyana 171, 172
Gautama-Dharmasūtra 137
Gaupāyana 16-17
graha 204

ghṛta 120
Ghoṣā 1, 10, 13-16, 27, 33, 35, 68, 70, 72, 74-75, 114, 125, 127, 131-33, 138-39, 143, 168-69, 171, 197, 210, 217, 228, 232-34, 249, 270, 278-79, 286

catur-viṁśa 201
Caṇḍī 24, 189
Candra 119
citrakalpa 235
cāturmāsya 196
cāndramasī 198
cāndramasīṣṭi 198
Cyavana 169

Jagatī 197
jāra 126-27, 145
jāspatyam 6, 131
Juhū 23, 92-93, 119, 123, 188-89, 222
juhū 57-58
Jaimini 111, 139
Jaiminīya Brāhmaṇa 178, 180
Jñāna Sūkta 25

tatpuruṣa 62
Taranta 113
Tārā 119
tīrtha 204
Tugra 169-70
Tuṣita 184
Taittirīya Brāhmaṇa 141, 180, 191
Taittirīya Saṁhitā 56, 107, 111, 120, 157, 159, 180
Triṣṭubh 40, 43
Tvaṣṭṛ 157

Dakṣiṇā 1, 22, 29, 35, 89, 116, 119, 184, 212, 221, 234
dakṣiṇā 21
dampatī 110, 122, 133
darśapūrṇamāsa 79, 196, 198
Daśagva 187
daśarātra 204

dānastuti 7, 38, 59
dāsa 141
Divya 22, 89, 184
Dīrghatamas 37-38, 142
Durga 3, 43, 45, 51, 88
duhitṛ 125
dṛṣad 199
dṛṣṭānta 222
devadāsī 161
devara 137
Devala Kāśyapa 236
devaśunī 184
Devī-sūkta 24, 141, 189

Dharma-śāstra 109, 136
Dharma-sūtra 107, 137
dhenu 34

nadī 1, 47
Navagva Aṅgiras 187
Nābhānediṣṭha Mānava 269
Nārāyaṇa 198
nārāśaṁsī 38, 218
nārī 7,
Nighaṇṭu 14, 56, 58, 159
Nirukta 3-4, 12, 18-19, 25, 43, 45, 49-51, 78, 88, 95, 111, 130, 137, 148-49, 159, 172, 179, 189
Niruktakāra 38
Nirṛti 66, 152, 166
niyoga 138, 111
Nivāvarī 1, 11, 35, 114, 286
nivid 56, 158
Niṣat 33, 35, 115, 126, 131, 205, 286
Niṣad 1
Nīti-mañjarī 7, 59
nṛmedha 256
Nodhā Gautama 237

Paṅkti 17, 99, 200
pañca mahāyajña 132
Pañcaviṁśa Brāhmaṇa 88
Paṇi 22-23, 76, 90, 119, 184-85, 188, 212, 256
pati 126, 175
patidvíṣaḥ 62
patnīsaṁyāja 79, 198
Padma Purāṇa 178
Parāśara Śāktya 210
pariṇayya 111
Parjanya 174, 191
paryāya 202
pavitreṣṭi 196
pāṭhā 27, 202
Pāṇḍu 126, 134
Pāṇini 82
Pārvatī 183
Pijavana 48
pitṛ 131
puṁsavana 107
punarbhū 138
Purandhi 191
Purāṇa 11, 21, 87, 90, 115, 119, 140, 165, 184
Purumitra 71, 169
puruṣa 24
puruṣamedha 256
Purūravas 20-21, 86-88, 116, 118, 134, 144, 182-84, 220, 232, 251
Puloman 104
pūrva-pakṣa 139, 202-03

Pūrvamīmāṁsā 139
Pūrvamīmāṁsā Sūtra 111, 139
Pūṣan 130, 175-76
Pṛthivī 151-52, 192
Pṛśni 174-75
pṛṣṭhya ṣaḍaha 200
Paippalāda Saṁhitā 34
Paura Ātreya 276-77
paurṇamāsī 192
Paulomī 31
Paulomī Śacī 30, 107, 132, 143
prakṛta 222
Pragātha Kāṇva 278
Pragātha Maṇḍala 7
Prajāpati 19, 22, 63-64, 89, 130, 152, 176, 178, 180, 212, 237
Prajāpati Vaiśvāmitra 210
Pratardana Daivodāsi 237
pratigara 204
praśāstṛ 202
prasāda-guṇa 214
prahelikā 220
prāṇa 173
prātar-anuvāka 16
prātaḥ-savana 202-03
Prāsahā 178, 180
Playoga 8, 59

Bandhu 16, 171-72
Balarāma 178
baliharaṇa 123
bahuvrīhī 62
Bārhaspatya Bharadvāja 237
Bāṣkala Mantropaniṣad 24, 189
Budha 183
Bhāgavata Purāṇa 119
Bhāguri 10, 163
Bhāradvāja 98, 123, 188, 192, 222
Bhāradvājī 25
Bhāvayavya 37-38, 41
Bhāva-vṛtta 27
bhrātṛ 123
Bhujyu 169-70
Bhūmi 34
Bṛhatī 43
Bṛhadāraṇyaka Upaniṣad 13, 111, 165
Bṛhaddevatā 1-5, 7-11, 13, 16-17, 19-20, 22-24, 26-27, 29-30, 32, 34-35, 38, 41-43, 47-48, 54-57, 59, 67, 99, 104, 113-14, 116-17, 120, 127-28, 133, 149, 153-57, 160-63, 165, 167-68, 171, 173, 178-79, 181-82, 184-85, 188-89, 192, 199, 206
Bṛhaspati 22-23, 25, 92, 95, 119, 123, 178, 185-89, 191
Baudhāyana Śrautaśūtra 20
Baudhāyana-Smṛti 18
brahmakilviṣa 23, 123
brahmacarya 108, 139, 200
brahmacārin 108, 132
Brahmajāyā Juhū 1, 188
Brahman 23, 93, 108, 119, 141, 182, 188
brahmayajña 108, 204
brahmavādinī 132, 192
bramavādin 114
brāhmaṇa 33, 56, 94-95, 191, 199, 131, 148, 152, 158, 166, 194, 198, 201, 288
brāhmaṇācchaṁsin 200
brāhma-śastra 202-03

Bhṛgu 217
bhojyā 41

Maghavan 100
madhu 120
madhyama-svara 204
Manu 136, 183
mantra-viniyoga 196
Mamatā 115, 125, 139, 142
Mammaṭa Bhaṭṭa 220
Marut 109, 151, 174
marutvatīya śastra 56, 158
marya 126
Mahābhārata 12, 49, 53, 87, 119, 126, 134, 136, 138, 141, 155, 181, 193
Mahābhāṣya 126
Mahāpaṅkti 26, 99
mahā-vrata 202-03
mahiṣa 105
mahiṣī 159
Mahīdhara 31
mādhyandina-savana 201
Mānasa 20, 183
mānasa-graha 204
mānasa-stotra 204
Māndhātṛ 26, 192
Mārkaṇḍeya Purāṇa 24
Mātariśvan 23
mālopamā 216-17, 224
Mitra 12, 20, 65, 78, 93, 183, 189
Mīḍhuṣī 152
mīmāṁsaka 195
Mīmāṁsā 126
Mudgalānī 113, 140
Mṛtyubandhu 88
Medhā 1, 29, 35, 121, 152
Medhātithi 8, 59, 277
Medhā-Sūkta 35
maitrāvaruṇa 202
mauñjī 198

yajamāna 198
Yajurveda 186
Yama 11-13, 29-30, 63-67, 120, 128-29, 165-67, 184, 187, 197, 204, 216, 231, 249
yamaka 214, 216, 217, 221, 223
Yama-Yamī sūkta (hymn) 209-10
Yama Vaivasvata 268
Yamī 1, 8, 11-13, 29-30, 35, 63-67, 103, 120, 127-29, 139, 152, 164-67, 197, 213, 216, 224, 231, 249, 286
Yamī Vaivasatī 11, 30, 115-16, 203, 208, 249
Yājñavalkya 111, 136
Yājñavalkya-Smṛti 18
yājyā 196, 202
yādurī 42
yāmi mantra 204
yāśū 41
Yāska 10, 12, 18-19, 38, 48-49, 51, 53, 76, 78, 86, 95, 129-30, 137, 149, 163, 172, 182, 232
Yuvanāśva 26, 192
yoga 172
yoni 90
yoṣā 174

Rati 43, 195, 197
ratnahavis 158

Rathabīti 113
Rasā 22, 185, 188
Rākā 19
Rātrī 222, 231, 233, 235-37
Rātri-sūkta 201
Rāma 180-81
Rāmāyaṇa 141, 181
Rāṣṭrī 96
Rukmiṇī 12, 165
Ruci 184
Rudra 113, 141, 174, 191, 211
Rudravartanī 72
Rudrāṇī 153
rūpaka 214
Rebha 169
Romaśā 1-2, 8, 35, 37-38, 41-42, 115, 127, 132-33, 140, 153-54, 213, 231, 241, 256, 260
Raibhī 218

Lakṣaṇa-Śāstra 82
Lakṣmī 33, 121, 153, 224
Lākṣā 1, 34, 121-22
lājahoma 199
lāṭānuprāsa 224
Lāṭyāyana Brāhmaṇa 81
liṅga-pramāṇa 195
luptopamā 64, 216
laiṅgiko viniyoga 202
Lopāmudrā 1-4, 8, 30, 35, 37, 42-46, 114-15, 127-28, 132-33, 139, 154-56, 195, 207, 214, 241-42, 256, 260-61, 286

Vaṁśa-Maṇḍala 35
vajra 56
Vadhrimatī 71, 169-71
Vana-Parvan 155
Vandana 169
vayaḥ 87
Varapradā 155
Varuṇa 12, 20, 65, 78, 93, 102, 129, 183, 189
varuṇapraghāsa 127
Vala 184-85
vahatu 79
Vaśa 170
Vaśā 174
Vasiṣṭha-Sūtra 135
Vasiṣṭha-Smṛti 18
Vasu 87
Vasukra 32, 67, 168
Vasukra-Patnī 32, 35, 67, 115, 122, 167, 286
Vāc 1, 23-25, 31, 35, 95-97, 113, 115, 119, 153, 159, 188, 190, 212, 222, 251, 286
Vācaspati 188, 191
Vāc-sūkta 95
Vācya Vaiśvāmitra 237
Vājasaneyī Saṁhitā 31
Vātāpi 156
Vātsyāyana 134
Vāmadeva 4-5, 54-55, 117, 156-58, 256, 267
Vāmana 227
Vāyu 151
Vāyu Purāṇa 87
Vālakhilya sūkta (hymn) 36
vāvātā 180
Vikramorvaśīyam 21
vidatha 110, 142

Vidarbha 155
Vidyāraṇya 34
viniyoga 25, 194-95, 197
Vipāś 4, 47-50, 156, 195, 231, 233, 237
Viprabandhu 16, 171
Vimada 169
Vilisteṅgā 178
Vivasvant 11, 13, 29, 63, 103, 164-65, 167, 173, 186-87, 213, 216
vivāha 79
viśeṣaviniyogo laiṅgika 195
Viśpalā 113, 140, 169
Viśvakarman 212
Viśvanātha Kavirāja 220
Viśvamanā Vaiyaśva 268
Viśvavārā 1, 5-6, 35, 56-57, 125, 132, 139, 142, 160, 208, 215, 235, 242-43, 256, 260-61, 286
Viśvāmitra 4, 47-53, 121, 125, 177, 195, 210, 233
Viśvāvasu 118, 175
Viśvedevāḥ 26, 193
Viṣuva 202-03
Viṣṇu 83, 95, 158, 180-81
Viṣṇu Purāṇa 21, 87, 119
Vīramitrodaya 132
Vṛtra 56, 141, 150, 158
vṛtraghnī 141
vṛttyanuprāsa 216, 223
Vṛṣan 103
Vṛṣākapi 19-20, 82-86, 118, 134, 173, 179-81, 200, 220, 250, 256
Vedī 203
Vyaṁśa 55, 117
vrata 200
vratacārin 108

Śaṁyur Bārhaspatya 267
śaṁyuvāka 198
Śakra 168
Śacī 30, 35, 104, 115, 152, 178, 213, 186
Śatapatha Brāhmaṇa 20-21, 86-87, 100, 128, 131-32, 159, 171, 178, 182
Śabara 139
Śabda Brahman 95, 189-90
śabdālaṁkāra 220
Śayu 170
Śaśīyasī 113
śaśramāṇā 241
Śaśvatī 1, 7-8, 11, 35, 59-60, 115, 127-28, 132-33, 196-97, 245, 286
Śākaṭāyana 38
Śākapuṇi 38
Śāṅkhāyana-Gṛhyasūtra 121
Śāṭyāyana Brāhmaṇa 9-10, 61-62, 140, 162-64
śilpa-śastra 200
Śiva 183
Śiśupālavadha 61
śyena 158
Śrī (Lakṣmī) 1, 33-35, 121, 143, 153, 224
Śrī Sūkta 33
Śutudrī 4, 47-50, 156, 195, 231, 233, 237,
Śundhyuva 169
Śaunaka 10, 42, 164, 173, 199
Śraddhā 1, 28, 35, 101-02, 116, 119

Śrutabandhu 16, 171
śrutyanuprāsa 216
Śrautaśūtra 33, 131, 194
Śvetaketu 134-35

Ṣaḍguruśiṣya 4, 20, 24, 183

Satī 135-36, 138
saṁstava 20
satra 203
satya 173
sapatnī-bādhana 27
sado-maṇḍapa 204
sadyodvāhā 132
saptapadī gamana 199
Saptaśatī 24, 189
Saptavadhri 170
samana 142
Saramā 1, 22-23, 90, 92, 119, 184-88, 212, 221, 256, 260, 262, 271-72
Saraṇyu 64, 174, 186-87
Sarasvatī 19, 141, 153
Sarvānukramaṇī 3, 5, 8, 13, 16, 19-20, 26-27, 29, 32, 43, 48, 54, 56-57, 59, 63, 67, 83, 87, 90, 104, 114, 119, 161, 165, 167-68, 171, 184, 192-93
Sarvānukramaṇī-Bhāṣya 4-5, 54-55, 156
Savitṛ 17, 48, 50-51, 76, 78, 117-18, 172, 175-77, 208, 211
sākamedha 196
Sāmayik Patra 228
Sāmaveda 26, 204
Sāmidhenī 6, 57, 196
Sāyaṇa 3-10, 12, 14-15, 19-20, 22, 24, 29, 36, 41-44, 46, 48, 50-53, 55-105, 117, 119, 137-38, 156, 158, 161-64, 169, 171, 179, 183-84, 187-88, 192, 194-95, 197, 200-02, 204, 216-18, 220-21, 224, 248, 253
sārameya 186-87
Sārparājñī 1, 31-32, 104, 116, 120, 204, 233, 236, 252
sālāvṛka 232
Sāvitrī 1, 17, 28, 172, 174, 234
Sikatā 1, 11, 35, 114, 286
Sinīvālī 19
Sindhu 39
Sītā 34, 180
sutyā-dina 194
Sudās 47-48, 156
Subandhu 16-17, 171-72
subhagā 169
Subhadrā 12, 165, 178
Suyajña 184
Suhastya 13, 169, 171
sūktaviniyoga laiṅgika 195-97
Sūrya 18-19, 64-65, 172-79, 208, 211, 218-19, 234
Sūryā 1, 17, 28, 72, 76-78, 81-82, 108-10, 117, 131-32, 172-76, 178, 189, 192, 197-98, 200, 208, 211, 218-19, 228, 234, 278, 280
Sūryā sūkta 131, 198-200
senā 178, 180
Sobhari 25
soma 4, 8-9, 17-18, 44-46, 61, 69-70, 78, 86, 133, 150, 155, 162-64, 168, 172-78, 183, 187, 189, 194, 203-04, 211, 218, 229, 234, 237

Soma-Sūryā 177
Sauparṇa sūkta 33, 205
saurī 198
stotra 203-04
stotriya-anurūpa 201
stotriya tṛca 201
stoma 203
strīdhana 111
smṛti 111, 138
Svanaya 37-39, 127, 153, 241, 256
svabhāvokti 214-15, 218-19, 222, 224, 226, 235
Svayambhū Manu 184
svayaṁvara 72, 109
Svarbhānu 5
sviṣṭakṛt 196

Hanumant 181
Hari 184
Harivaṁśa 21
Harṣacarita 215
Havirdhāna Āṅgirasa 209
havirdhāna śakaṭa 72
Hiraṇyagarbha 24, 212
Hiranyastūpa 236
Hiraṇyahasta 171
hotṛ 198, 204-05